Love Me,
Love Me Not

11

IO SAKISAKA

Contents

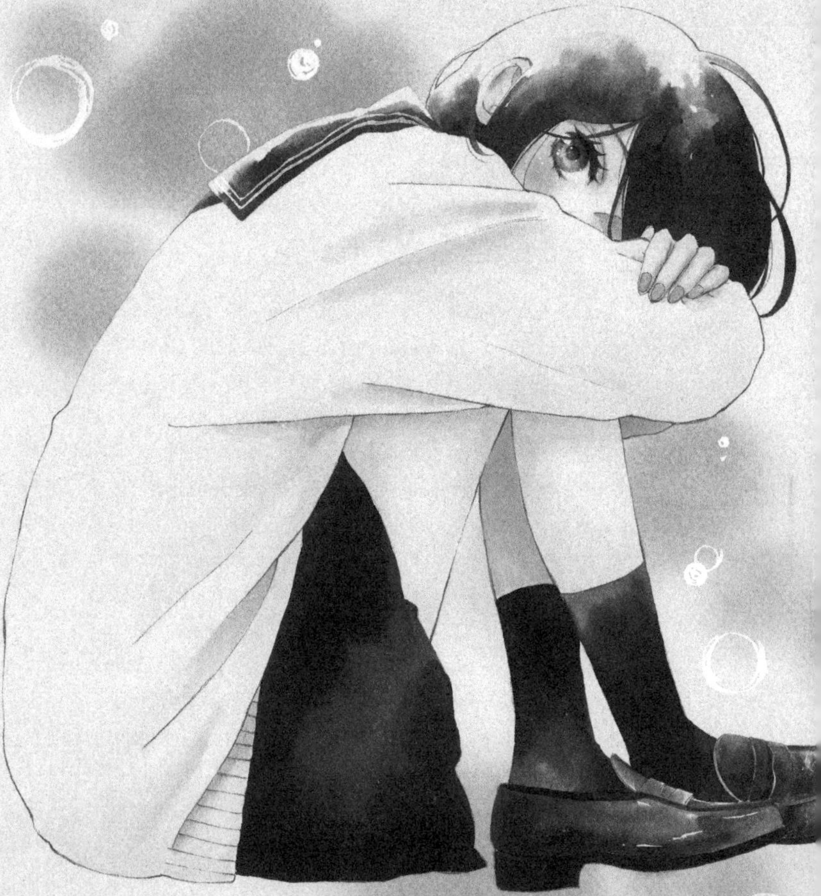

Love Me, Love Me Not

Piece 41

GREETINGS

Hello, I'm Io Sakisaka. Thank you so much for picking up volume 11 of *Love Me, Love Me Not*.

I like working just before the sun rises with the curtains open to the semidarkness. I've always liked the quiet when no one is around, with just the birds chirping. When I was in grade school, I wasn't allowed to go outside if I woke up too early. But because I really wanted to see what it was like outside, I would open the windows and watch excitedly as it gradually grew light. So even when I'm facing a deadline, I'm able to work cheerfully during this time of day. Strangely though, as soon as the sun fully rises, the magic disappears and reality intrudes. It's almost violent. Forgive me. I'll move my hand super hard and draw, so forgive me. Somehow I've managed to complete this volume while going back and forth between being relaxed and frantic. It would really please me if you all can read it feeling relaxed the whole time.

Io Sakisaka

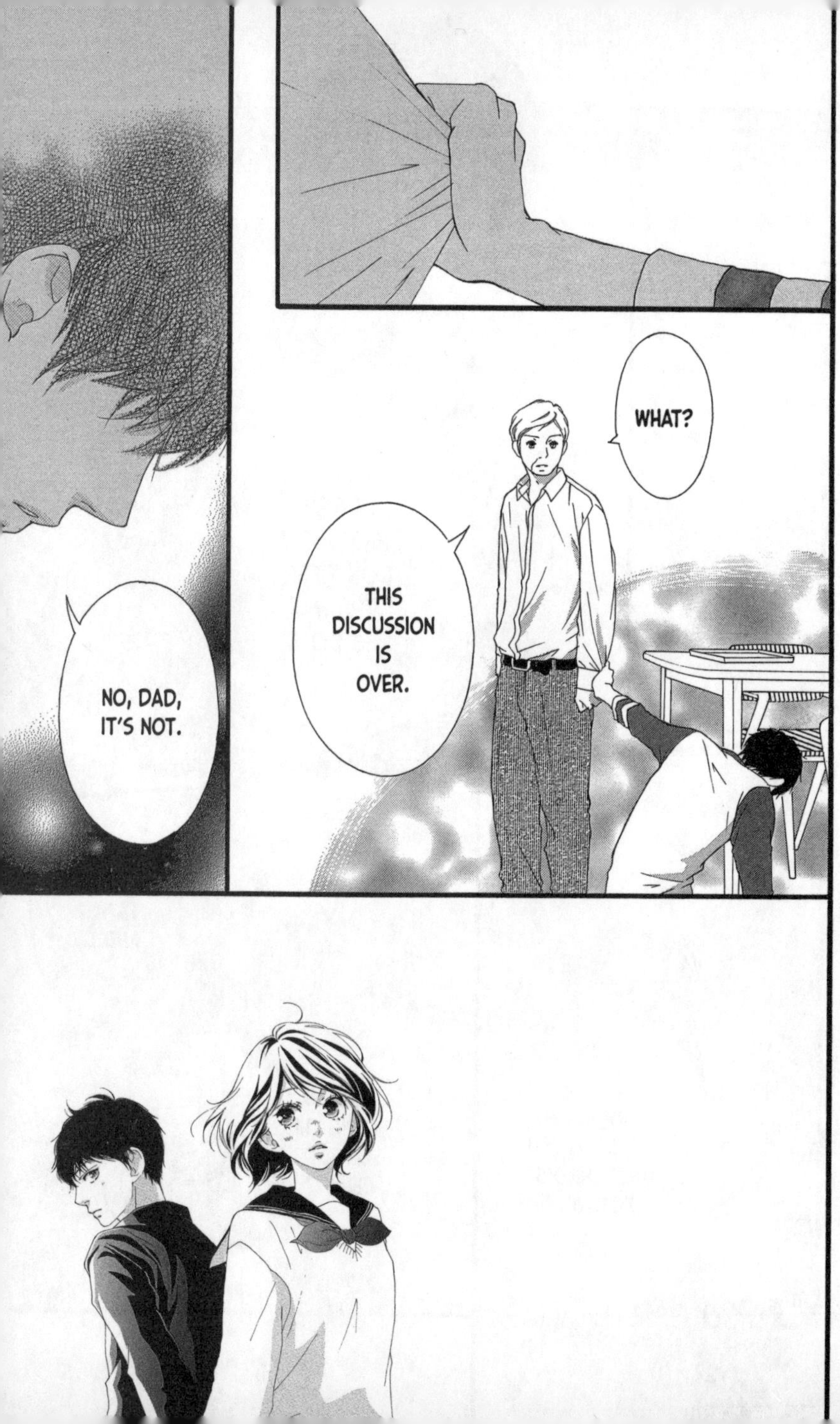
WHAT?
THIS DISCUSSION IS OVER.
NO, DAD, IT'S NOT.

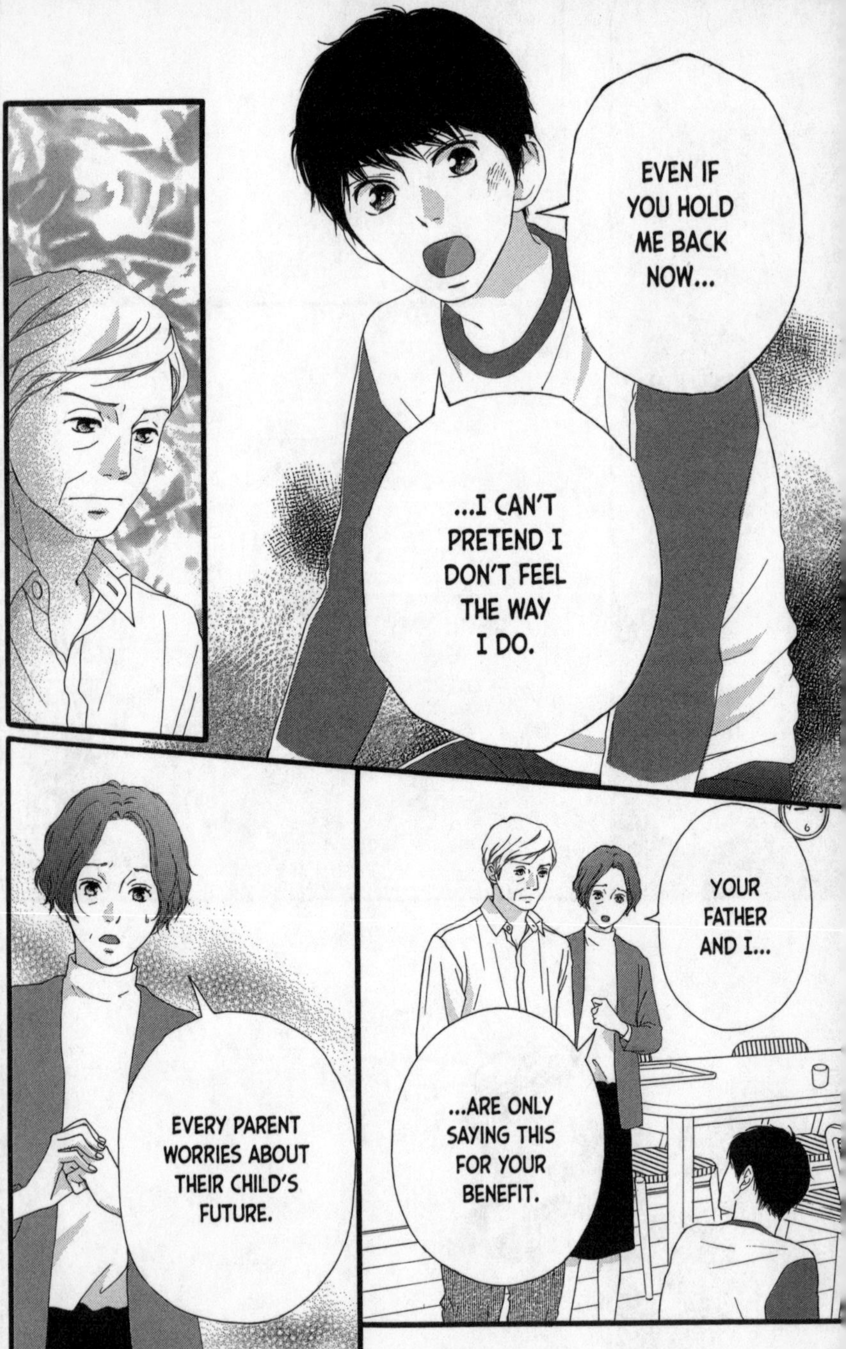
EVEN IF YOU HOLD ME BACK NOW...
...I CAN'T PRETEND I DON'T FEEL THE WAY I DO.
YOUR FATHER AND I...
...ARE ONLY SAYING THIS FOR YOUR BENEFIT.
EVERY PARENT WORRIES ABOUT THEIR CHILD'S FUTURE.

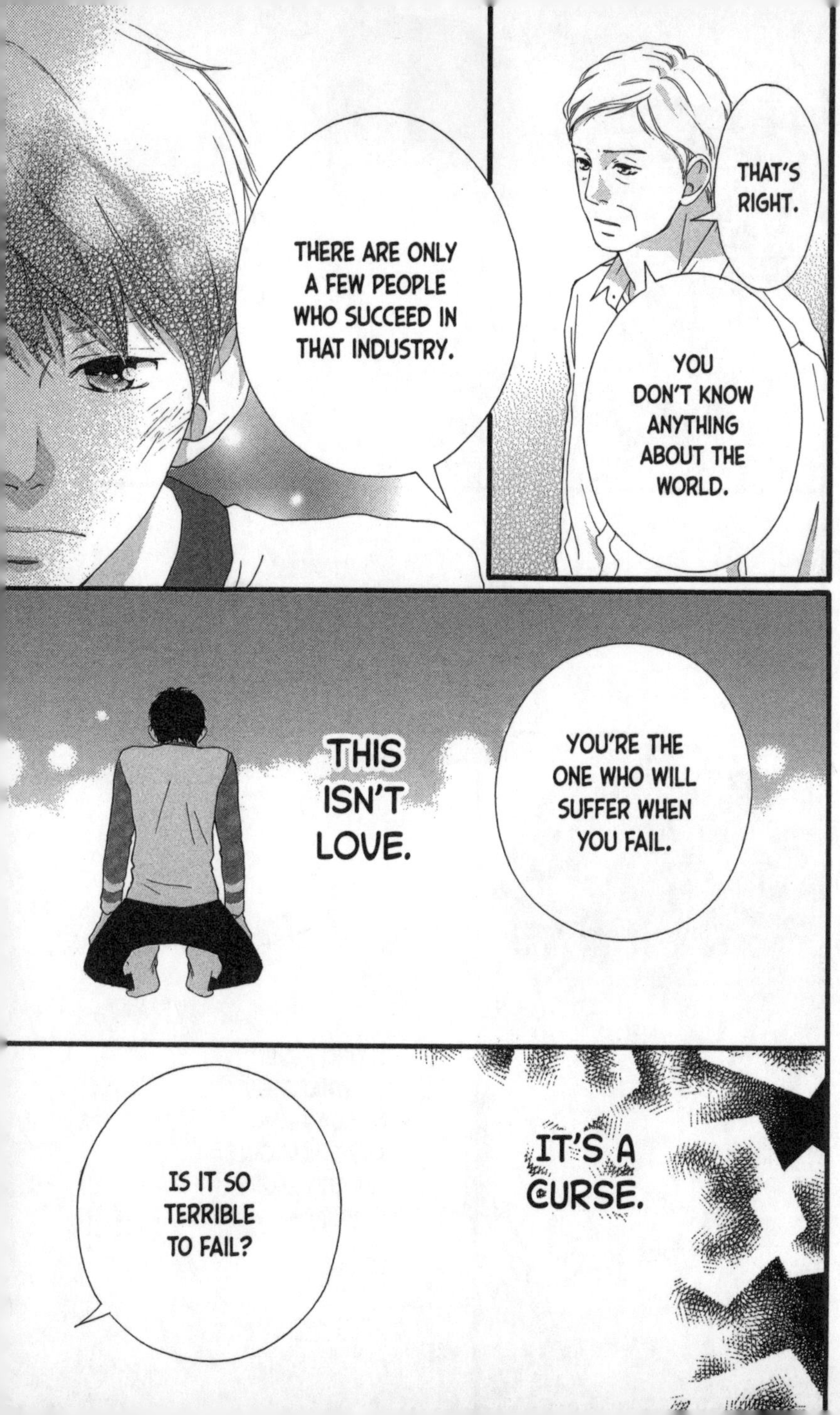

THAT'S RIGHT.
YOU DON'T KNOW ANYTHING ABOUT THE WORLD.
THERE ARE ONLY A FEW PEOPLE WHO SUCCEED IN THAT INDUSTRY.
YOU'RE THE ONE WHO WILL SUFFER WHEN YOU FAIL.
THIS ISN'T LOVE.
IT'S A CURSE.
IS IT SO TERRIBLE TO FAIL?

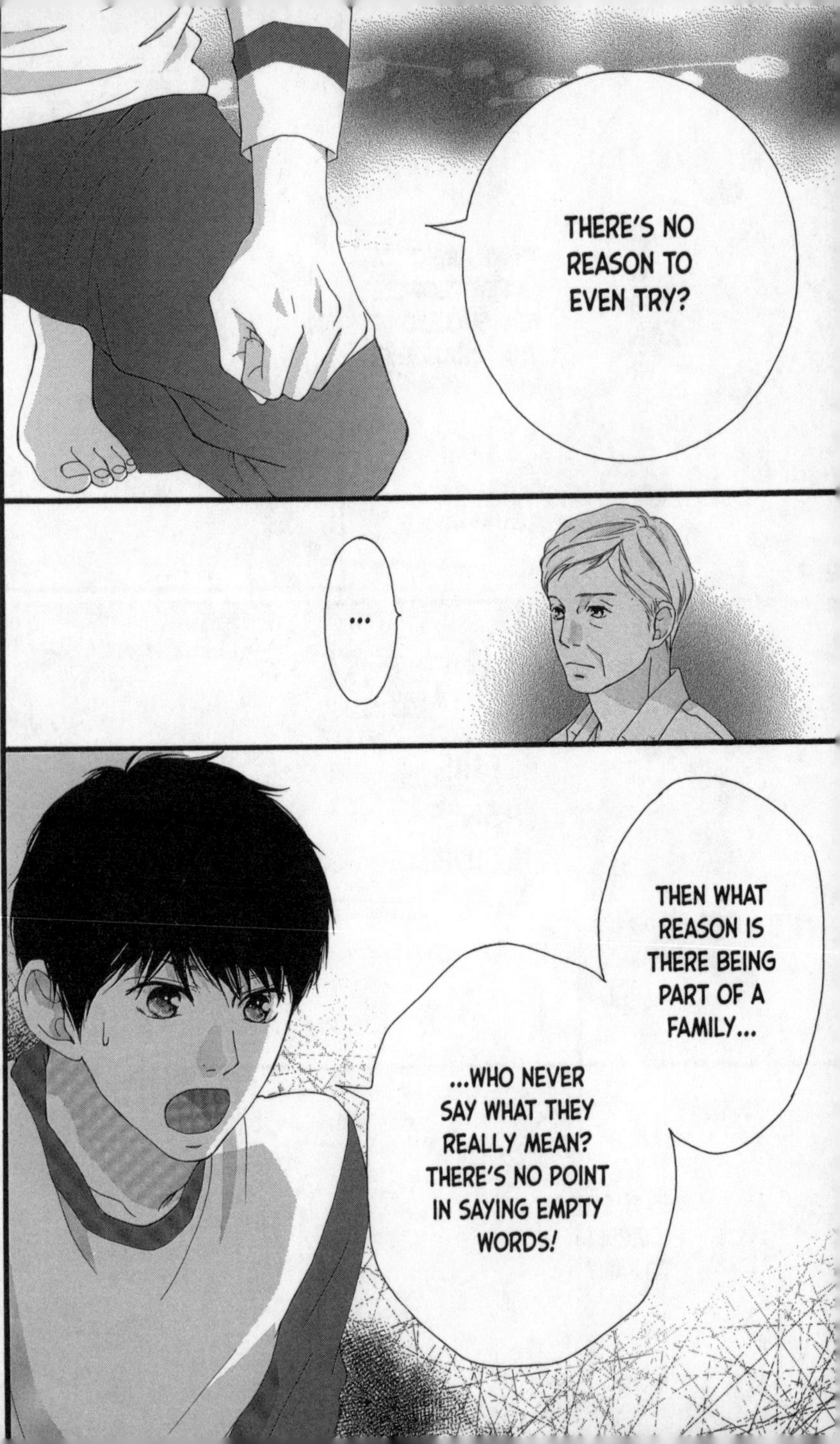
THERE'S NO REASON TO EVEN TRY?
...
THEN WHAT REASON IS THERE BEING PART OF A FAMILY...
...WHO NEVER SAY WHAT THEY REALLY MEAN? THERE'S NO POINT IN SAYING EMPTY WORDS!

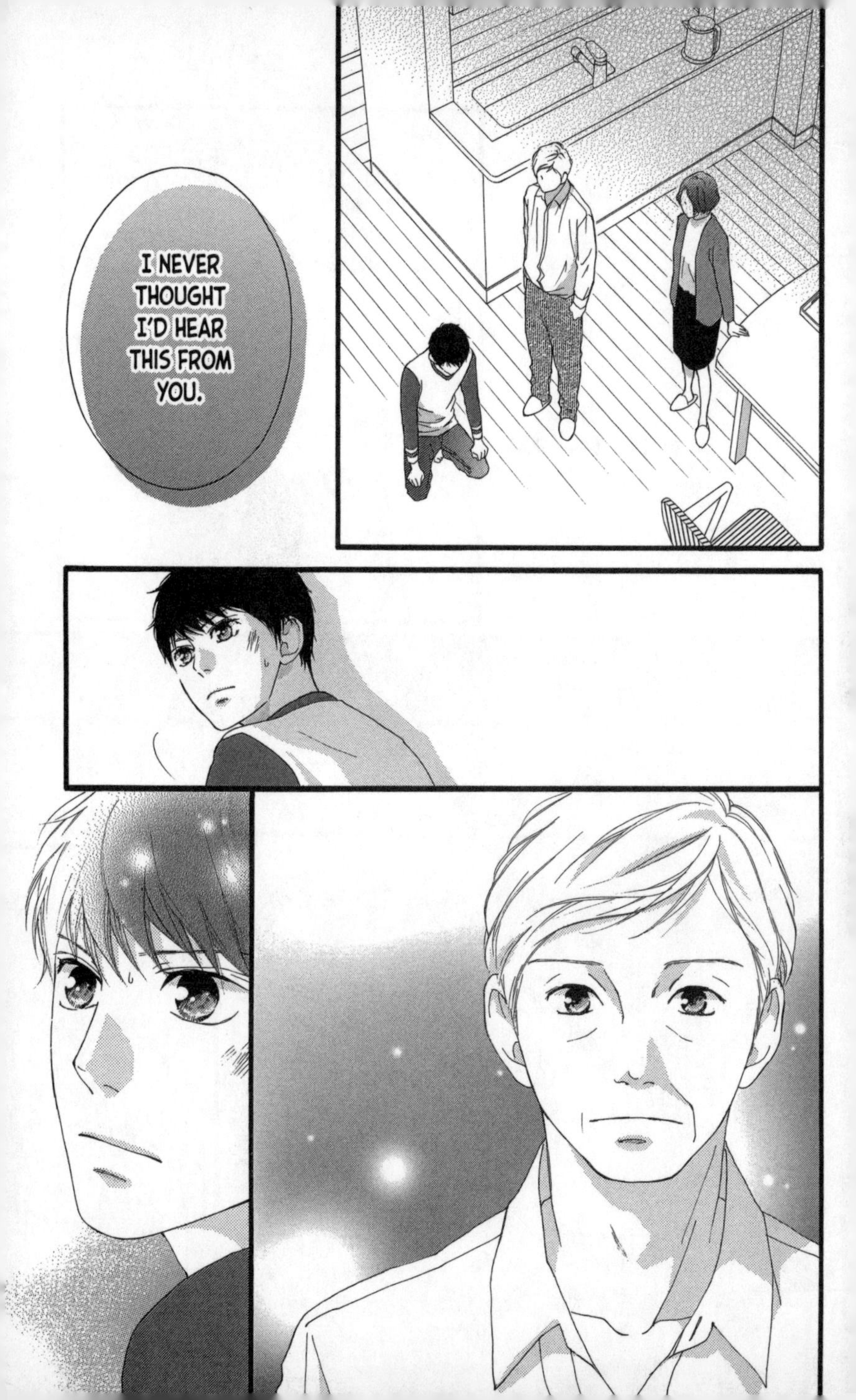
I NEVER THOUGHT I'D HEAR THIS FROM YOU.

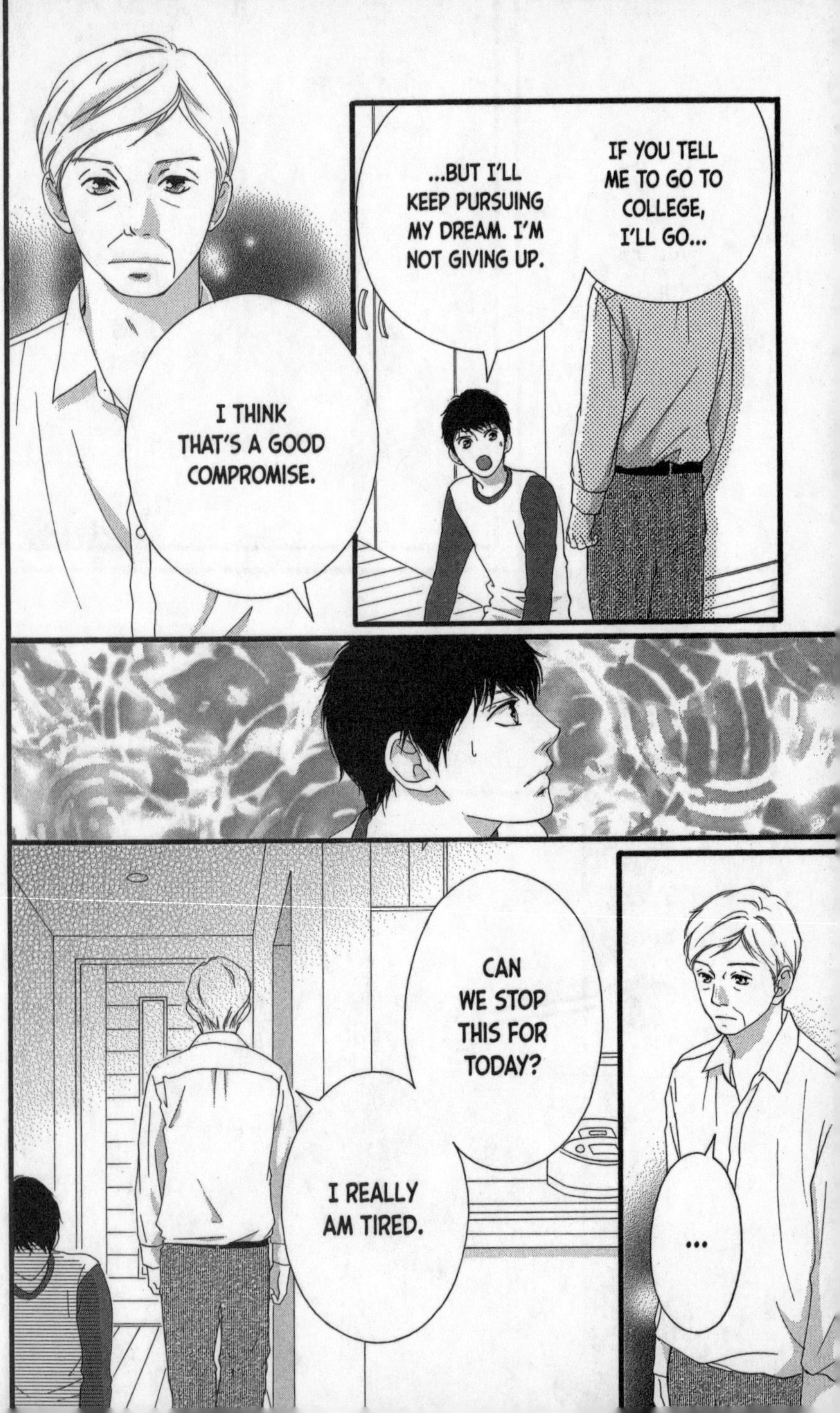

IF YOU TELL ME TO GO TO COLLEGE, I'LL GO...
...BUT I'LL KEEP PURSUING MY DREAM. I'M NOT GIVING UP.
I THINK THAT'S A GOOD COMPROMISE.
...
CAN WE STOP THIS FOR TODAY?
I REALLY AM TIRED.

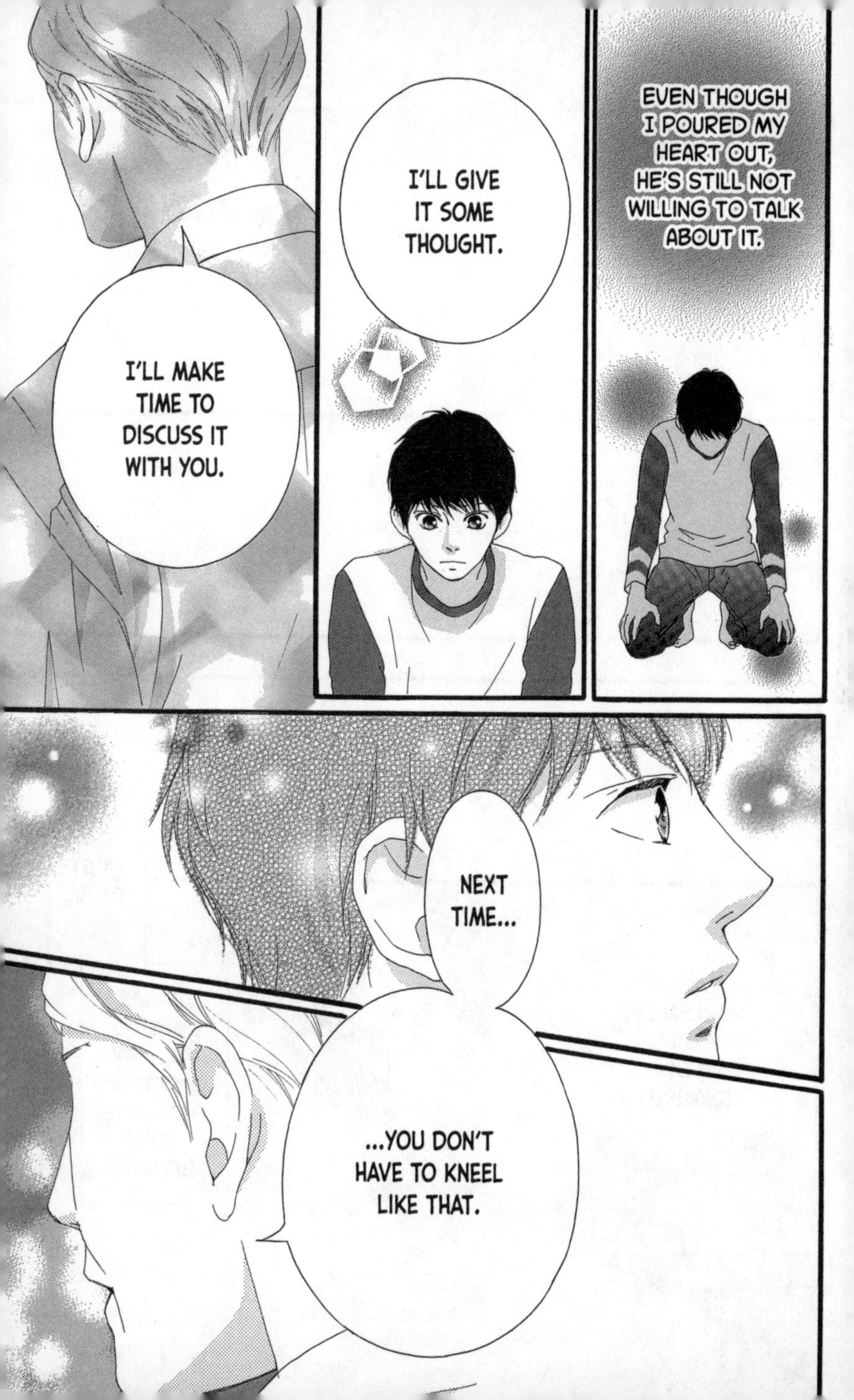
EVEN THOUGH I POURED MY HEART OUT, HE'S STILL NOT WILLING TO TALK ABOUT IT.
I'LL GIVE IT SOME THOUGHT.
I'LL MAKE TIME TO DISCUSS IT WITH YOU.
NEXT TIME...
...YOU DON'T HAVE TO KNEEL LIKE THAT.

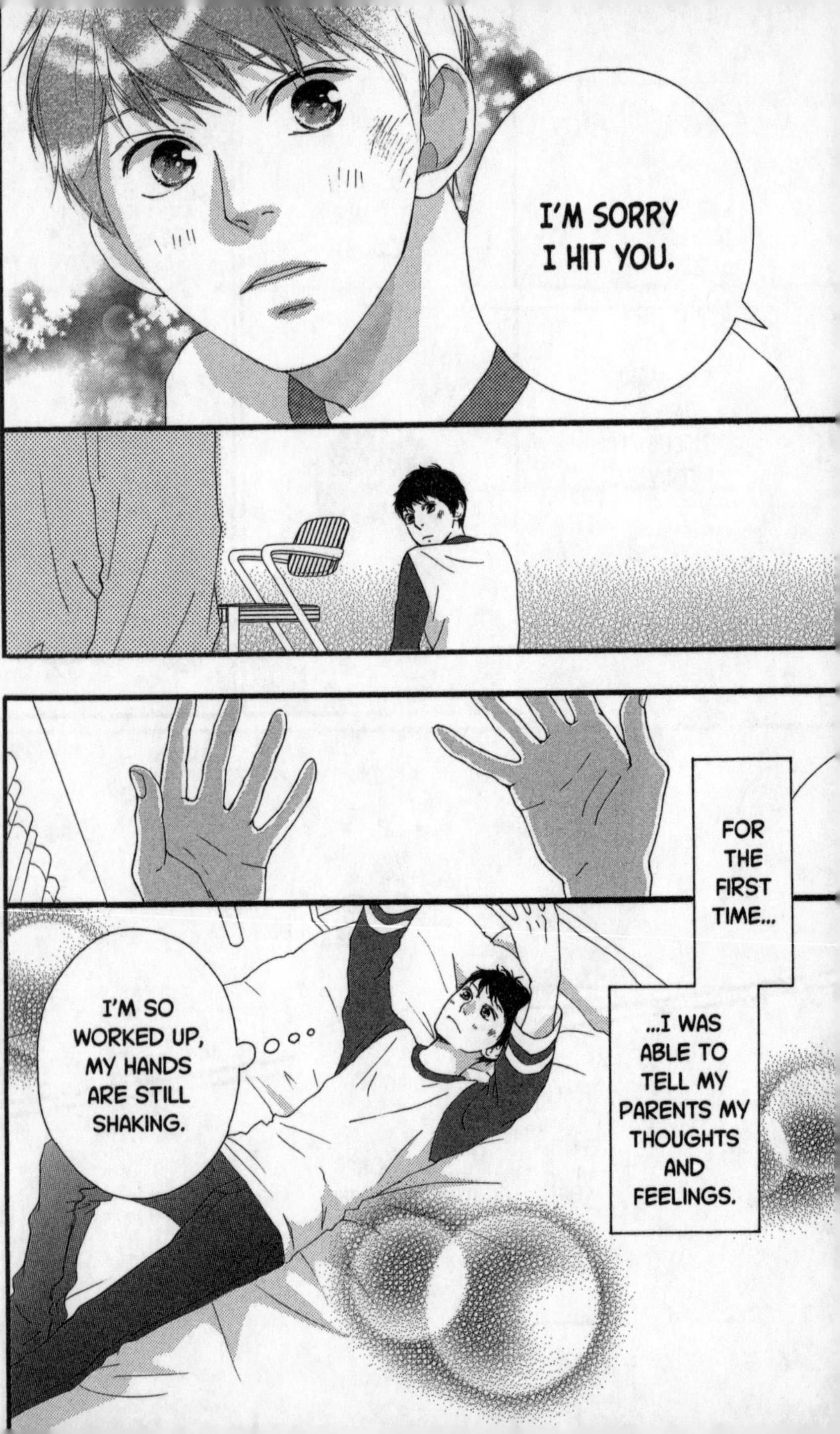
I'M SORRY I HIT YOU.
FOR THE FIRST TIME...
...I WAS ABLE TO TELL MY PARENTS MY THOUGHTS AND FEELINGS.
I'M SO WORKED UP, MY HANDS ARE STILL SHAKING.

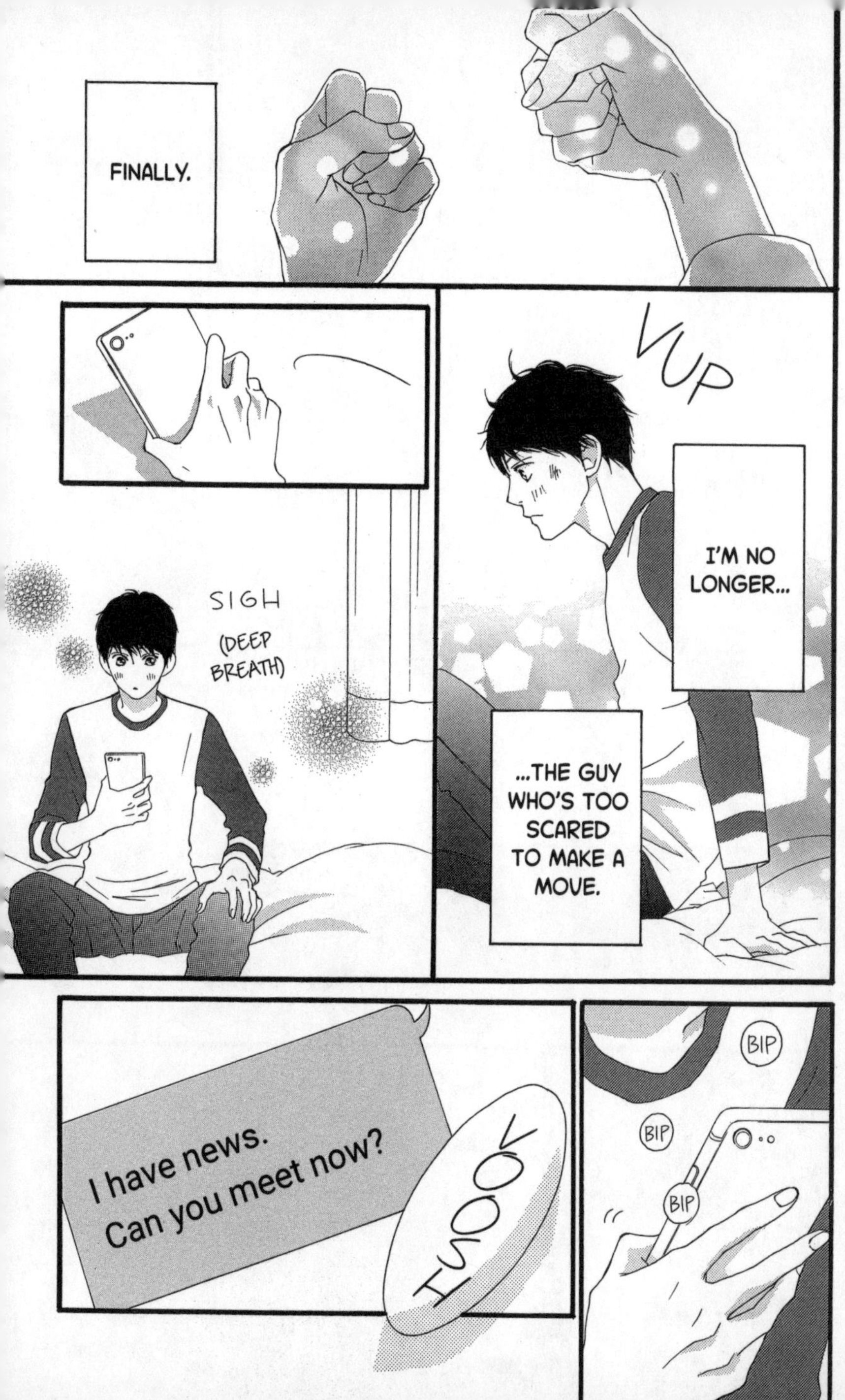
FINALLY.
VUP
I'M NO LONGER...
...THE GUY WHO'S TOO SCARED TO MAKE A MOVE.
SIGH
(DEEP BREATH)
BIP
BIP
BIP
I have news. Can you meet now?
VOOSH

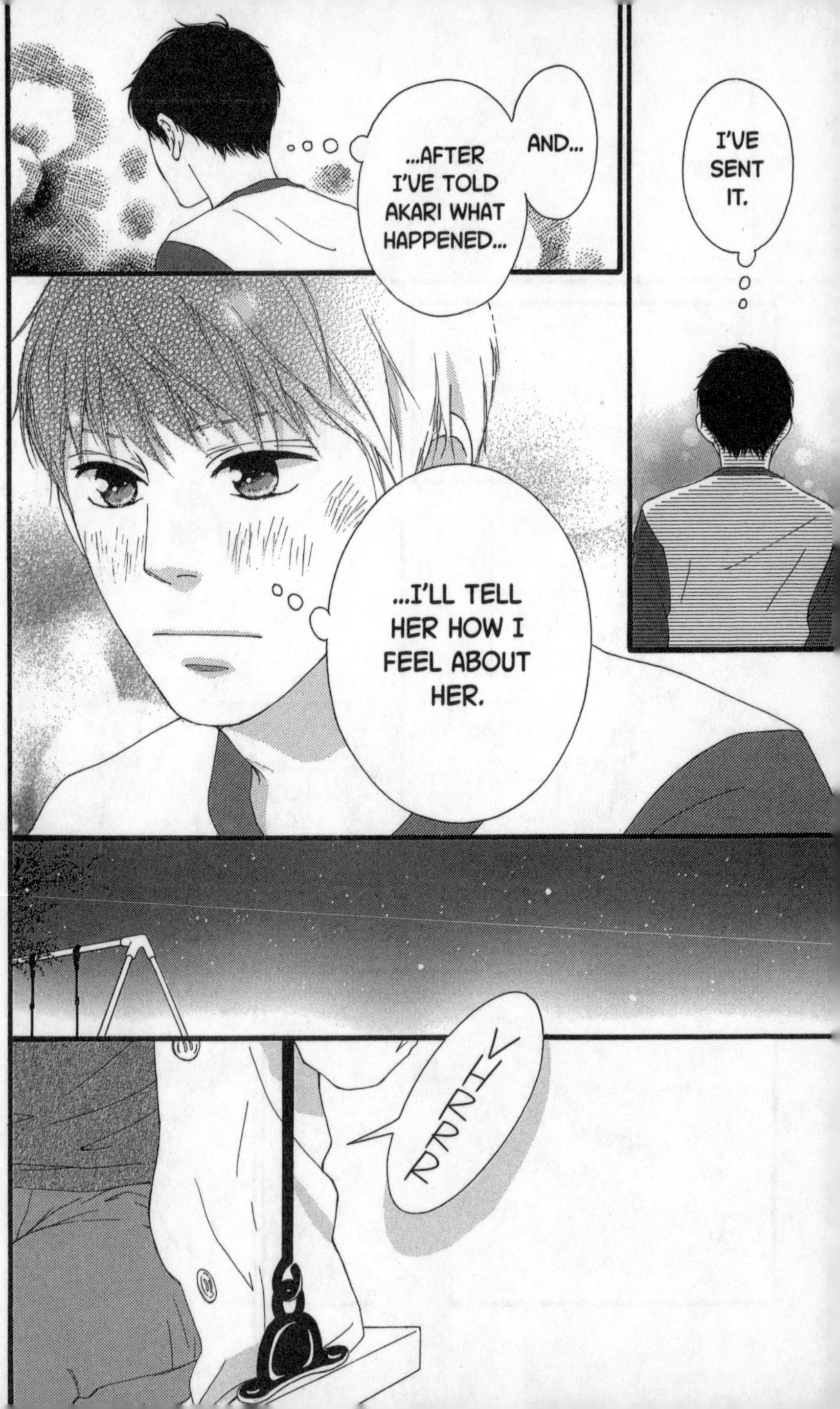
I'VE SENT IT.
AND...
...AFTER I'VE TOLD AKARI WHAT HAPPENED...
...I'LL TELL HER HOW I FEEL ABOUT HER.
VRRRR

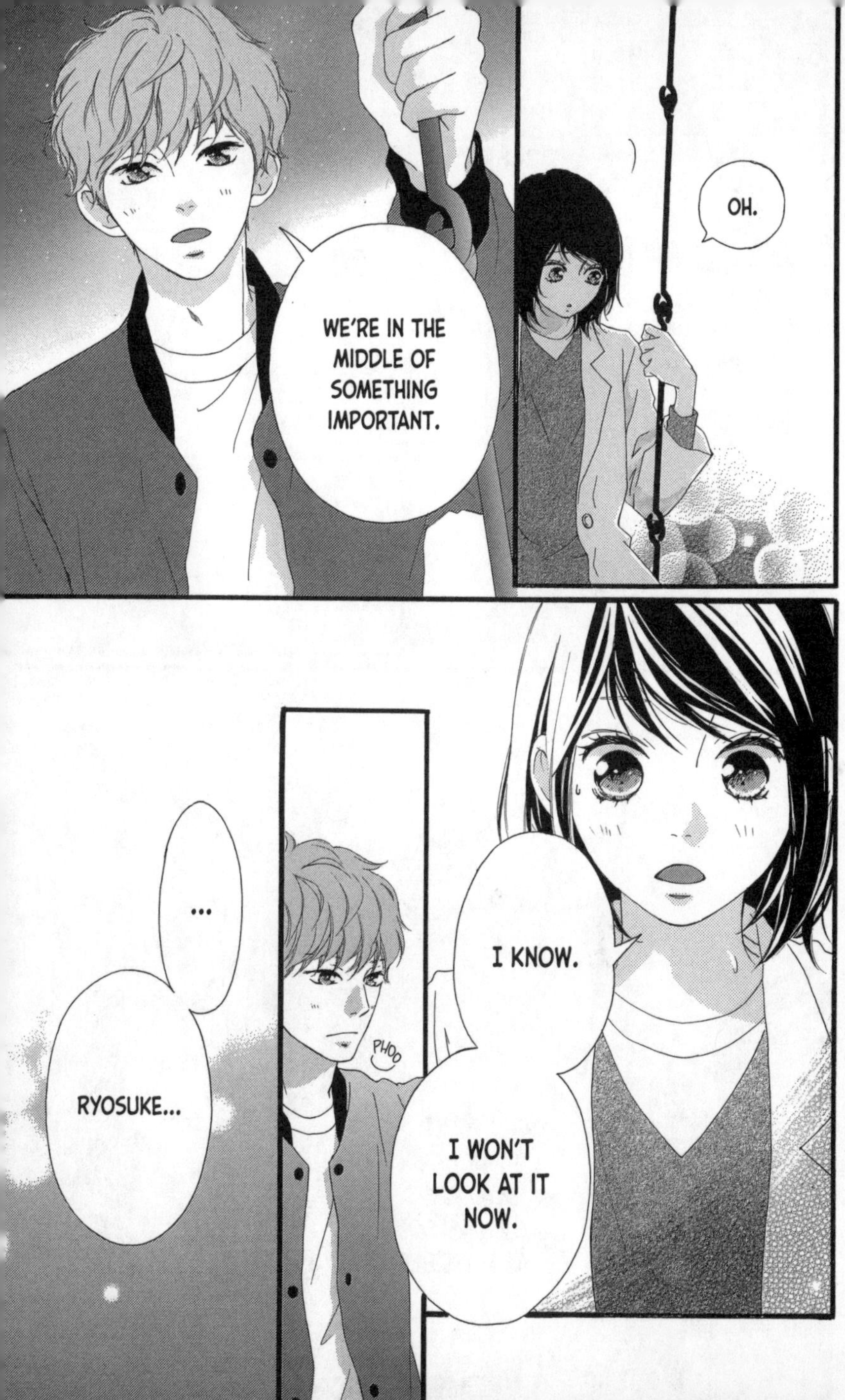
OH.
WE'RE IN THE MIDDLE OF SOMETHING IMPORTANT.
I KNOW.
I WON'T LOOK AT IT NOW.
PHOO
...
RYOSUKE...

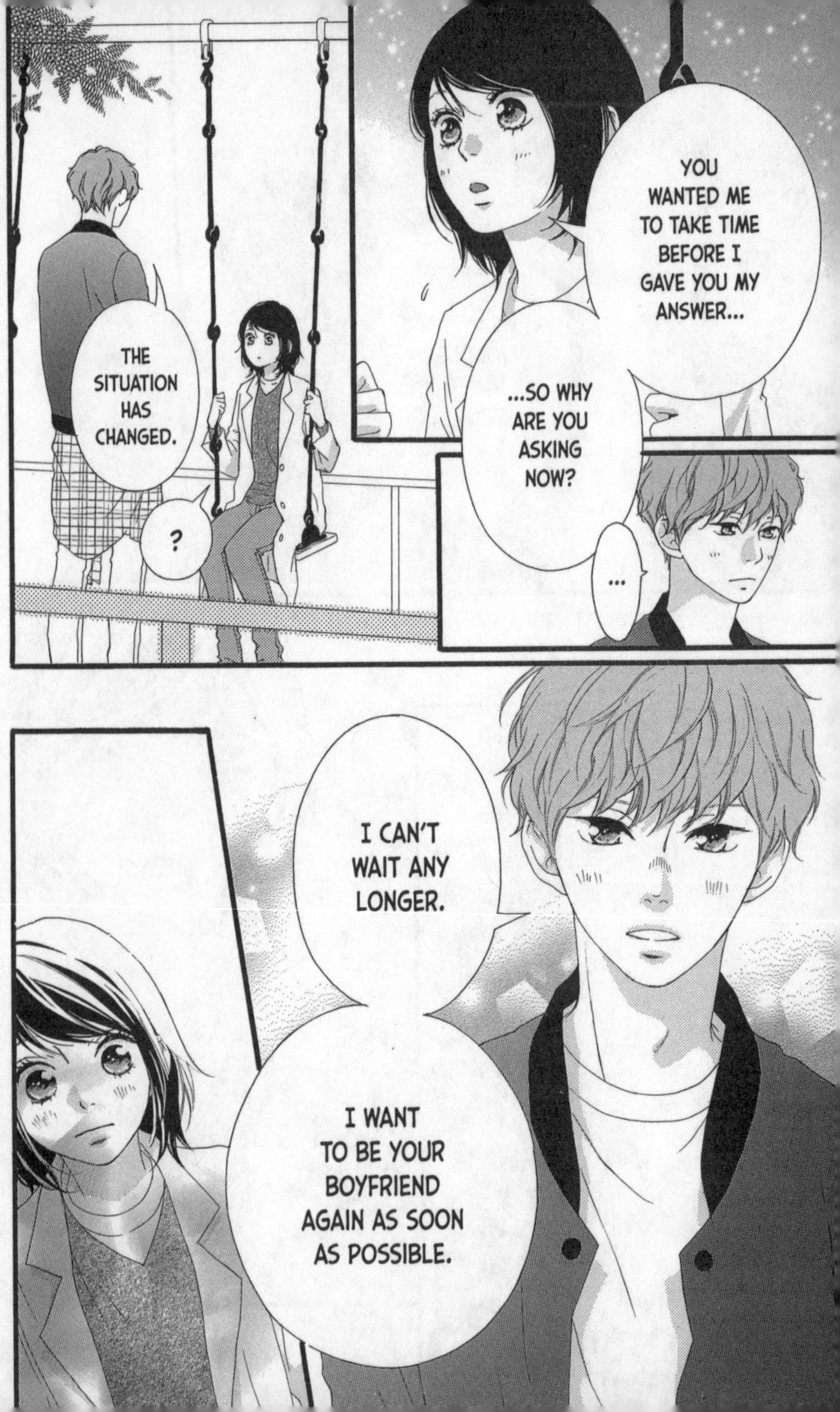
YOU WANTED ME TO TAKE TIME BEFORE I GAVE YOU MY ANSWER...
...SO WHY ARE YOU ASKING NOW?
...
THE SITUATION HAS CHANGED.
?
I CAN'T WAIT ANY LONGER.
I WANT TO BE YOUR BOYFRIEND AGAIN AS SOON AS POSSIBLE.

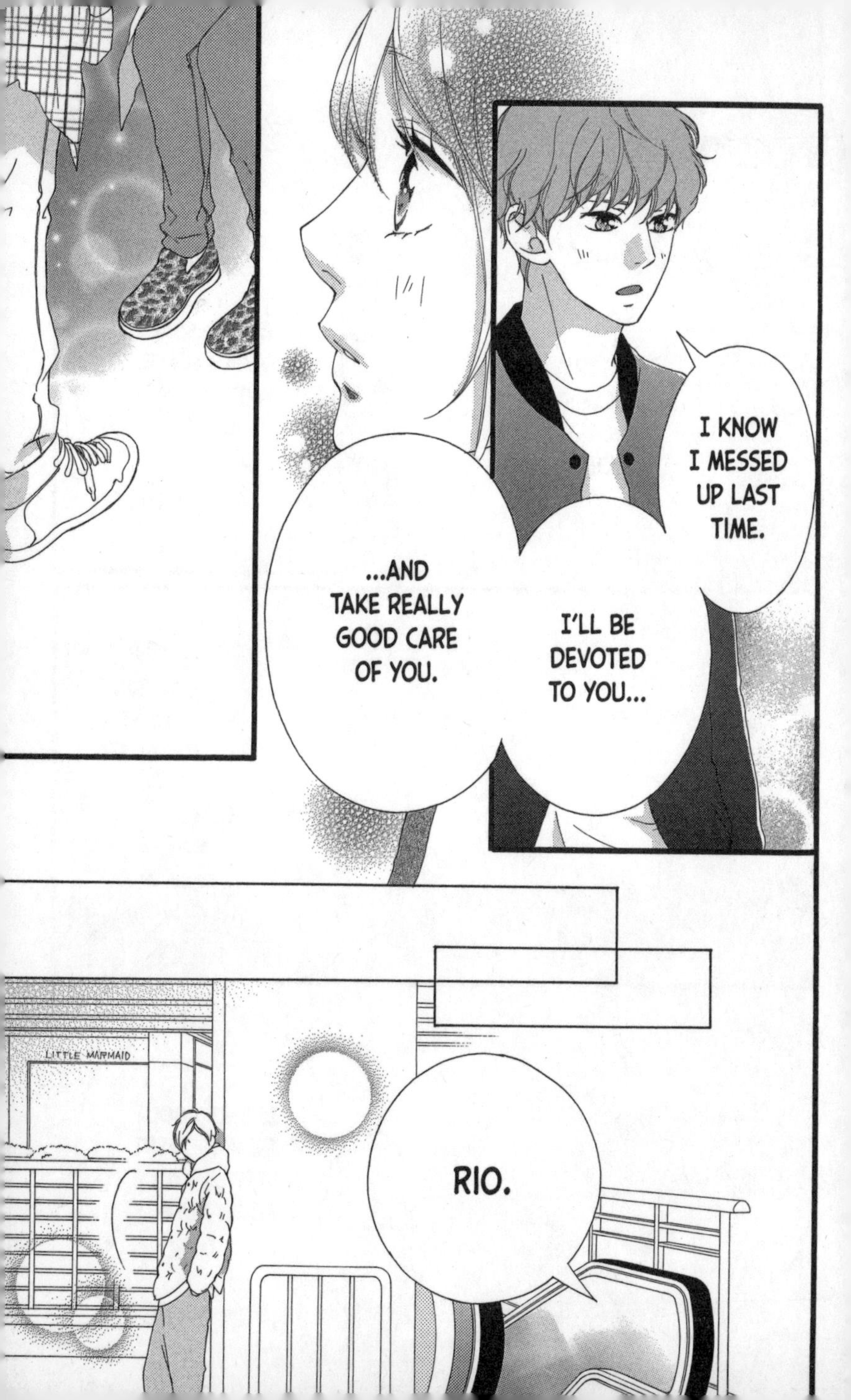
I KNOW I MESSED UP LAST TIME.
I'LL BE DEVOTED TO YOU...
...AND TAKE REALLY GOOD CARE OF YOU.
RIO.
LITTLE MARMAID

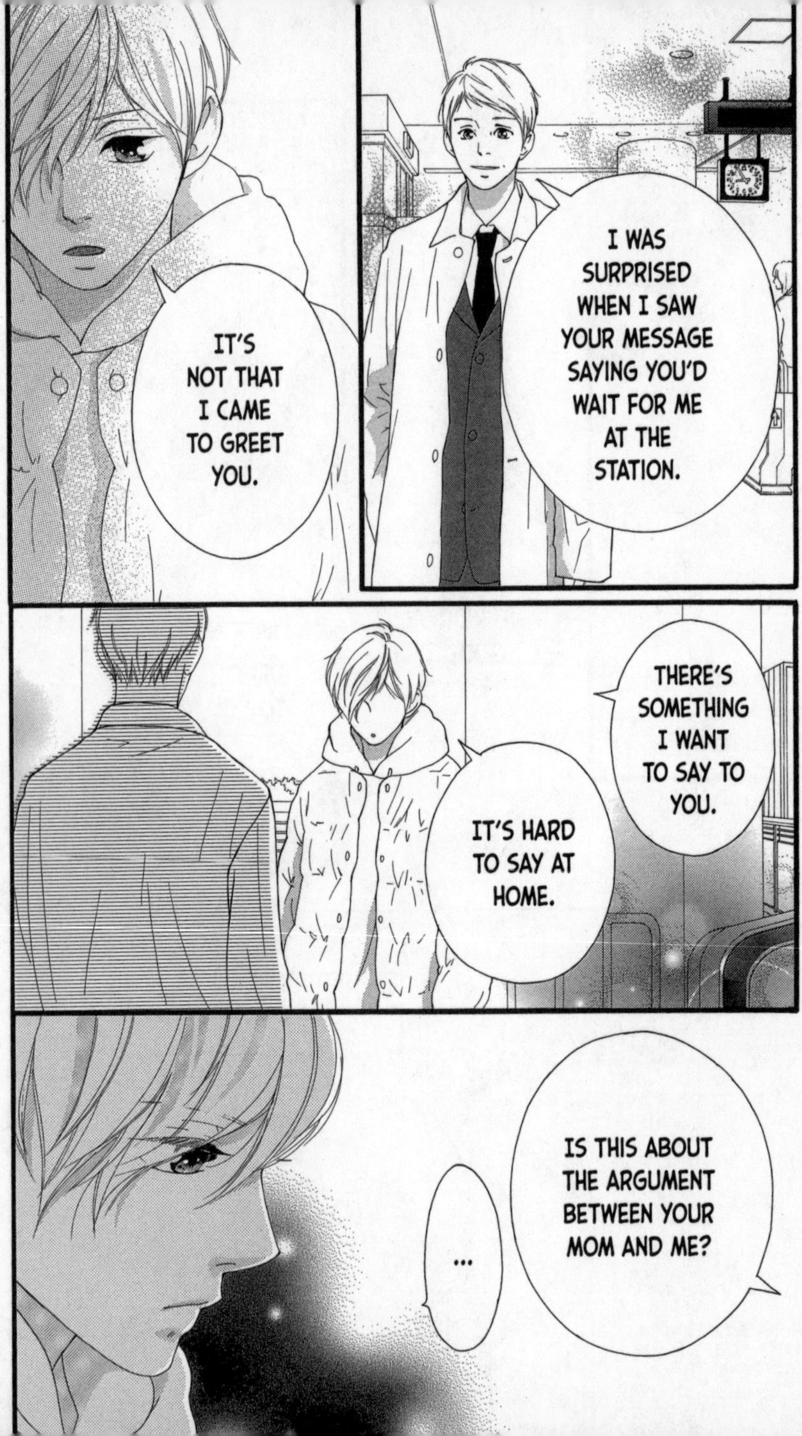
I WAS SURPRISED WHEN I SAW YOUR MESSAGE SAYING YOU'D WAIT FOR ME AT THE STATION.
IT'S NOT THAT I CAME TO GREET YOU.
THERE'S SOMETHING I WANT TO SAY TO YOU.
IT'S HARD TO SAY AT HOME.
IS THIS ABOUT THE ARGUMENT BETWEEN YOUR MOM AND ME?
...

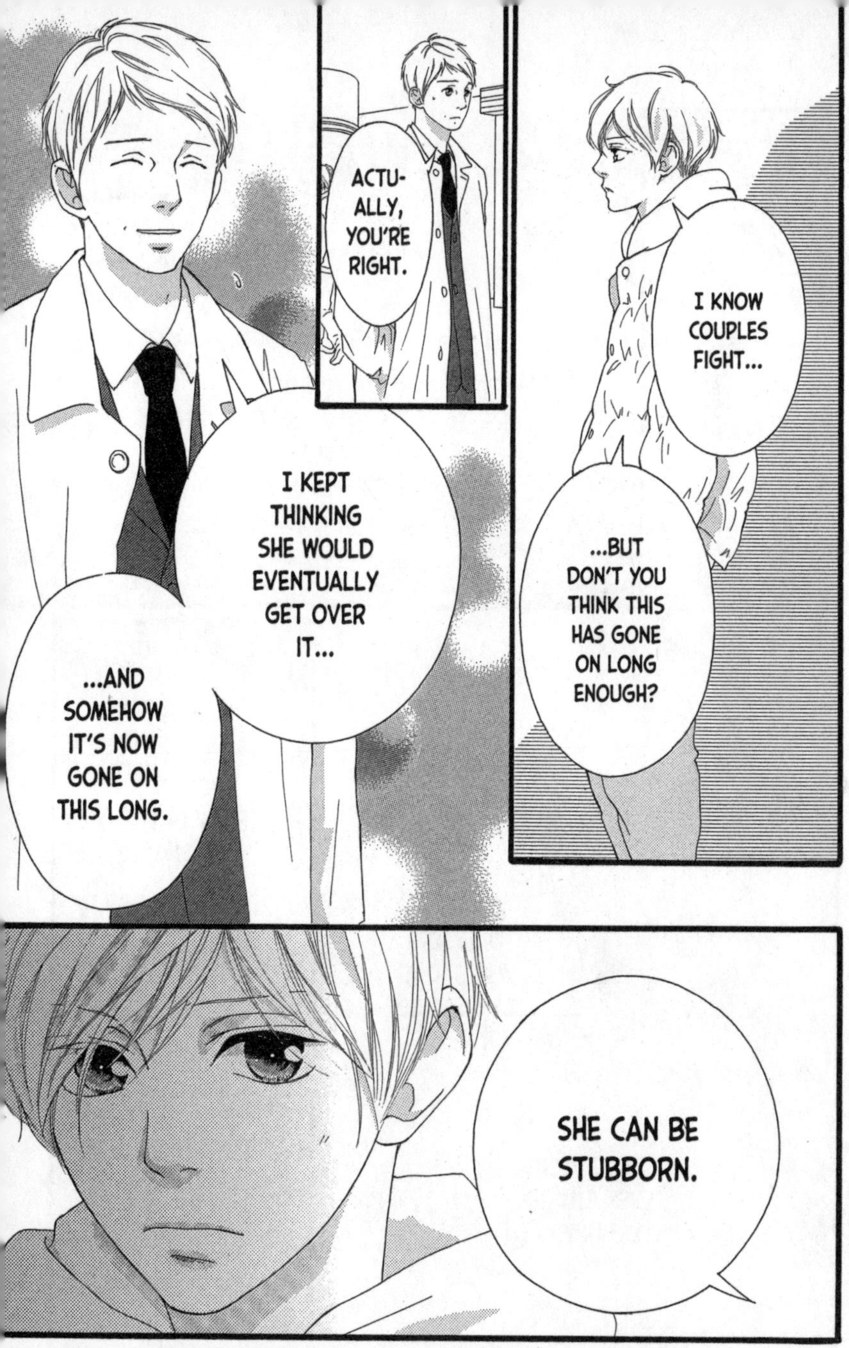
I KNOW COUPLES FIGHT...
...BUT DON'T YOU THINK THIS HAS GONE ON LONG ENOUGH?
ACTU-ALLY, YOU'RE RIGHT.
I KEPT THINKING SHE WOULD EVENTUALLY GET OVER IT...
...AND SOMEHOW IT'S NOW GONE ON THIS LONG.
SHE CAN BE STUBBORN.

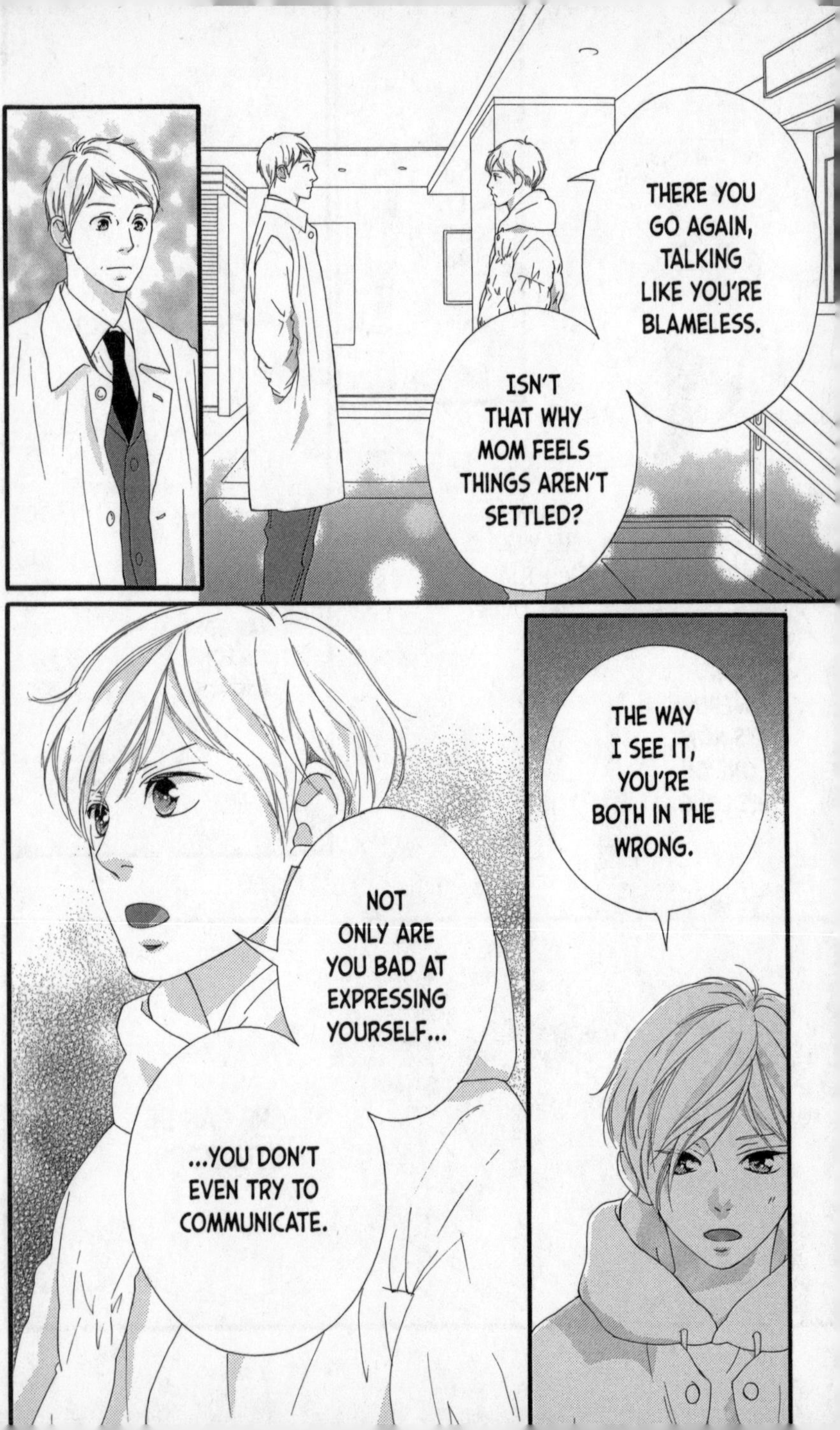
THERE YOU GO AGAIN, TALKING LIKE YOU'RE BLAMELESS.
ISN'T THAT WHY MOM FEELS THINGS AREN'T SETTLED?
THE WAY I SEE IT, YOU'RE BOTH IN THE WRONG.
NOT ONLY ARE YOU BAD AT EXPRESSING YOURSELF...
...YOU DON'T EVEN TRY TO COMMUNICATE.

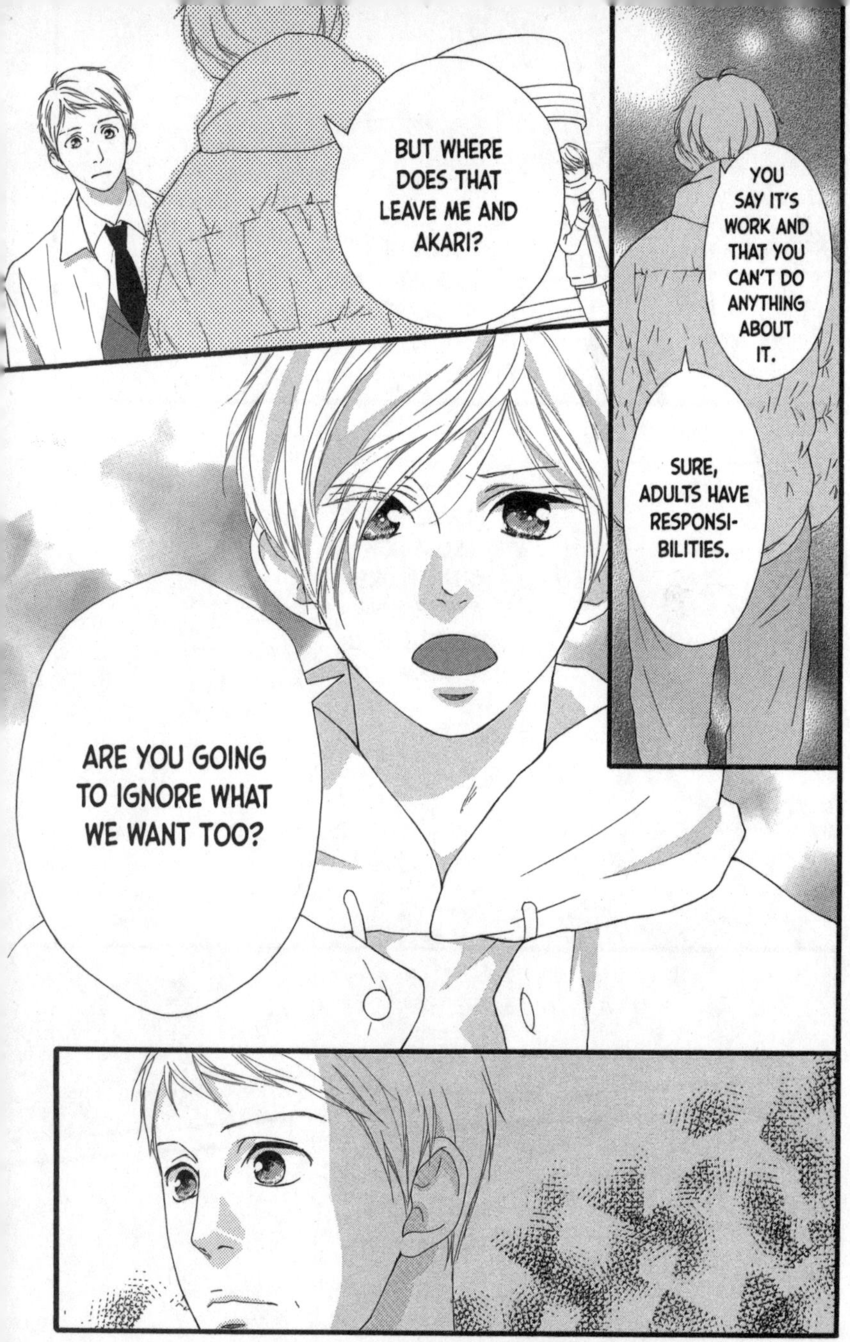
YOU SAY IT'S WORK AND THAT YOU CAN'T DO ANYTHING ABOUT IT.
SURE, ADULTS HAVE RESPONSI-BILITIES.
BUT WHERE DOES THAT LEAVE ME AND AKARI?
ARE YOU GOING TO IGNORE WHAT WE WANT TOO?

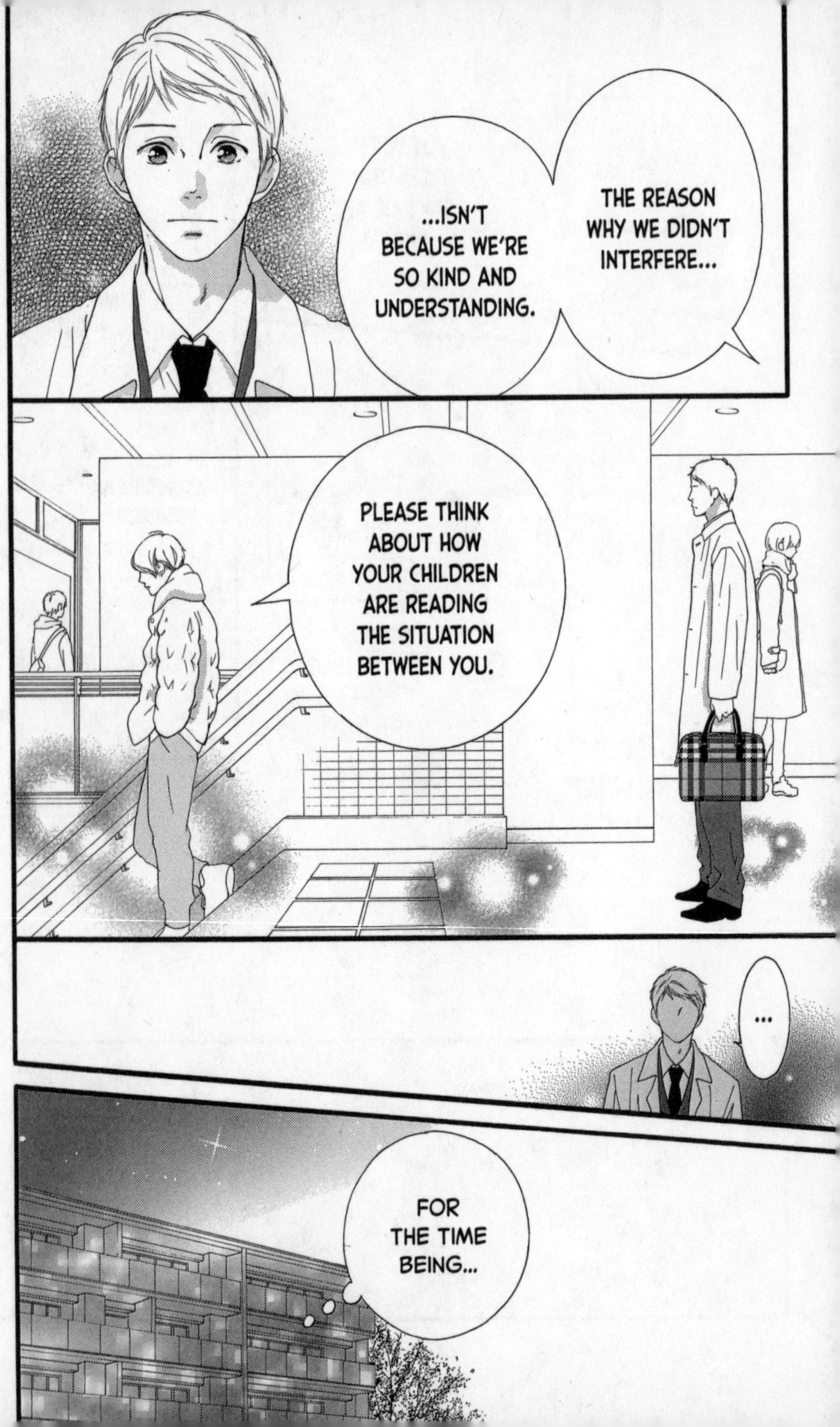
THE REASON WHY WE DIDN'T INTERFERE...
...ISN'T BECAUSE WE'RE SO KIND AND UNDERSTANDING.
PLEASE THINK ABOUT HOW YOUR CHILDREN ARE READING THE SITUATION BETWEEN YOU.
...
FOR THE TIME BEING...

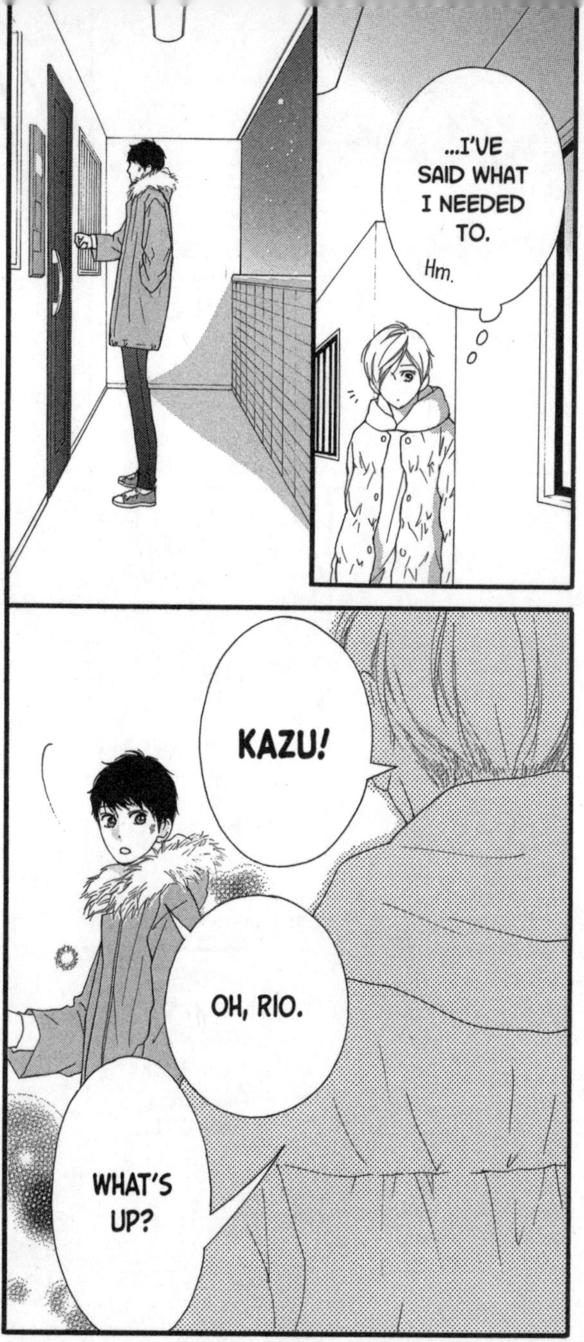
...I'VE SAID WHAT I NEEDED TO.
Hm.
KAZU!
OH, RIO.
WHAT'S UP?

I usually sit all the time while working. Especially when I start drawing, I stay in the same position all day. I thought about using a pedometer to see how little I actually move, but I wasn't sure I could accept the number, so I decided against it. It's not good. I feel sorry for my body, so I've decided that while I'm working, I'll do radio calisthenics every morning. I was very lackadaisical about these exercises in grade school, but when you get passionate about how precisely you can do them, they become fun. My body is happy from being stretched, and I feel awake. It's exactly what I needed. Maybe this is something the very lazy me can continue... If one of these days I make it to the third or fourth level, I will let you know! (*laugh*)

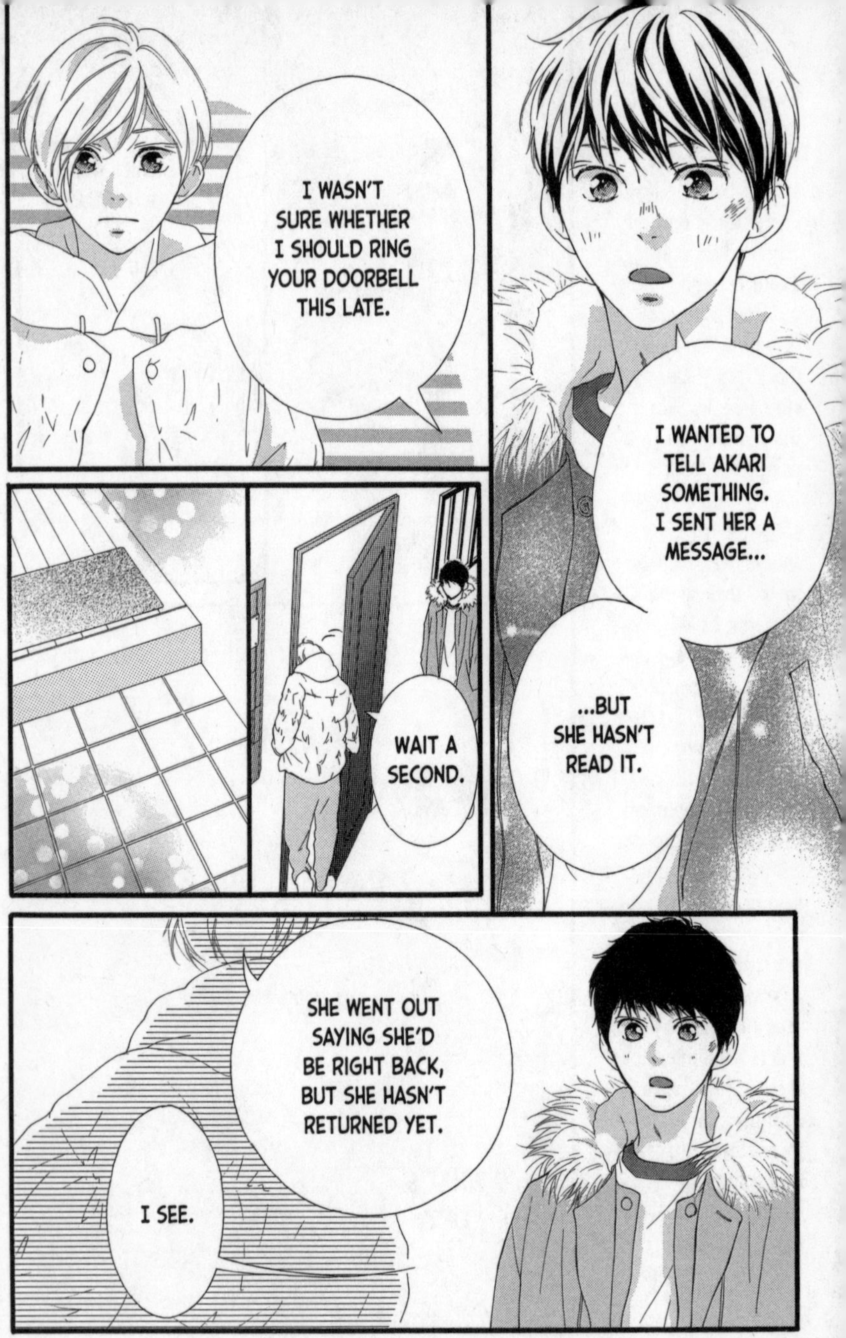
I WANTED TO TELL AKARI SOMETHING. I SENT HER A MESSAGE...
...BUT SHE HASN'T READ IT.
I WASN'T SURE WHETHER I SHOULD RING YOUR DOORBELL THIS LATE.
WAIT A SECOND.
SHE WENT OUT SAYING SHE'D BE RIGHT BACK, BUT SHE HASN'T RETURNED YET.
I SEE.

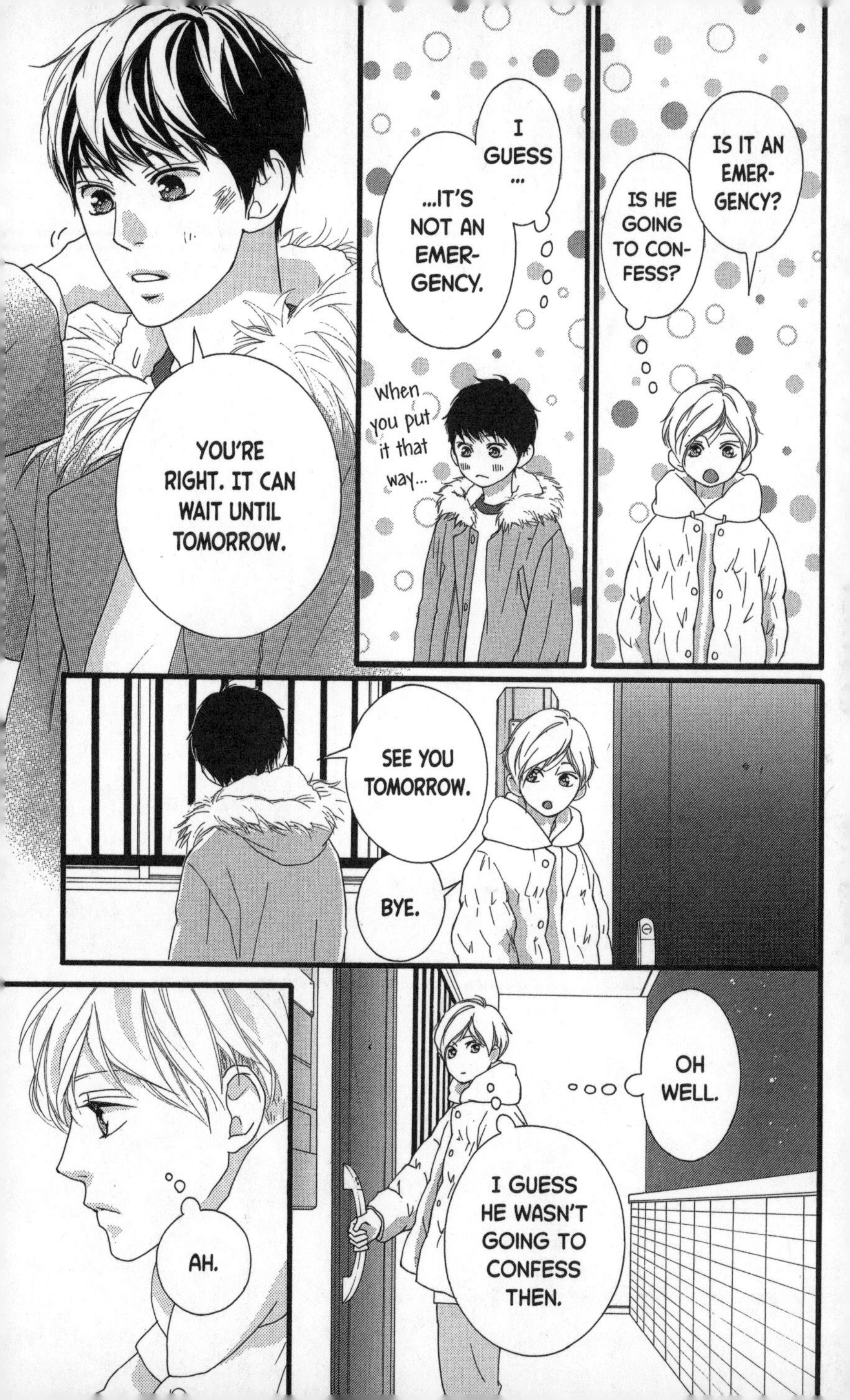
IS IT AN EMERGENCY?
IS HE GOING TO CONFESS?
I GUESS...
...IT'S NOT AN EMERGENCY.
When you put it that way...
YOU'RE RIGHT. IT CAN WAIT UNTIL TOMORROW.
SEE YOU TOMORROW.
BYE.
OH WELL.
I GUESS HE WASN'T GOING TO CONFESS THEN.
AH.

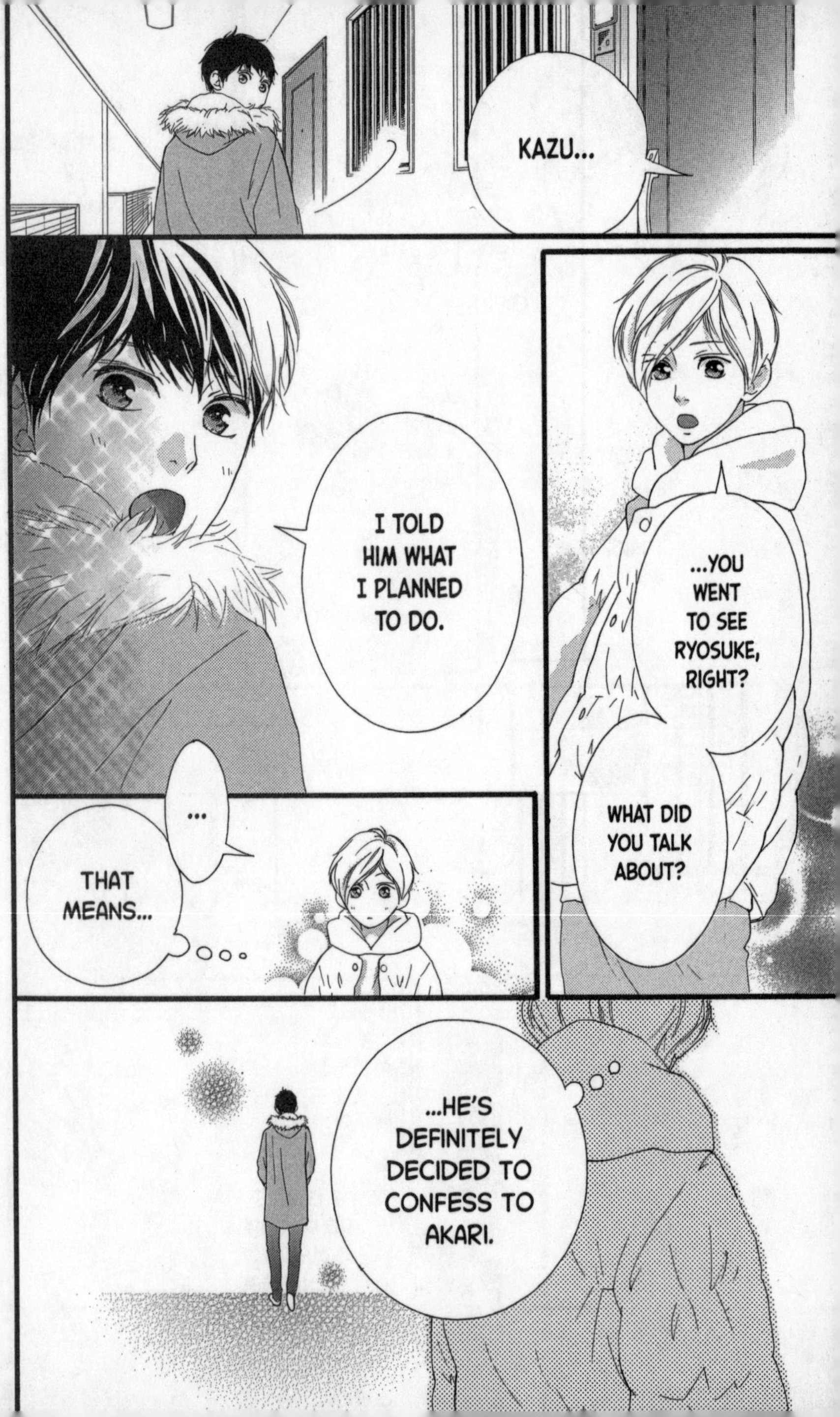
KAZU...
...YOU WENT TO SEE RYOSUKE, RIGHT?
WHAT DID YOU TALK ABOUT?
I TOLD HIM WHAT I PLANNED TO DO.
...
THAT MEANS...
...HE'S DEFINITELY DECIDED TO CONFESS TO AKARI.

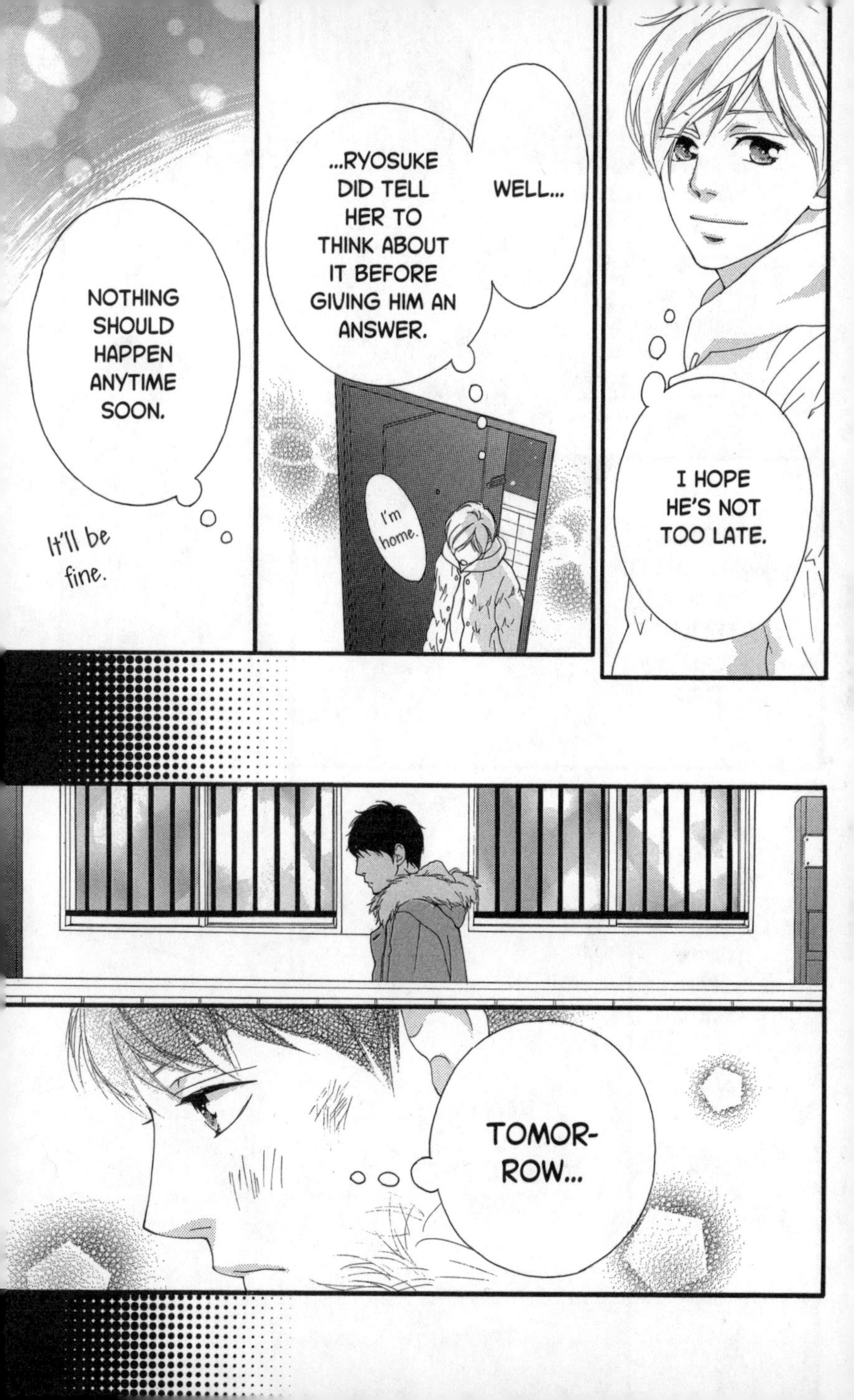
I HOPE HE'S NOT TOO LATE.
WELL...
...RYOSUKE DID TELL HER TO THINK ABOUT IT BEFORE GIVING HIM AN ANSWER.
I'm home.
NOTHING SHOULD HAPPEN ANYTIME SOON.
It'll be fine.
TOMOR-ROW...

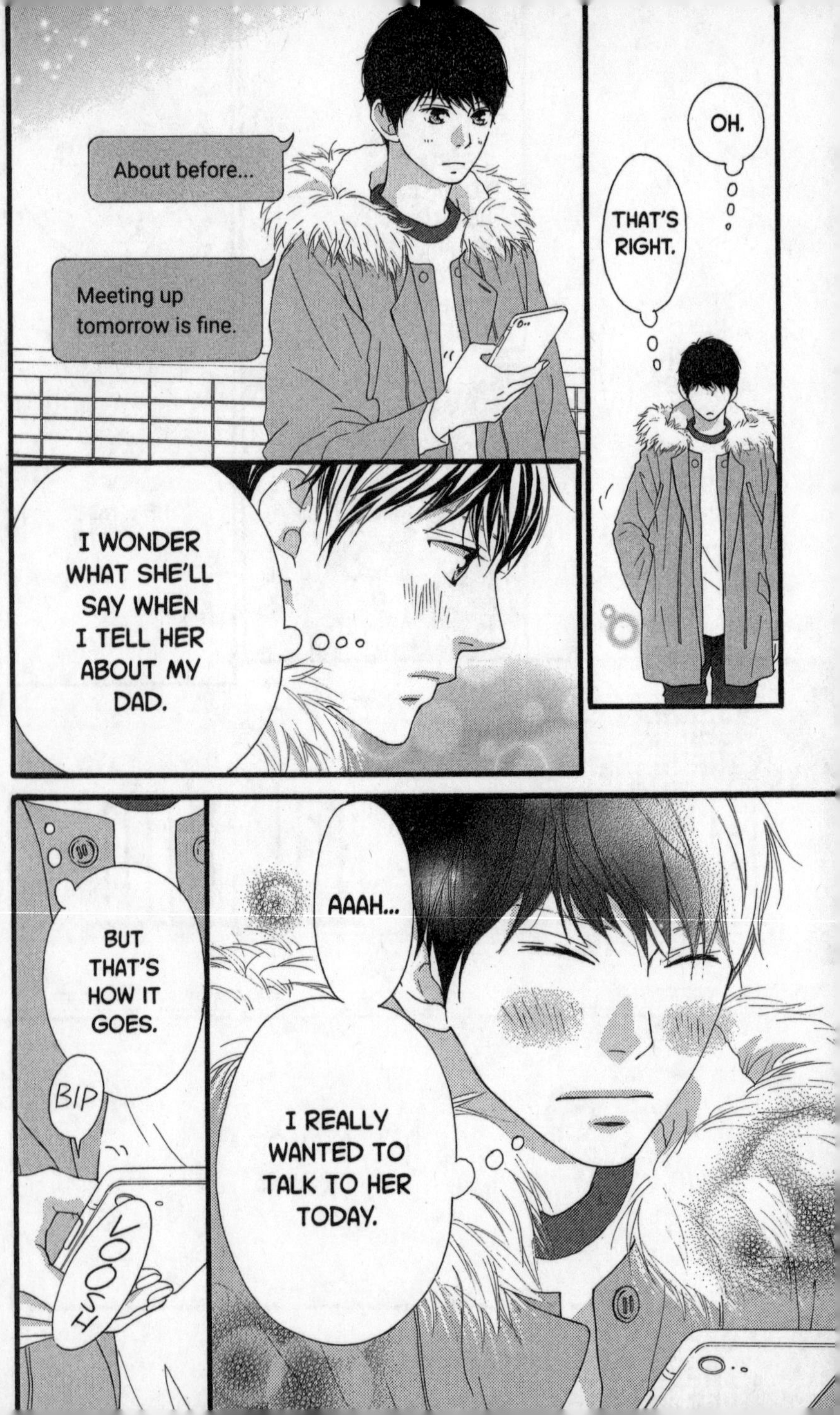
OH.
THAT'S RIGHT.
About before...
Meeting up tomorrow is fine.
I WONDER WHAT SHE'LL SAY WHEN I TELL HER ABOUT MY DAD.
AAAH...
I REALLY WANTED TO TALK TO HER TODAY.
BUT THAT'S HOW IT GOES.
BIP
VOOOSH

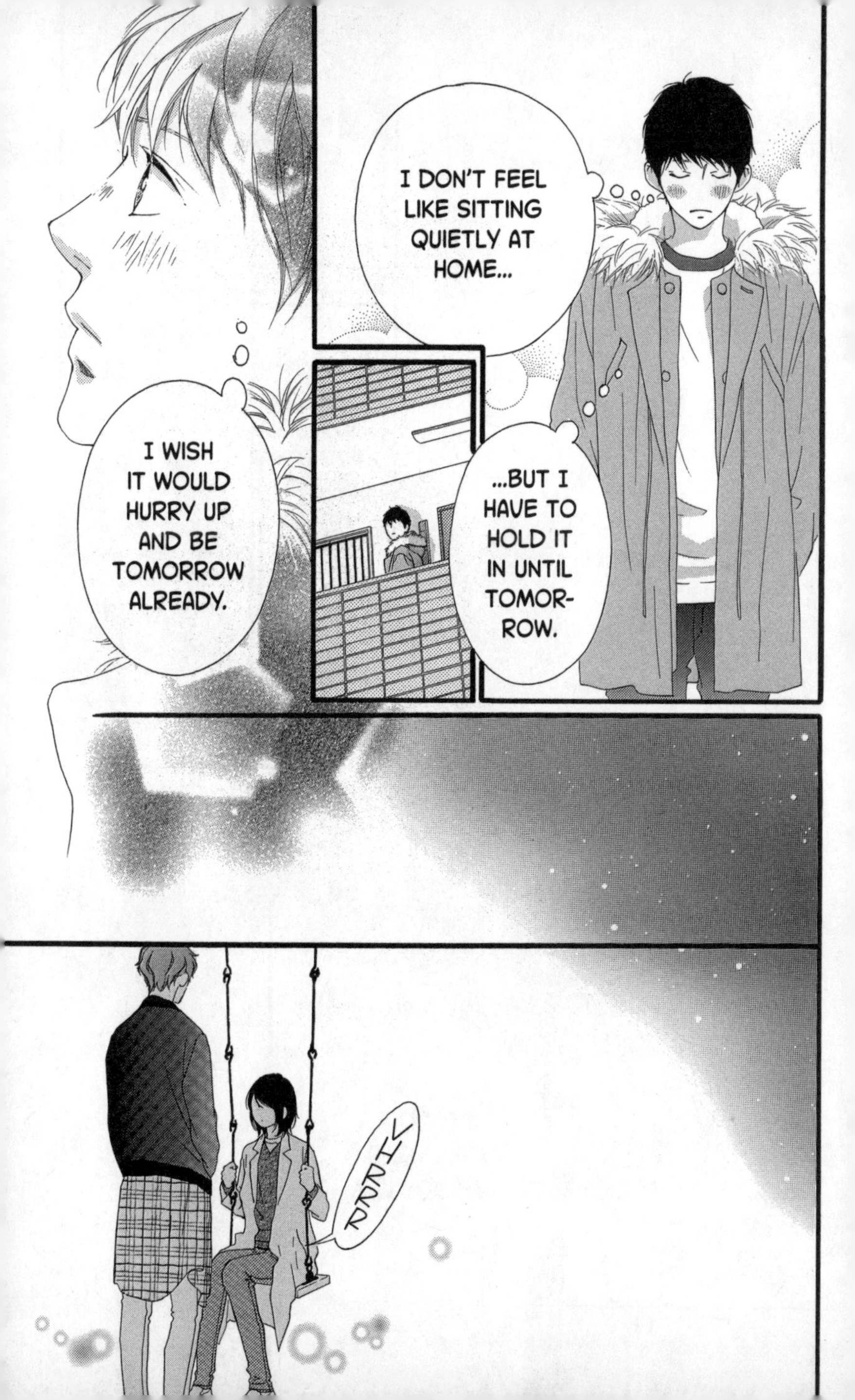
I DON'T FEEL LIKE SITTING QUIETLY AT HOME...
...BUT I HAVE TO HOLD IT IN UNTIL TOMORROW.
I WISH IT WOULD HURRY UP AND BE TOMORROW ALREADY.
VHRRR

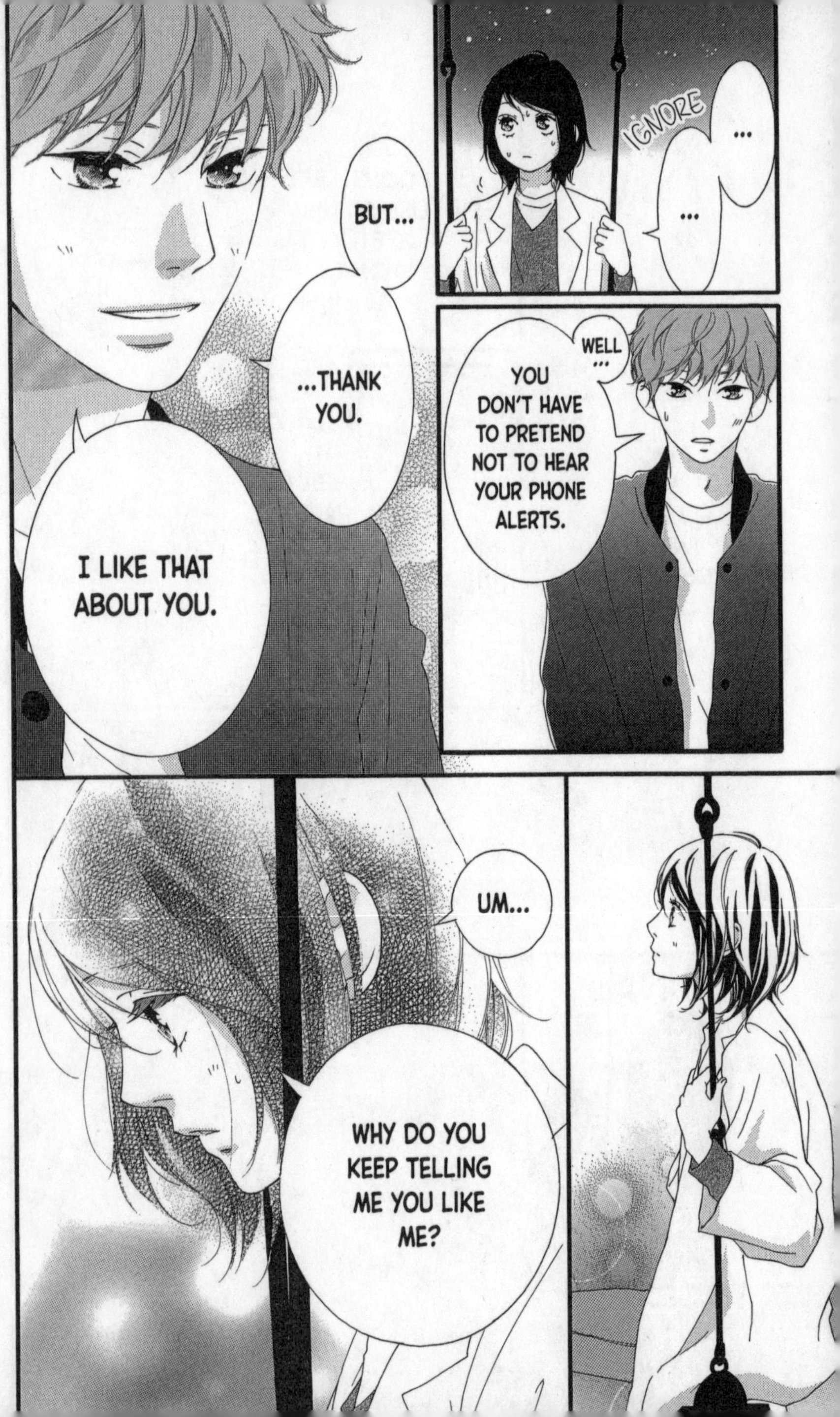
IGNORE
...
...
WELL...
YOU DON'T HAVE TO PRETEND NOT TO HEAR YOUR PHONE ALERTS.
BUT...
...THANK YOU.
I LIKE THAT ABOUT YOU.
UM...
WHY DO YOU KEEP TELLING ME YOU LIKE ME?

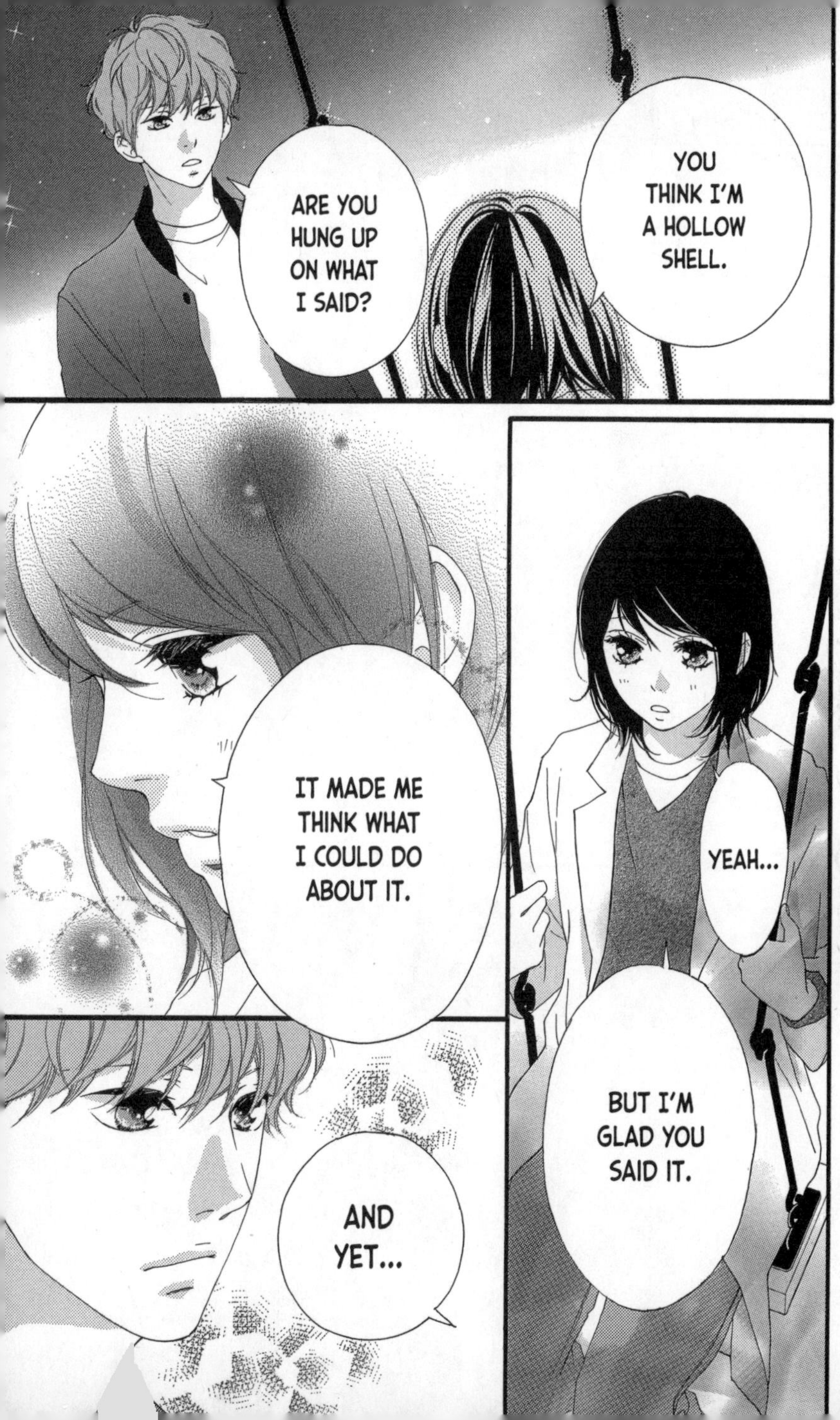
YOU THINK I'M A HOLLOW SHELL.
ARE YOU HUNG UP ON WHAT I SAID?
YEAH...
BUT I'M GLAD YOU SAID IT.
IT MADE ME THINK WHAT I COULD DO ABOUT IT.
AND YET...

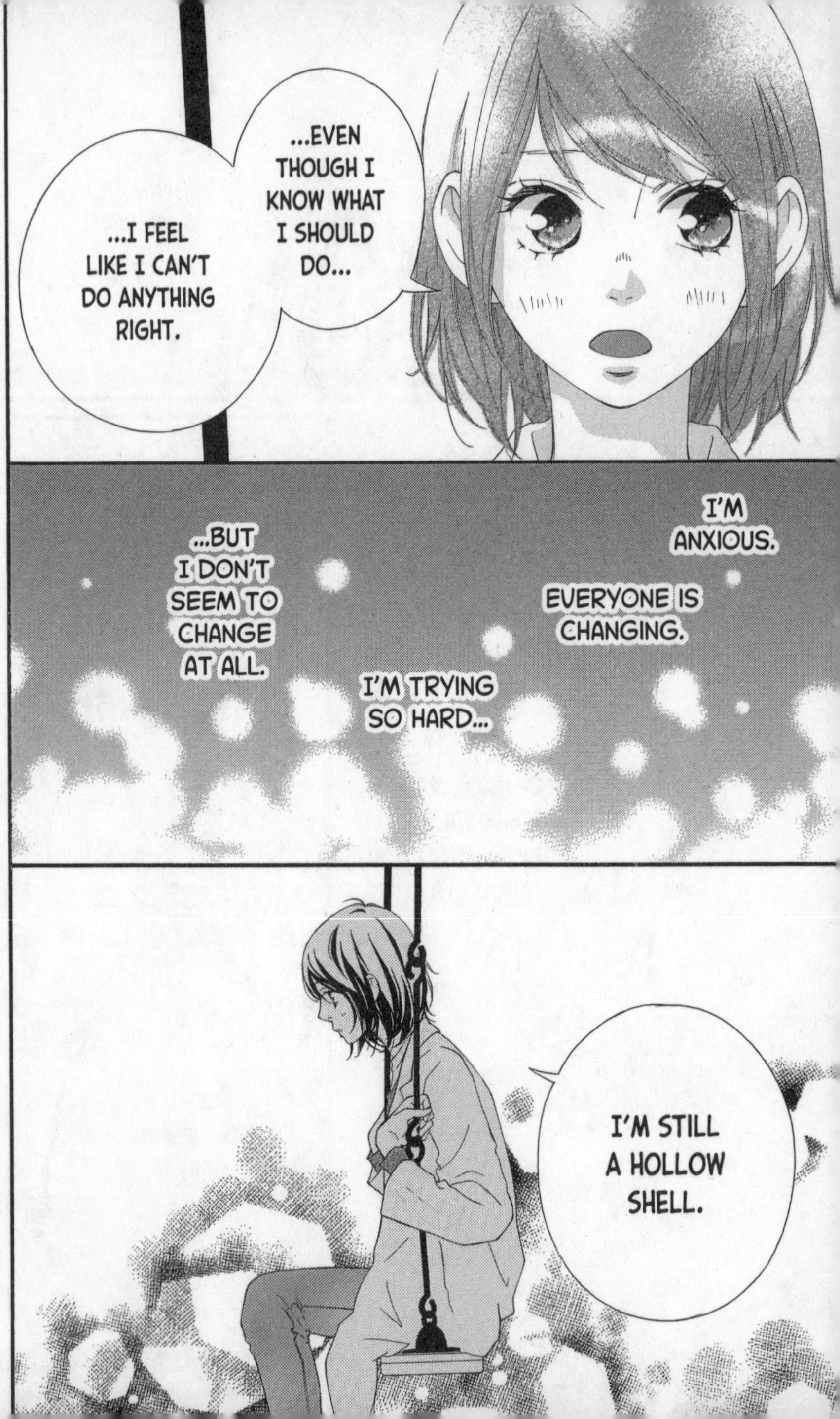
...EVEN THOUGH I KNOW WHAT I SHOULD DO...
...I FEEL LIKE I CAN'T DO ANYTHING RIGHT.
I'M ANXIOUS.
EVERYONE IS CHANGING.
I'M TRYING SO HARD...
...BUT I DON'T SEEM TO CHANGE AT ALL.
I'M STILL A HOLLOW SHELL.

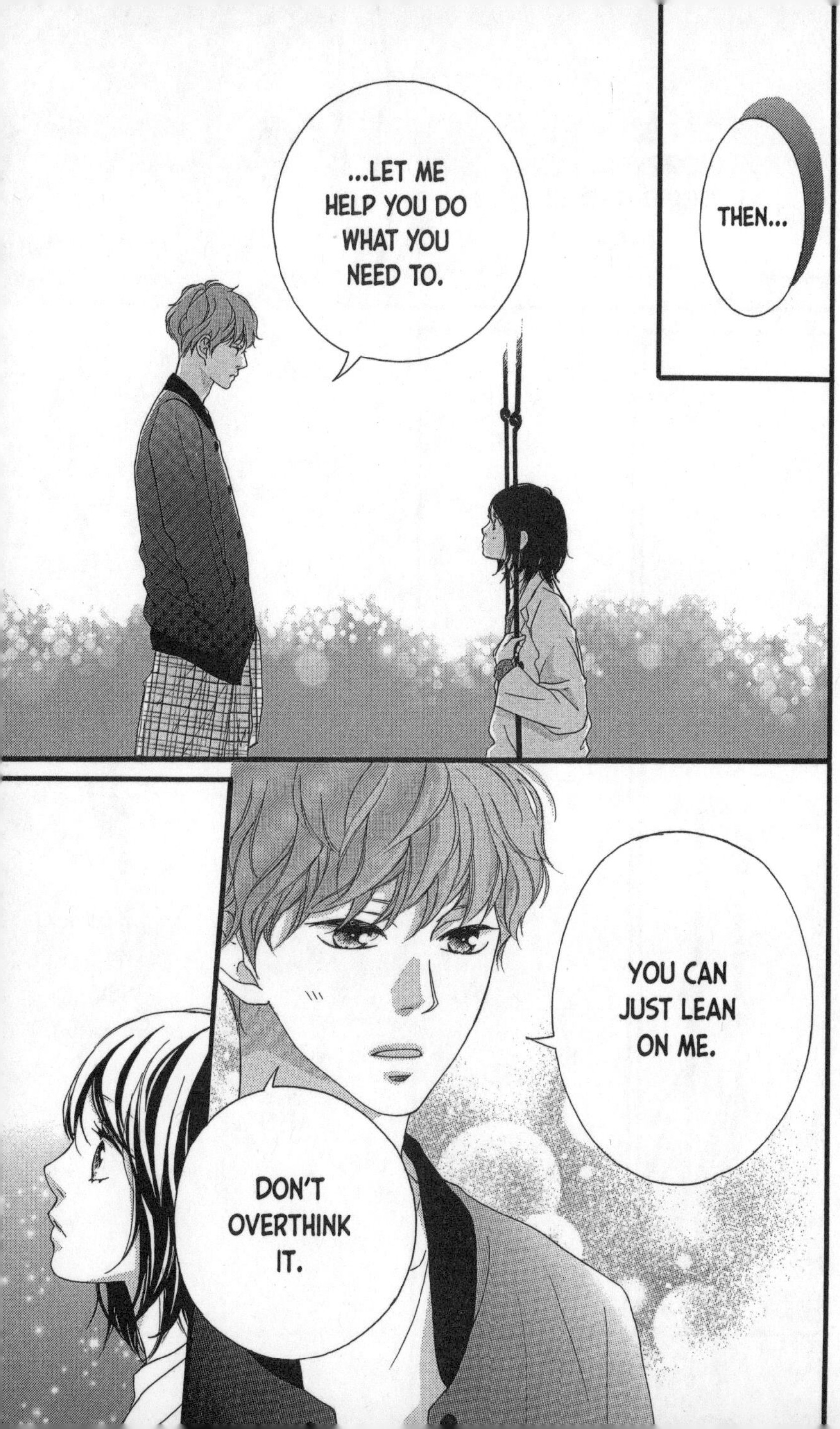
THEN...
...LET ME HELP YOU DO WHAT YOU NEED TO.
YOU CAN JUST LEAN ON ME.
DON'T OVERTHINK IT.

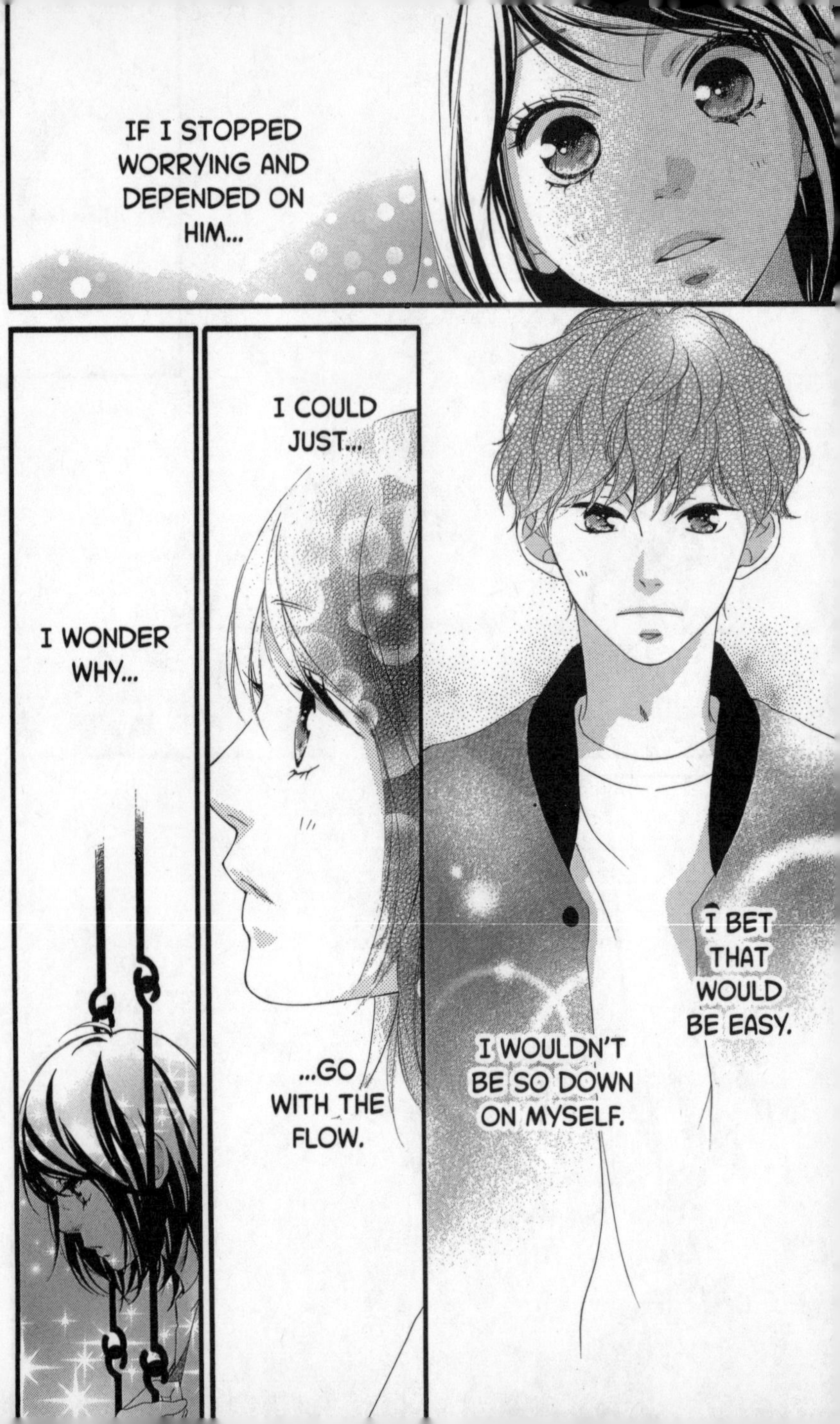
IF I STOPPED WORRYING AND DEPENDED ON HIM...
I BET THAT WOULD BE EASY.
I WOULDN'T BE SO DOWN ON MYSELF.
I COULD JUST...
...GO WITH THE FLOW.
I WONDER WHY...

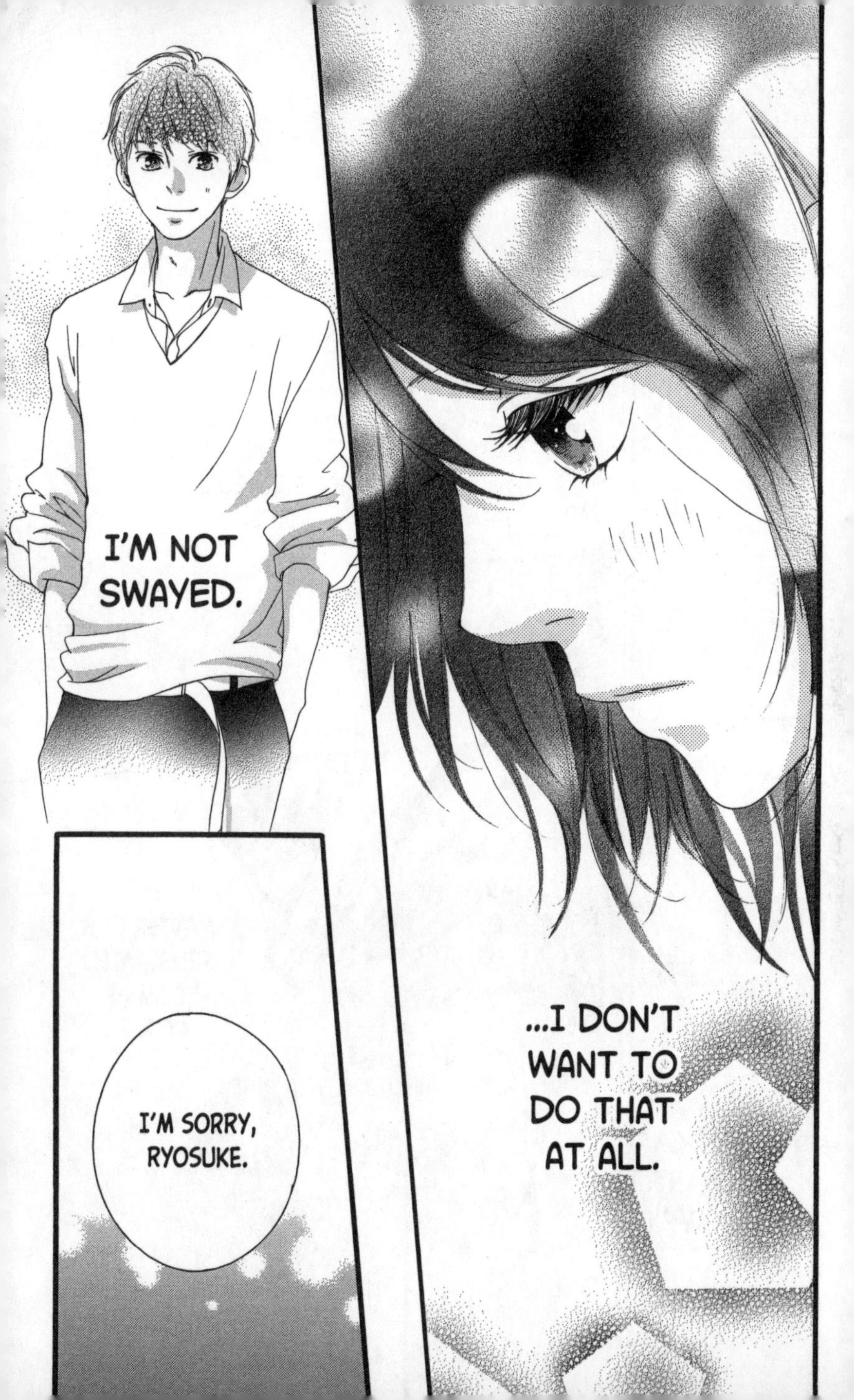
...I DON'T WANT TO DO THAT AT ALL.
I'M NOT SWAYED.
I'M SORRY, RYOSUKE.

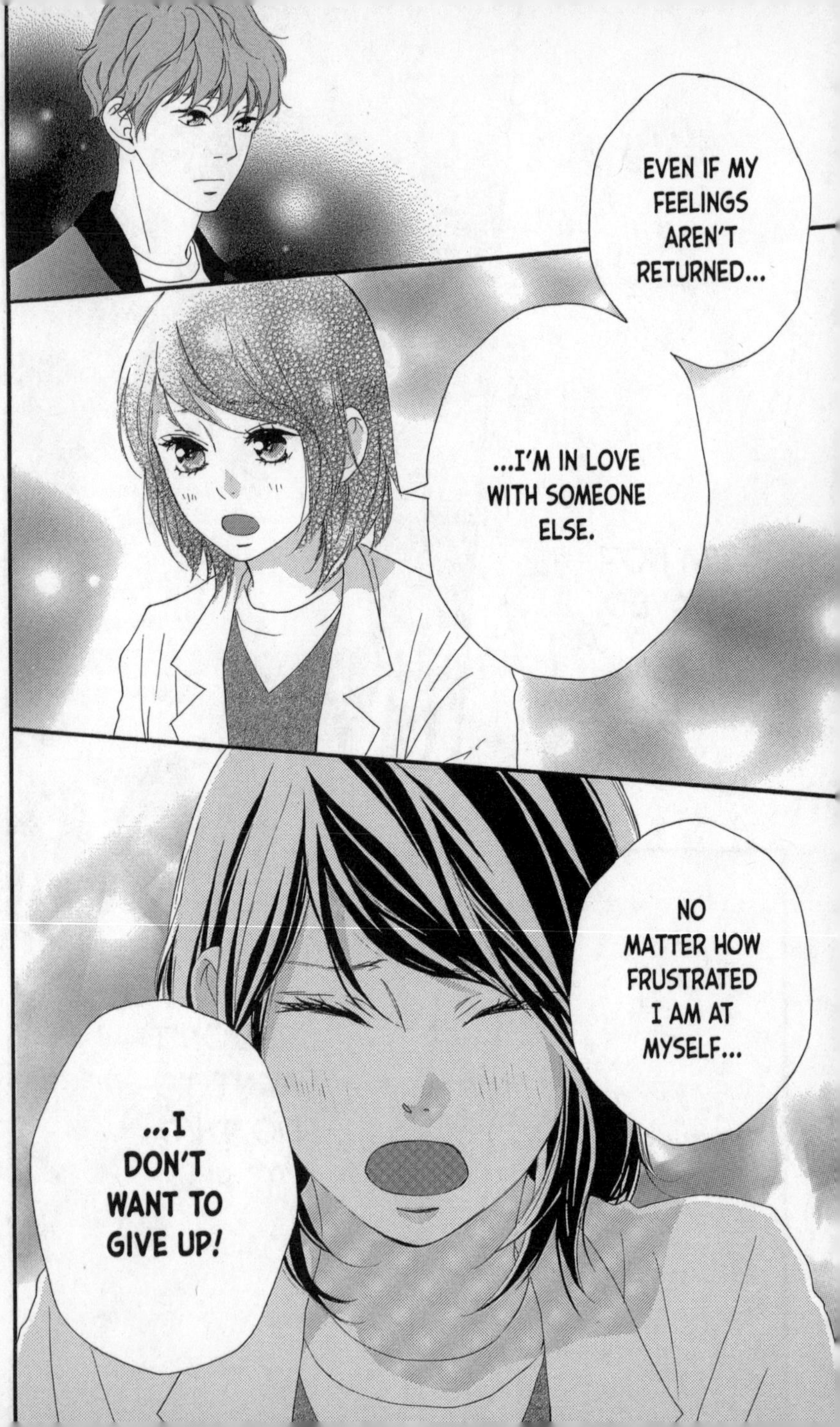
EVEN IF MY FEELINGS AREN'T RETURNED...
...I'M IN LOVE WITH SOMEONE ELSE.
NO MATTER HOW FRUSTRATED I AM AT MYSELF...
...I DON'T WANT TO GIVE UP!

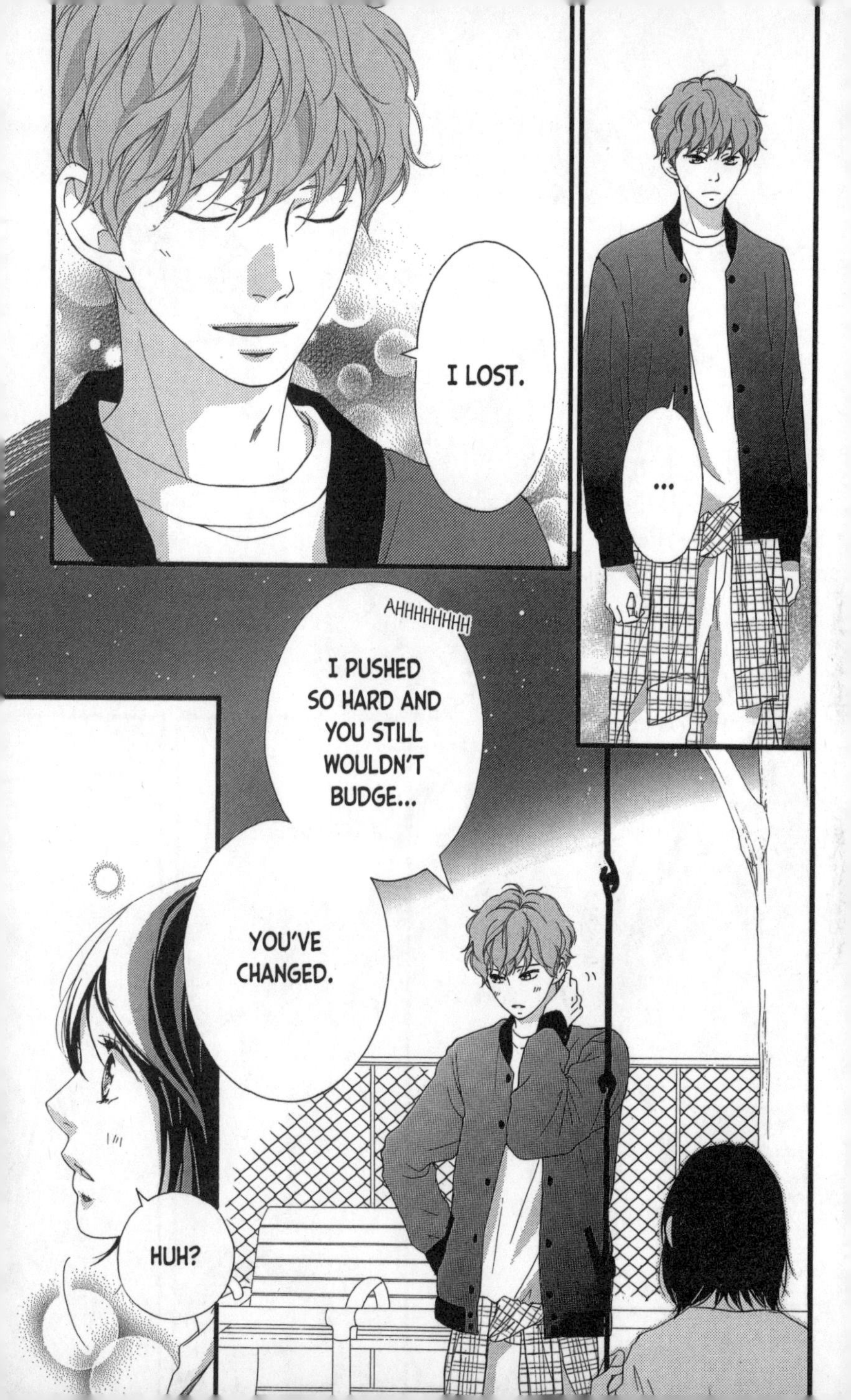
...
I LOST.
AHHHHHHHH
I PUSHED SO HARD AND YOU STILL WOULDN'T BUDGE...
YOU'VE CHANGED.
HUH?

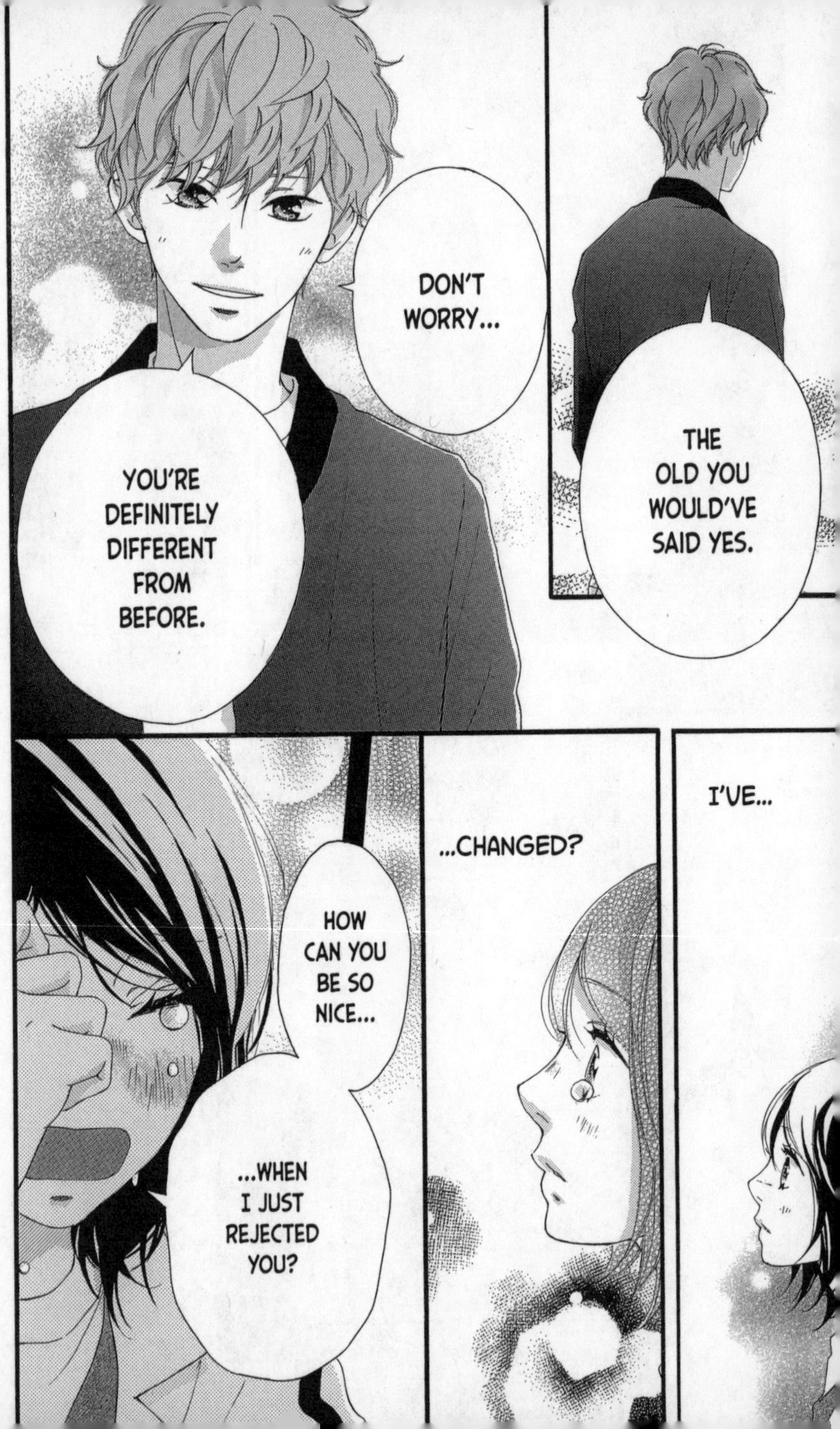
THE OLD YOU WOULD'VE SAID YES.
DON'T WORRY...
YOU'RE DEFINITELY DIFFERENT FROM BEFORE.
I'VE...
...CHANGED?
HOW CAN YOU BE SO NICE...
...WHEN I JUST REJECTED YOU?

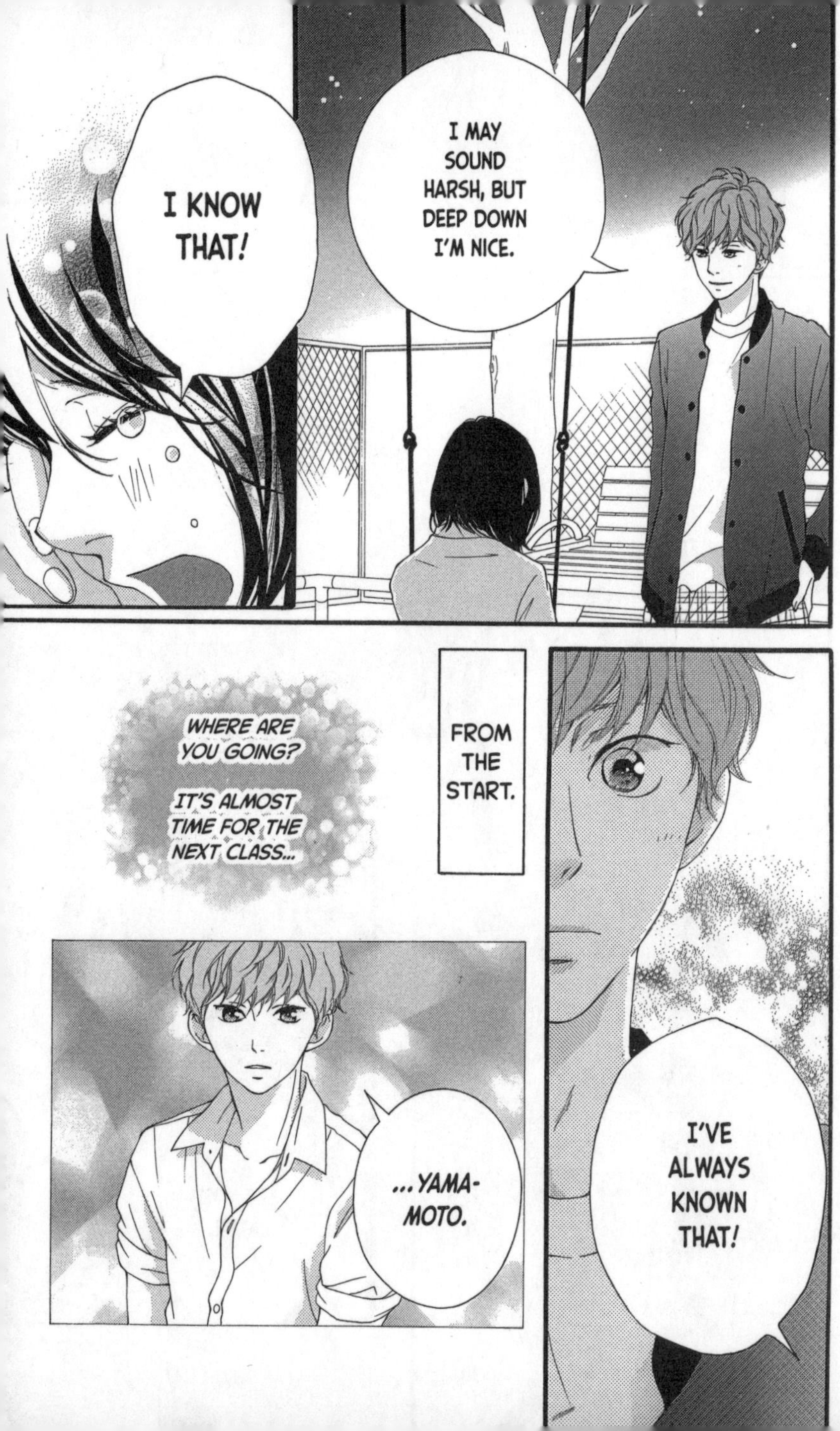
I MAY SOUND HARSH, BUT DEEP DOWN I'M NICE.
I KNOW THAT!
I'VE ALWAYS KNOWN THAT!
FROM THE START.
WHERE ARE YOU GOING?
IT'S ALMOST TIME FOR THE NEXT CLASS...
...YAMA-MOTO.

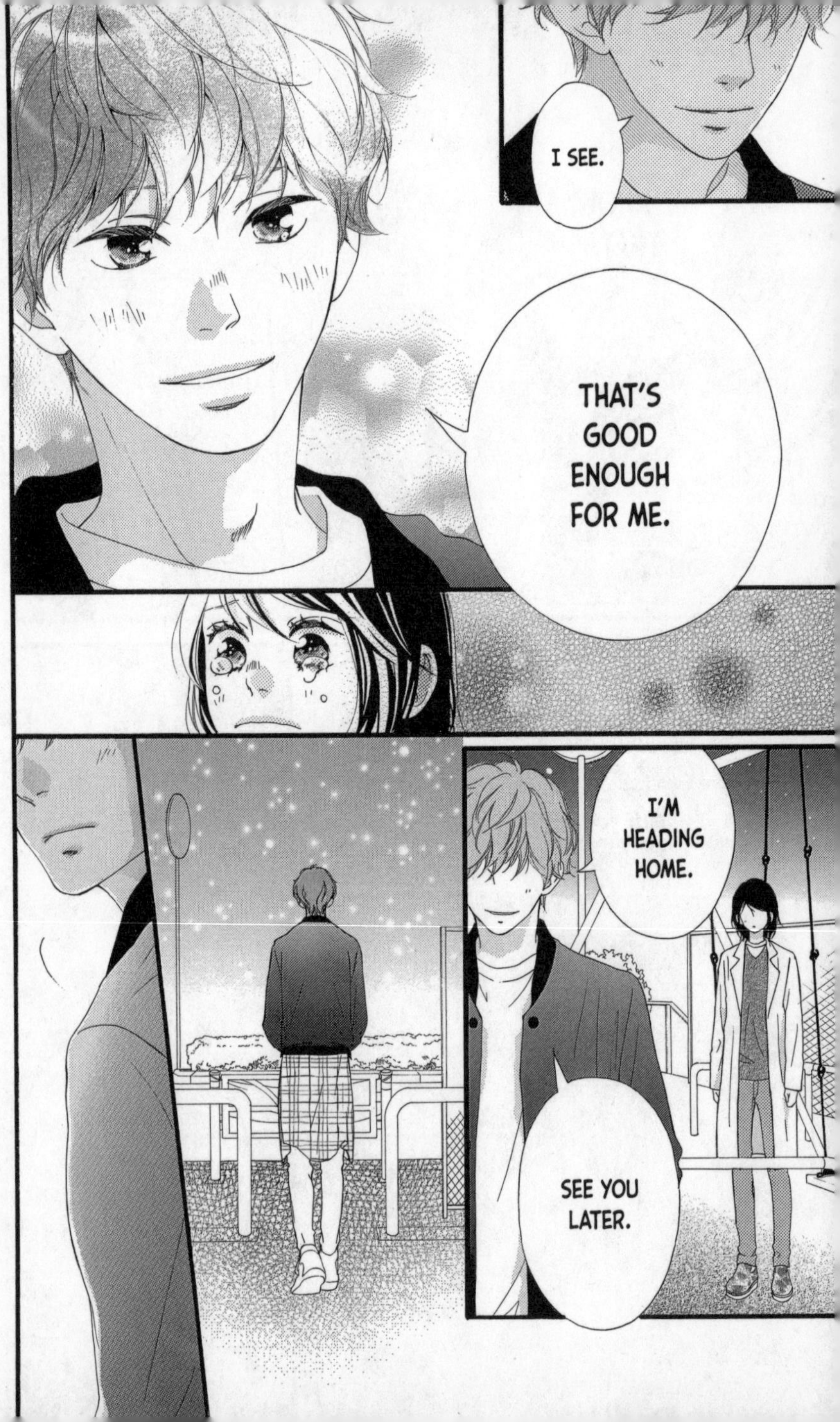
I SEE.
THAT'S GOOD ENOUGH FOR ME.
I'M HEADING HOME.
SEE YOU LATER.

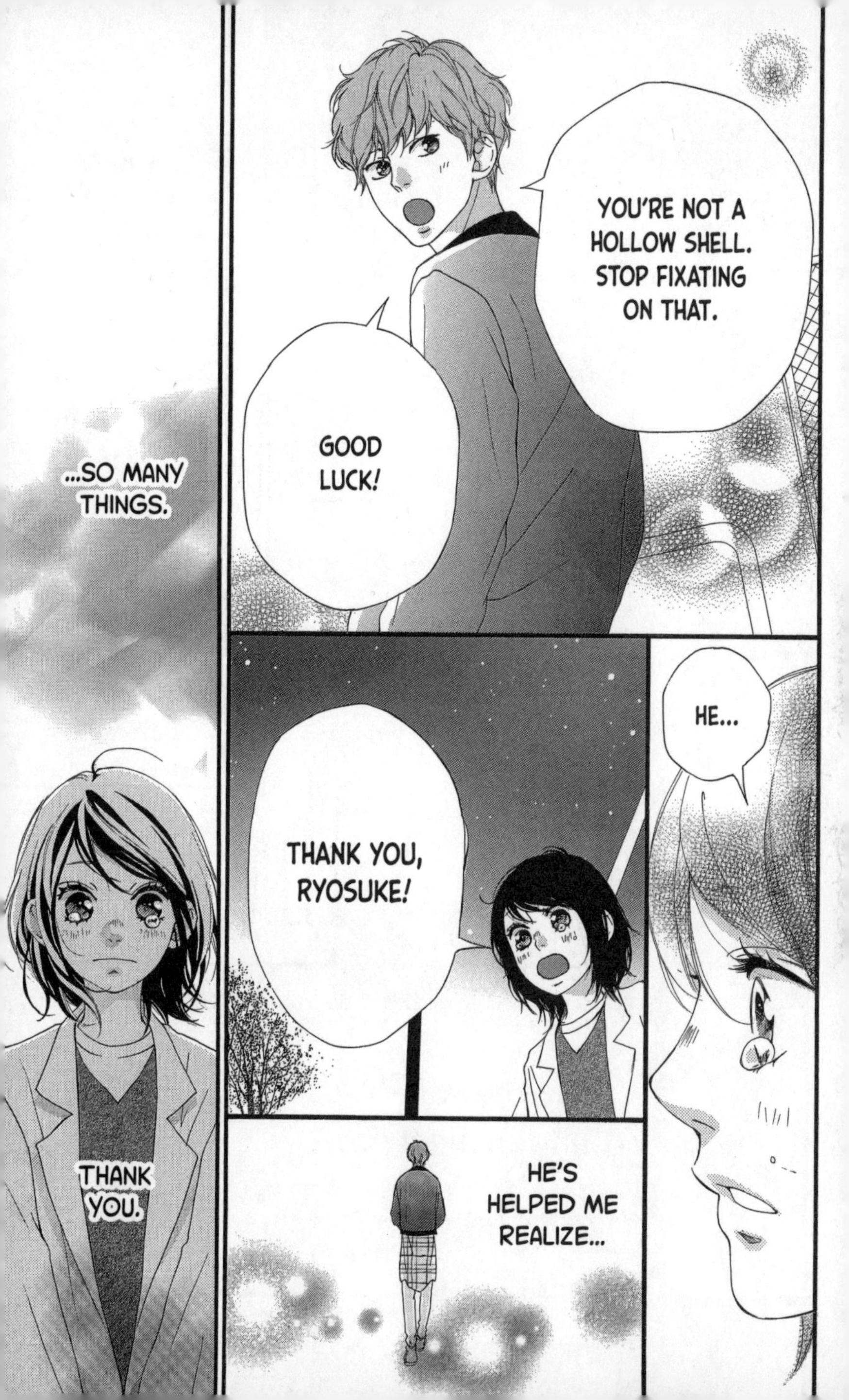
YOU'RE NOT A HOLLOW SHELL. STOP FIXATING ON THAT.
GOOD LUCK!
HE...
THANK YOU, RYOSUKE!
HE'S HELPED ME REALIZE...
...SO MANY THINGS.
THANK YOU.

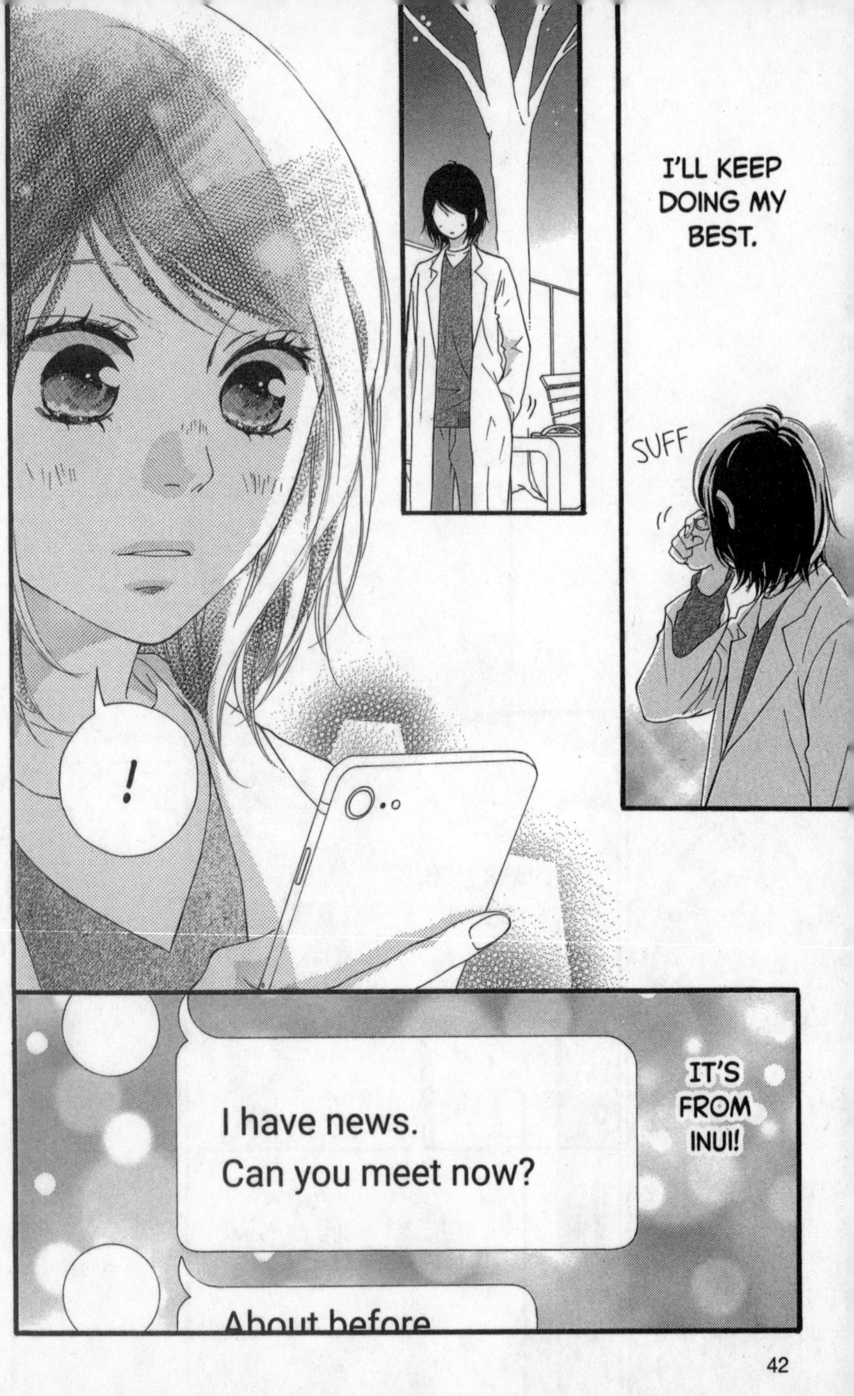
I'LL KEEP DOING MY BEST.
SUFF
!
IT'S FROM INUI!
I have news.
Can you meet now?
About before

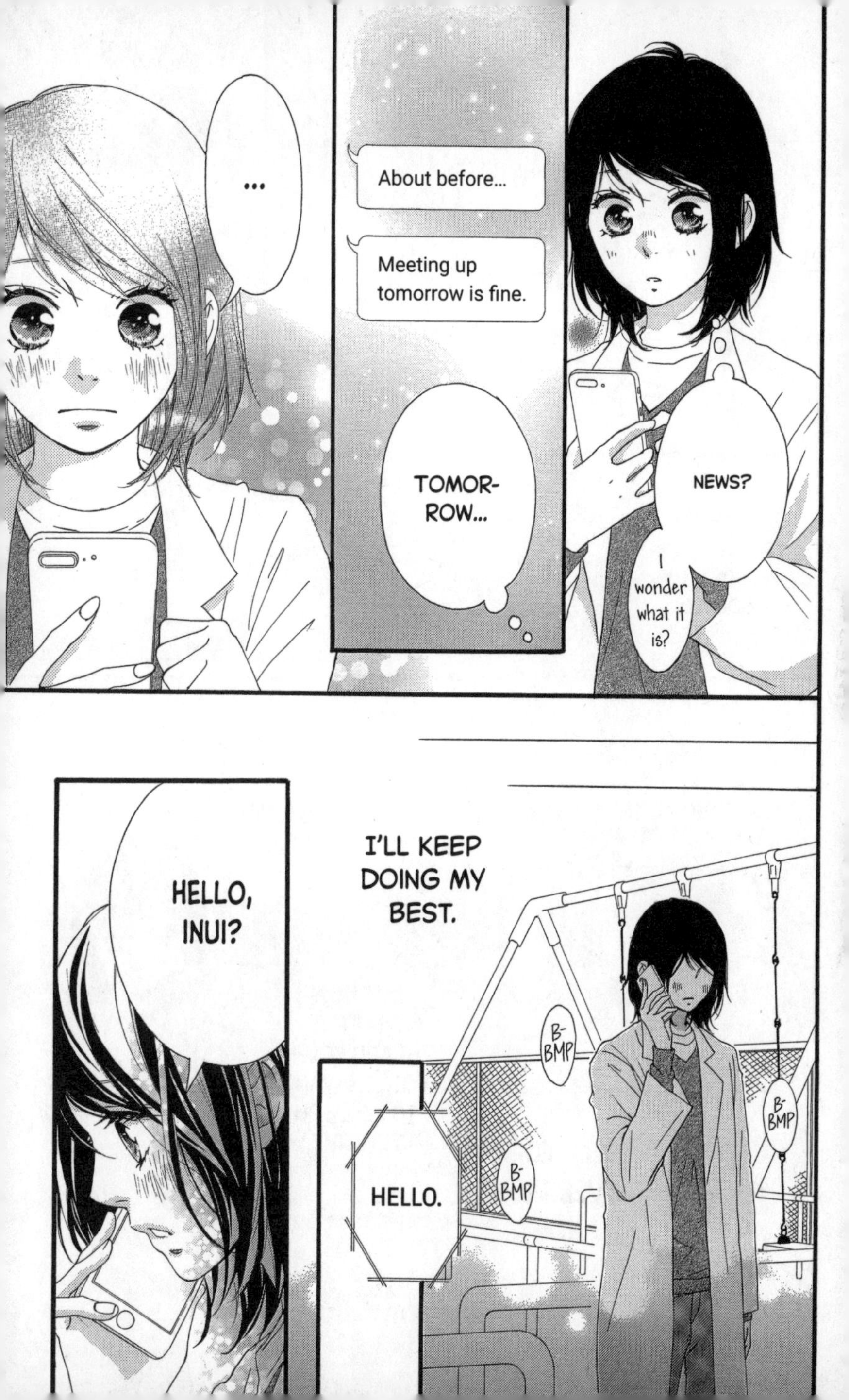
NEWS?
I wonder what it is?
About before...
Meeting up tomorrow is fine.
TOMOR-ROW...
...
I'LL KEEP DOING MY BEST.
B-BMP
B-BMP
B-BMP
HELLO.
HELLO, INUI?

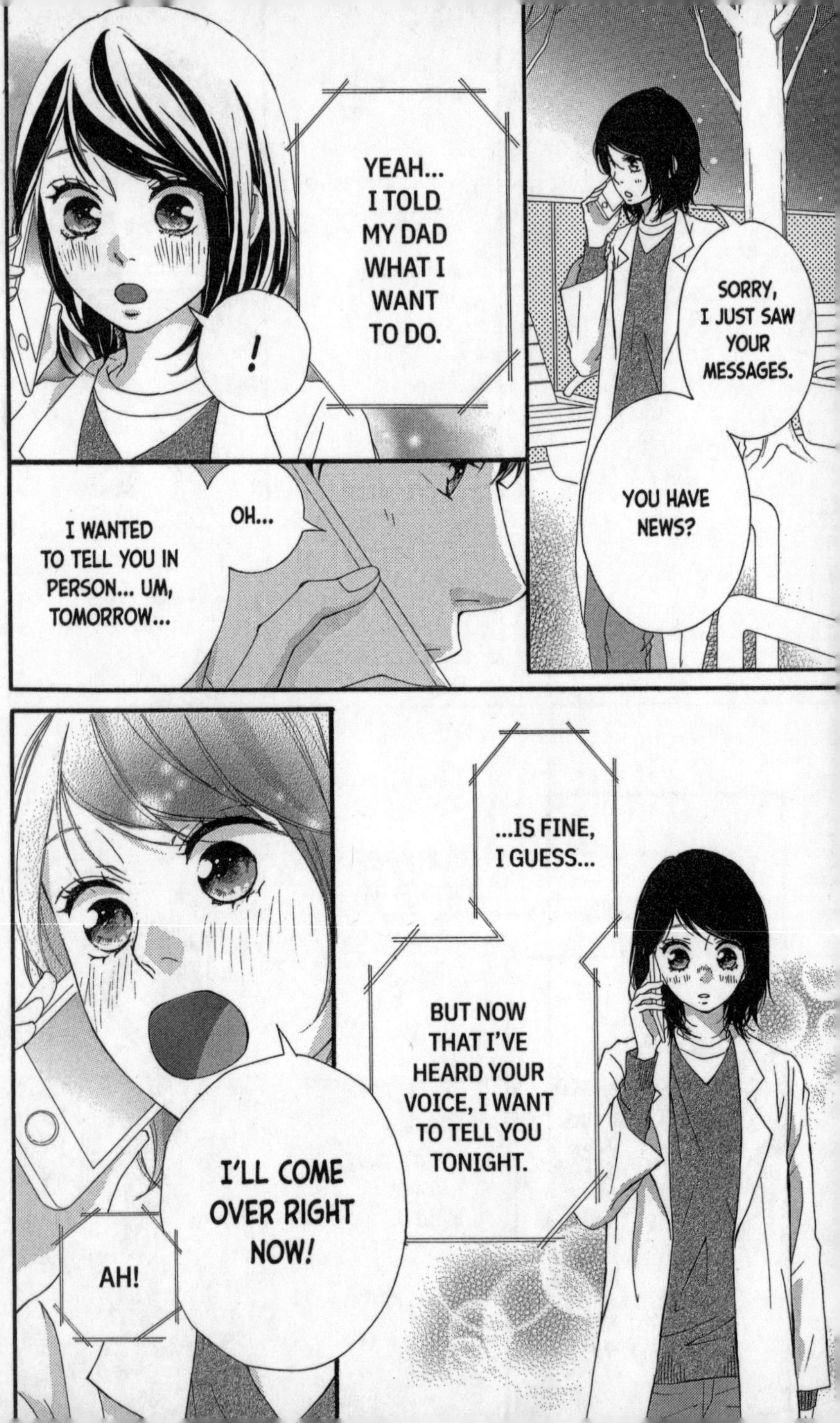

SORRY, I JUST SAW YOUR MESSAGES.
YOU HAVE NEWS?
YEAH... I TOLD MY DAD WHAT I WANT TO DO.
!
OH...
I WANTED TO TELL YOU IN PERSON... UM, TOMORROW...
...IS FINE, I GUESS...
BUT NOW THAT I'VE HEARD YOUR VOICE, I WANT TO TELL YOU TONIGHT.
I'LL COME OVER RIGHT NOW!
AH!

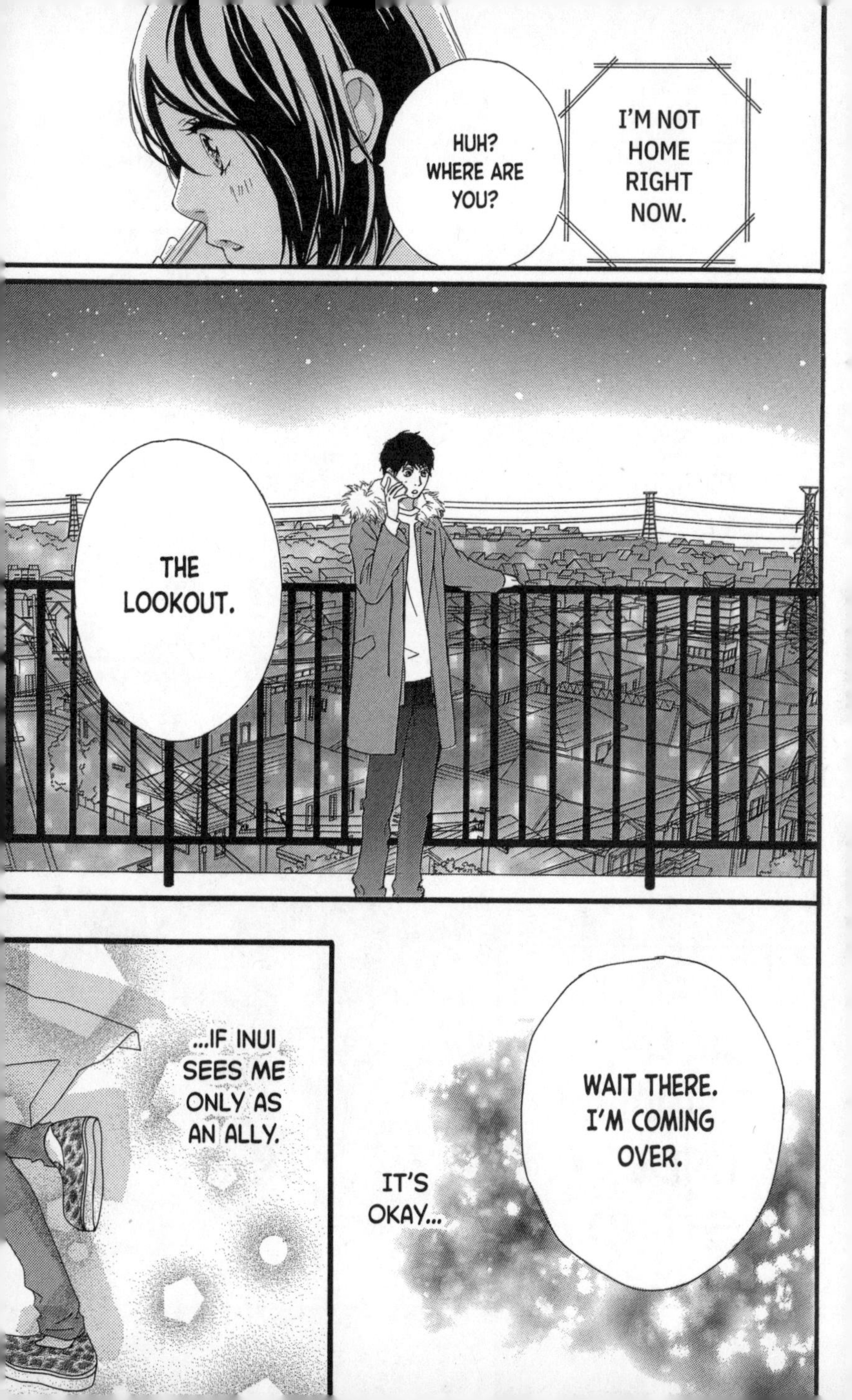
I'M NOT HOME RIGHT NOW.
HUH? WHERE ARE YOU?
THE LOOKOUT.
WAIT THERE. I'M COMING OVER.
IT'S OKAY...
...IF INUI SEES ME ONLY AS AN ALLY.

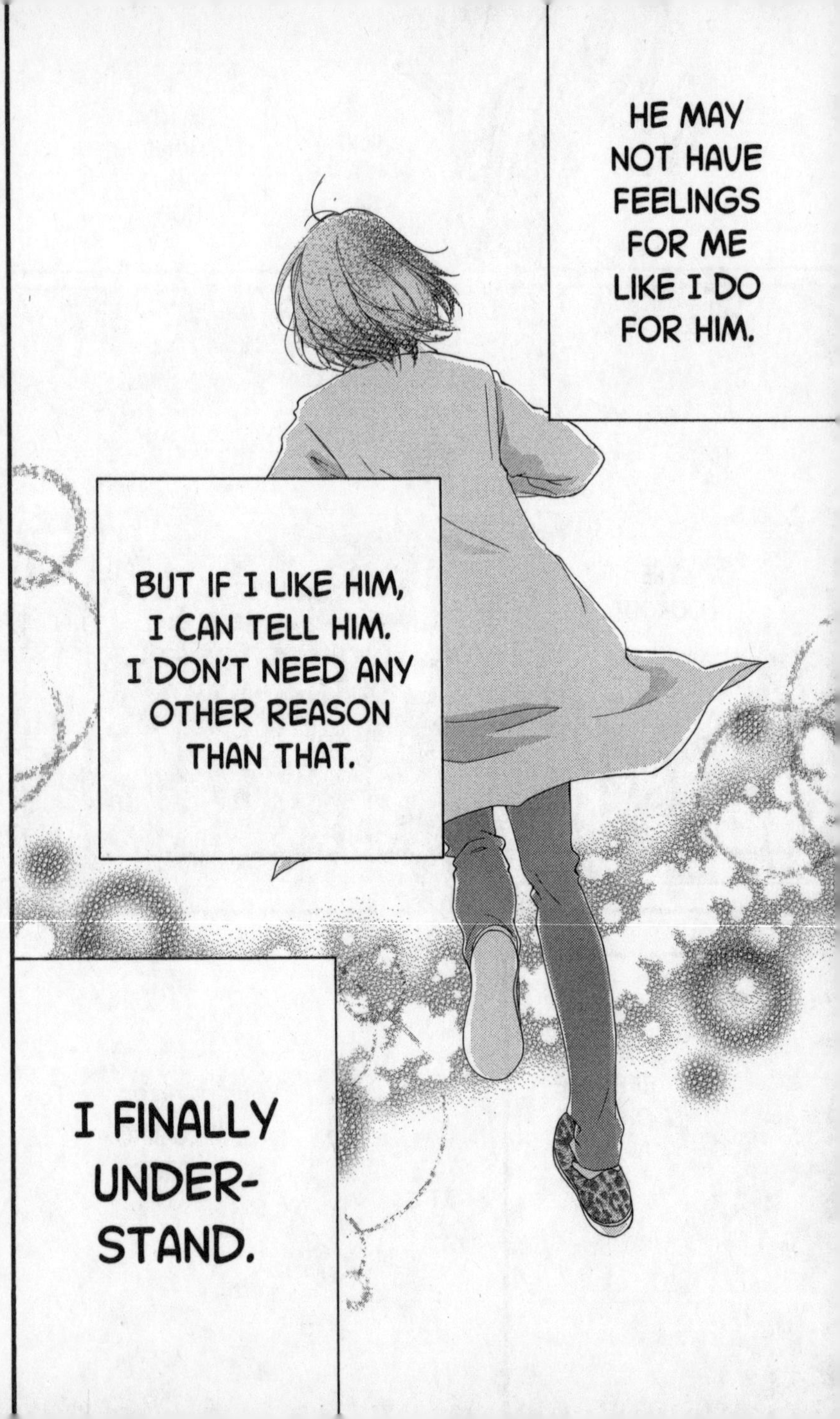
HE MAY NOT HAVE FEELINGS FOR ME LIKE I DO FOR HIM.
BUT IF I LIKE HIM, I CAN TELL HIM. I DON'T NEED ANY OTHER REASON THAN THAT.
I FINALLY UNDER-STAND.

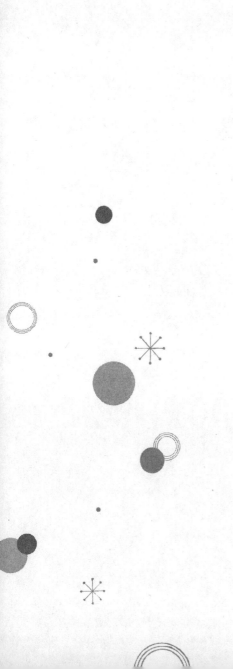

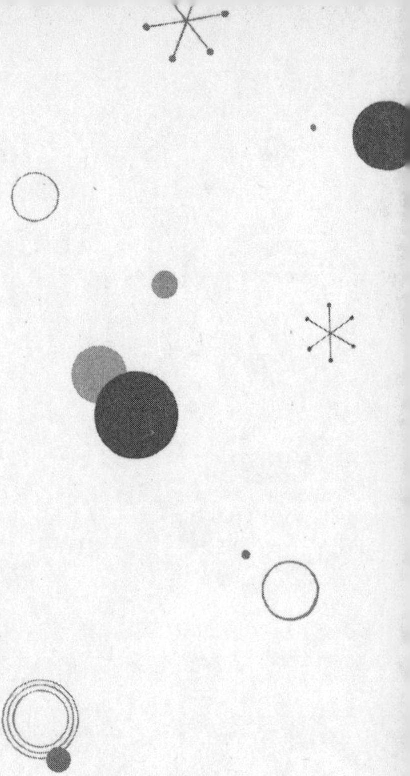

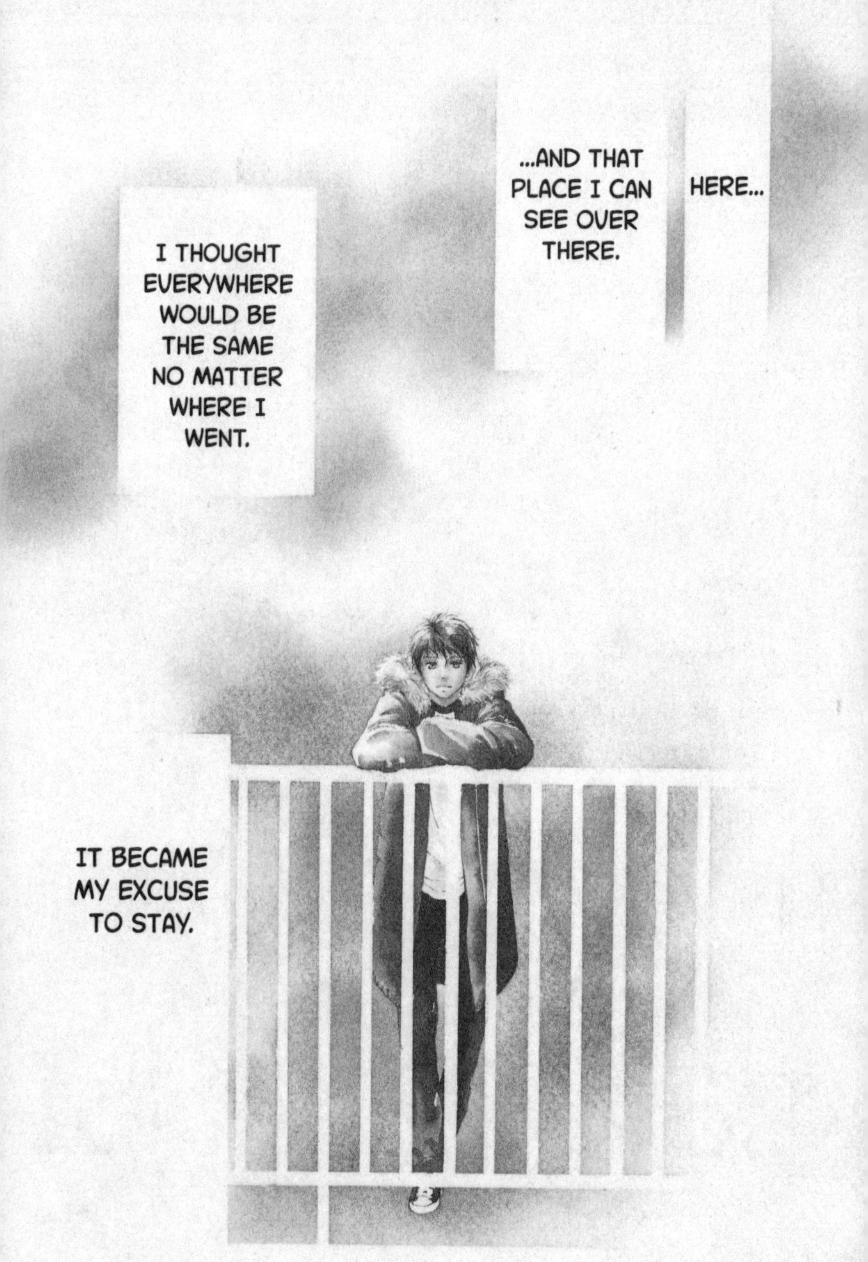
HERE...
...AND THAT PLACE I CAN SEE OVER THERE.
I THOUGHT EVERYWHERE WOULD BE THE SAME NO MATTER WHERE I WENT.
IT BECAME MY EXCUSE TO STAY.

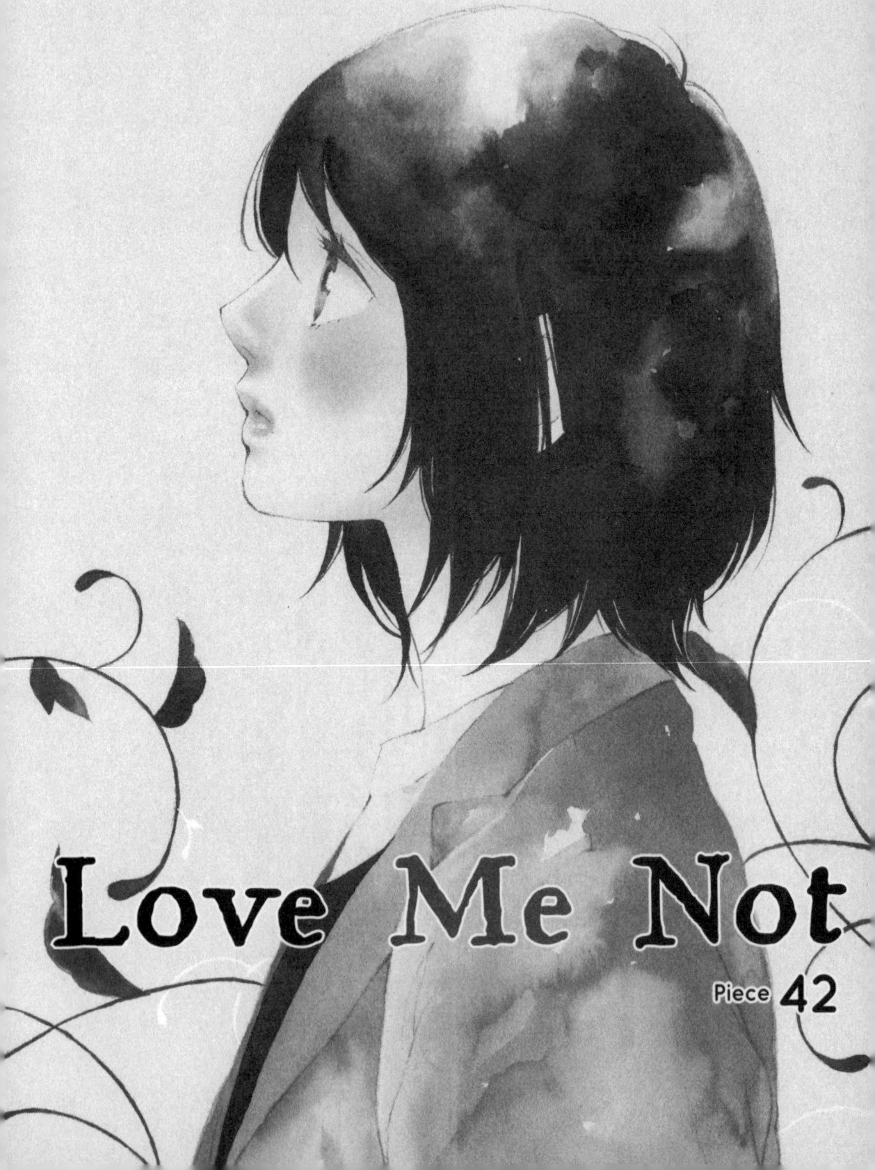
Love Me Not
Piece 42

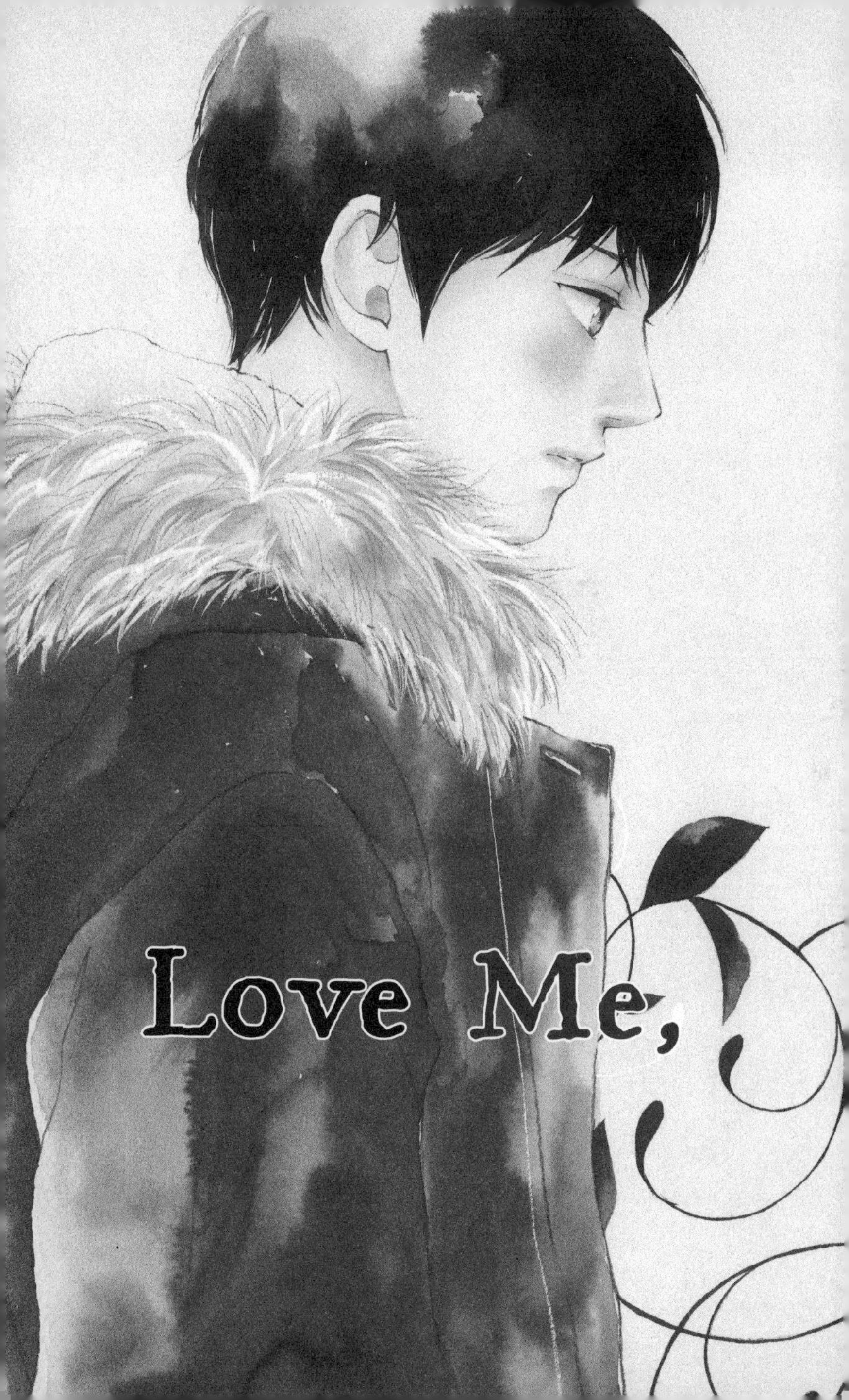
Love Me,

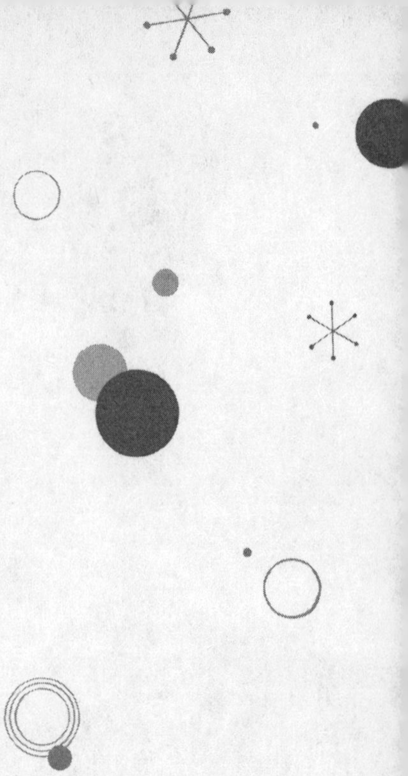

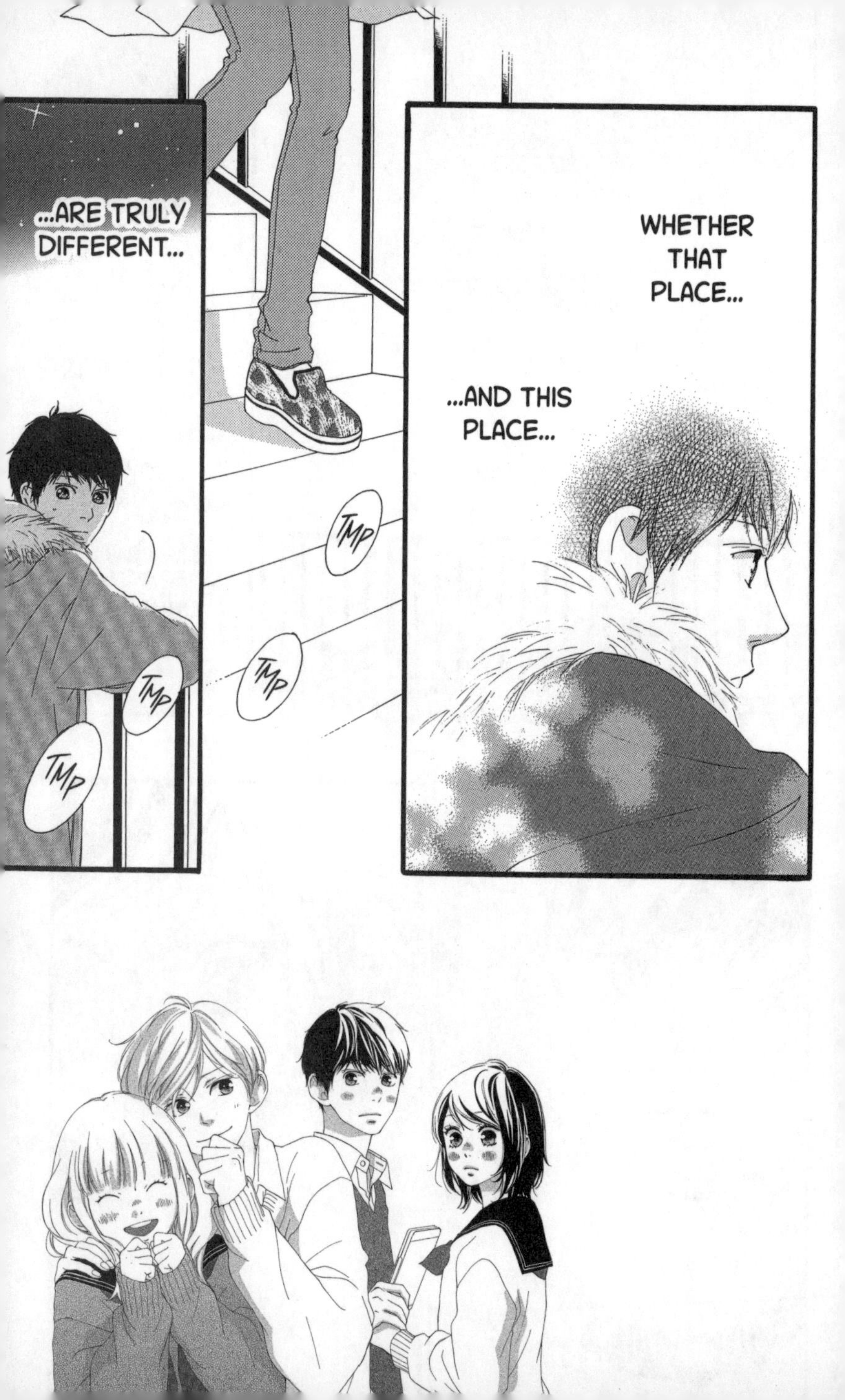
WHETHER THAT PLACE...
...AND THIS PLACE...
TMP
TMP
...ARE TRULY DIFFERENT...
TMP
TMP

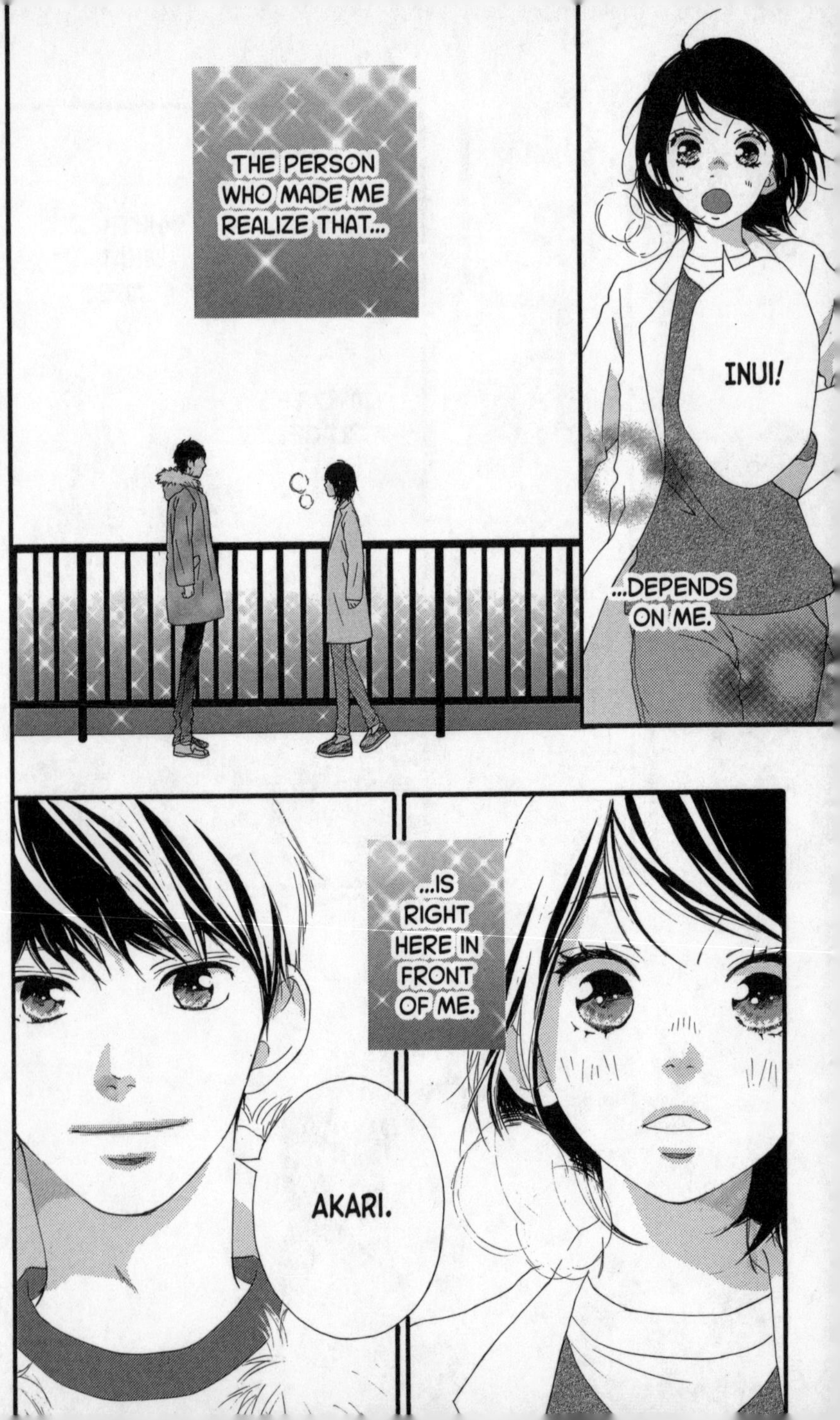
INUI!
...DEPENDS ON ME.
THE PERSON WHO MADE ME REALIZE THAT...
...IS RIGHT HERE IN FRONT OF ME.
AKARI.

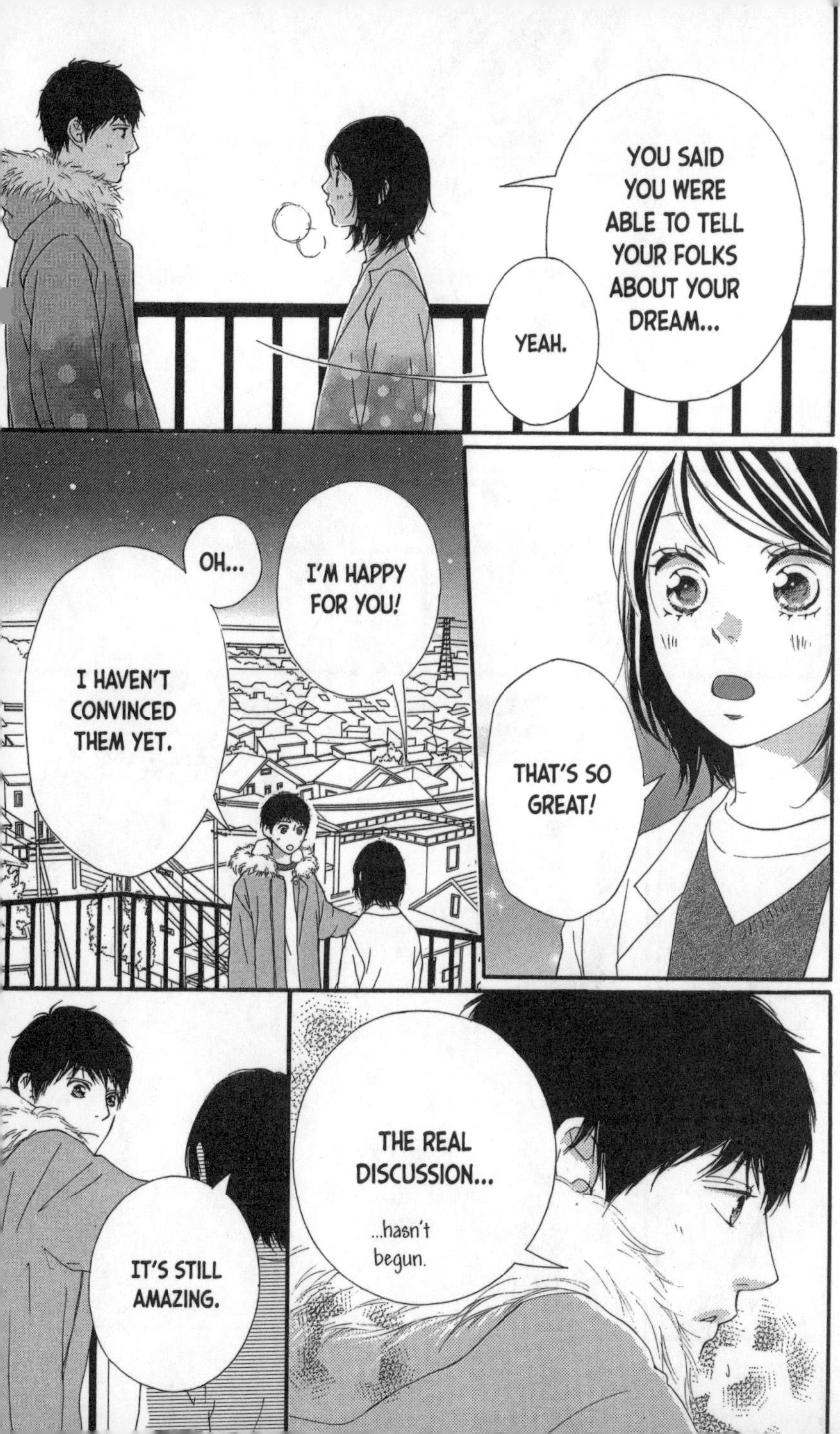
YOU SAID YOU WERE ABLE TO TELL YOUR FOLKS ABOUT YOUR DREAM...
YEAH.
THAT'S SO GREAT!
I'M HAPPY FOR YOU!
OH...
I HAVEN'T CONVINCED THEM YET.
THE REAL DISCUSSION...
...hasn't begun.
IT'S STILL AMAZING.

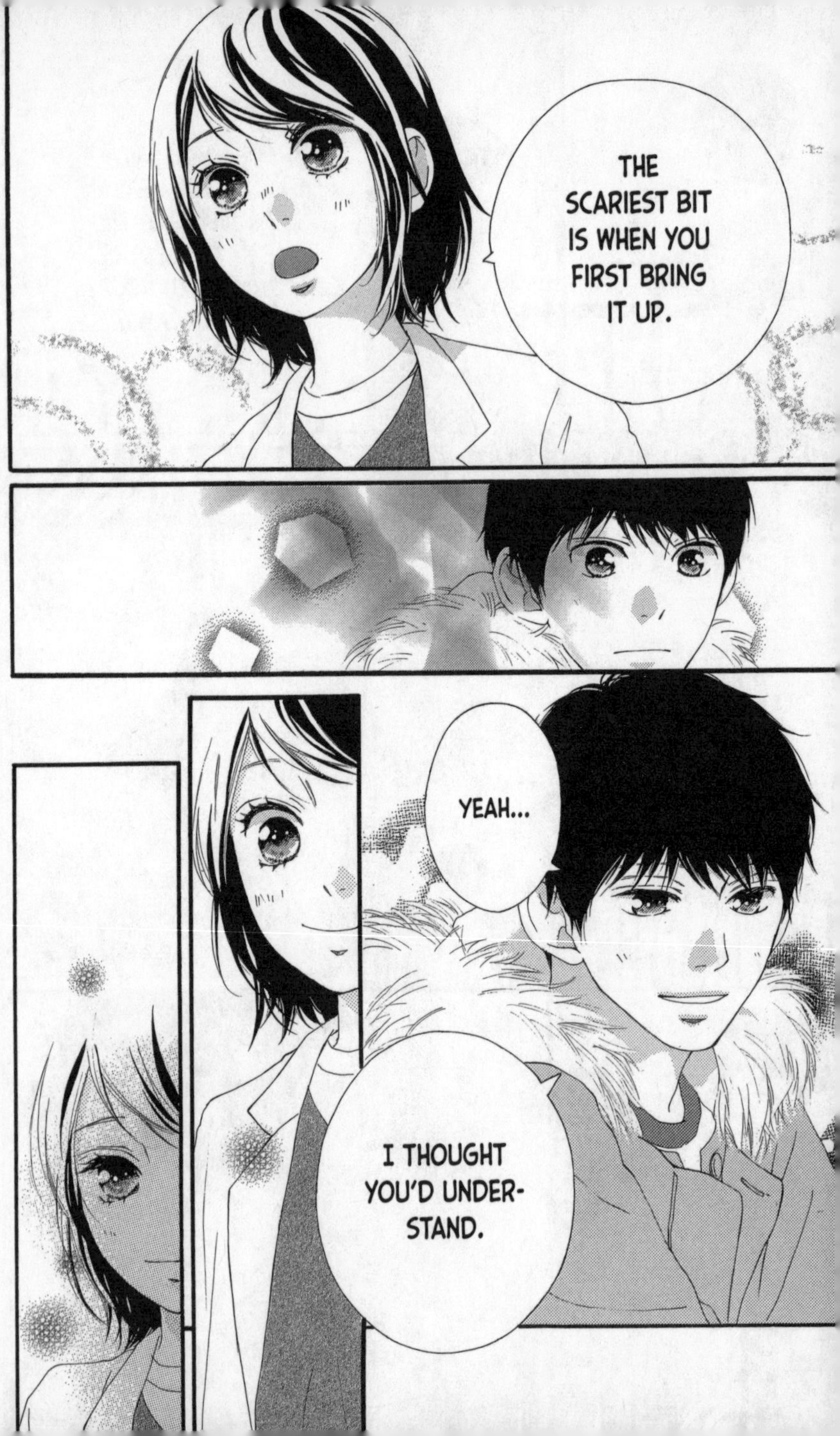
THE SCARIEST BIT IS WHEN YOU FIRST BRING IT UP.
YEAH...
I THOUGHT YOU'D UNDER-STAND.

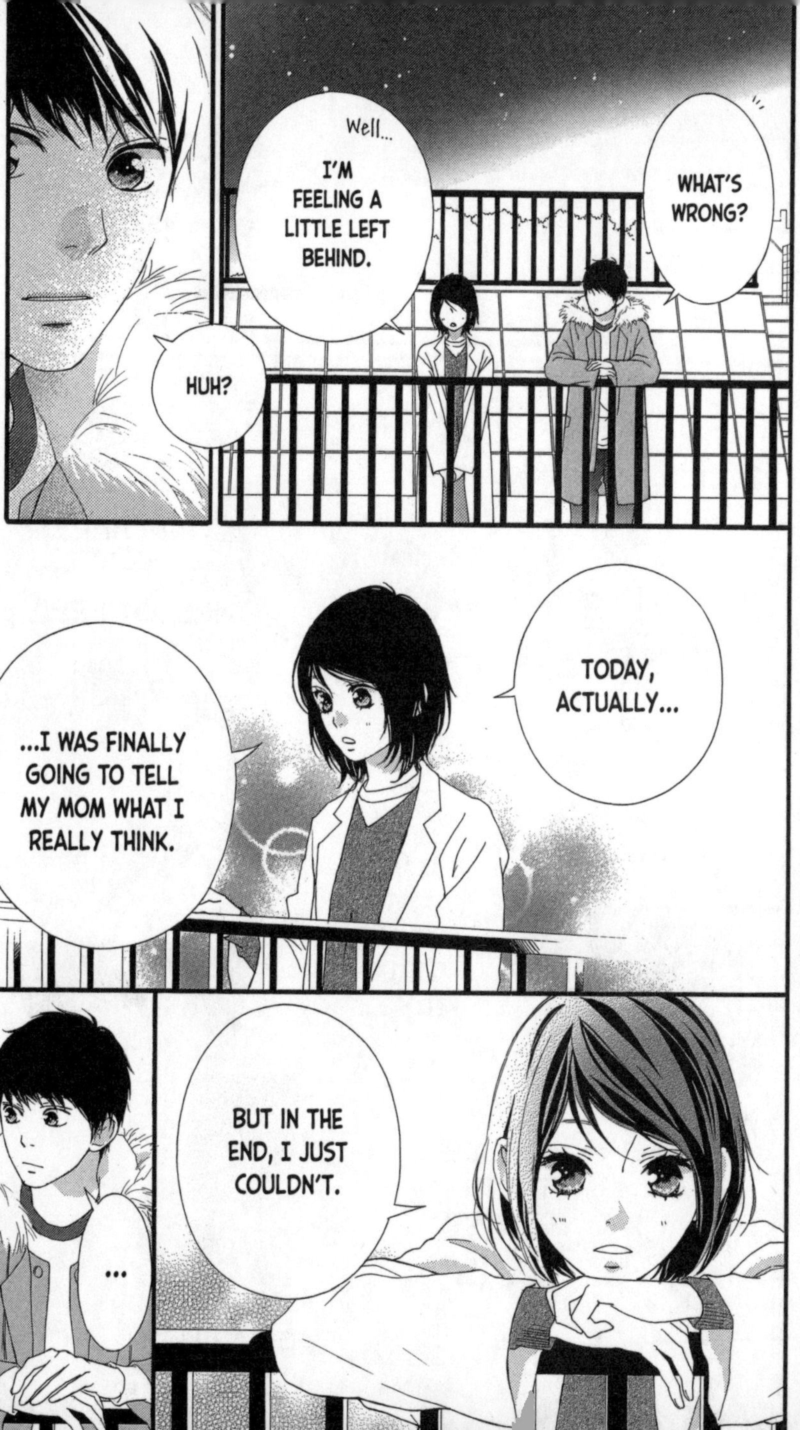
WHAT'S WRONG?
Well...
I'M FEELING A LITTLE LEFT BEHIND.
HUH?
TODAY, ACTUALLY...
...I WAS FINALLY GOING TO TELL MY MOM WHAT I REALLY THINK.
BUT IN THE END, I JUST COULDN'T.
...

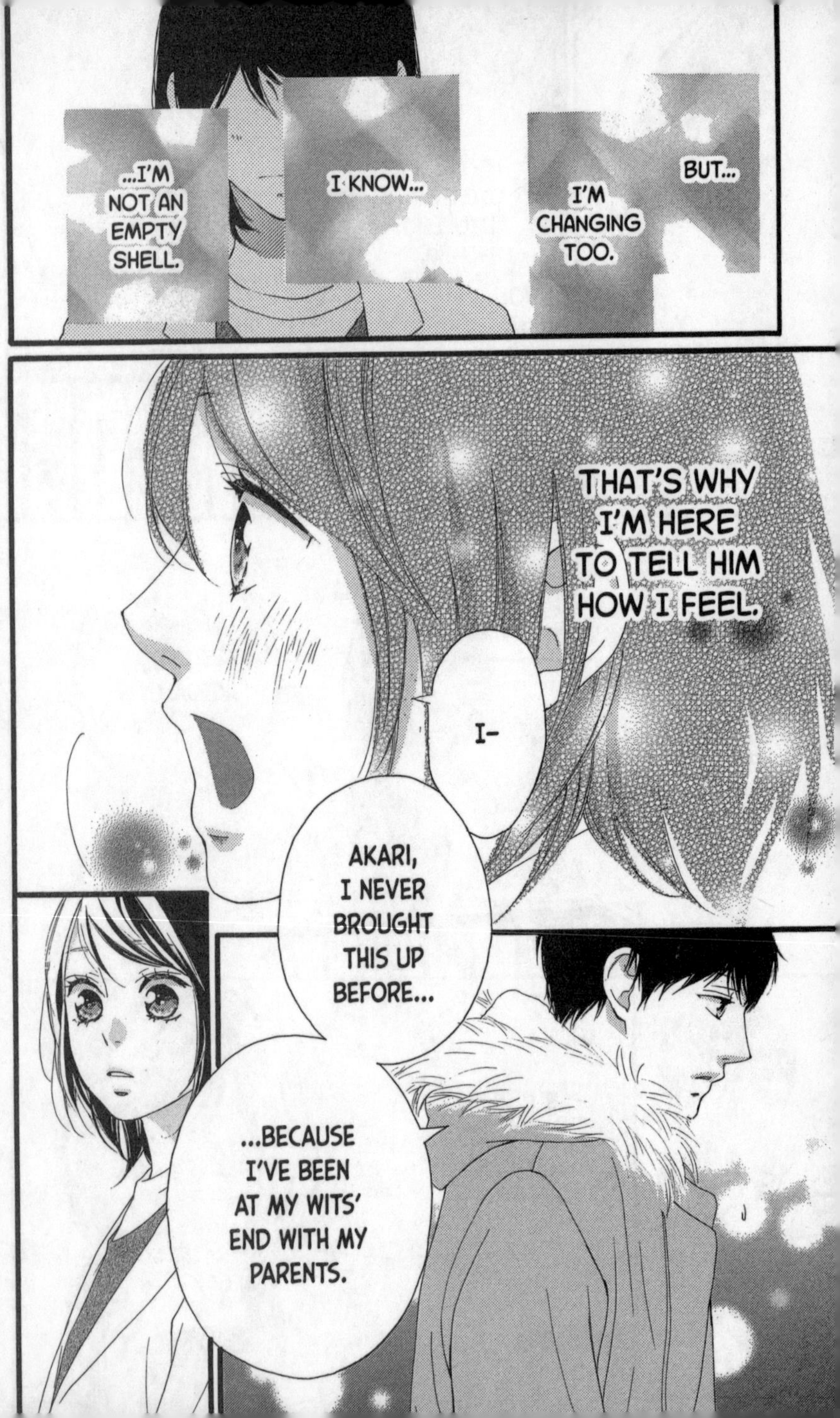
BUT...
I'M CHANGING TOO.
I KNOW...
...I'M NOT AN EMPTY SHELL.
THAT'S WHY I'M HERE TO TELL HIM HOW I FEEL.
I-
AKARI, I NEVER BROUGHT THIS UP BEFORE...
...BECAUSE I'VE BEEN AT MY WITS' END WITH MY PARENTS.

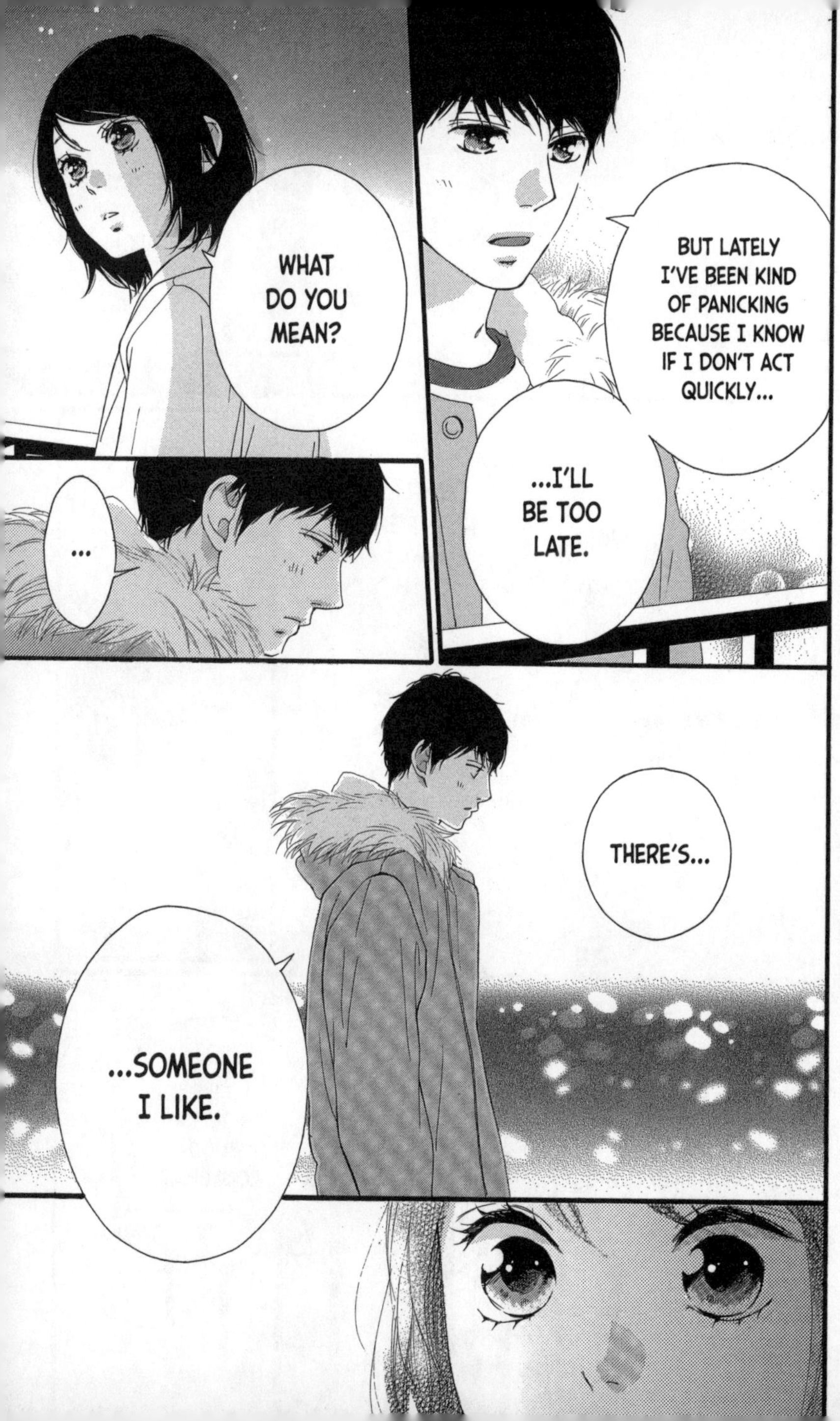
BUT LATELY I'VE BEEN KIND OF PANICKING BECAUSE I KNOW IF I DON'T ACT QUICKLY...
...I'LL BE TOO LATE.
WHAT DO YOU MEAN?
...
THERE'S...
...SOMEONE I LIKE.

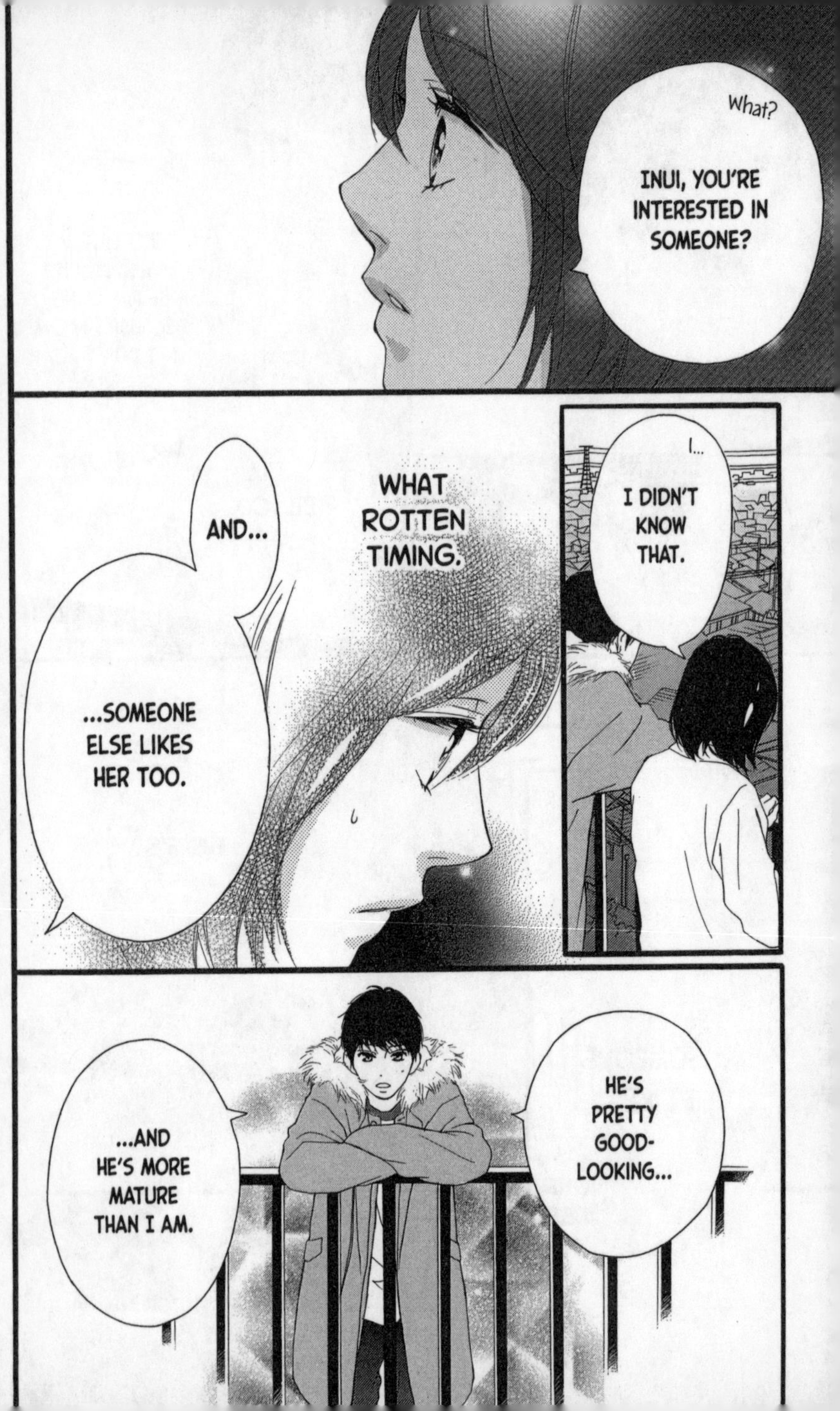
What?
INUI, YOU'RE INTERESTED IN SOMEONE?
I...
I DIDN'T KNOW THAT.
WHAT ROTTEN TIMING.
AND...
...SOMEONE ELSE LIKES HER TOO.
HE'S PRETTY GOOD-LOOKING...
...AND HE'S MORE MATURE THAN I AM.

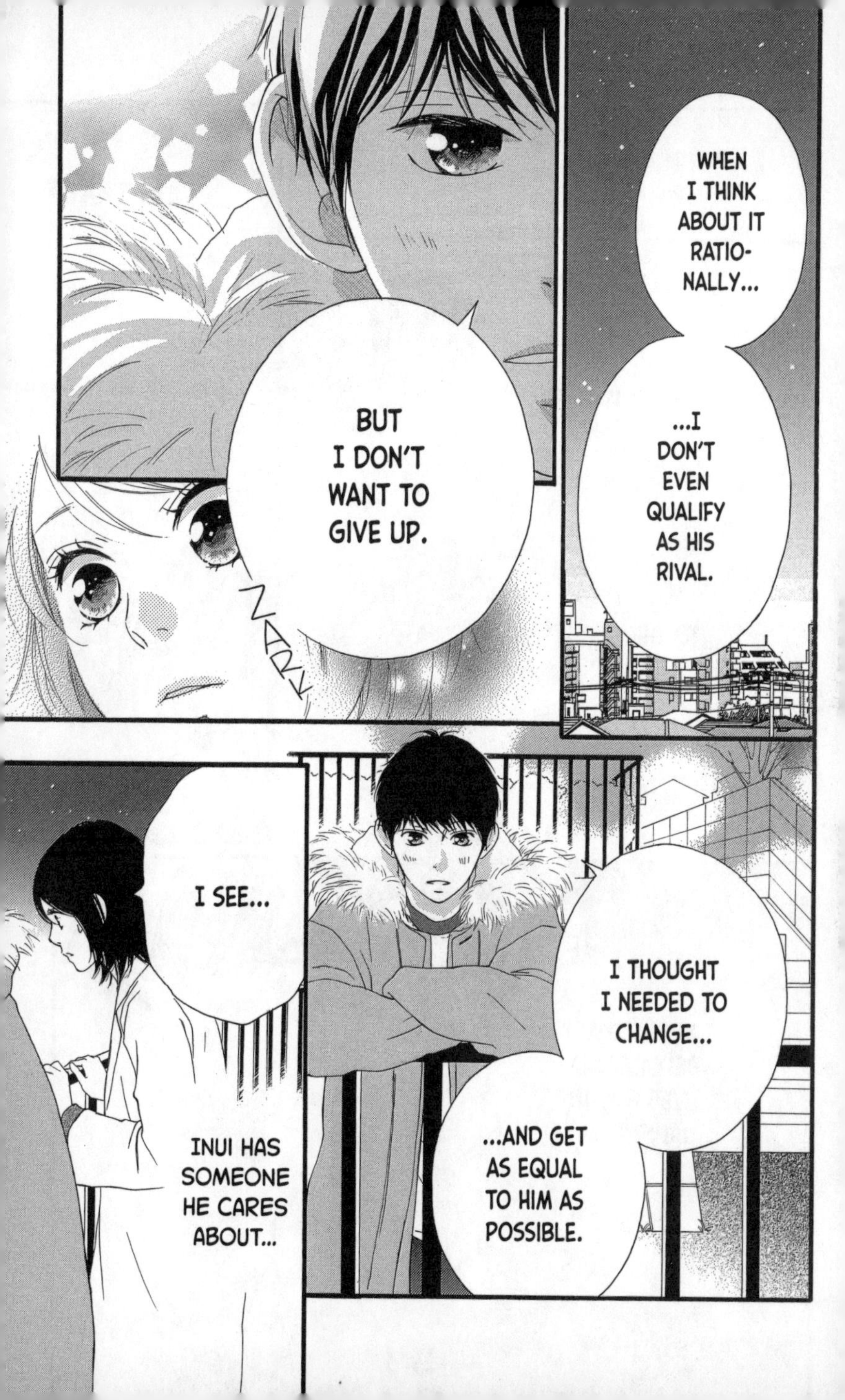
WHEN I THINK ABOUT IT RATIO-NALLY...
...I DON'T EVEN QUALIFY AS HIS RIVAL.
BUT I DON'T WANT TO GIVE UP.
NARY
I THOUGHT I NEEDED TO CHANGE...
...AND GET AS EQUAL TO HIM AS POSSIBLE.
I SEE...
INUI HAS SOMEONE HE CARES ABOUT...

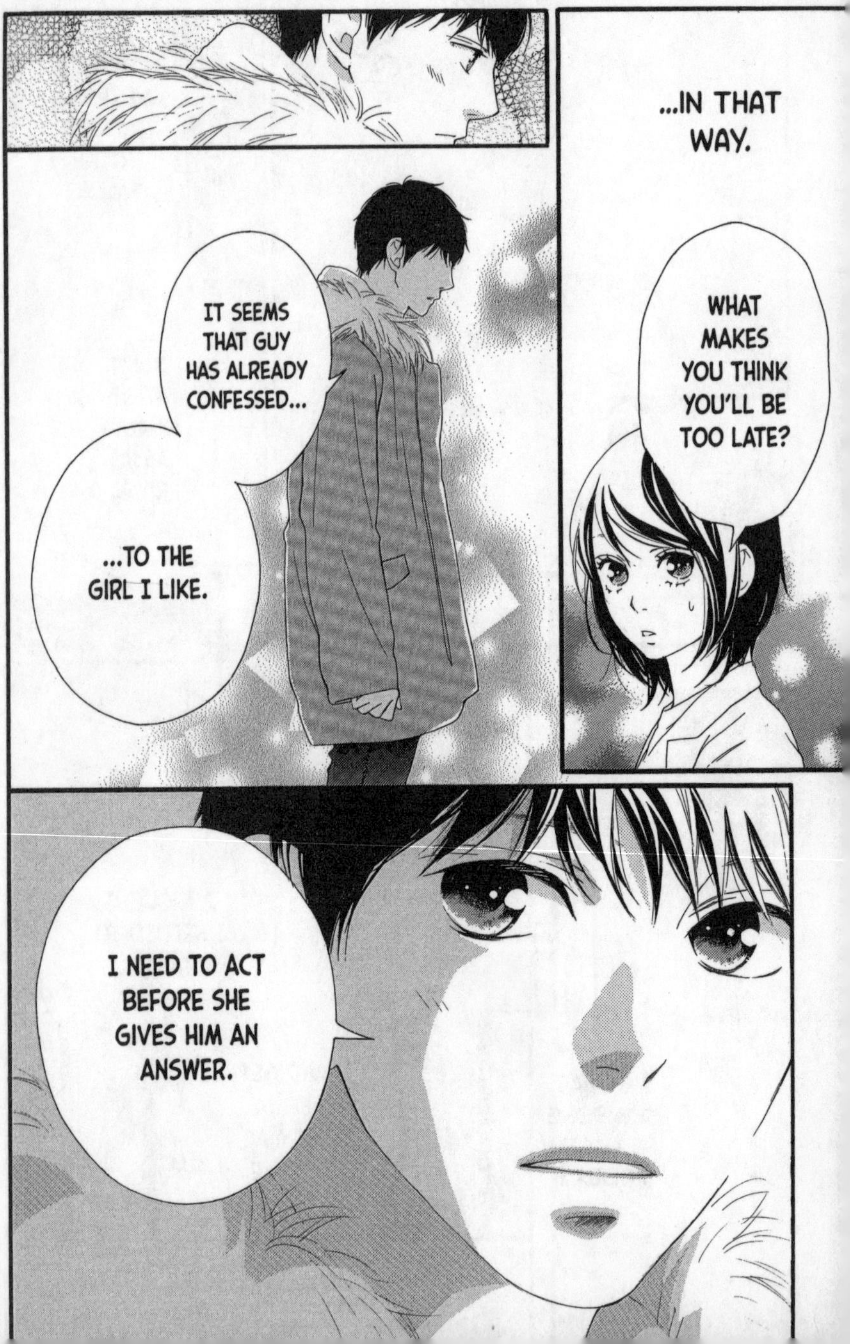
...IN THAT WAY.
WHAT MAKES YOU THINK YOU'LL BE TOO LATE?
IT SEEMS THAT GUY HAS ALREADY CONFESSED...
...TO THE GIRL I LIKE.
I NEED TO ACT BEFORE SHE GIVES HIM AN ANSWER.

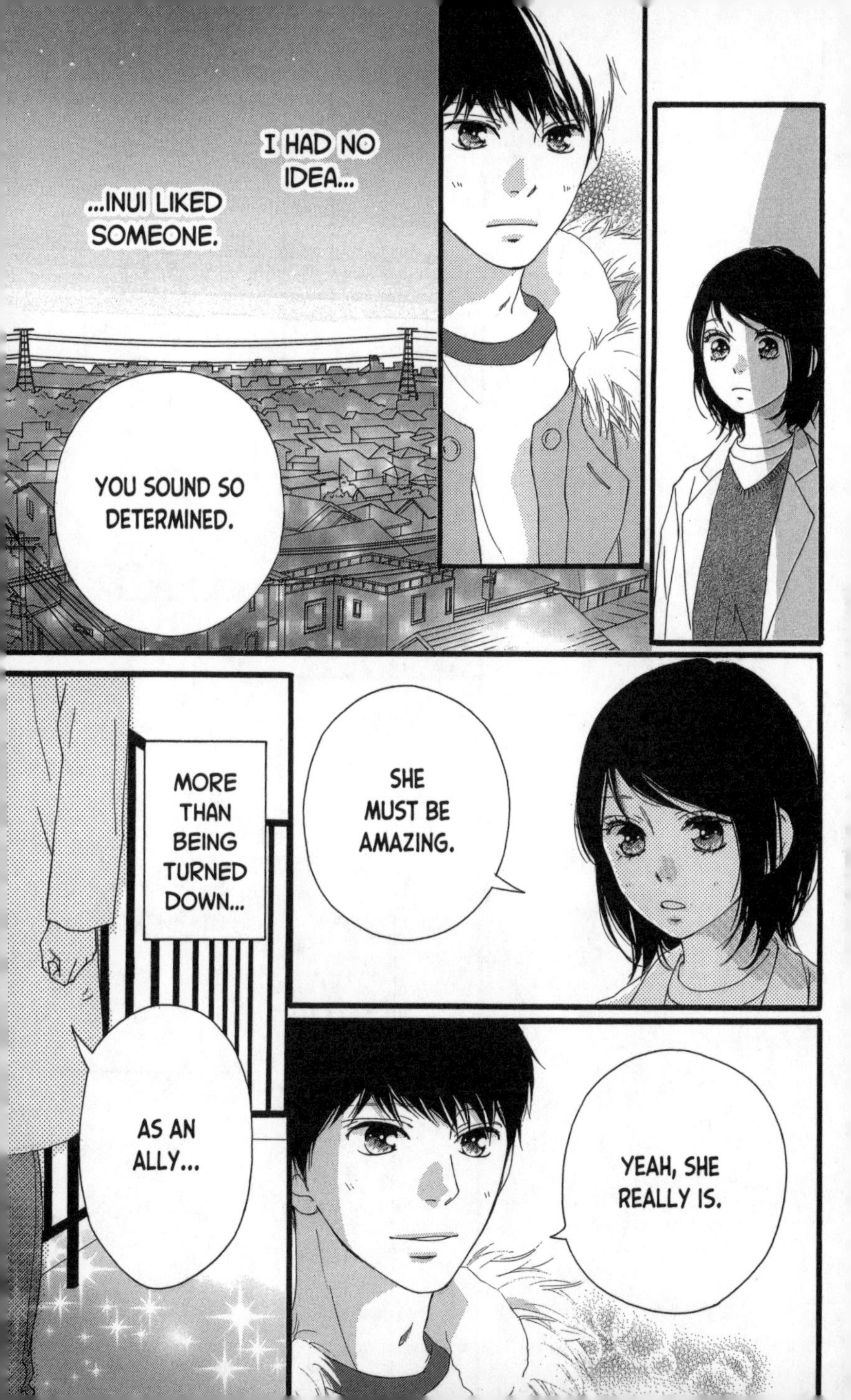
I HAD NO IDEA...
...INUI LIKED SOMEONE.
YOU SOUND SO DETERMINED.
SHE MUST BE AMAZING.
YEAH, SHE REALLY IS.
MORE THAN BEING TURNED DOWN...
AS AN ALLY...

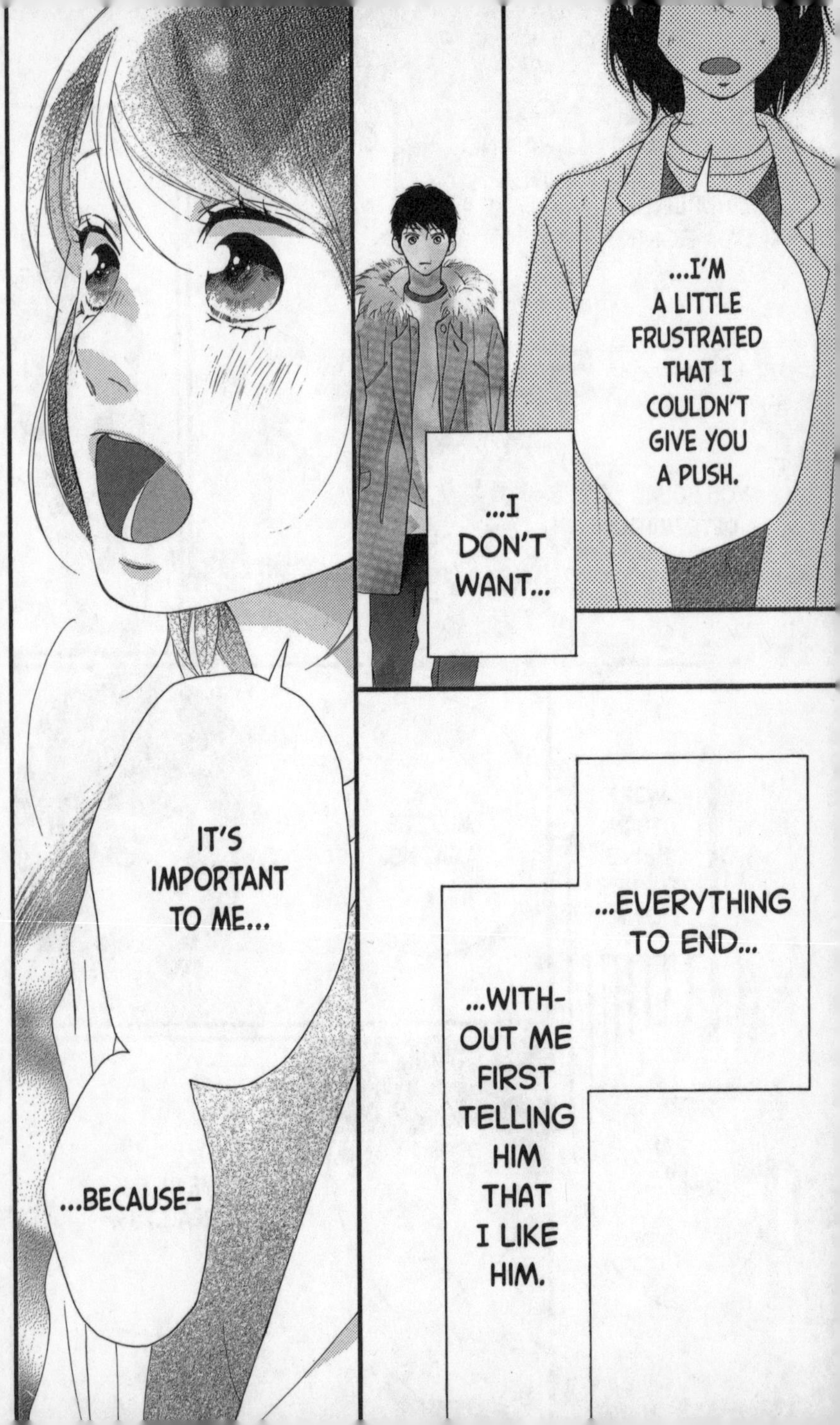
...I'M A LITTLE FRUSTRATED THAT I COULDN'T GIVE YOU A PUSH.
...I DON'T WANT...
...EVERYTHING TO END...
...WITH-OUT ME FIRST TELLING HIM THAT I LIKE HIM.
IT'S IMPORTANT TO ME...
...BECAUSE-

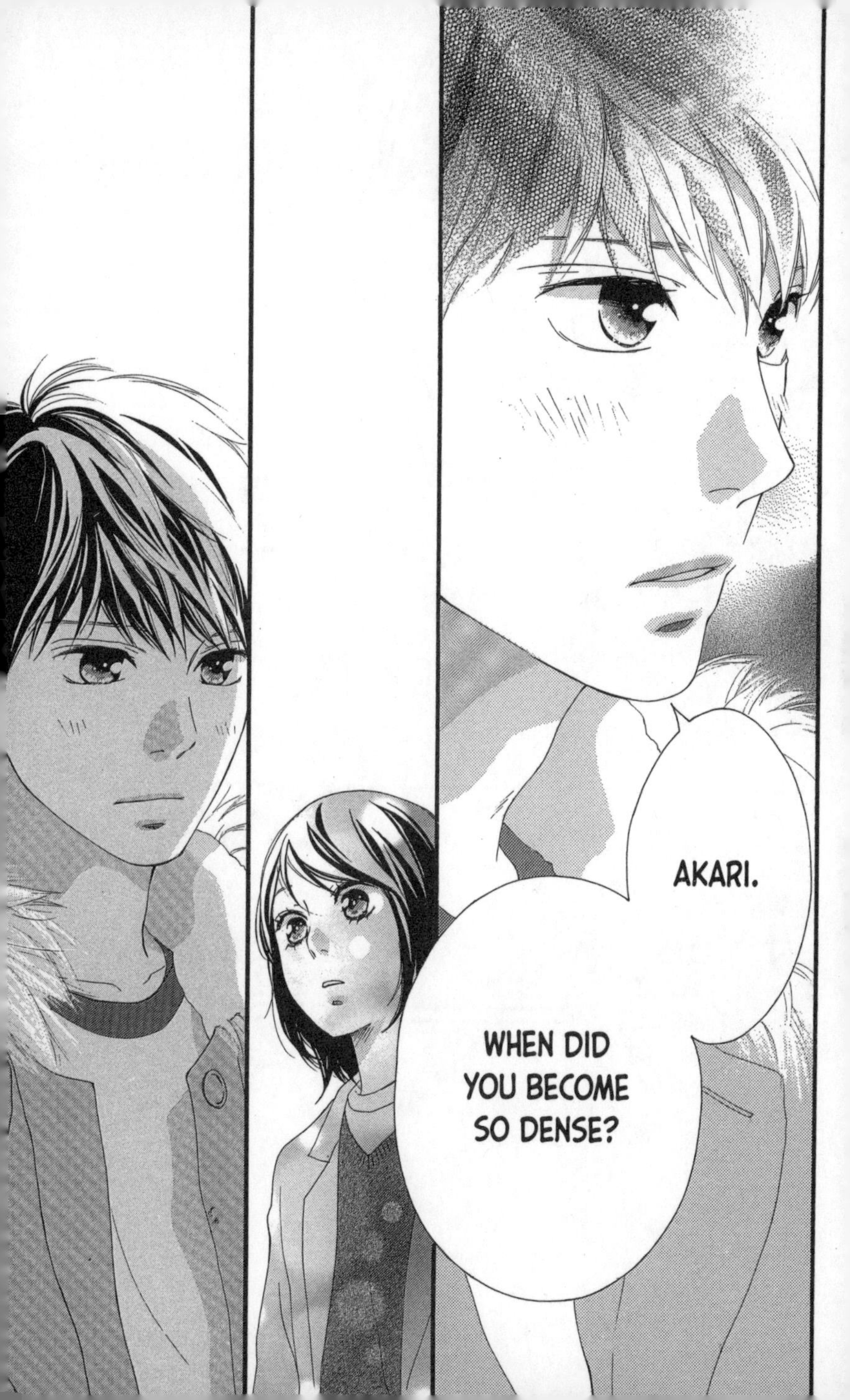
AKARI.
WHEN DID YOU BECOME SO DENSE?

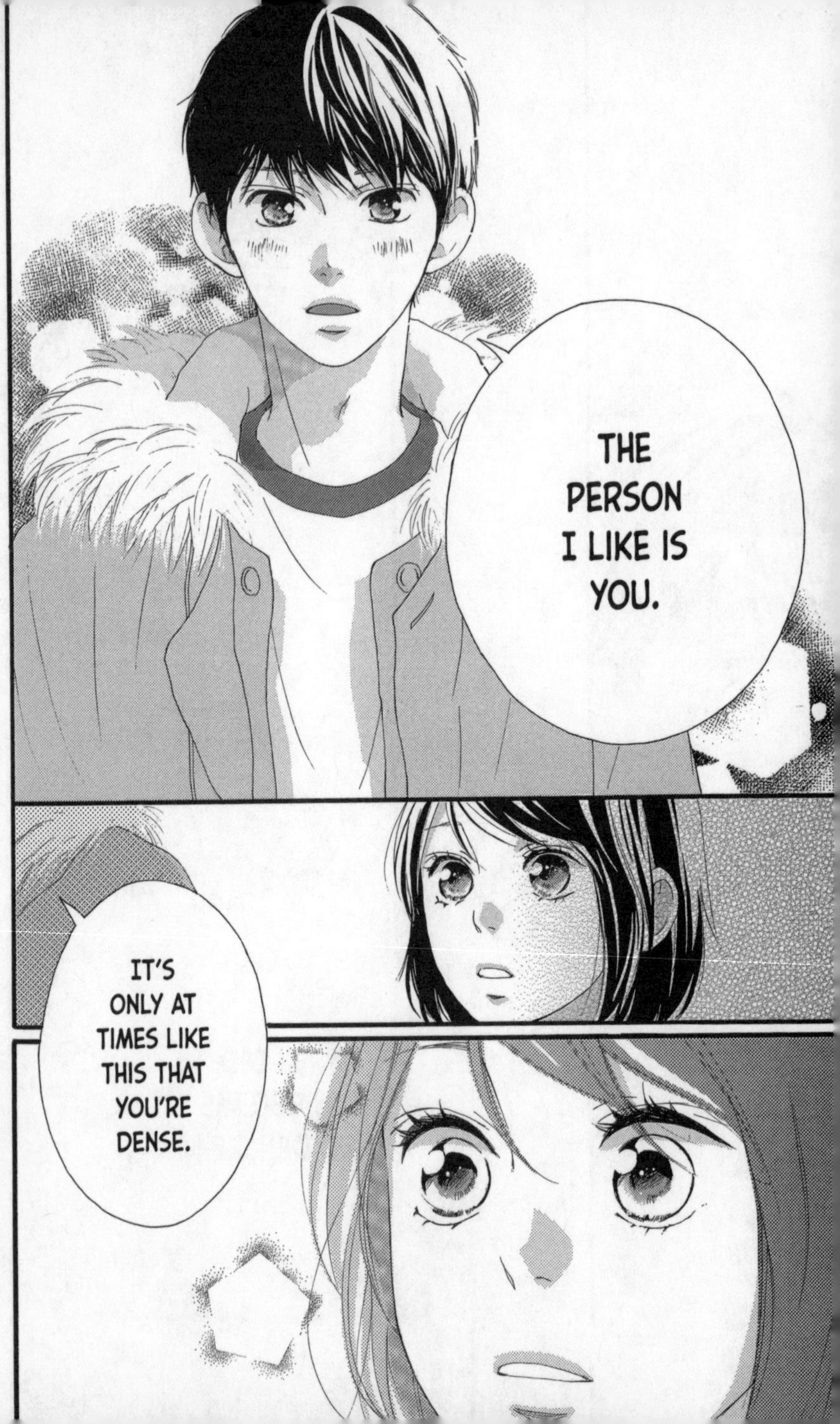
THE PERSON I LIKE IS YOU.
IT'S ONLY AT TIMES LIKE THIS THAT YOU'RE DENSE.

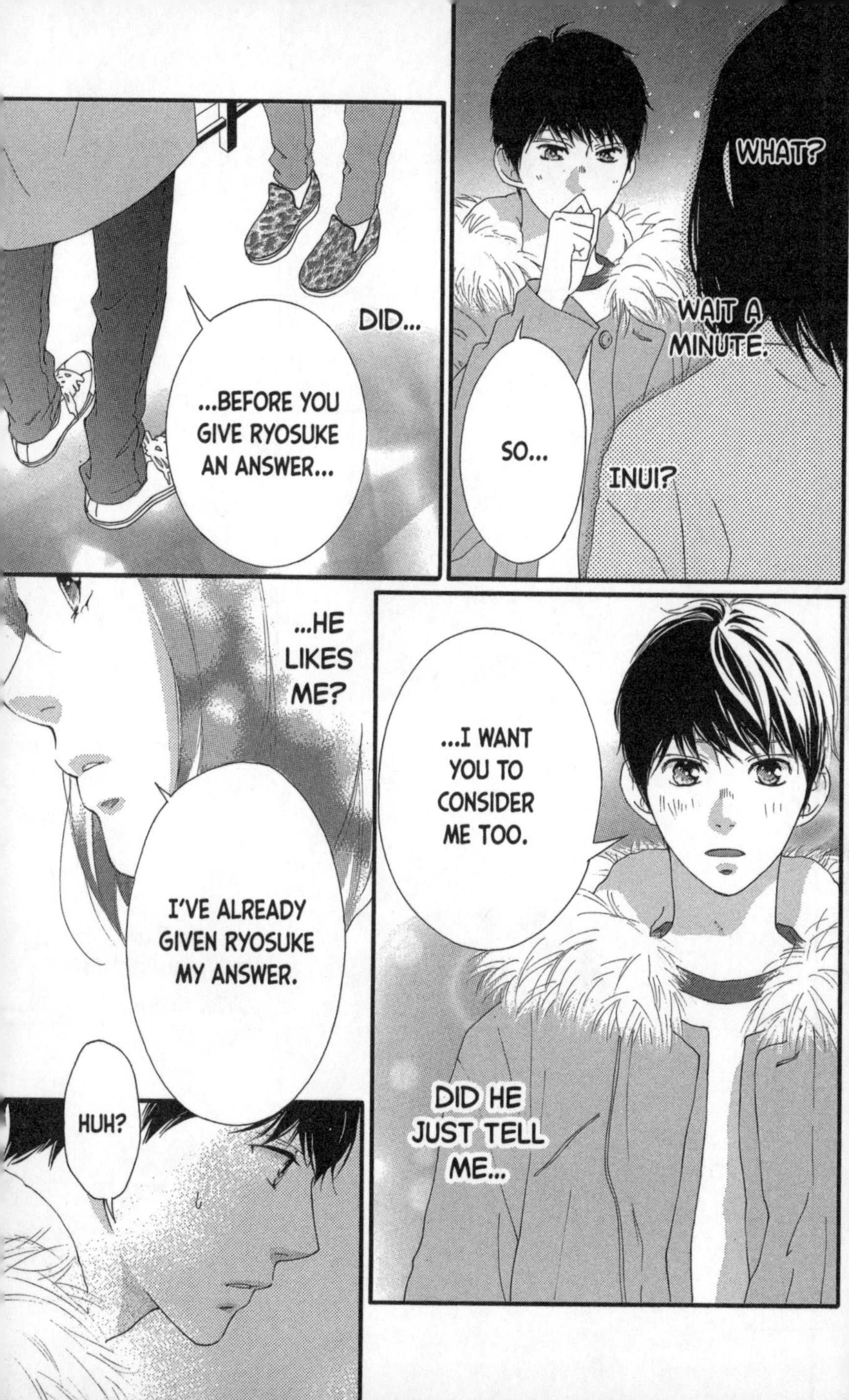
WHAT?
WAIT A MINUTE.
INUI?
SO...
DID...
...BEFORE YOU GIVE RYOSUKE AN ANSWER...
...I WANT YOU TO CONSIDER ME TOO.
DID HE JUST TELL ME...
...HE LIKES ME?
I'VE ALREADY GIVEN RYOSUKE MY ANSWER.
HUH?

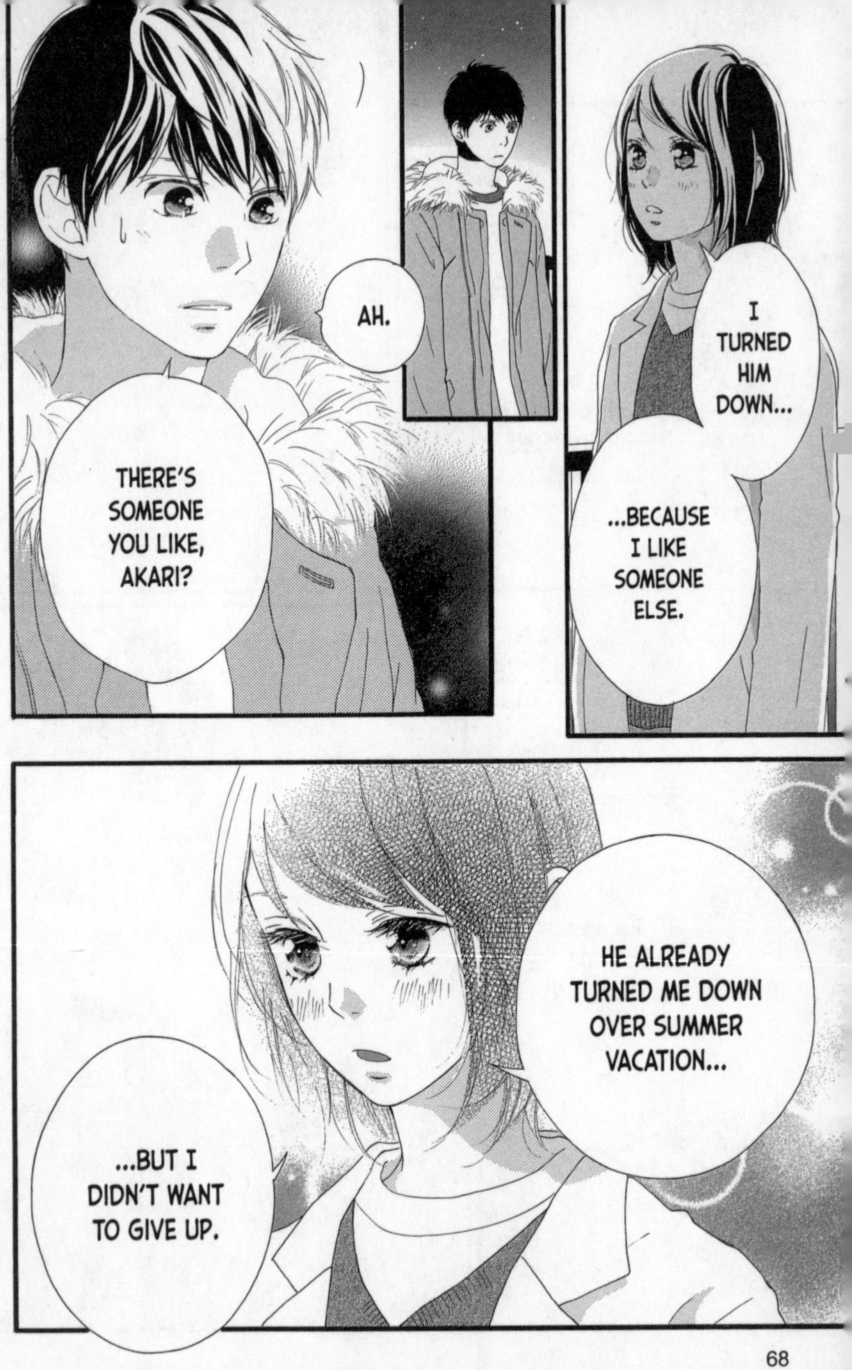
I TURNED HIM DOWN...
...BECAUSE I LIKE SOMEONE ELSE.
AH.
THERE'S SOMEONE YOU LIKE, AKARI?
HE ALREADY TURNED ME DOWN OVER SUMMER VACATION...
...BUT I DIDN'T WANT TO GIVE UP.

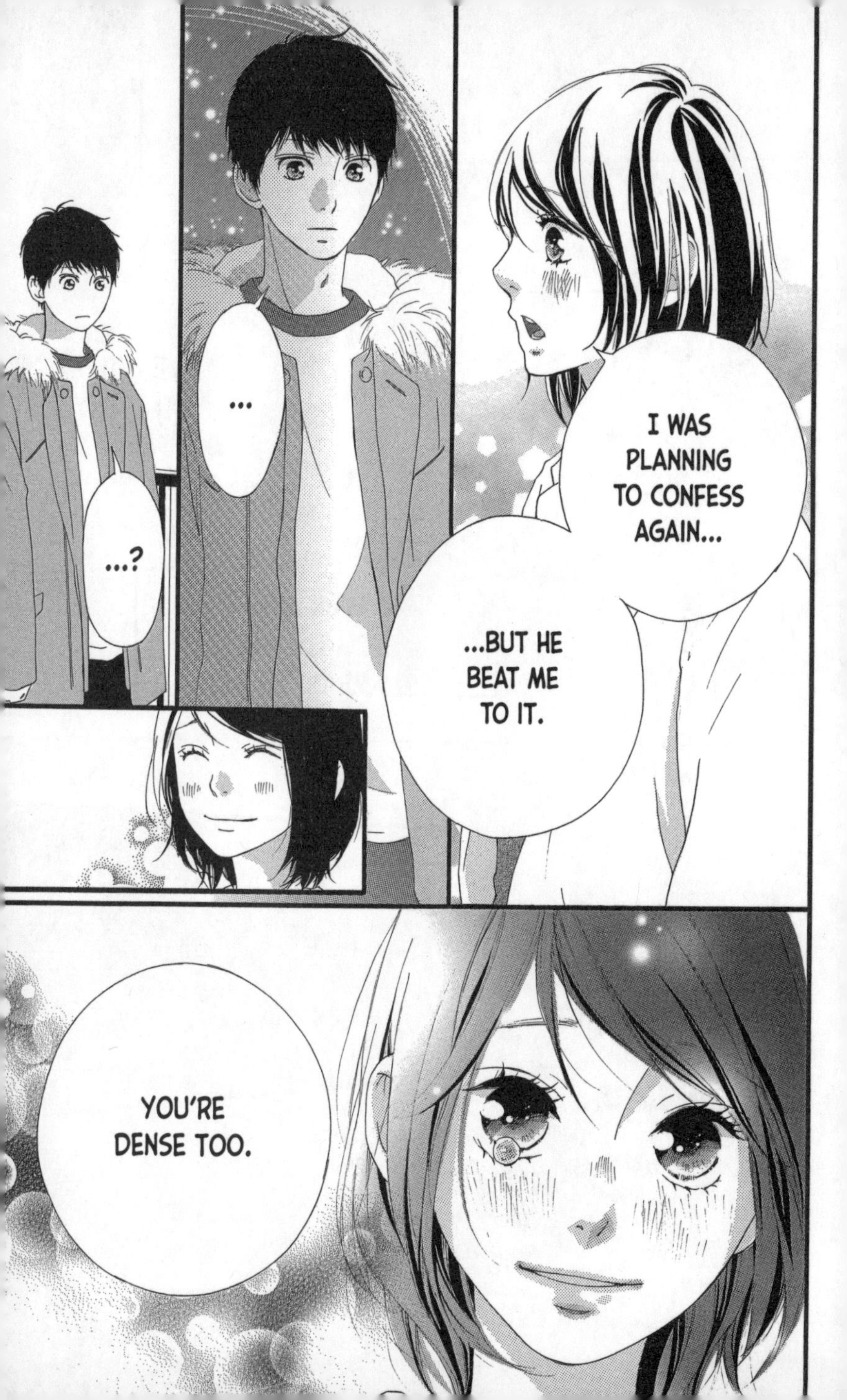
I WAS PLANNING TO CONFESS AGAIN...
...BUT HE BEAT ME TO IT.
...
...?
YOU'RE DENSE TOO.

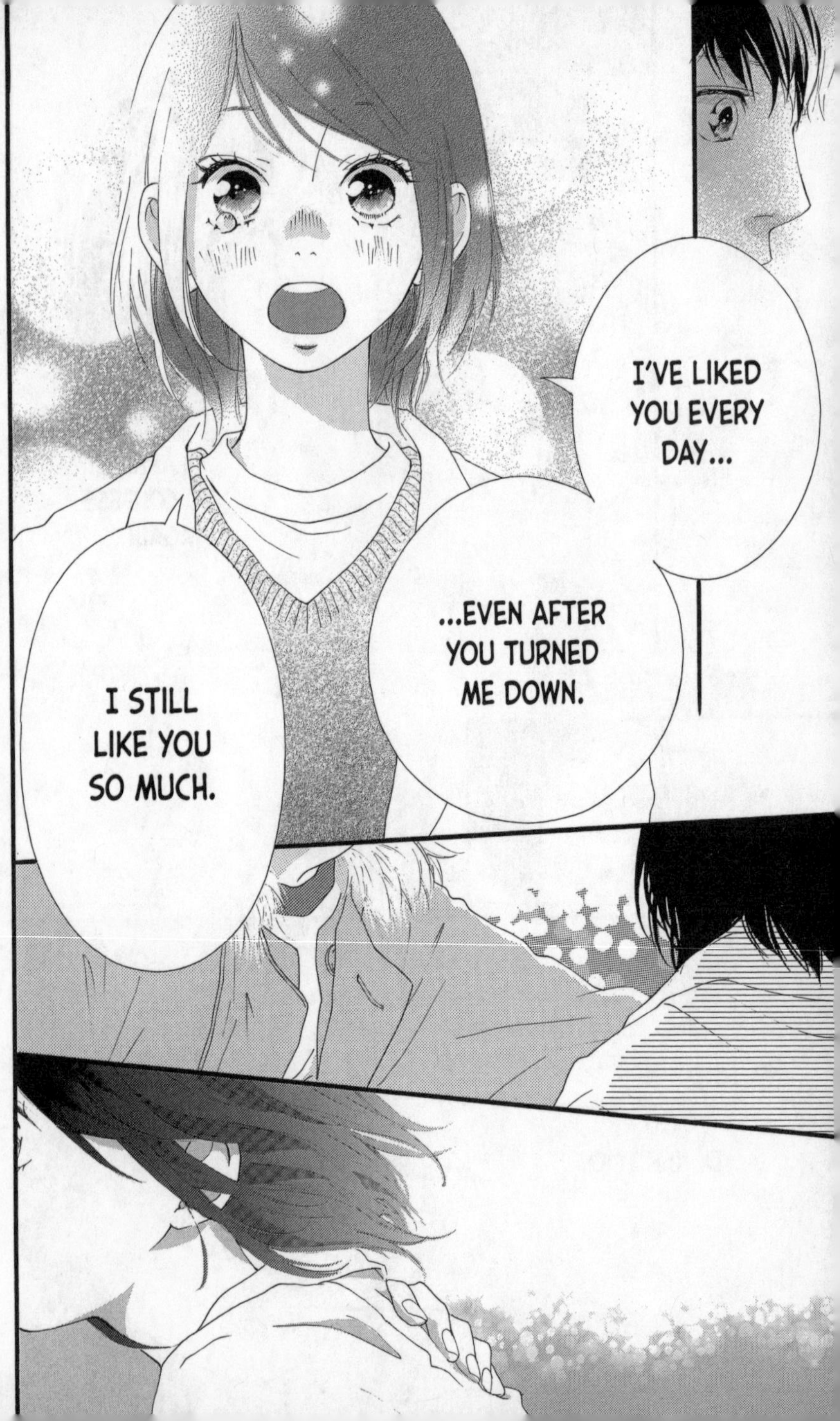
I'VE LIKED YOU EVERY DAY...
...EVEN AFTER YOU TURNED ME DOWN.
I STILL LIKE YOU SO MUCH.

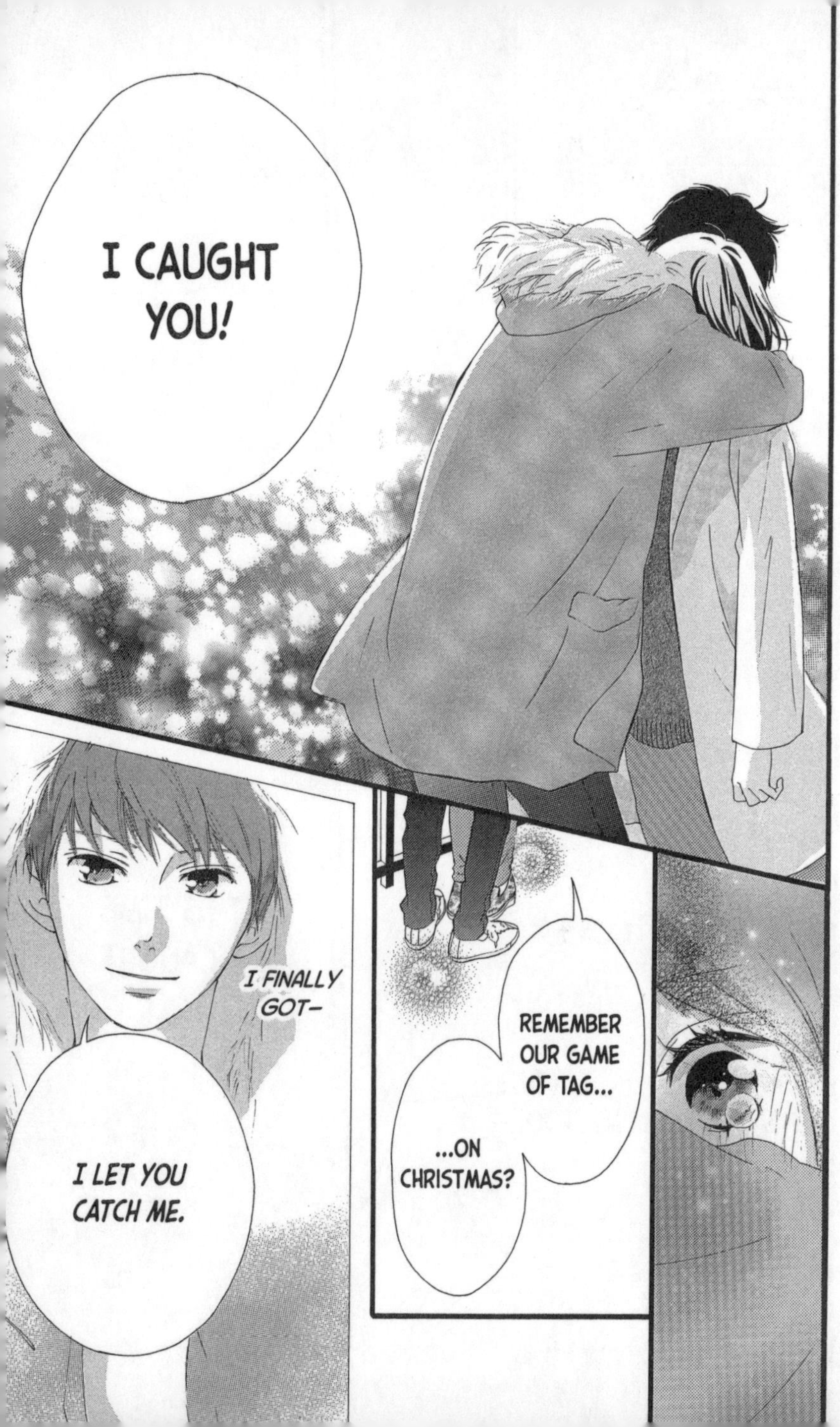
I CAUGHT YOU!
REMEMBER OUR GAME OF TAG...
...ON CHRISTMAS?
I FINALLY GOT—
I LET YOU CATCH ME.

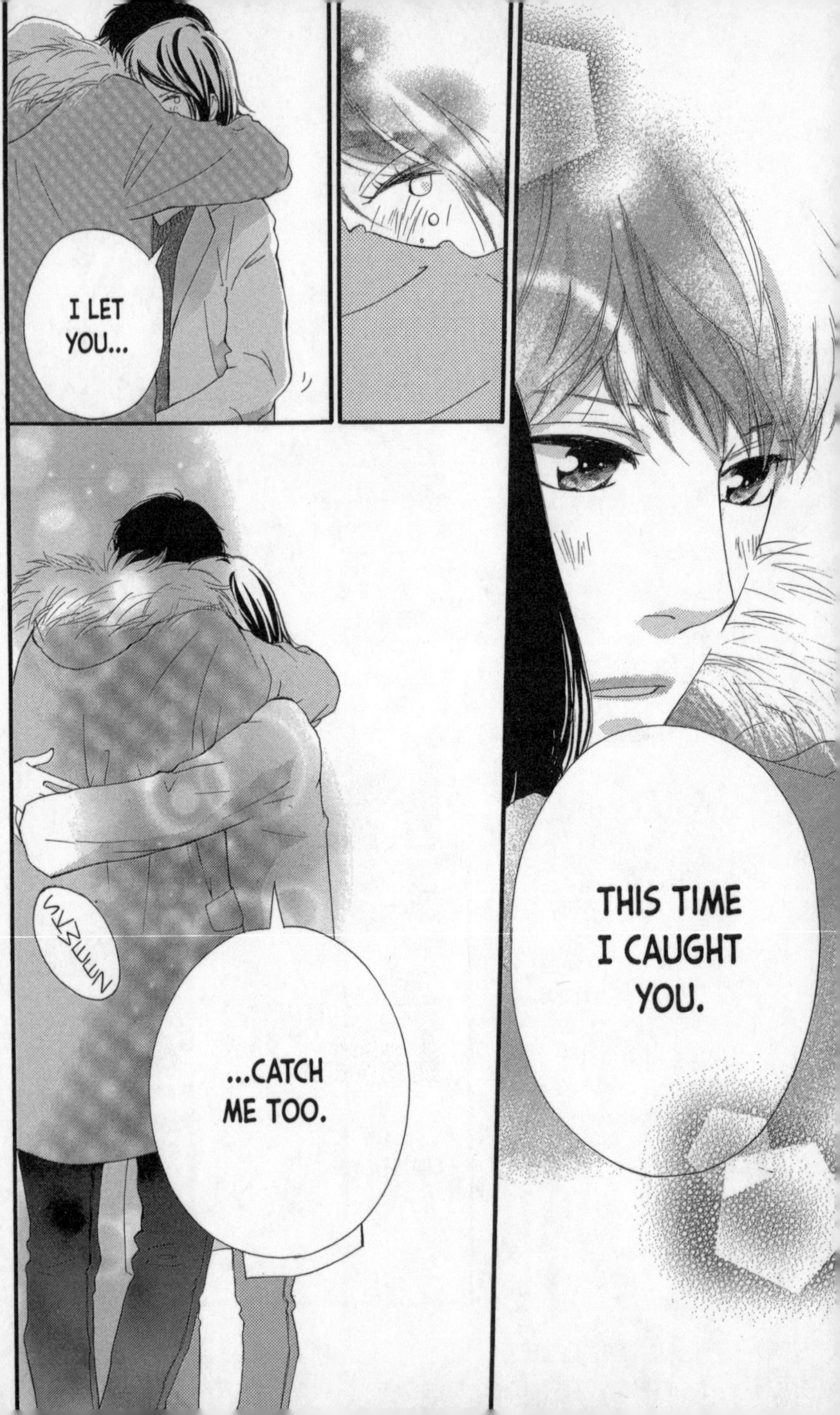
THIS TIME I CAUGHT YOU.
I LET YOU...
...CATCH ME TOO.

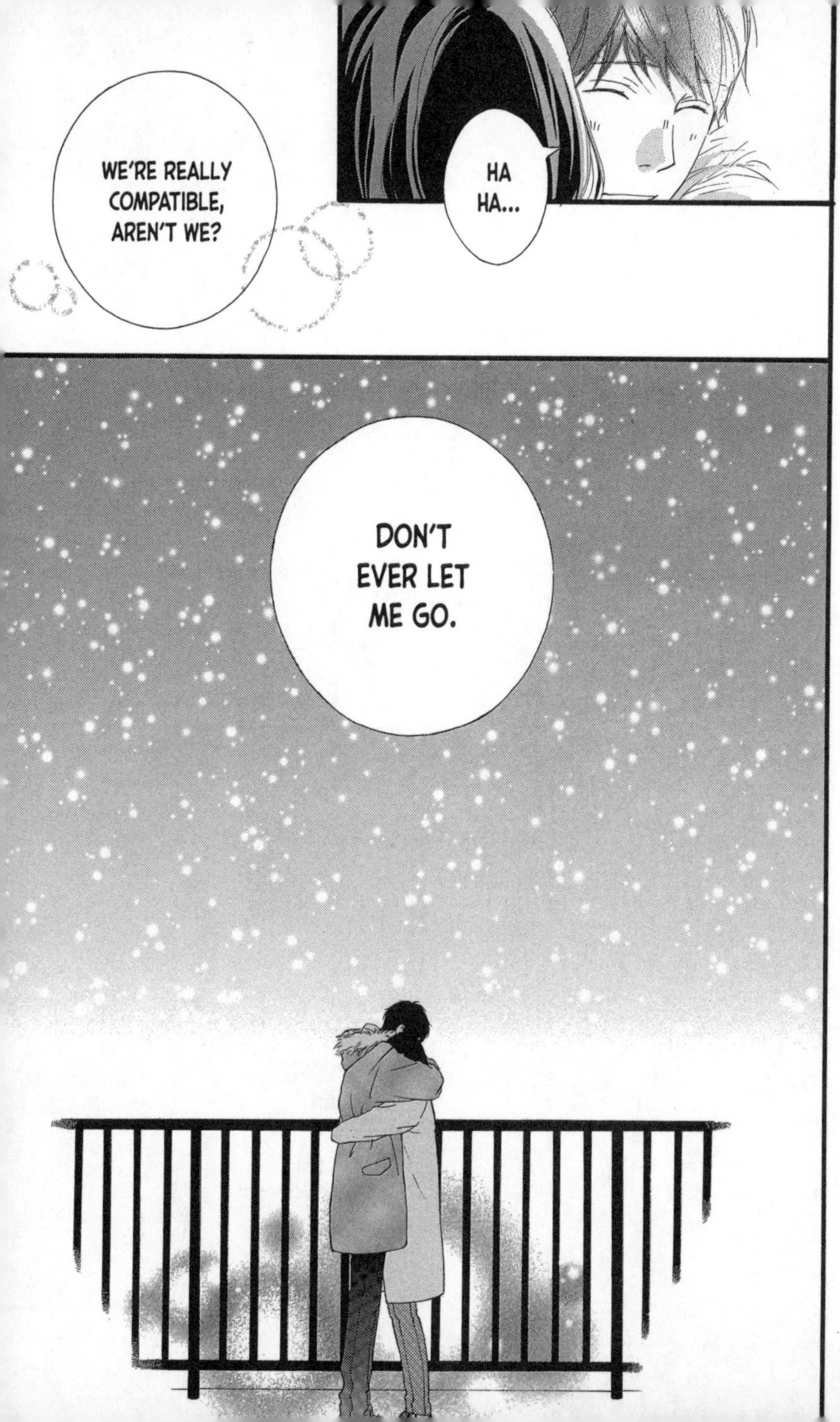
HA HA...
WE'RE REALLY COMPATIBLE, AREN'T WE?
DON'T EVER LET ME GO.

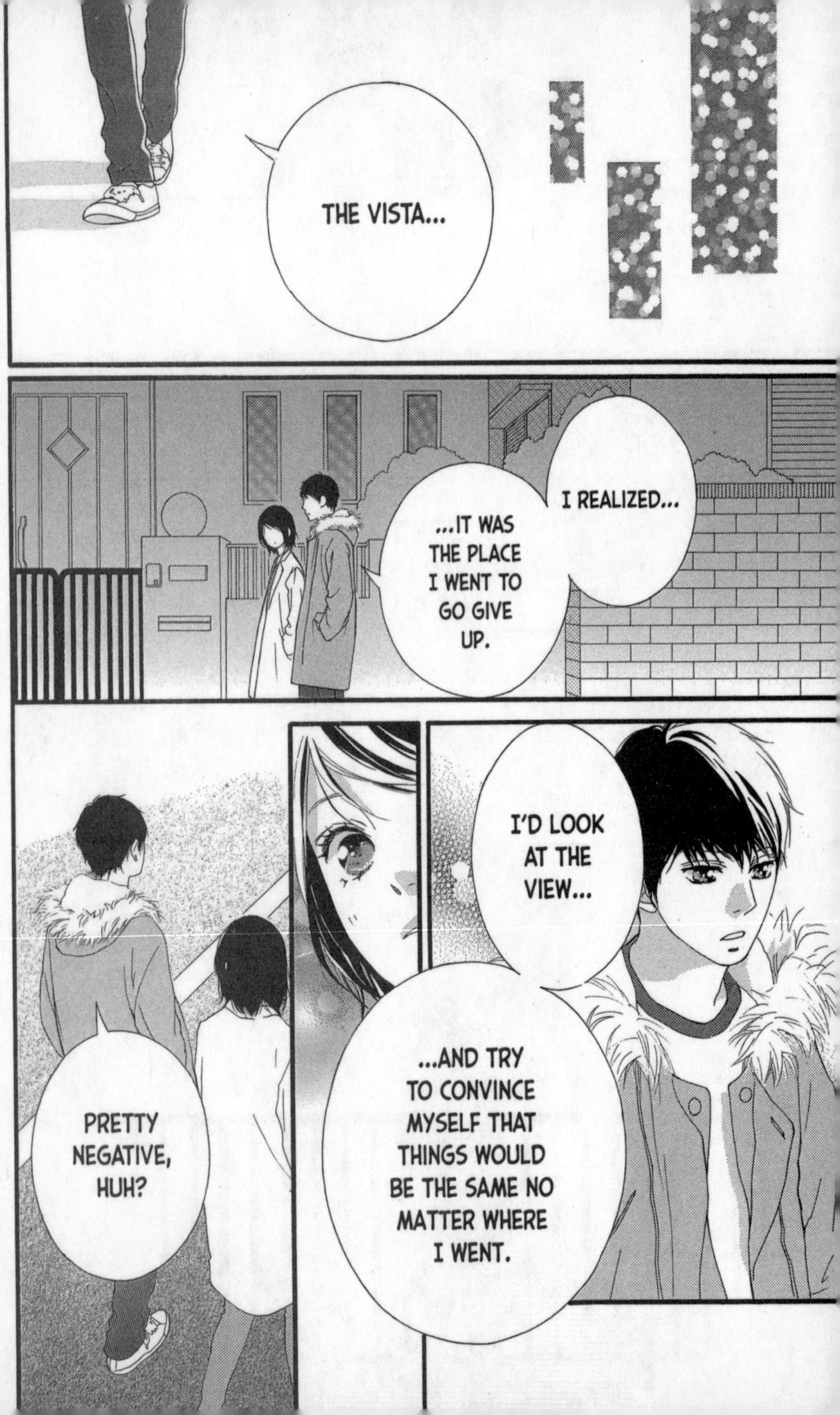
THE VISTA...
I REALIZED...
...IT WAS THE PLACE I WENT TO GO GIVE UP.
I'D LOOK AT THE VIEW...
...AND TRY TO CONVINCE MYSELF THAT THINGS WOULD BE THE SAME NO MATTER WHERE I WENT.
PRETTY NEGATIVE, HUH?

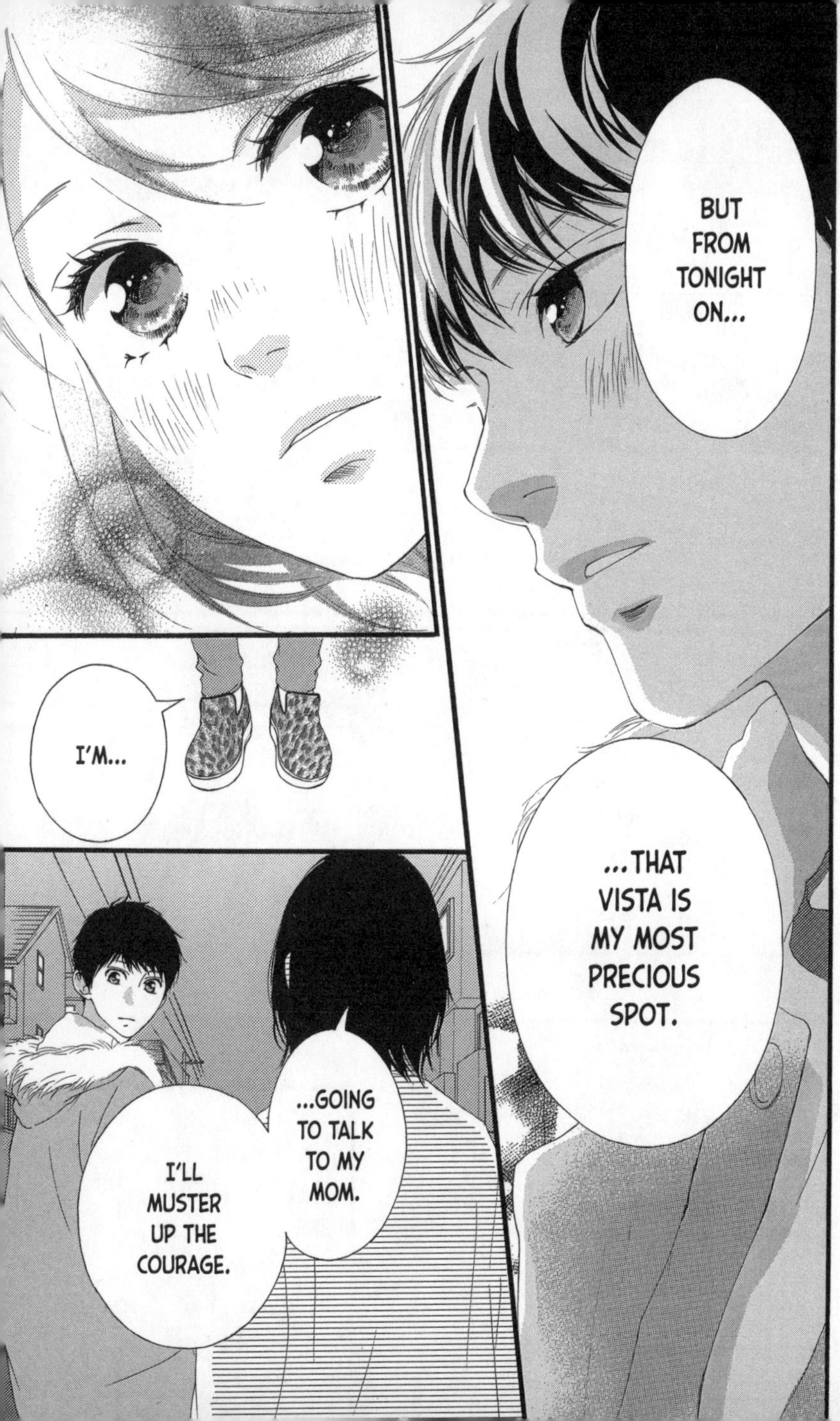
BUT FROM TONIGHT ON...
...THAT VISTA IS MY MOST PRECIOUS SPOT.
I'M...
...GOING TO TALK TO MY MOM.
I'LL MUSTER UP THE COURAGE.

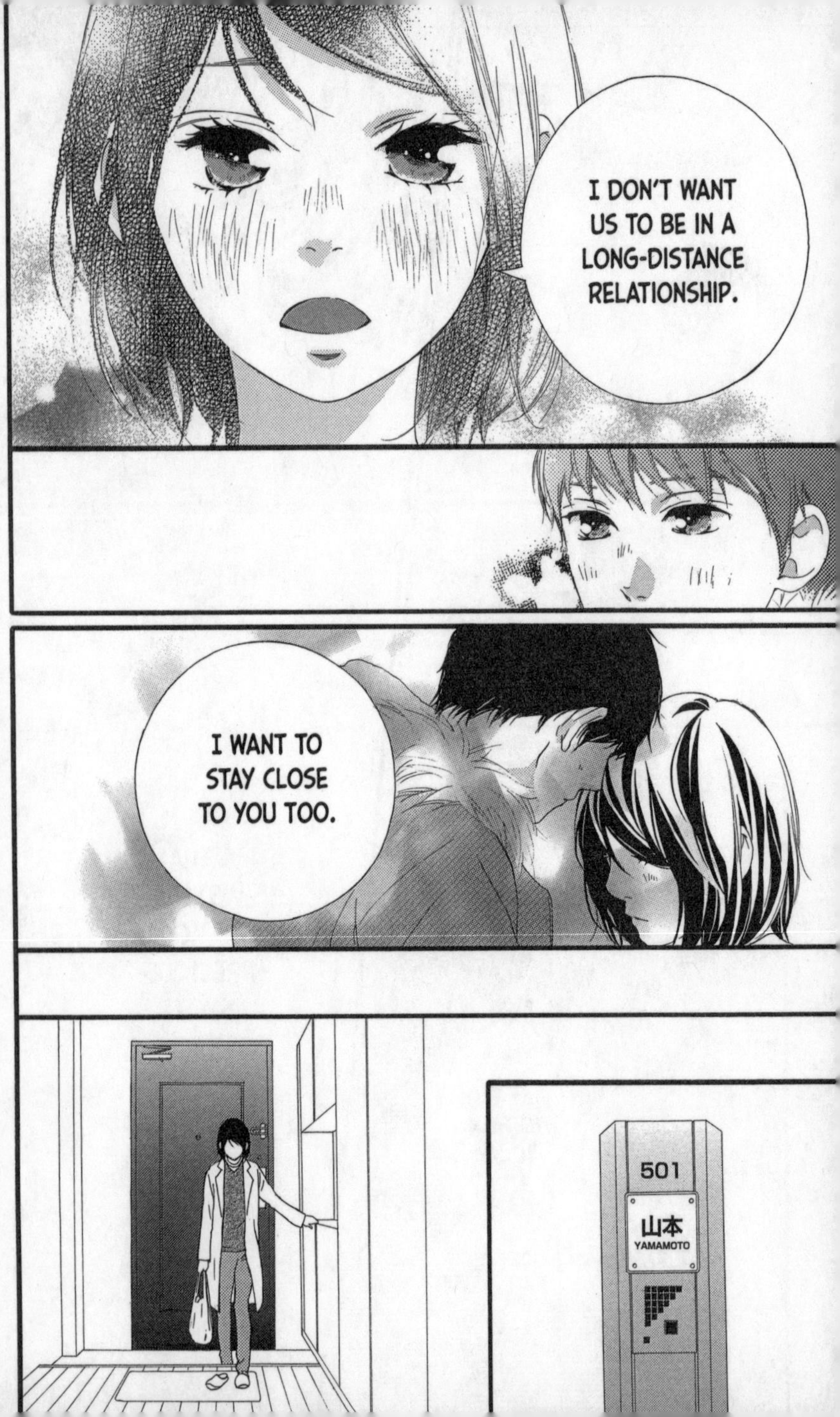
I DON'T WANT US TO BE IN A LONG-DISTANCE RELATIONSHIP.
I WANT TO STAY CLOSE TO YOU TOO.
501
山本
YAMAMOTO

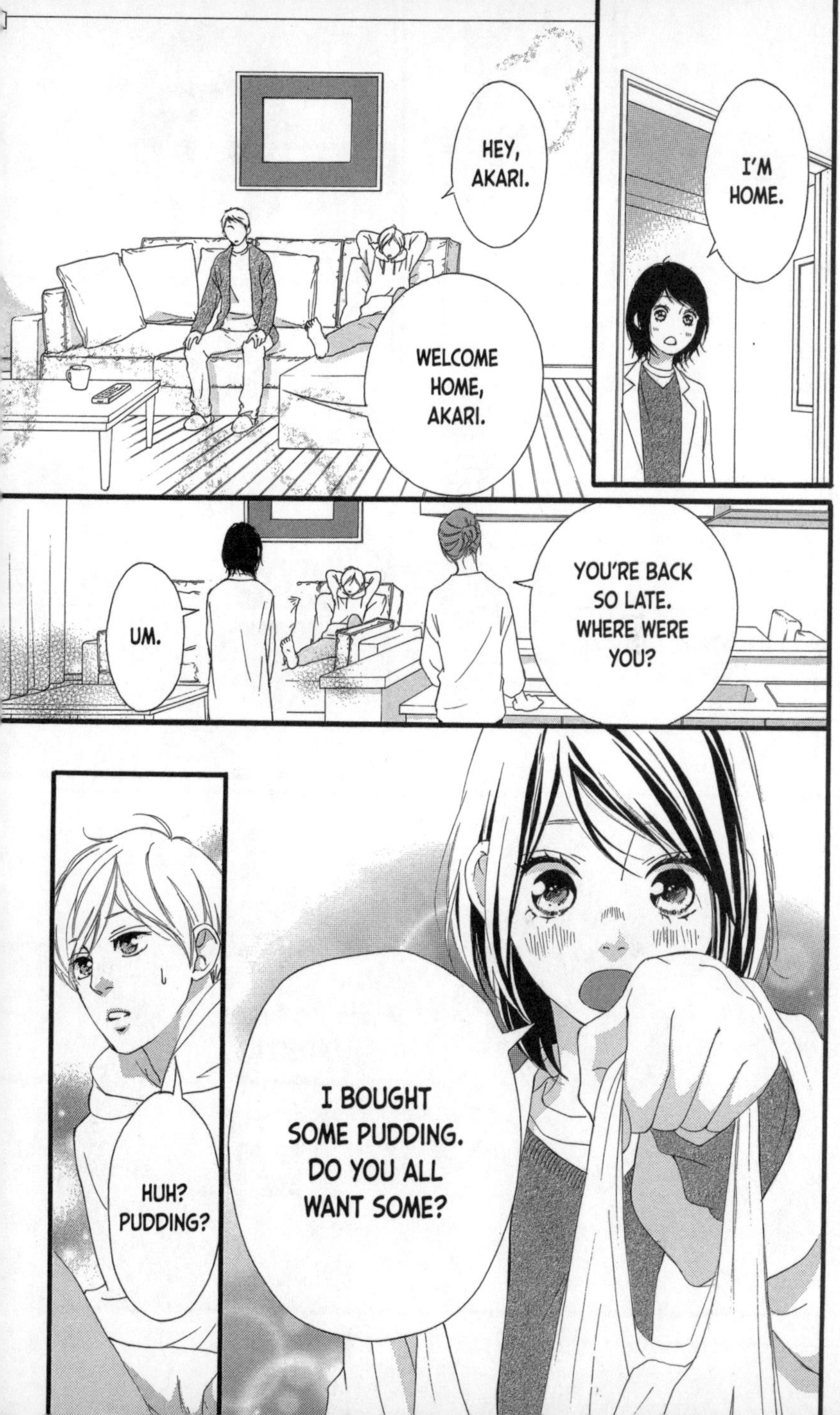
I'M HOME.
HEY, AKARI.
WELCOME HOME, AKARI.
YOU'RE BACK SO LATE. WHERE WERE YOU?
UM.
I BOUGHT SOME PUDDING. DO YOU ALL WANT SOME?
HUH? PUDDING?

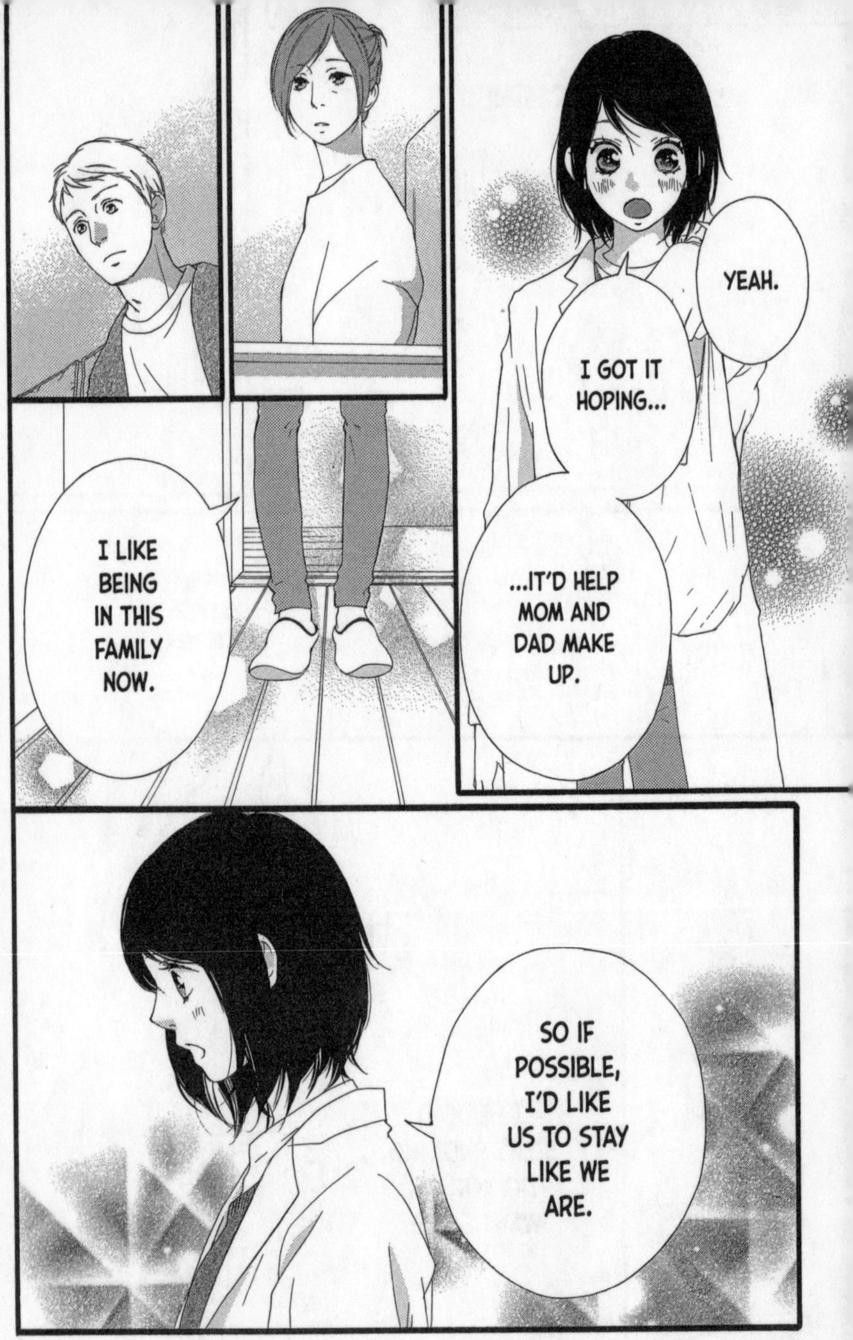
YEAH.
I GOT IT HOPING...
...IT'D HELP MOM AND DAD MAKE UP.
I LIKE BEING IN THIS FAMILY NOW.
SO IF POSSIBLE, I'D LIKE US TO STAY LIKE WE ARE.

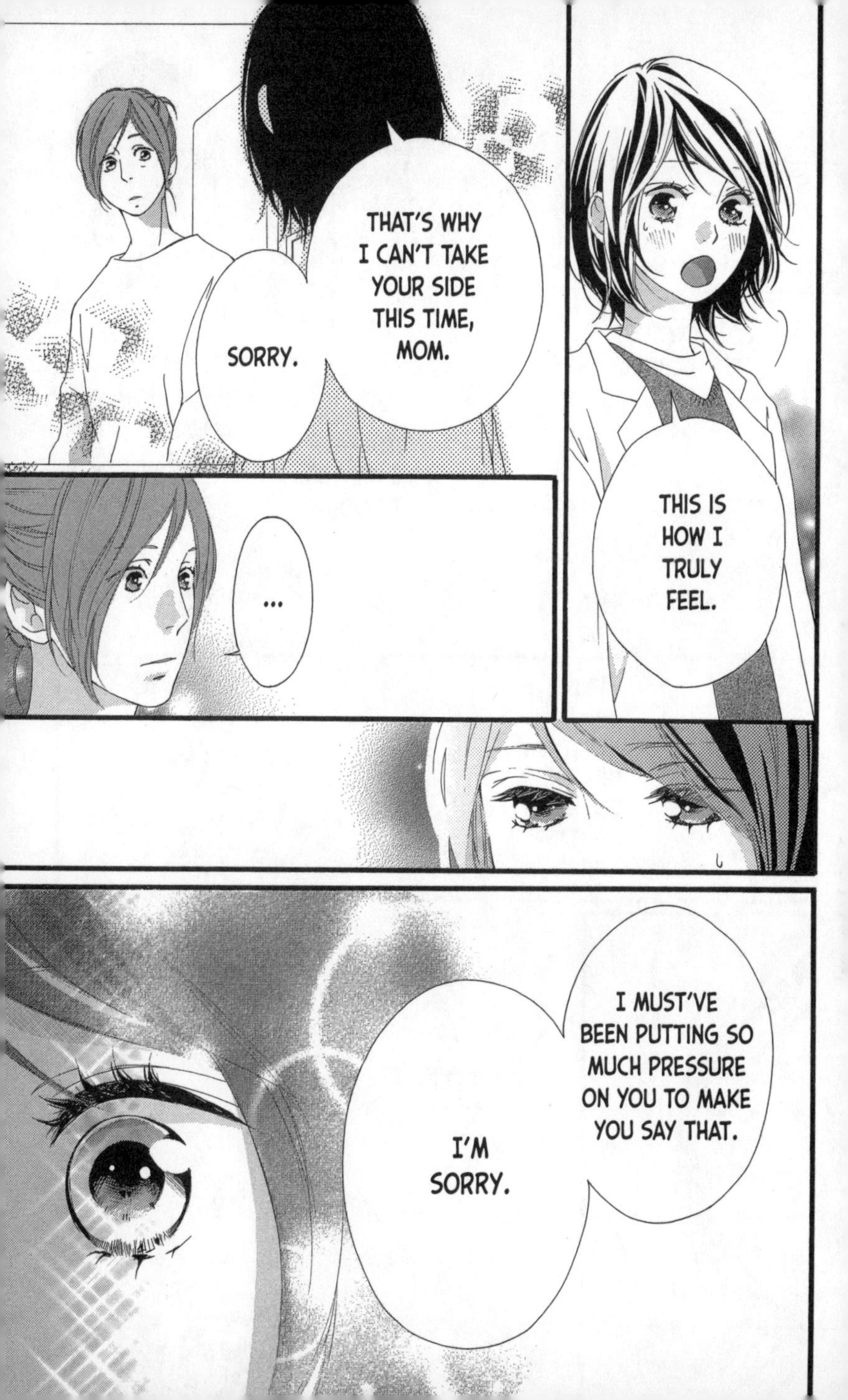
THIS IS HOW I TRULY FEEL.
THAT'S WHY I CAN'T TAKE YOUR SIDE THIS TIME, MOM.
SORRY.
...
I MUST'VE BEEN PUTTING SO MUCH PRESSURE ON YOU TO MAKE YOU SAY THAT.
I'M SORRY.

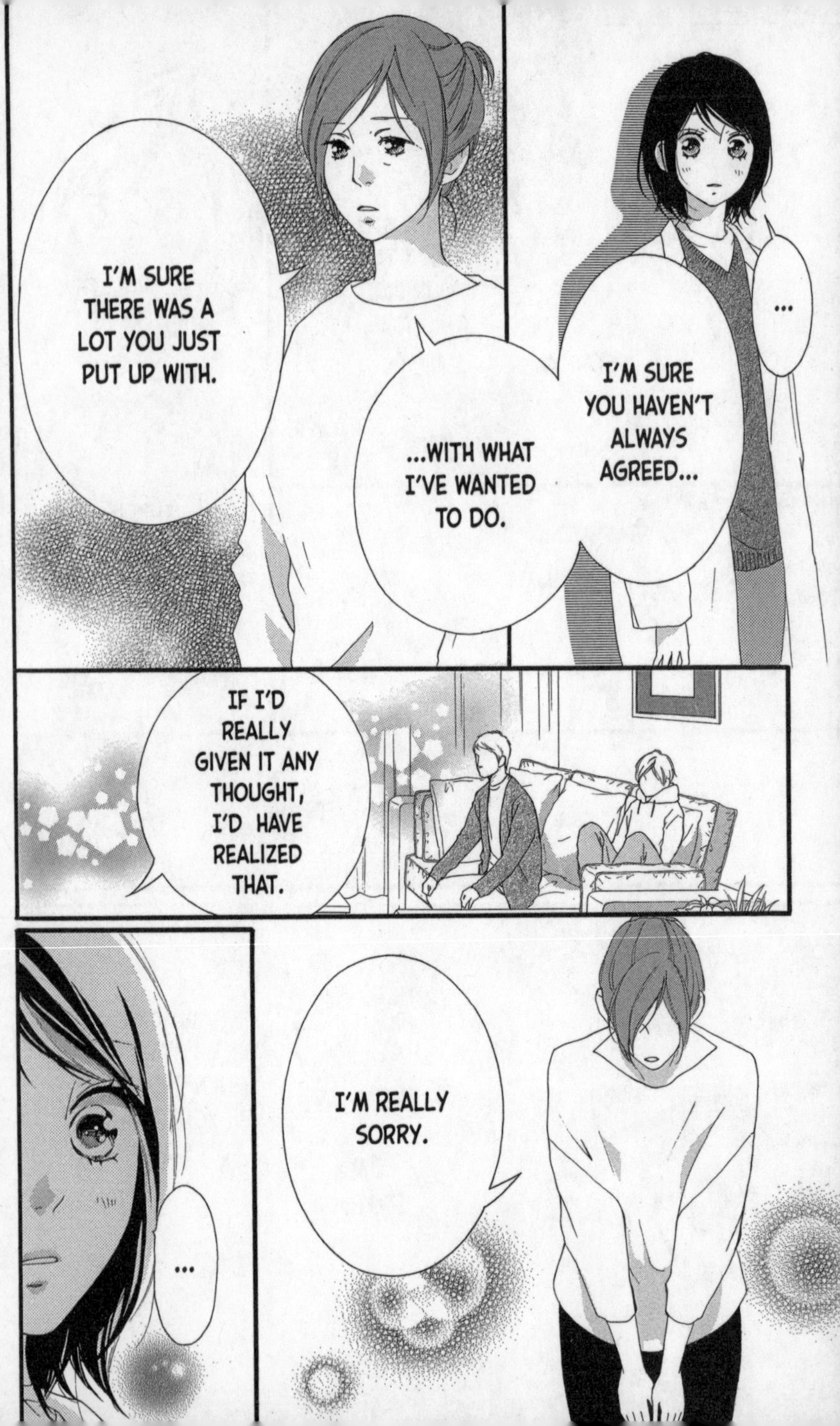
...
I'M SURE YOU HAVEN'T ALWAYS AGREED...
...WITH WHAT I'VE WANTED TO DO.
I'M SURE THERE WAS A LOT YOU JUST PUT UP WITH.
IF I'D REALLY GIVEN IT ANY THOUGHT, I'D HAVE REALIZED THAT.
I'M REALLY SORRY.
...

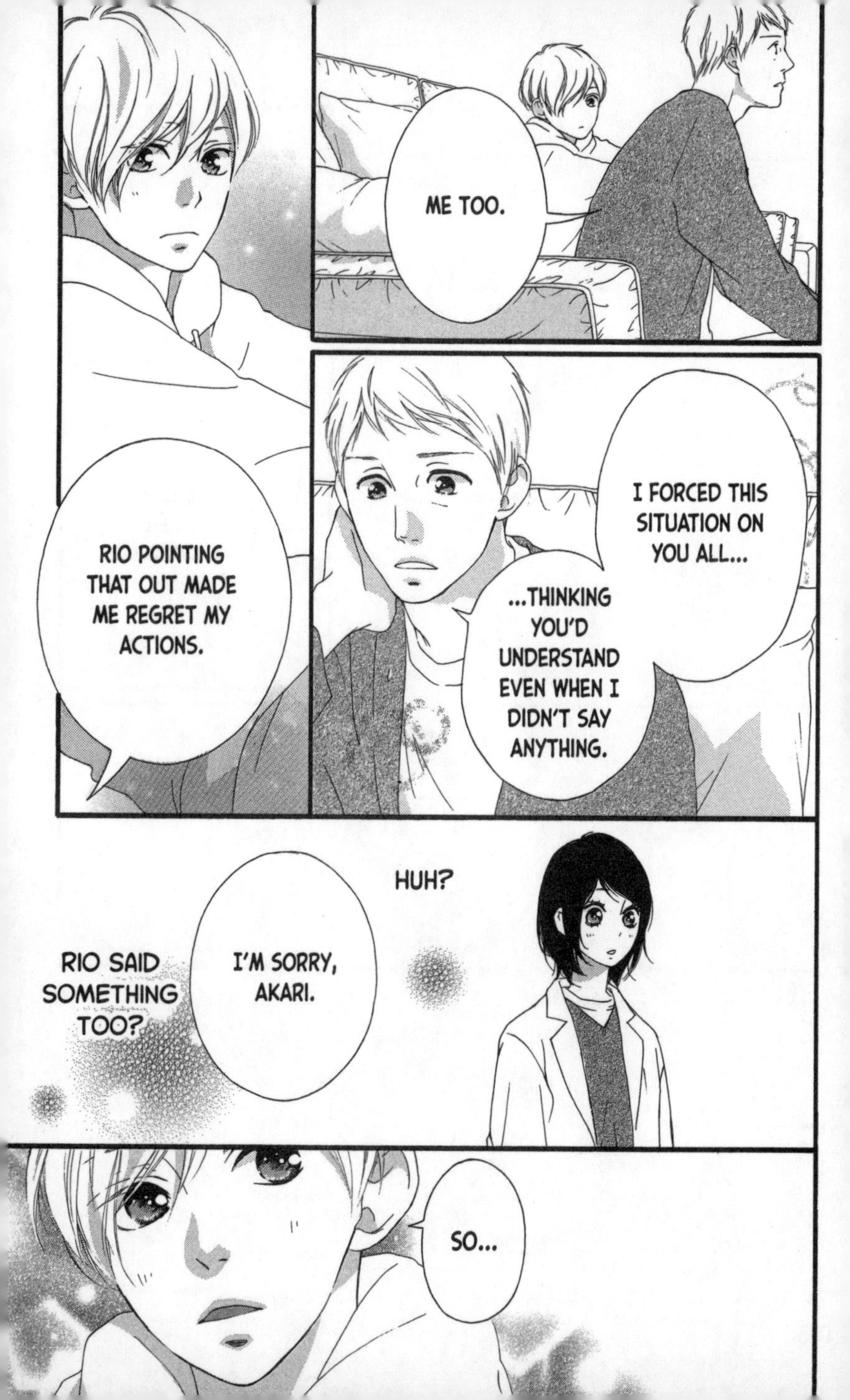
ME TOO.
I FORCED THIS SITUATION ON YOU ALL...
...THINKING YOU'D UNDERSTAND EVEN WHEN I DIDN'T SAY ANYTHING.
RIO POINTING THAT OUT MADE ME REGRET MY ACTIONS.
HUH?
I'M SORRY, AKARI.
RIO SAID SOMETHING TOO?
SO...

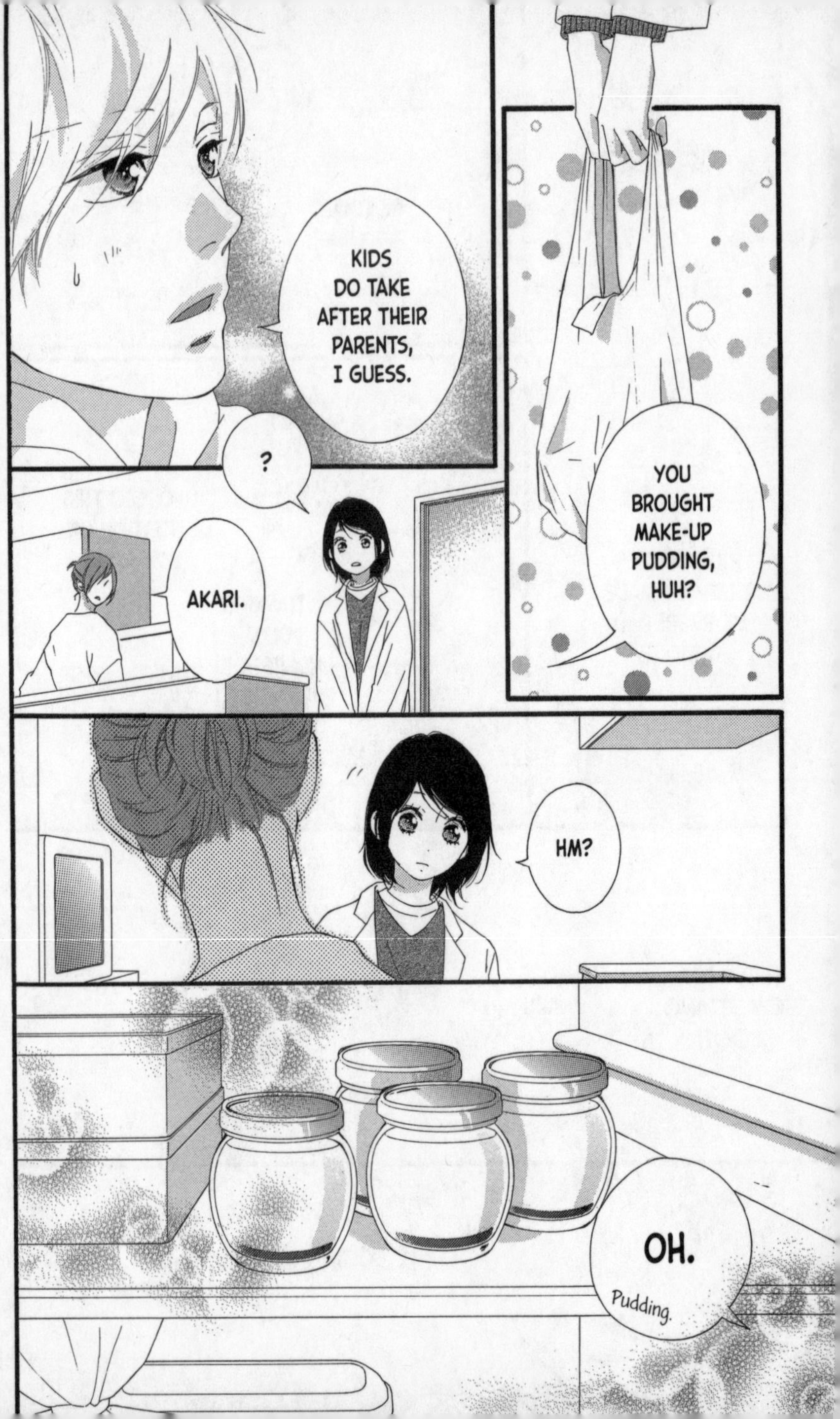
YOU BROUGHT MAKE-UP PUDDING, HUH?
KIDS DO TAKE AFTER THEIR PARENTS, I GUESS.
?
AKARI.
HM?
OH.
Pudding.

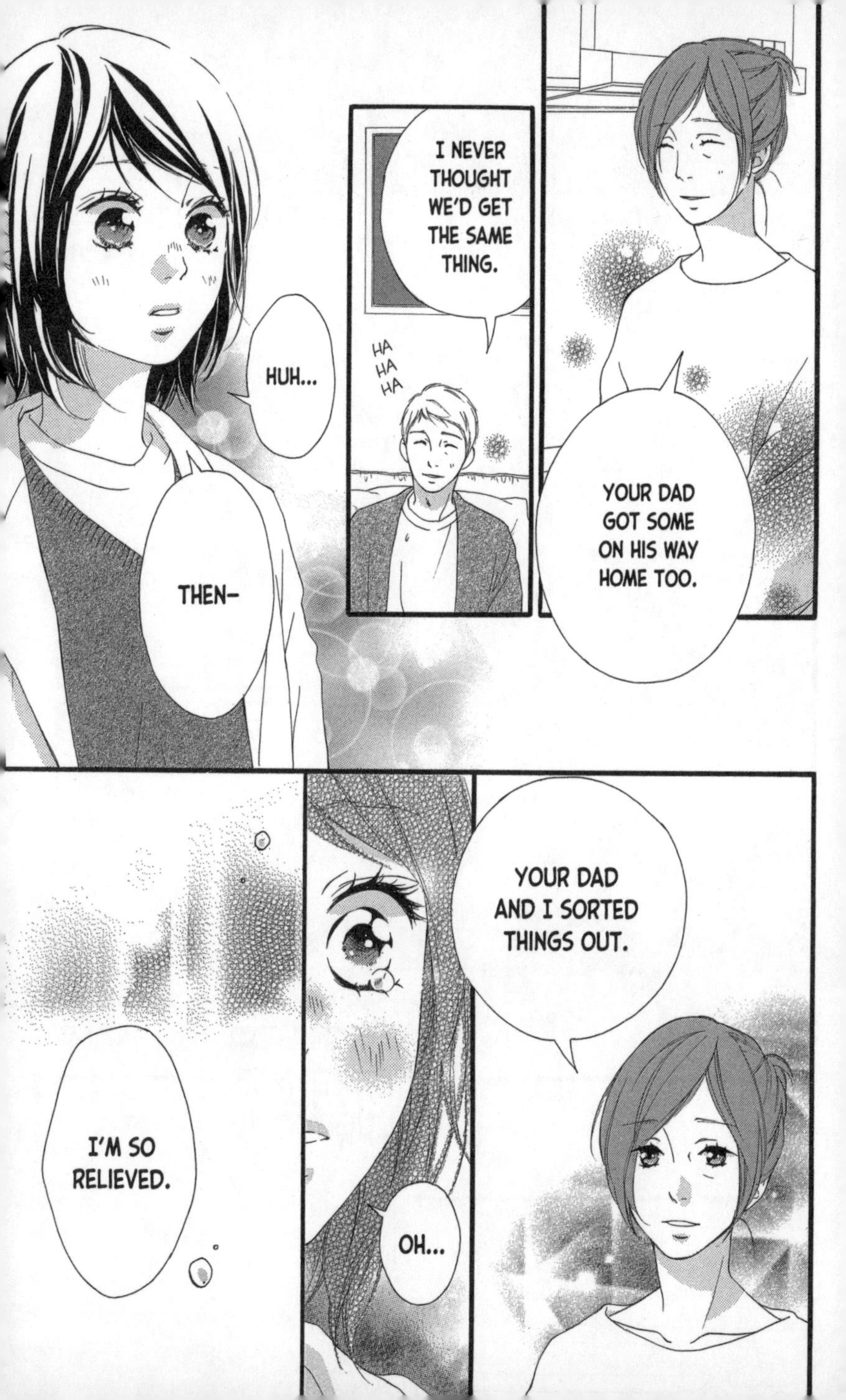
YOUR DAD GOT SOME ON HIS WAY HOME TOO.
I NEVER THOUGHT WE'D GET THE SAME THING.
HA HA HA
HUH...
THEN-
YOUR DAD AND I SORTED THINGS OUT.
OH...
I'M SO RELIEVED.

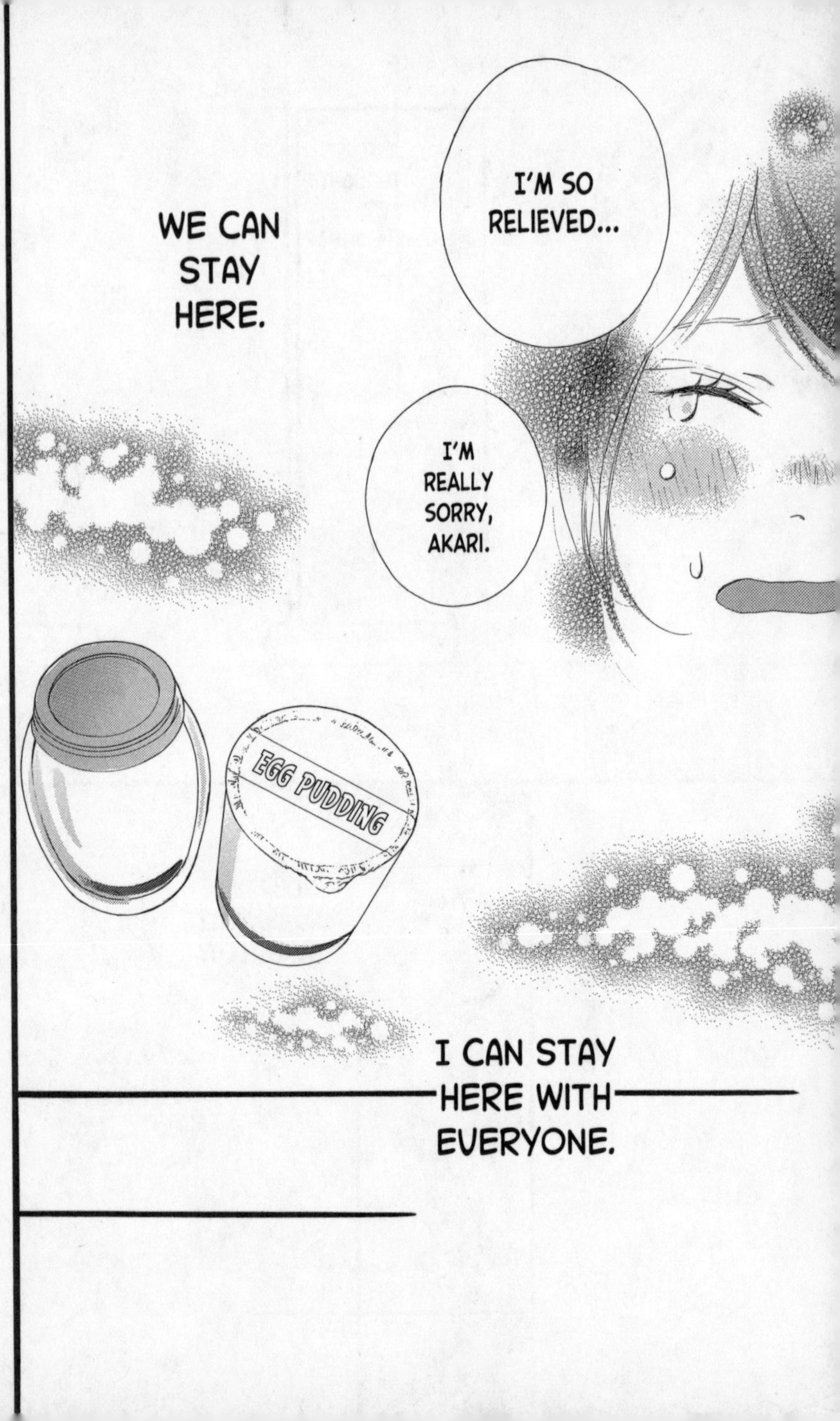
I'M SO RELIEVED...
I'M REALLY SORRY, AKARI.
WE CAN STAY HERE.
EGG PUDDING
I CAN STAY HERE WITH EVERYONE.

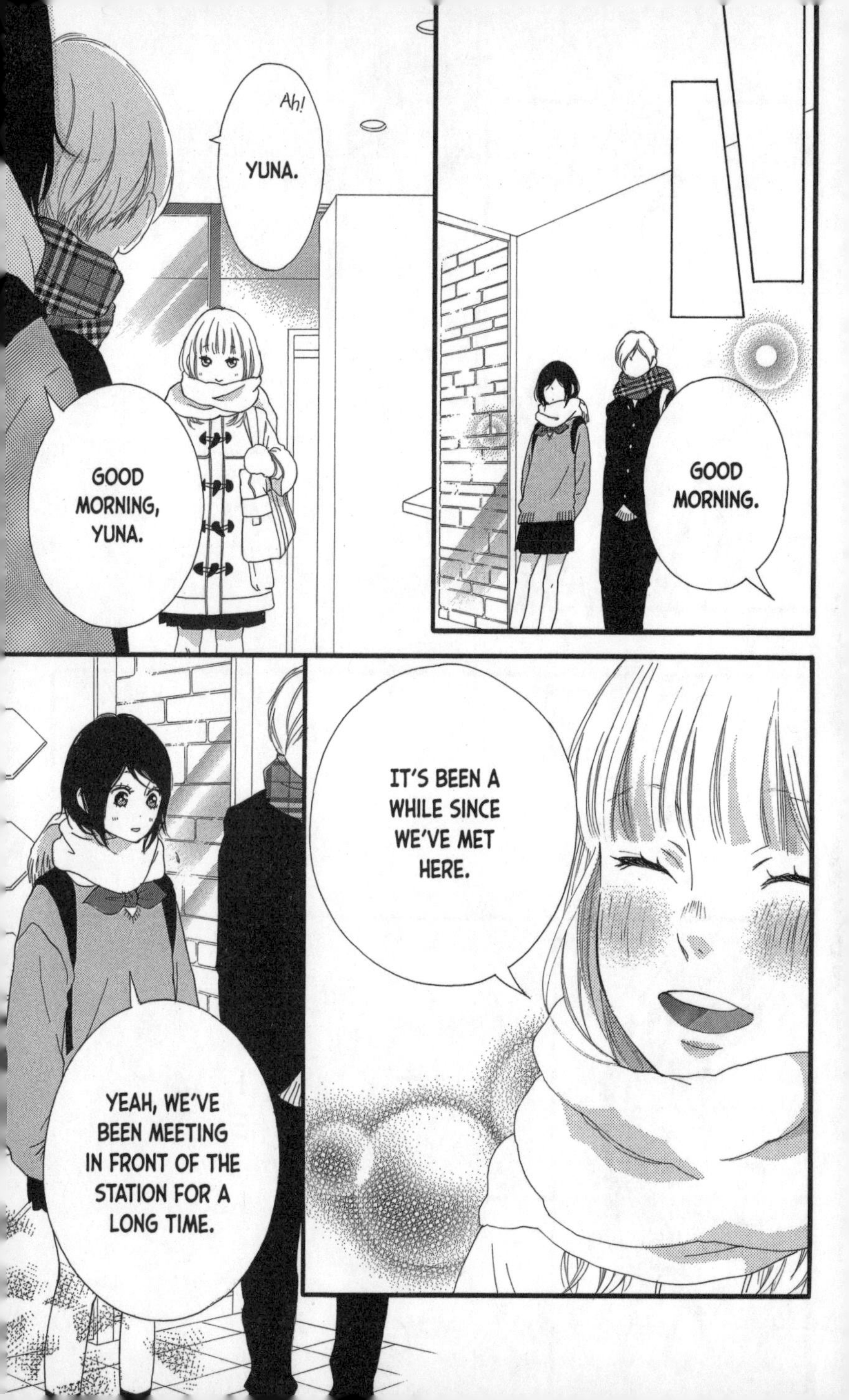
GOOD MORNING.
Ah!
YUNA.
GOOD MORNING, YUNA.
IT'S BEEN A WHILE SINCE WE'VE MET HERE.
YEAH, WE'VE BEEN MEETING IN FRONT OF THE STATION FOR A LONG TIME.

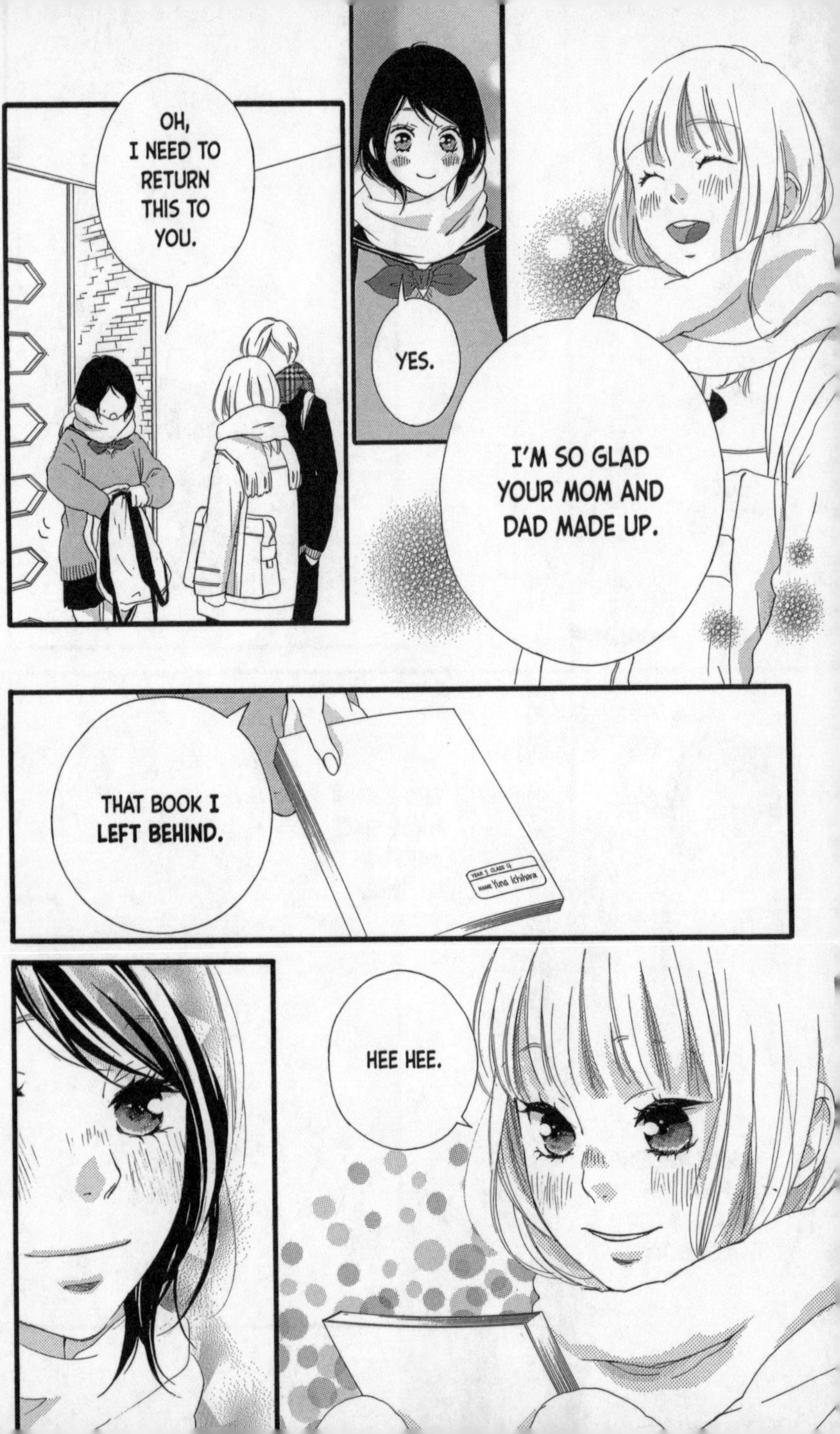
I'M SO GLAD YOUR MOM AND DAD MADE UP.
YES.
OH, I NEED TO RETURN THIS TO YOU.
THAT BOOK I LEFT BEHIND.
YEAR 1 CLASS 4
NAME Yuna Ichihara
HEE HEE.

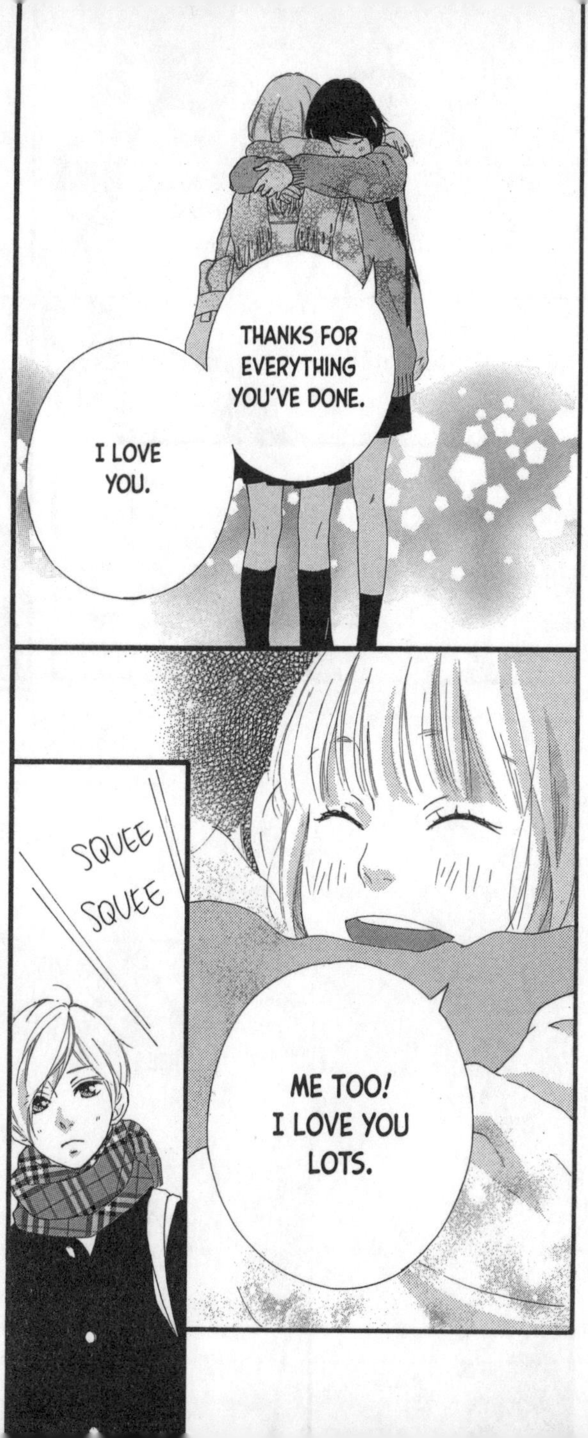
THANKS FOR EVERYTHING YOU'VE DONE.
I LOVE YOU.
ME TOO! I LOVE YOU LOTS.
SQUEE SQUEE

There's a game I'm really into right now. My interest began when I watched a live video of it. The video was really good, and I started feeling like I wanted to try it too. The game is called *Minecraft*, and it's a sandbox video game. It came out a while ago, but I'm really not up on games, so I've just now discovered it. I'm caught up in the excitement, but I've held off installing it for now. That's because I can easily picture myself ignoring things I need to do to play it. I really want to start it right now, but I'm holding back. Good for me. I'm so great. I tell myself that and endure. When I have a bit of time off from work, I'm planning to go digging for minerals to my heart's content.

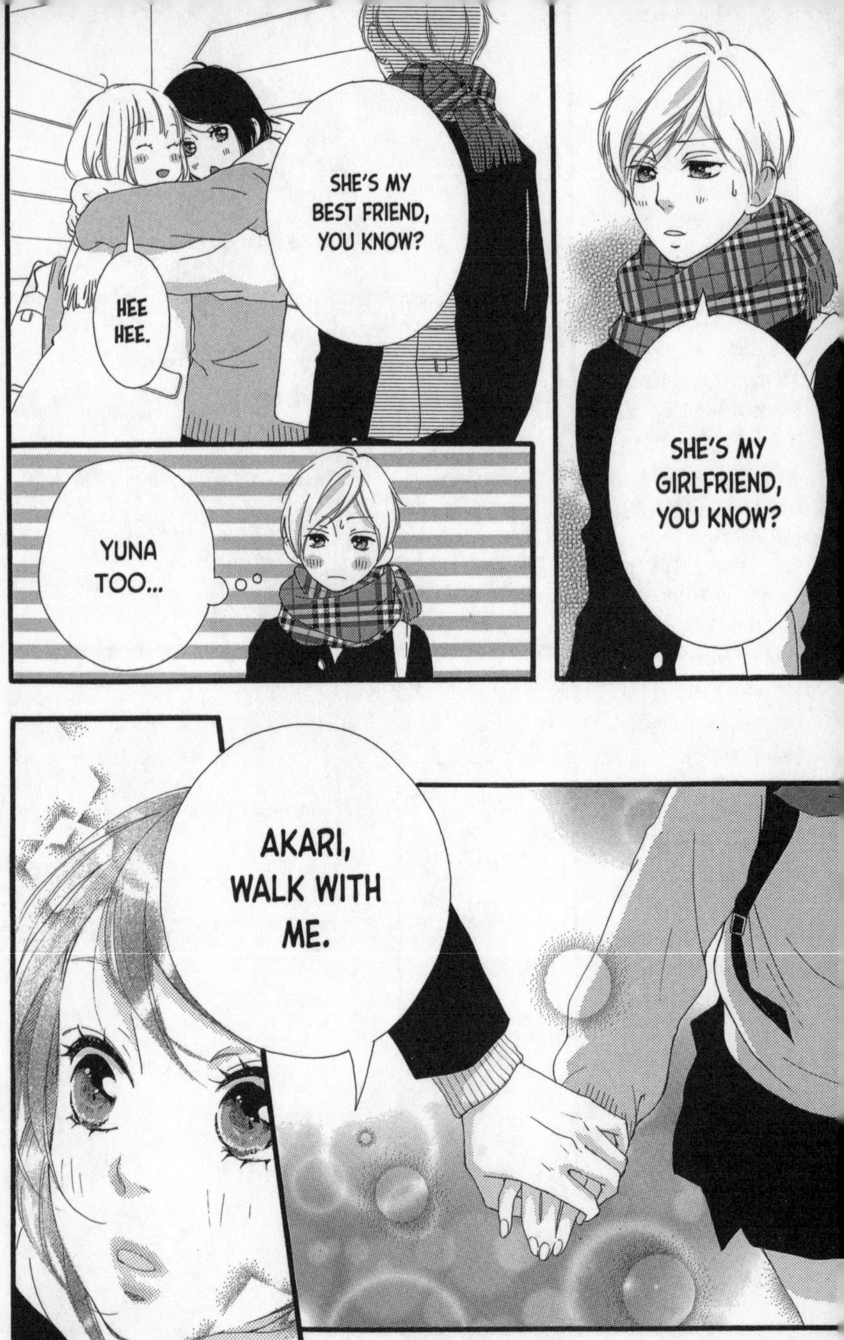
SHE'S MY GIRLFRIEND, YOU KNOW?
SHE'S MY BEST FRIEND, YOU KNOW?
HEE HEE.
YUNA TOO...
AKARI, WALK WITH ME.

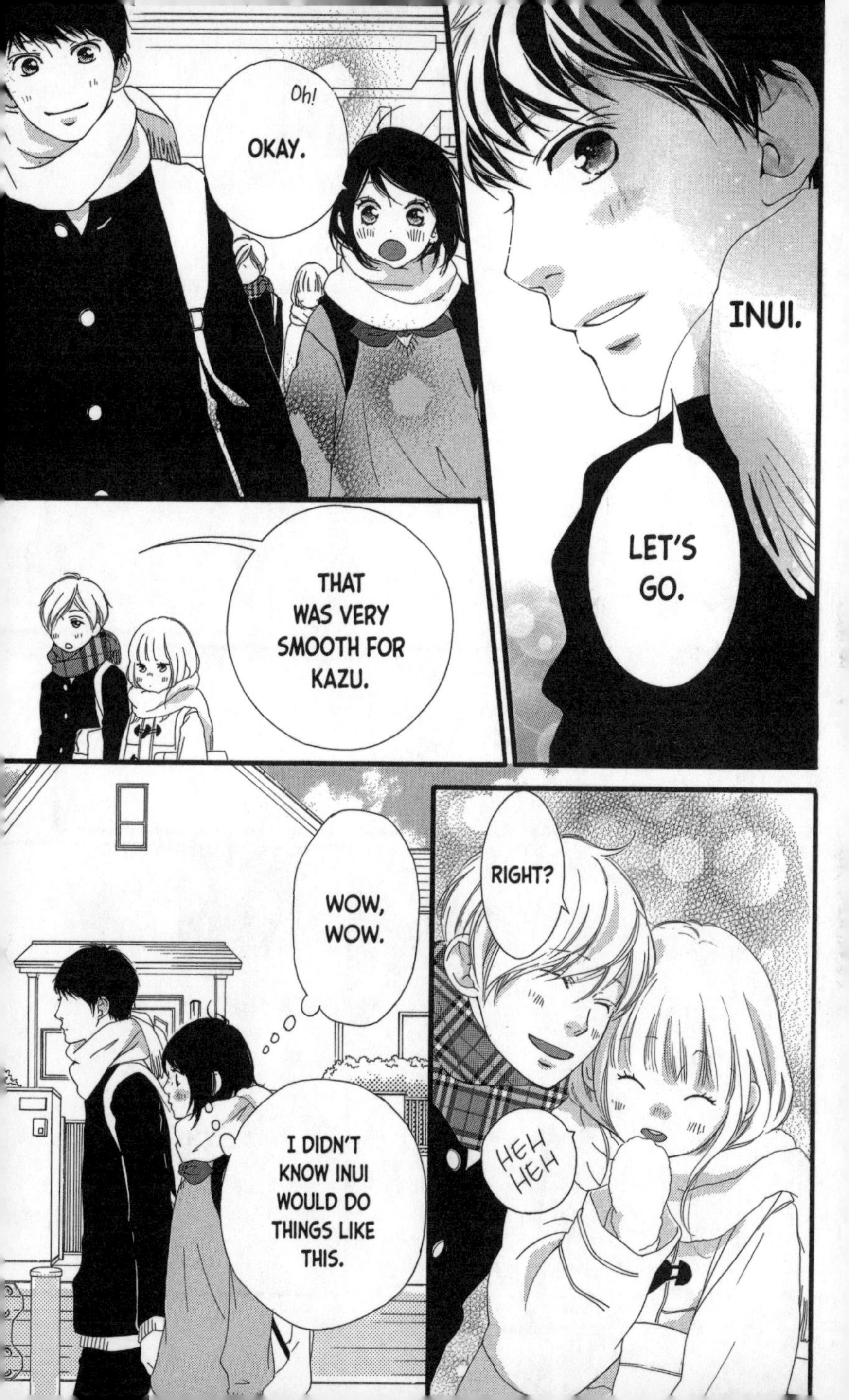
INUI.
LET'S GO.
Oh!
OKAY.
THAT WAS VERY SMOOTH FOR KAZU.
RIGHT?
HEH HEH
WOW, WOW.
I DIDN'T KNOW INUI WOULD DO THINGS LIKE THIS.

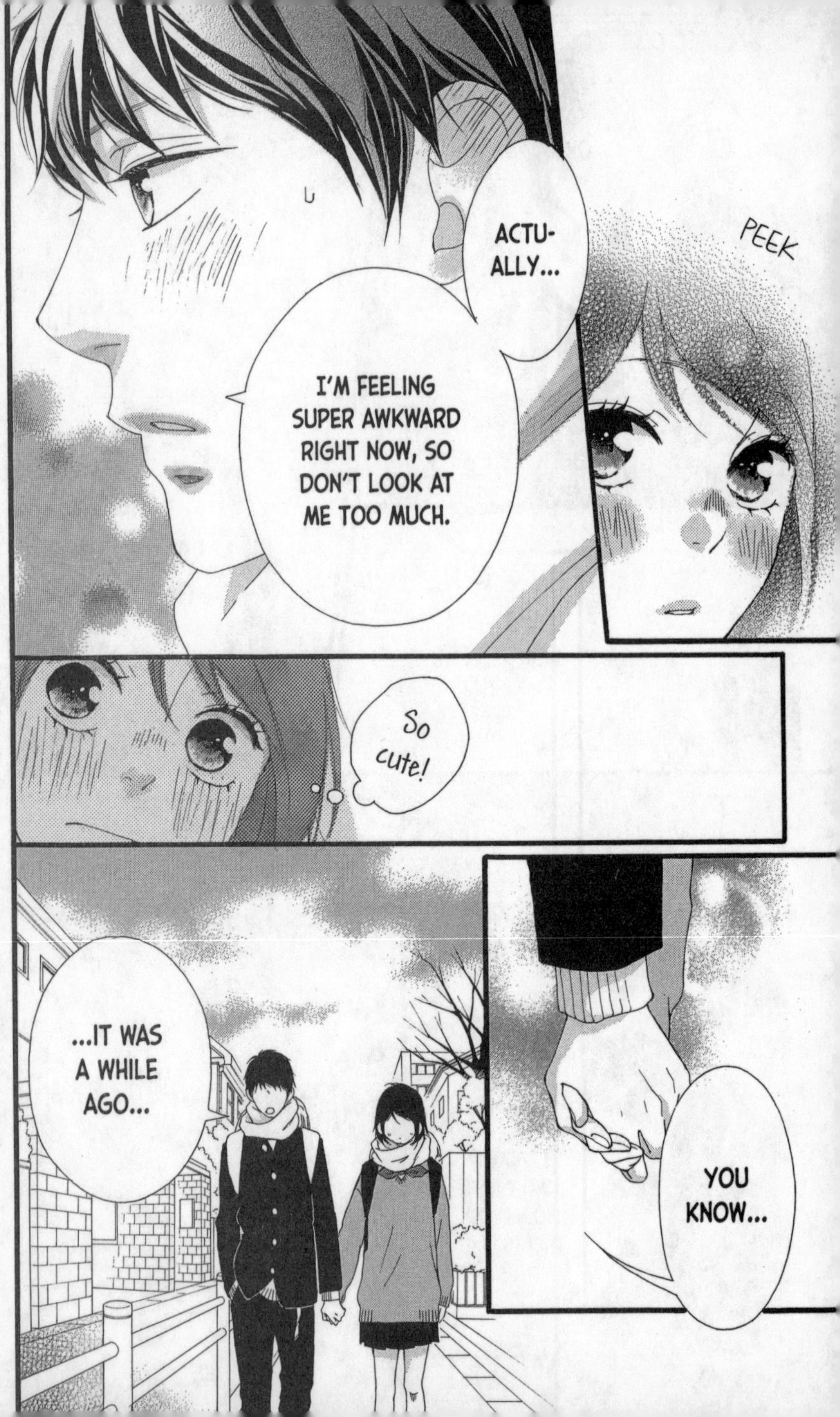
PEEK
ACTU-ALLY...
I'M FEELING SUPER AWKWARD RIGHT NOW, SO DON'T LOOK AT ME TOO MUCH.
So cute!
YOU KNOW...
...IT WAS A WHILE AGO...

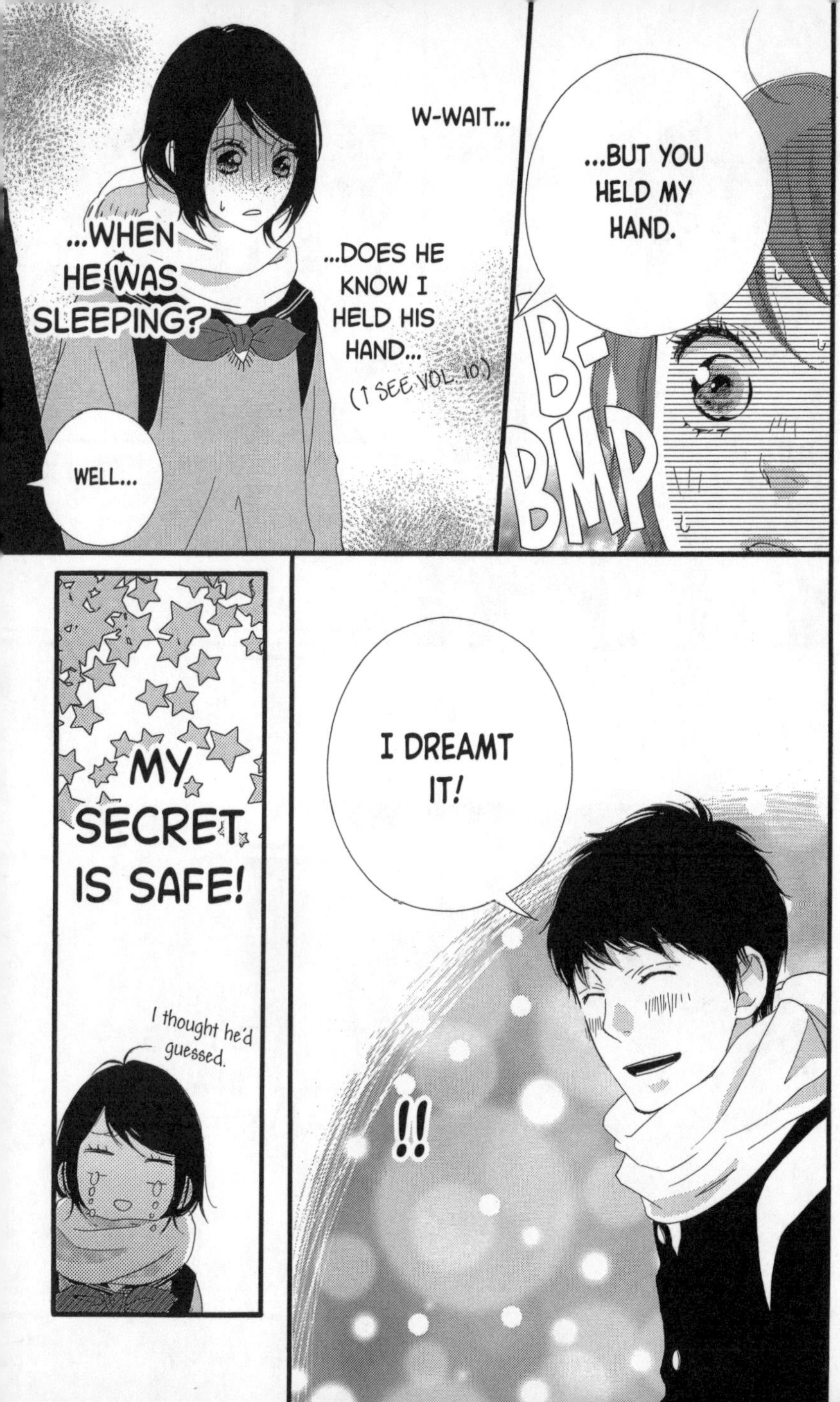
...BUT YOU HELD MY HAND.
B-BMP
W-WAIT...
...DOES HE KNOW I HELD HIS HAND...
(↑ SEE VOL. 10)
...WHEN HE WAS SLEEPING?
WELL...
I DREAMT IT!
!!
MY SECRET IS SAFE!
I thought he'd guessed.

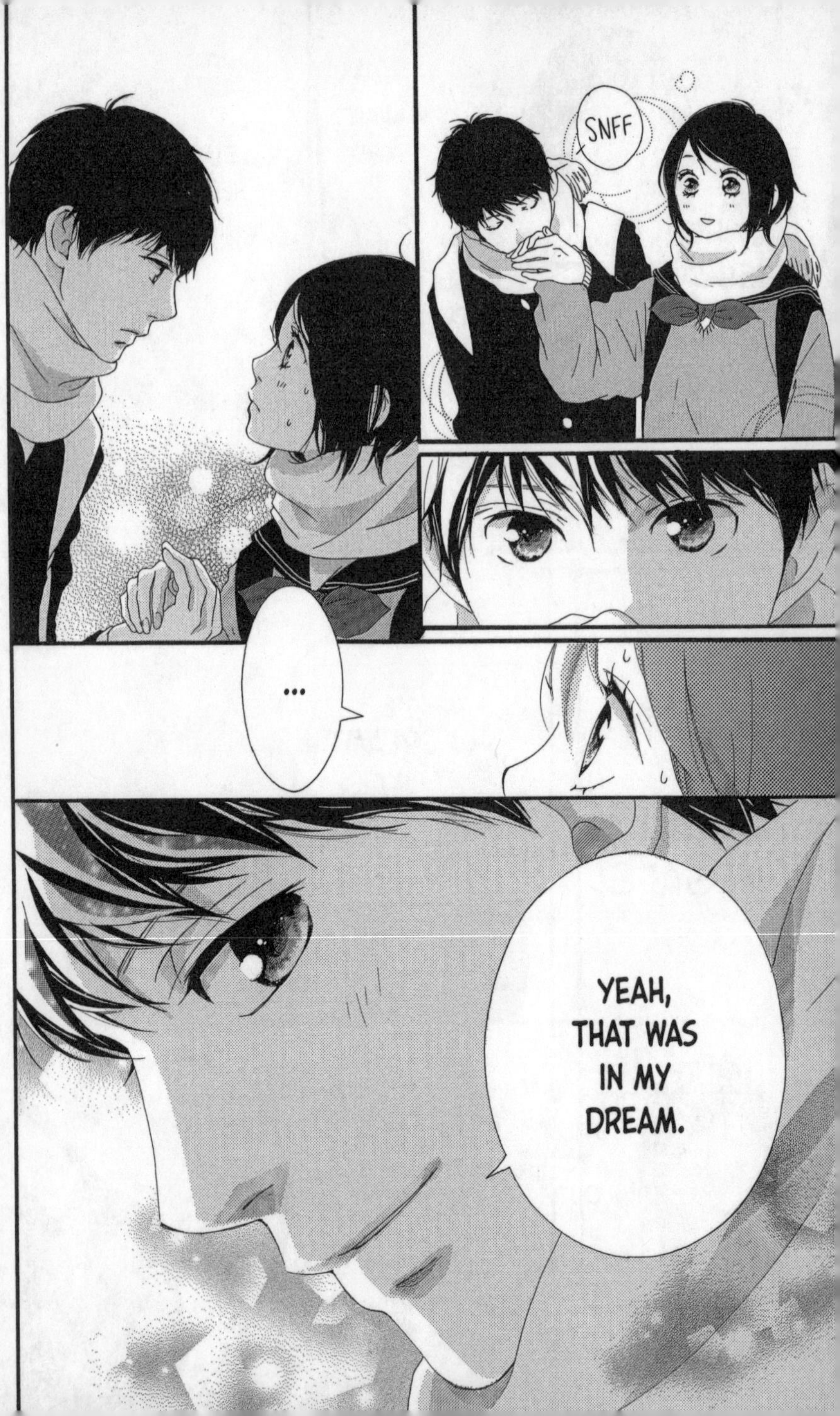
SNFF
...
YEAH, THAT WAS IN MY DREAM.

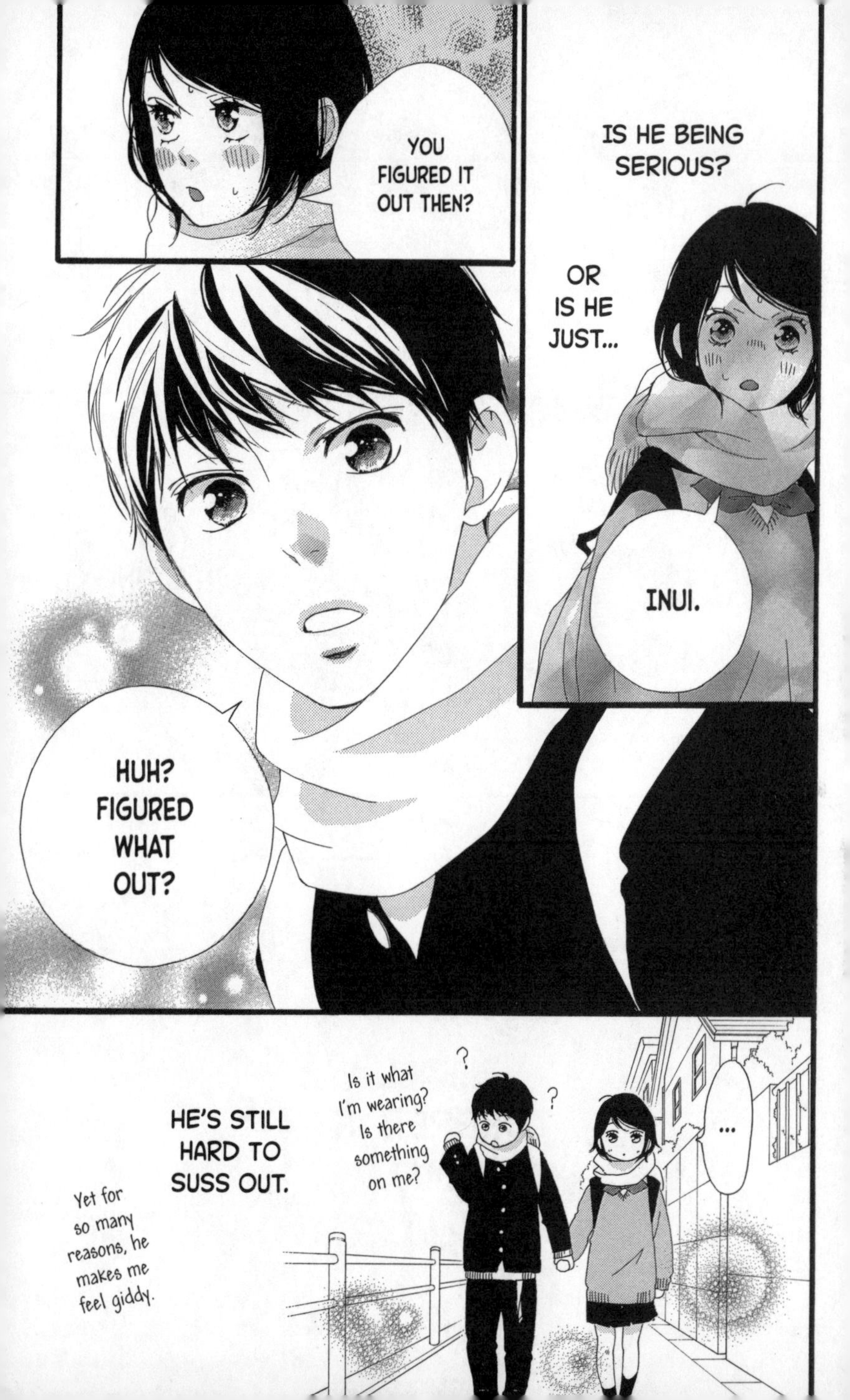
IS HE BEING SERIOUS?
OR IS HE JUST...
INUI.
YOU FIGURED IT OUT THEN?
HUH? FIGURED WHAT OUT?
...
?
?
Is it what I'm wearing? Is there something on me?
HE'S STILL HARD TO SUSS OUT.
Yet for so many reasons, he makes me feel giddy.

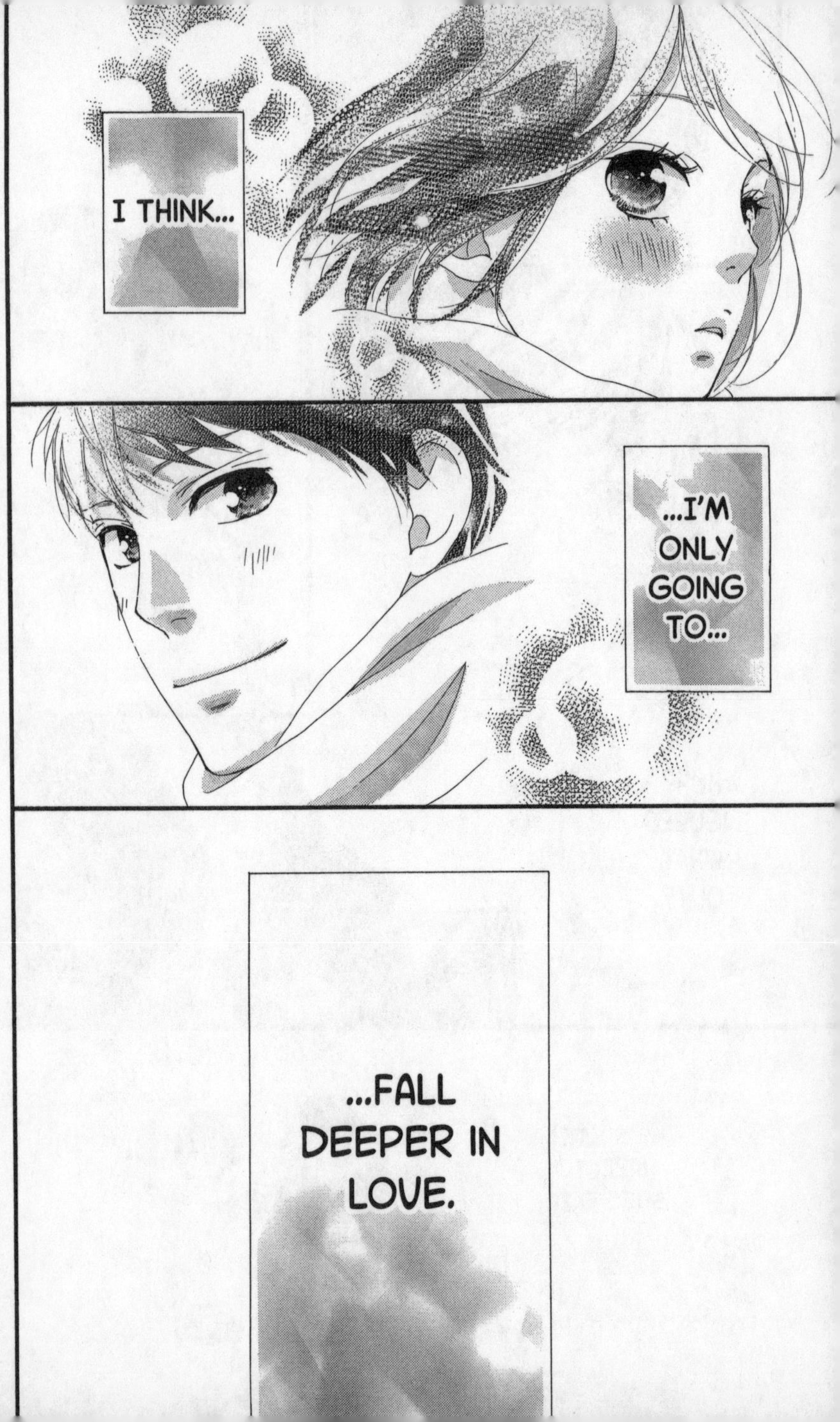
I THINK...
...I'M ONLY GOING TO...
...FALL DEEPER IN LOVE.

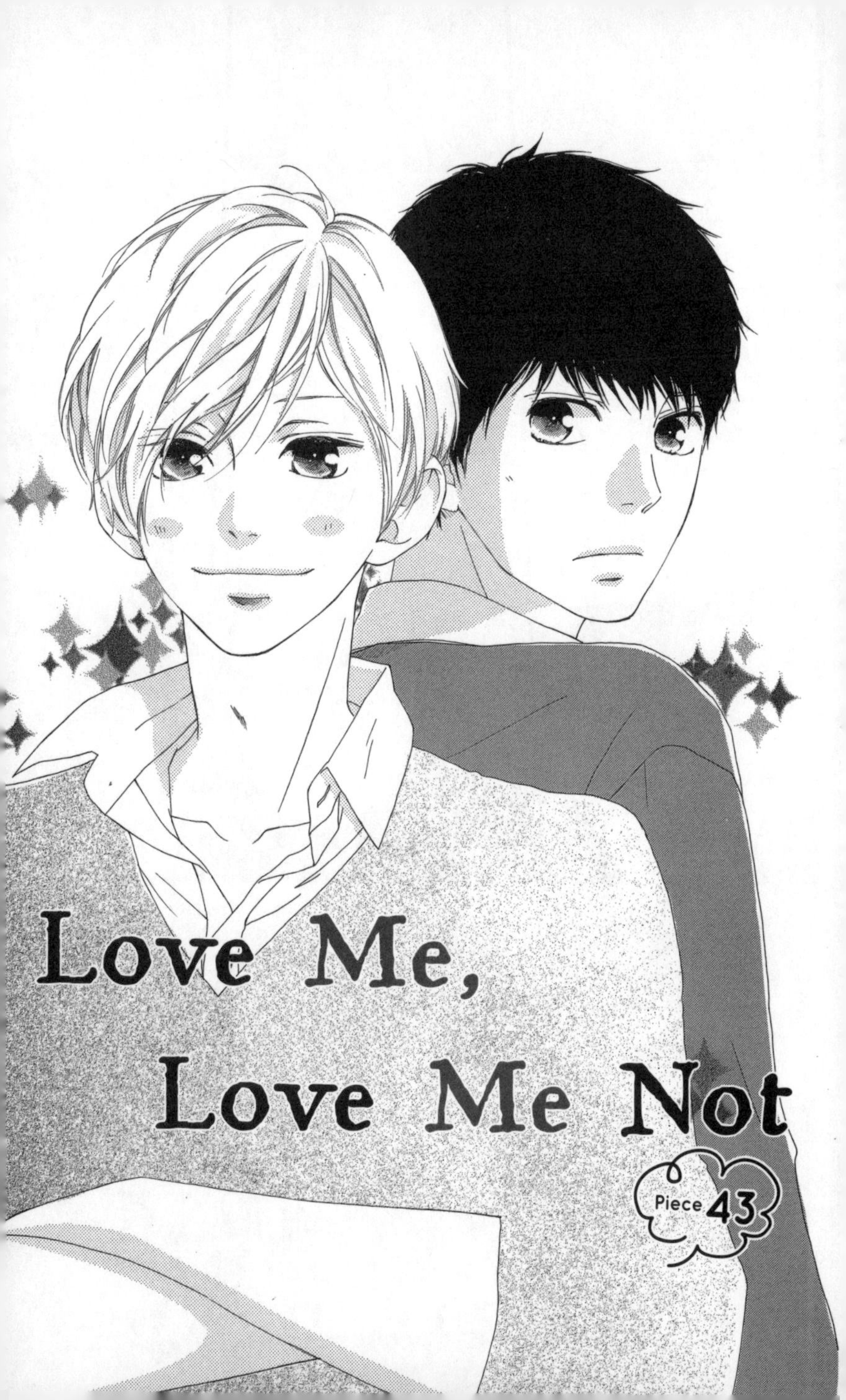
Love Me,
Love Me Not
Piece 43

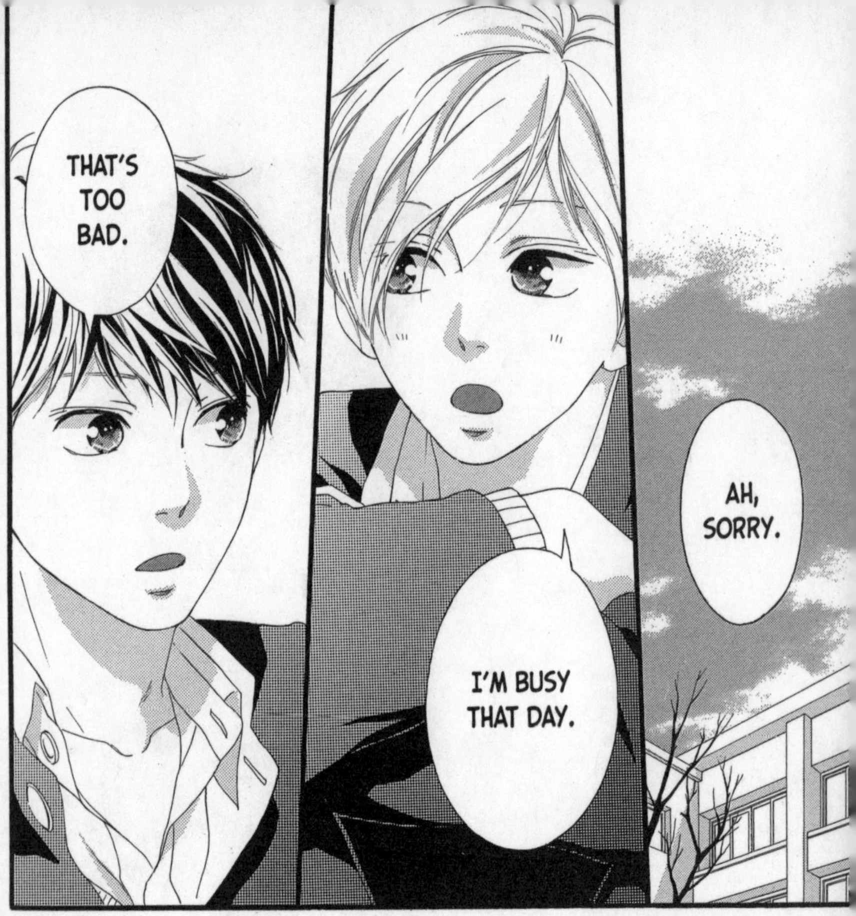
AH, SORRY.
I'M BUSY THAT DAY.
THAT'S TOO BAD.
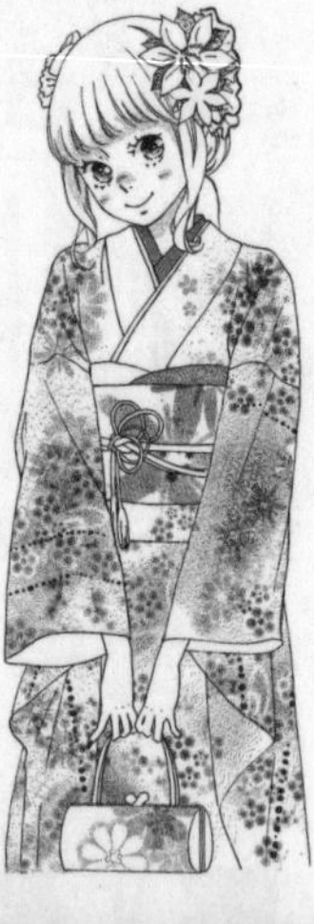

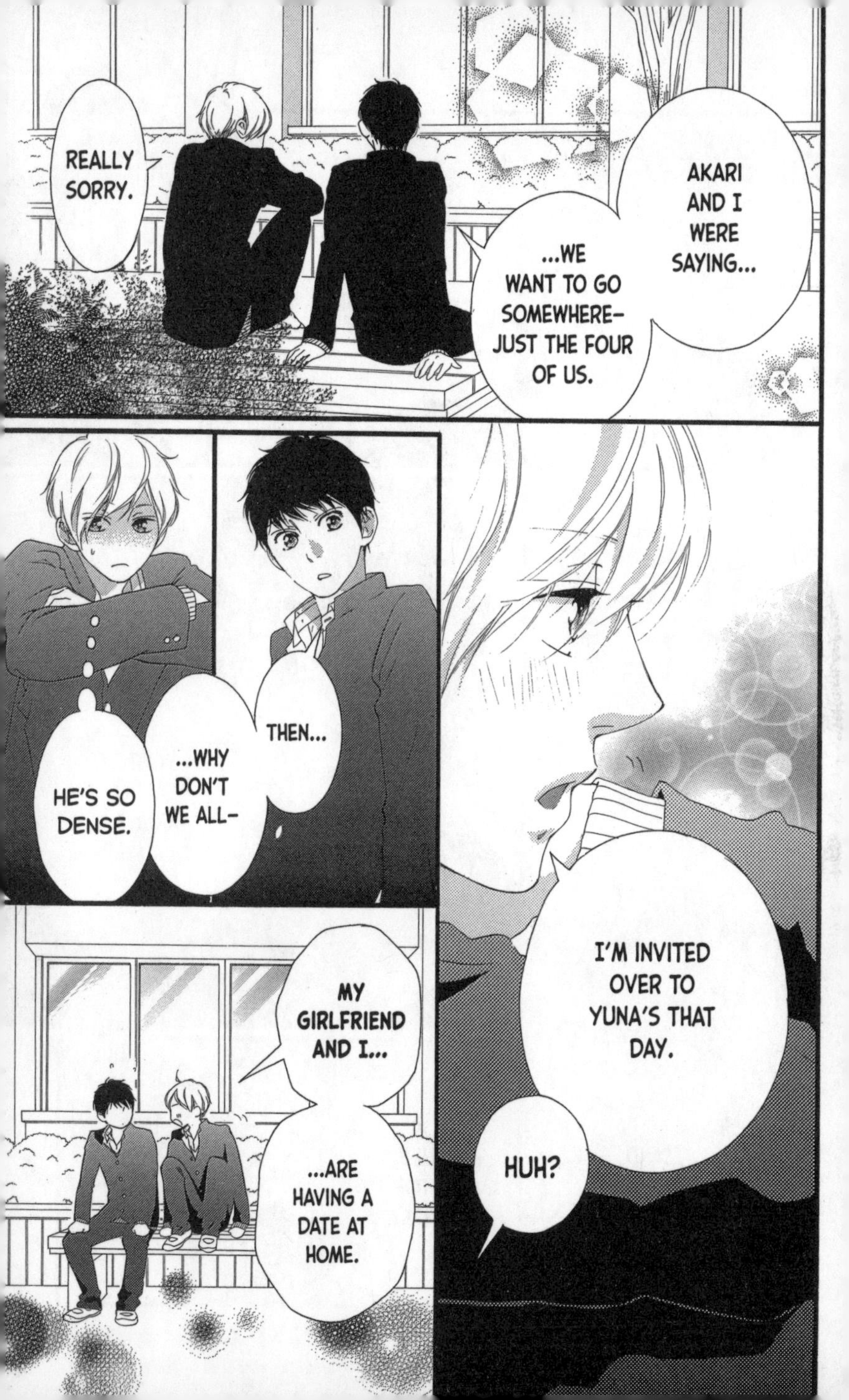
AKARI AND I WERE SAYING...
...WE WANT TO GO SOMEWHERE— JUST THE FOUR OF US.
REALLY SORRY.
THEN...
...WHY DON'T WE ALL—
HE'S SO DENSE.
MY GIRLFRIEND AND I...
...ARE HAVING A DATE AT HOME.
I'M INVITED OVER TO YUNA'S THAT DAY.
HUH?

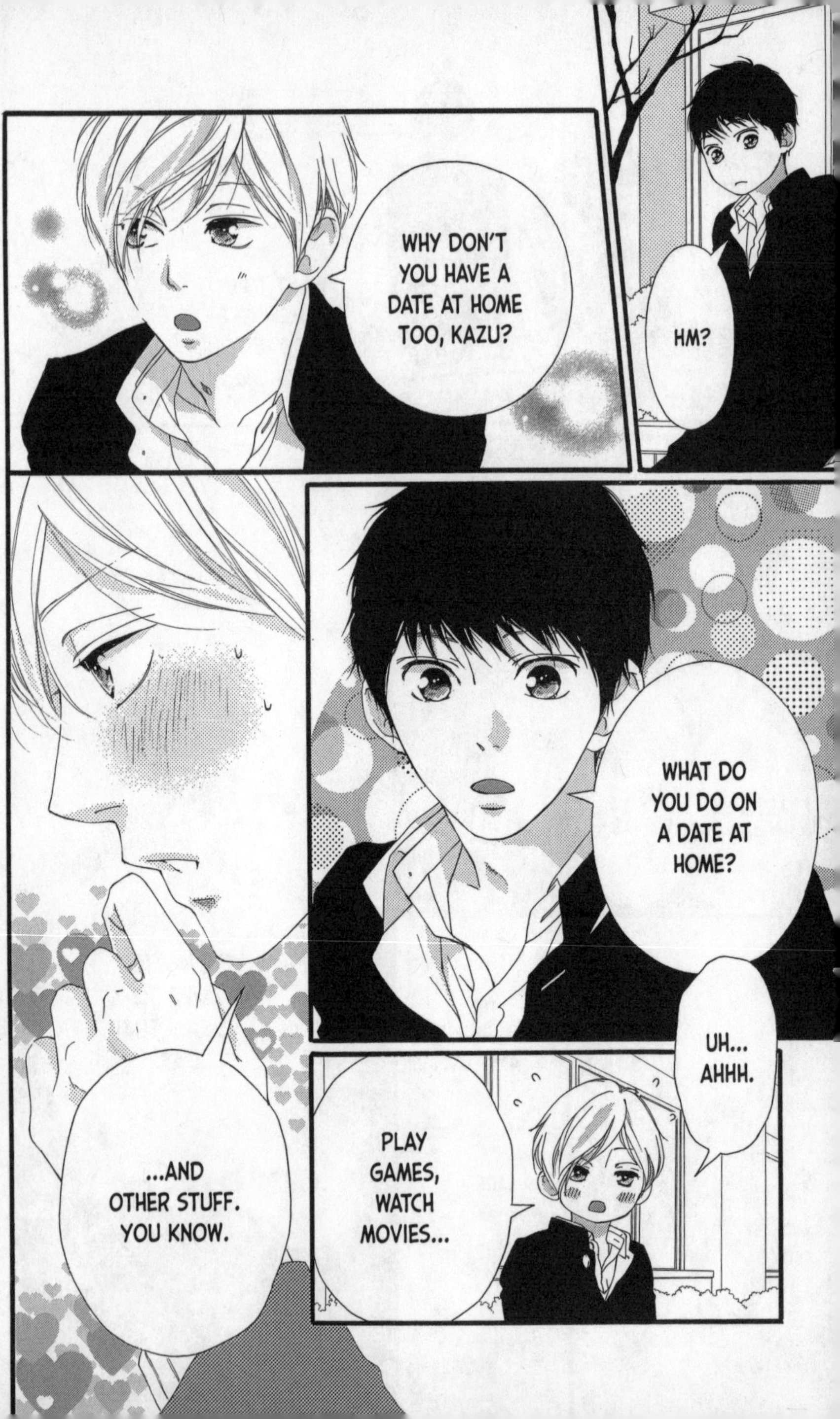
HM?
WHY DON'T YOU HAVE A DATE AT HOME TOO, KAZU?
WHAT DO YOU DO ON A DATE AT HOME?
UH... AHHH.
PLAY GAMES, WATCH MOVIES...
...AND OTHER STUFF. YOU KNOW.

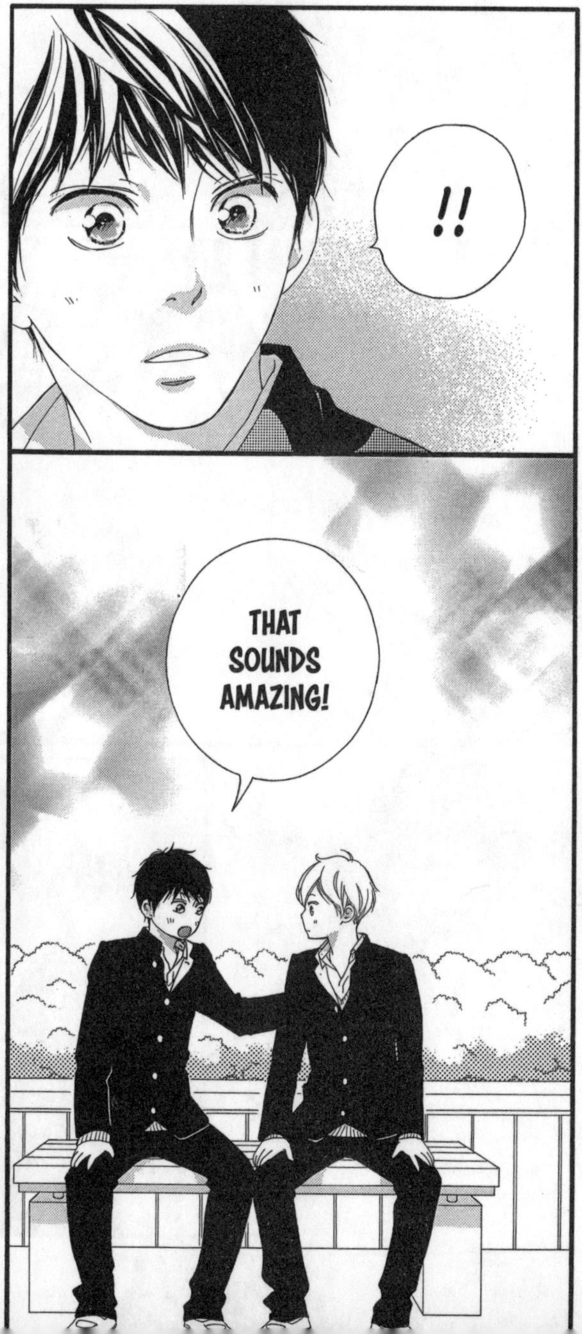
!!
THAT SOUNDS AMAZING!

I really look up to people who can use transparent watercolors. When I produce color pages, I use color ink. I thought I could get a different kind of warmth using watercolors, so I tried it. My goodness it's hard. It's partly because I'm used to color ink, but watercolor has a completely different feel, and I couldn't get the results I wanted using my usual methods. The other day I redid the same drawing three times. Depending on the paper you use, it's all different: the way the paint spreads out, the way the edges of the spread are created, the way the brushstroke appears on the paper, etc. I want to learn to use transparent watercolors in a way that best utilizes the medium, so I'm currently studying books and DVDs I bought on the topic. I'd love to watch a live demonstration by a pro. I'm sure it would look like magic. I want to swoon over that magic.

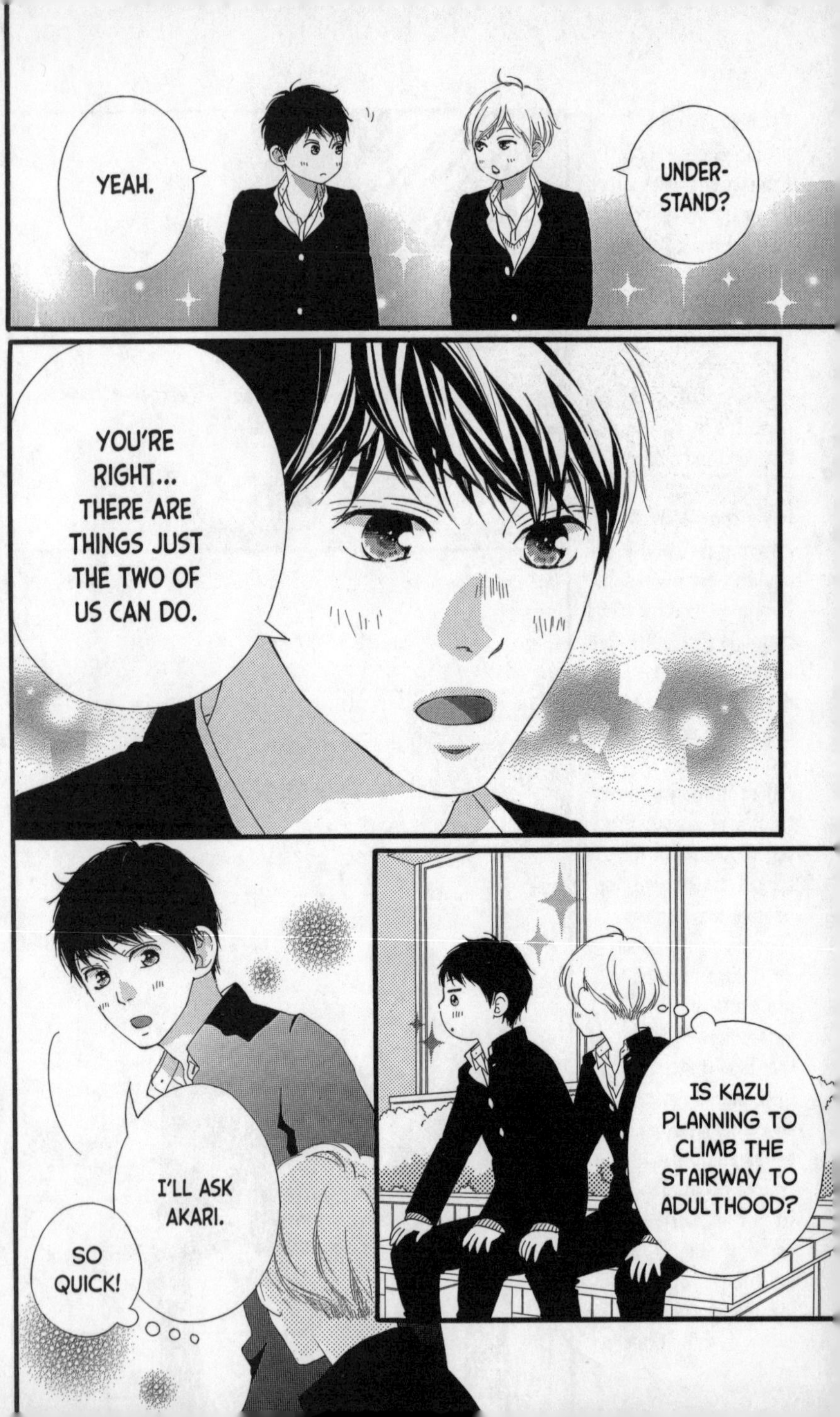
UNDER-STAND?
YEAH.
YOU'RE RIGHT... THERE ARE THINGS JUST THE TWO OF US CAN DO.
IS KAZU PLANNING TO CLIMB THE STAIRWAY TO ADULTHOOD?
I'LL ASK AKARI.
SO QUICK!

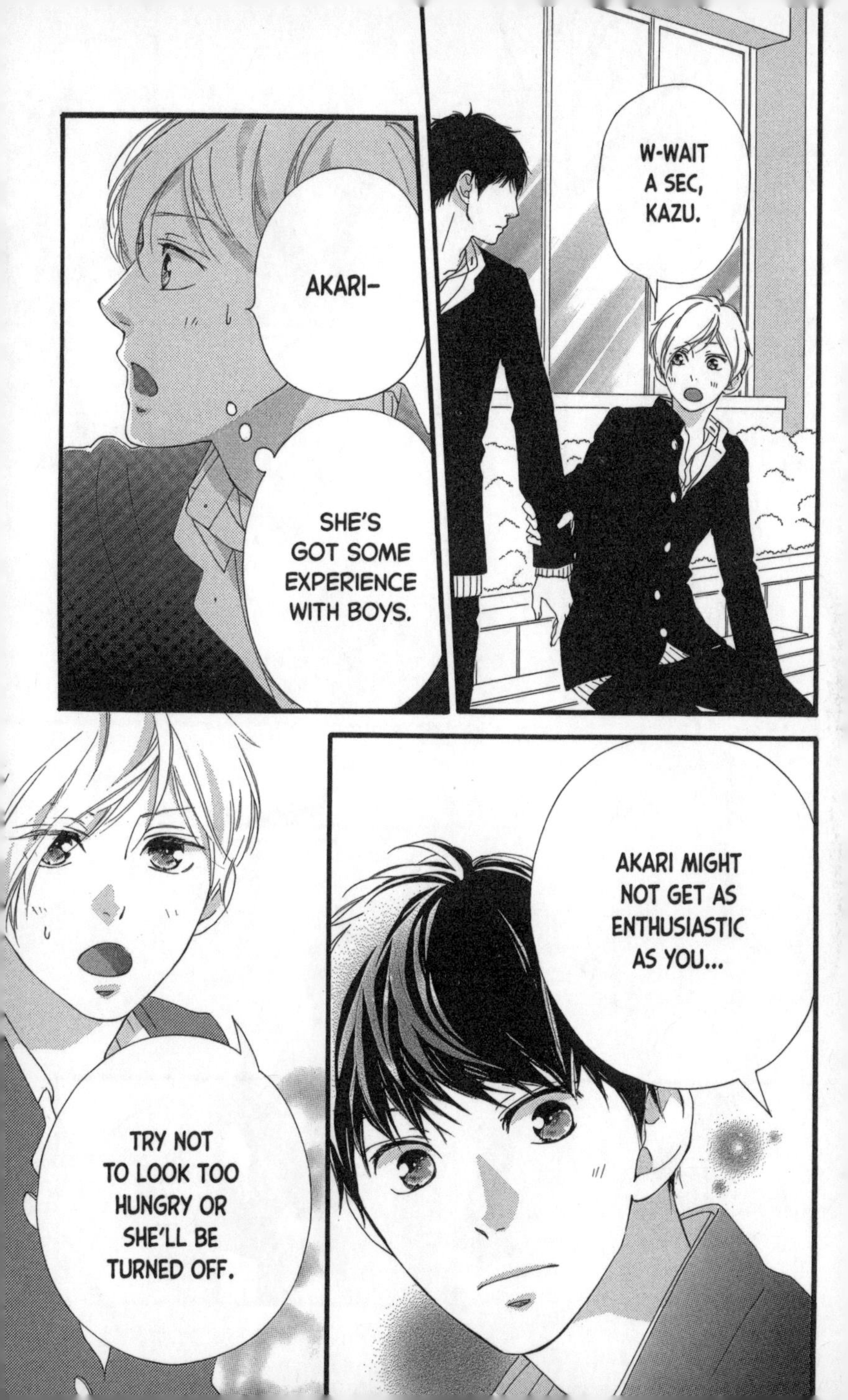
W-WAIT A SEC, KAZU.
AKARI–
SHE'S GOT SOME EXPERIENCE WITH BOYS.
AKARI MIGHT NOT GET AS ENTHUSIASTIC AS YOU...
TRY NOT TO LOOK TOO HUNGRY OR SHE'LL BE TURNED OFF.

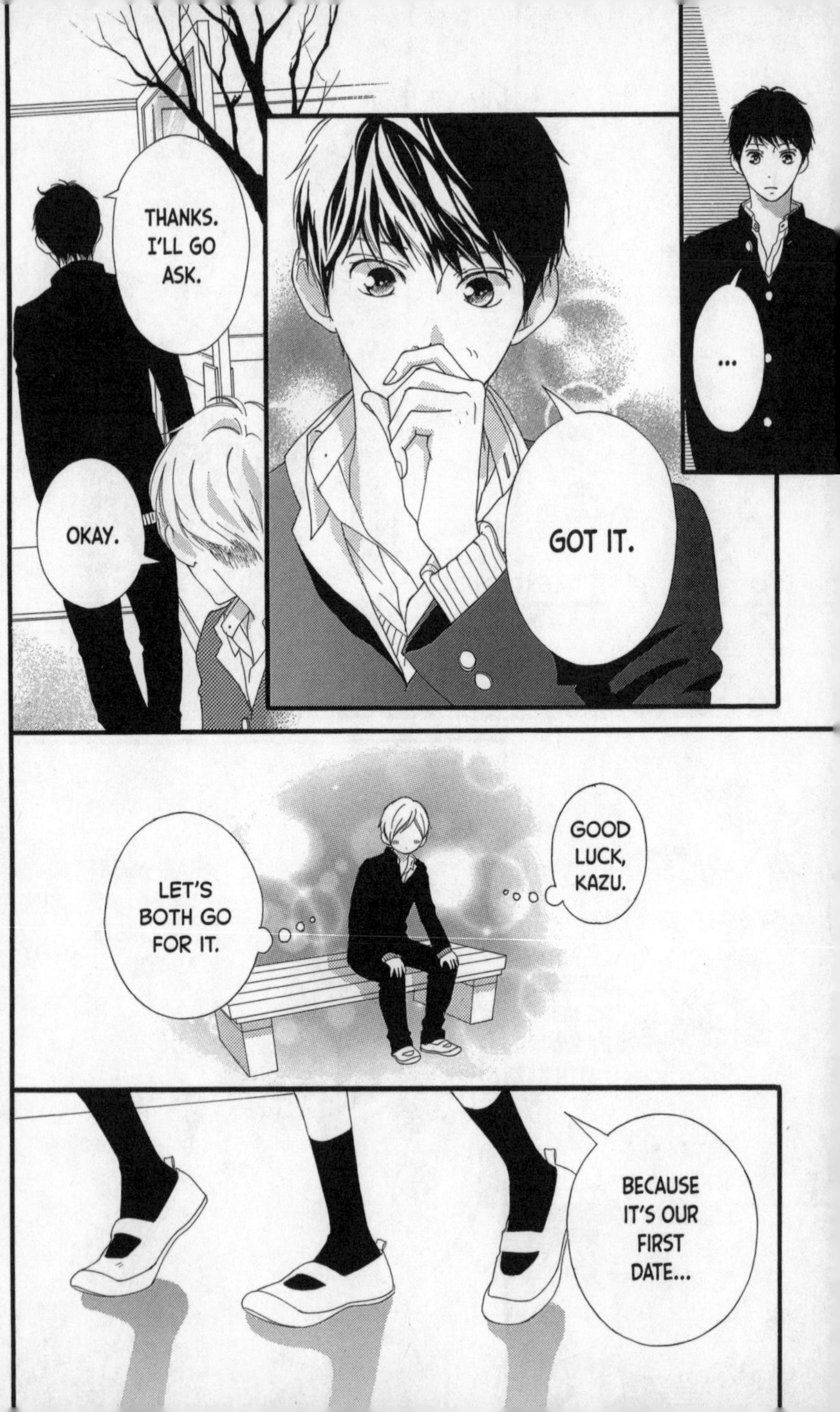
...
GOT IT.
THANKS. I'LL GO ASK.
OKAY.
GOOD LUCK, KAZU.
LET'S BOTH GO FOR IT.
BECAUSE IT'S OUR FIRST DATE...

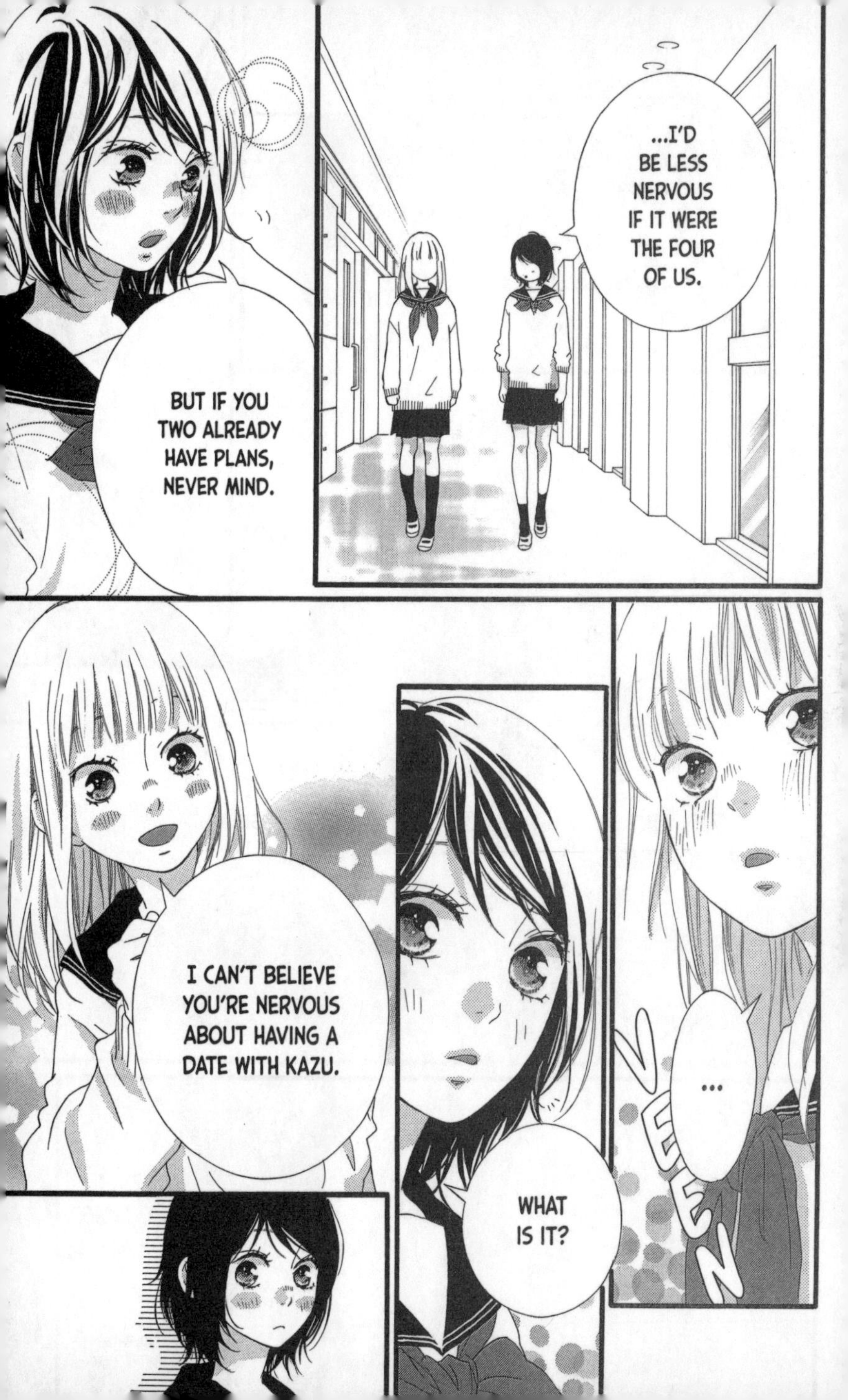
...I'D BE LESS NERVOUS IF IT WERE THE FOUR OF US.
BUT IF YOU TWO ALREADY HAVE PLANS, NEVER MIND.
...
WHAT IS IT?
I CAN'T BELIEVE YOU'RE NERVOUS ABOUT HAVING A DATE WITH KAZU.

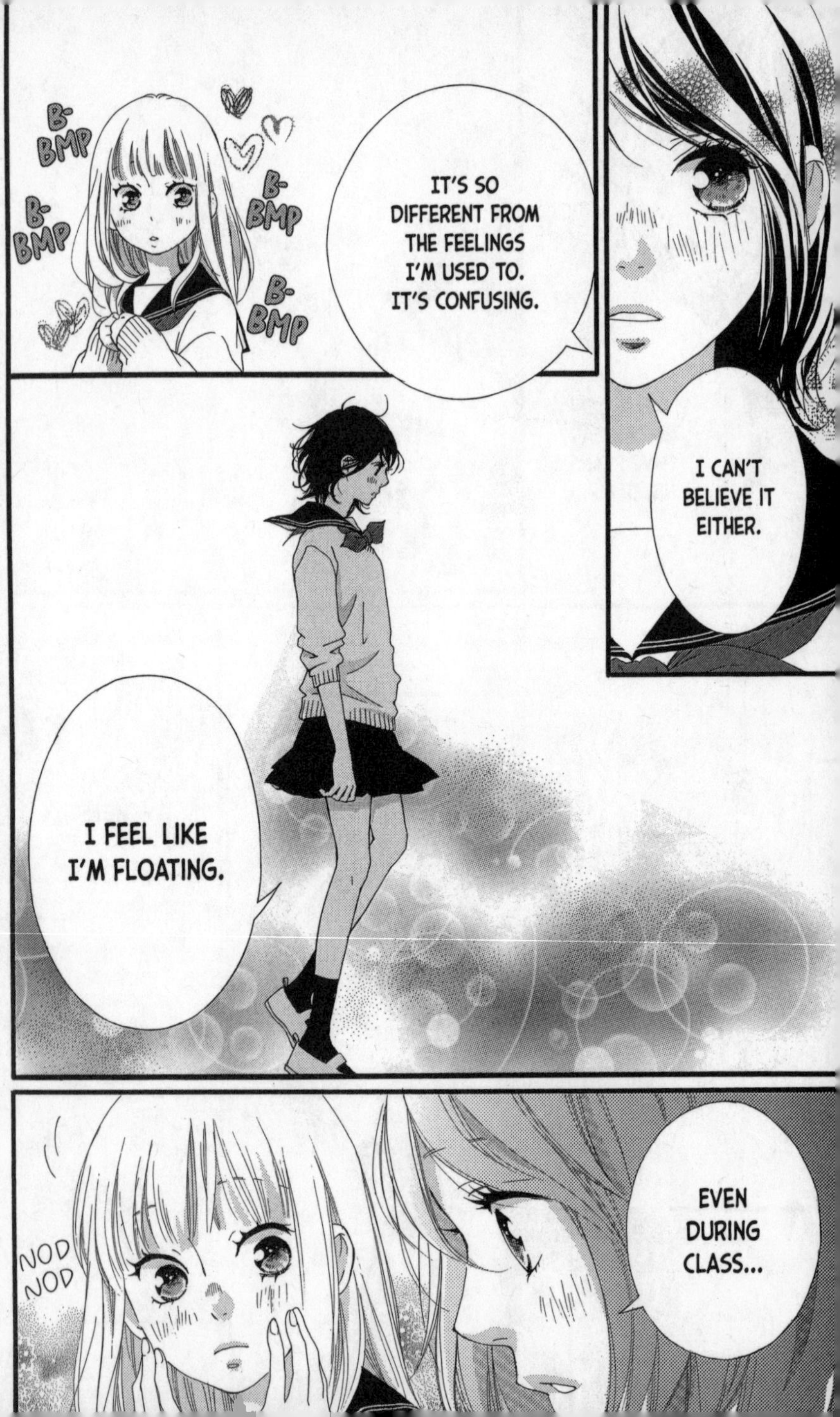
IT'S SO DIFFERENT FROM THE FEELINGS I'M USED TO. IT'S CONFUSING.
I CAN'T BELIEVE IT EITHER.
B-BMP
B-BMP
B-BMP
B-BMP
I FEEL LIKE I'M FLOATING.
EVEN DURING CLASS...
NOD NOD

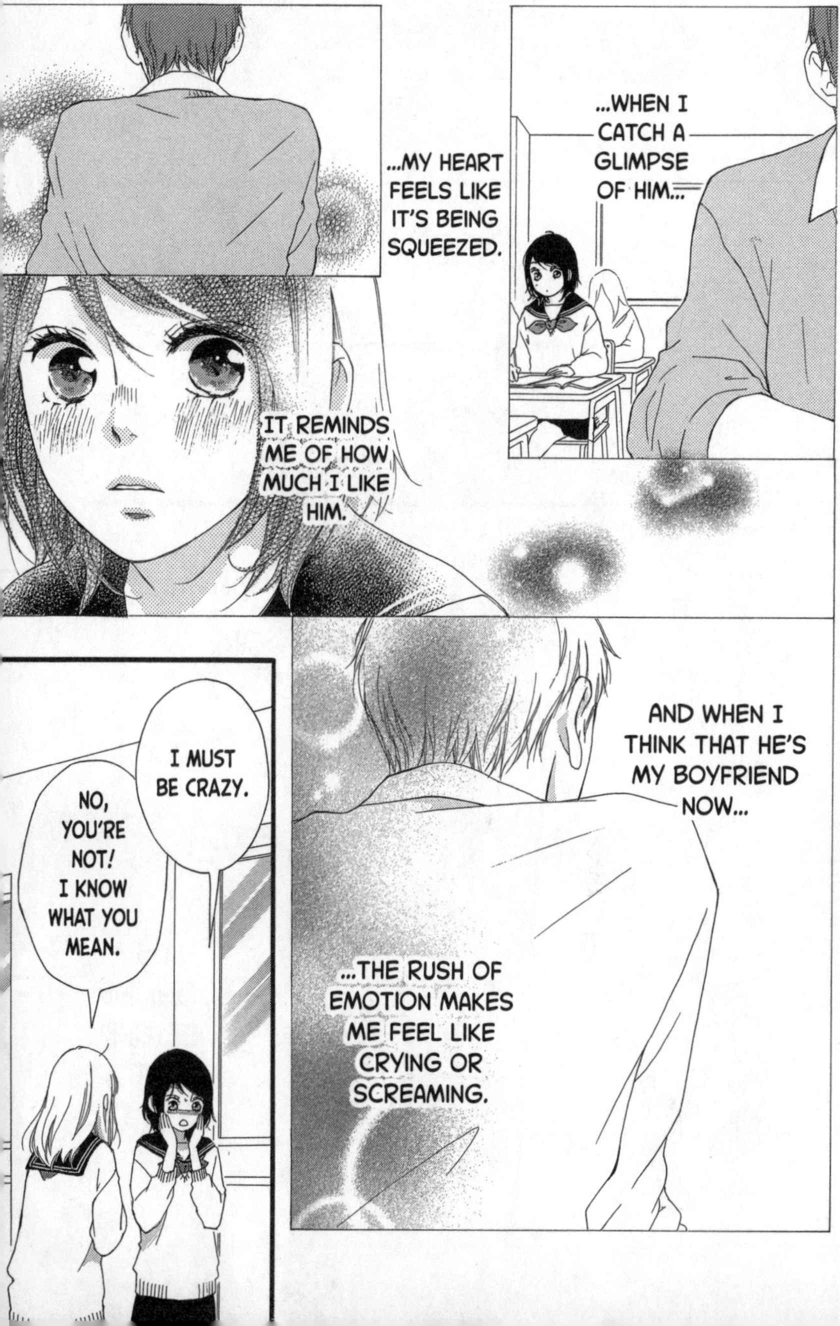
...WHEN I CATCH A GLIMPSE OF HIM...
...MY HEART FEELS LIKE IT'S BEING SQUEEZED.
IT REMINDS ME OF HOW MUCH I LIKE HIM.
AND WHEN I THINK THAT HE'S MY BOYFRIEND NOW...
...THE RUSH OF EMOTION MAKES ME FEEL LIKE CRYING OR SCREAMING.
I MUST BE CRAZY.
NO, YOU'RE NOT! I KNOW WHAT YOU MEAN.

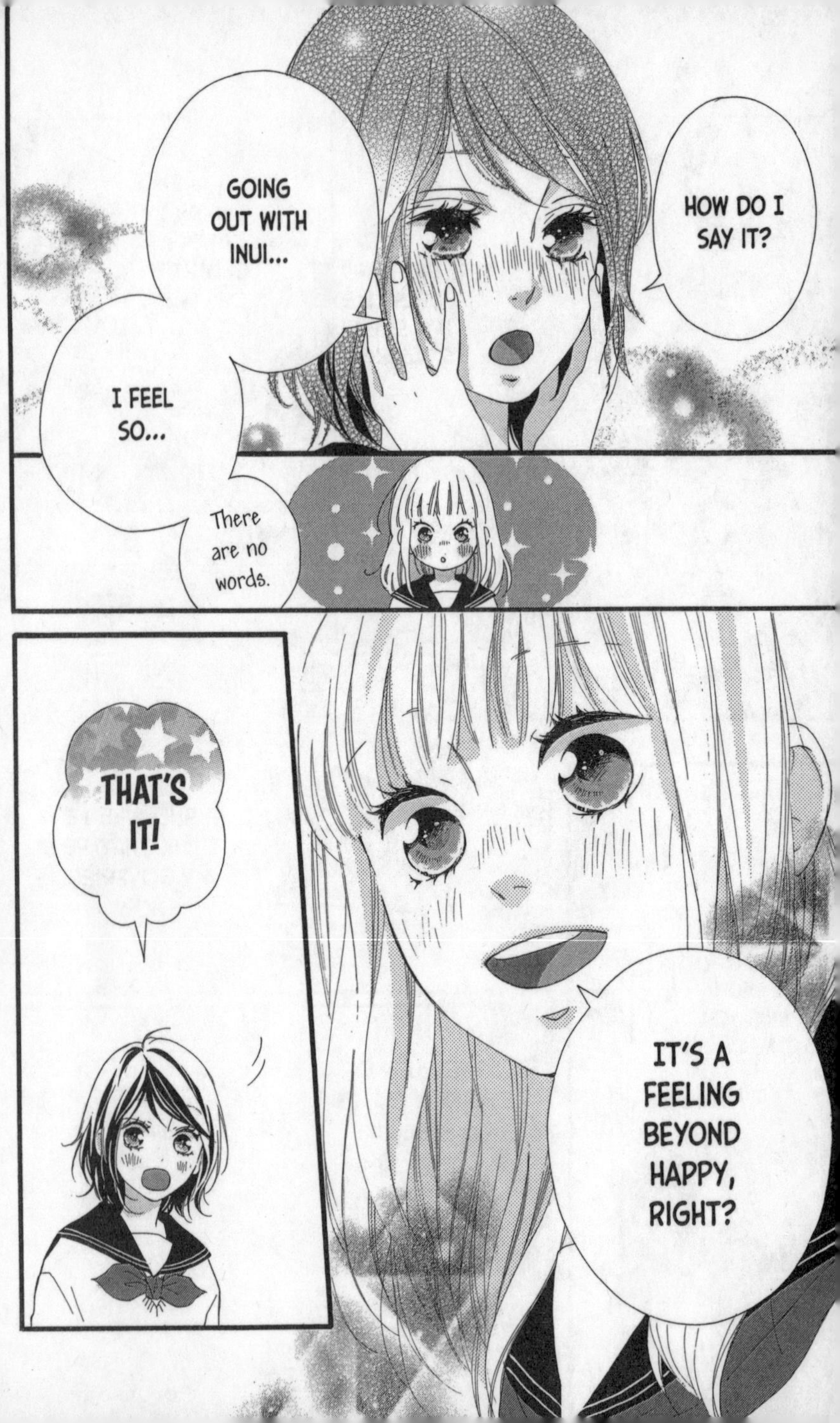
HOW DO I SAY IT?
GOING OUT WITH INUI...
I FEEL SO...
There are no words.
IT'S A FEELING BEYOND HAPPY, RIGHT?
THAT'S IT!

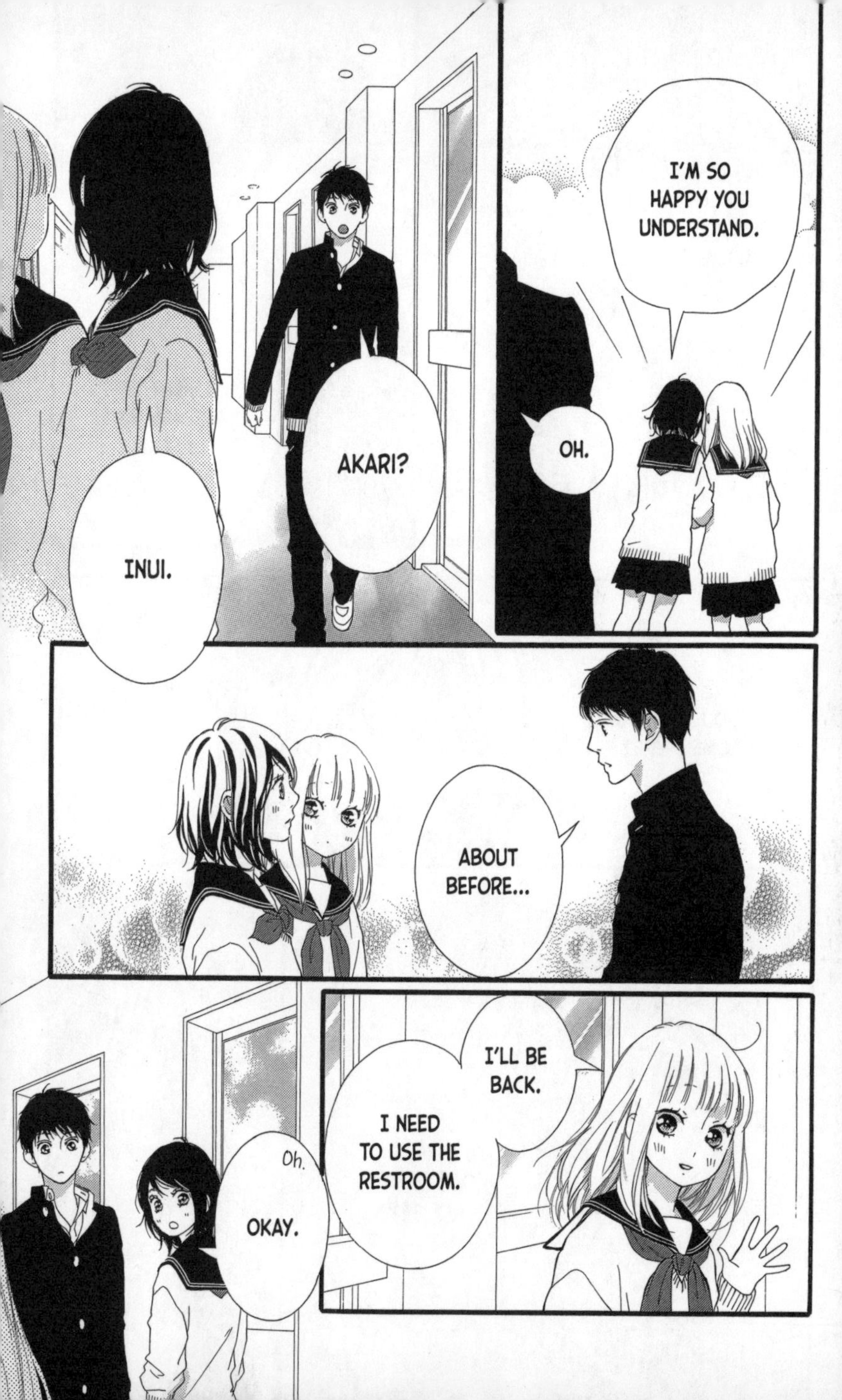
I'M SO HAPPY YOU UNDERSTAND.
OH.
AKARI?
INUI.
ABOUT BEFORE...
I'LL BE BACK.
I NEED TO USE THE RESTROOM.
Oh.
OKAY.

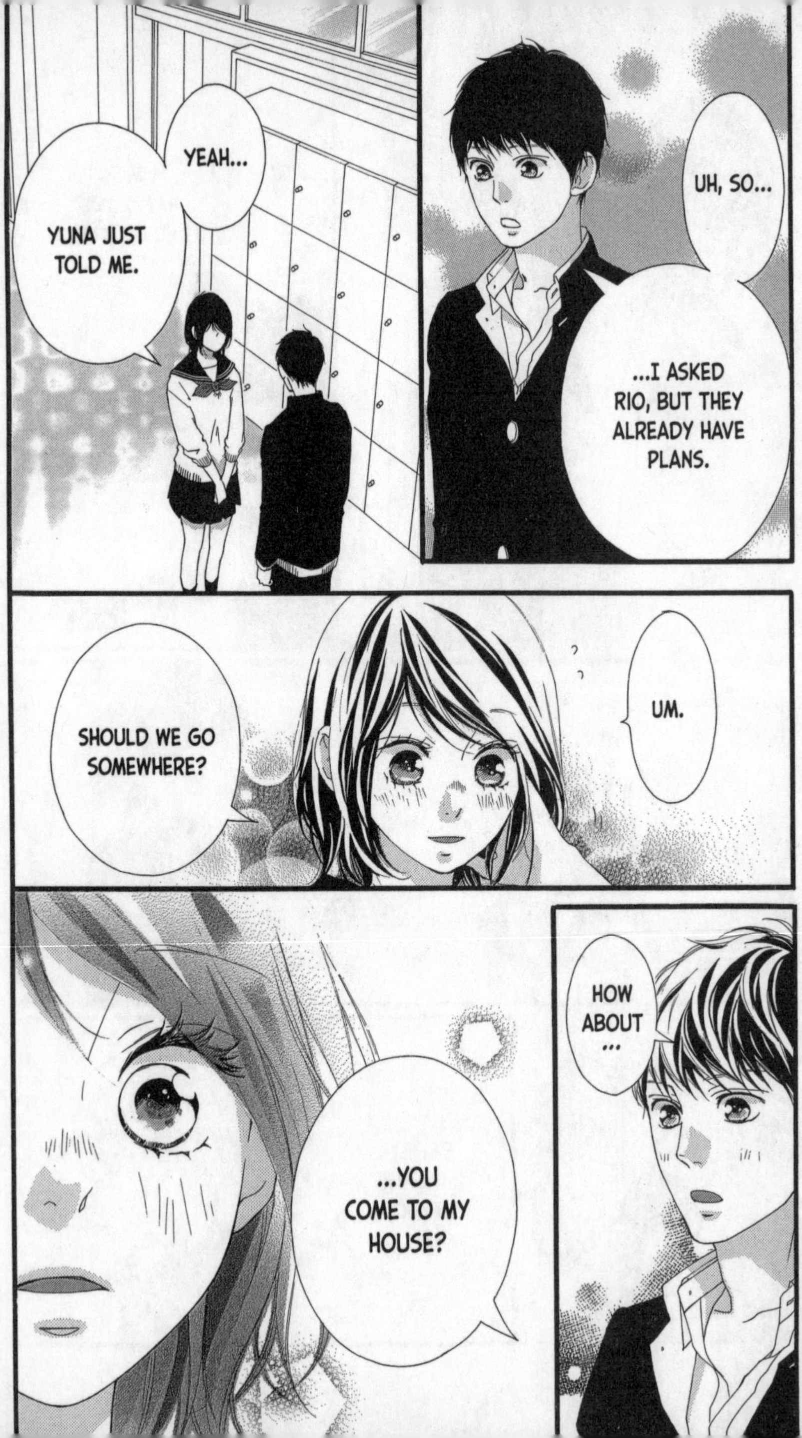
UH, SO...
...I ASKED RIO, BUT THEY ALREADY HAVE PLANS.
YEAH...
YUNA JUST TOLD ME.
UM.
SHOULD WE GO SOMEWHERE?
HOW ABOUT ...
...YOU COME TO MY HOUSE?

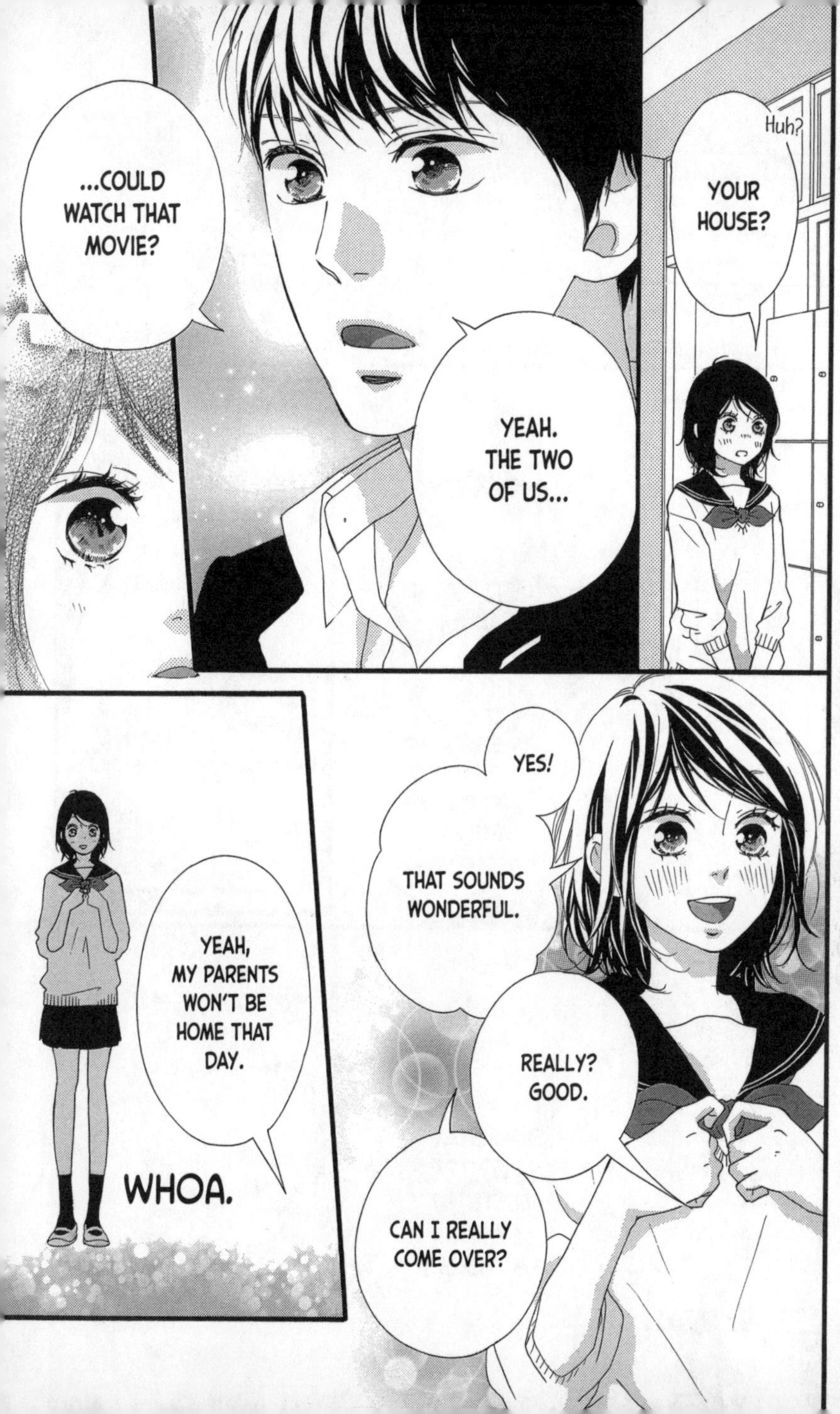
Huh?
YOUR HOUSE?
YEAH. THE TWO OF US...
...COULD WATCH THAT MOVIE?
YES!
THAT SOUNDS WONDERFUL.
REALLY? GOOD.
CAN I REALLY COME OVER?
YEAH, MY PARENTS WON'T BE HOME THAT DAY.
WHOA.

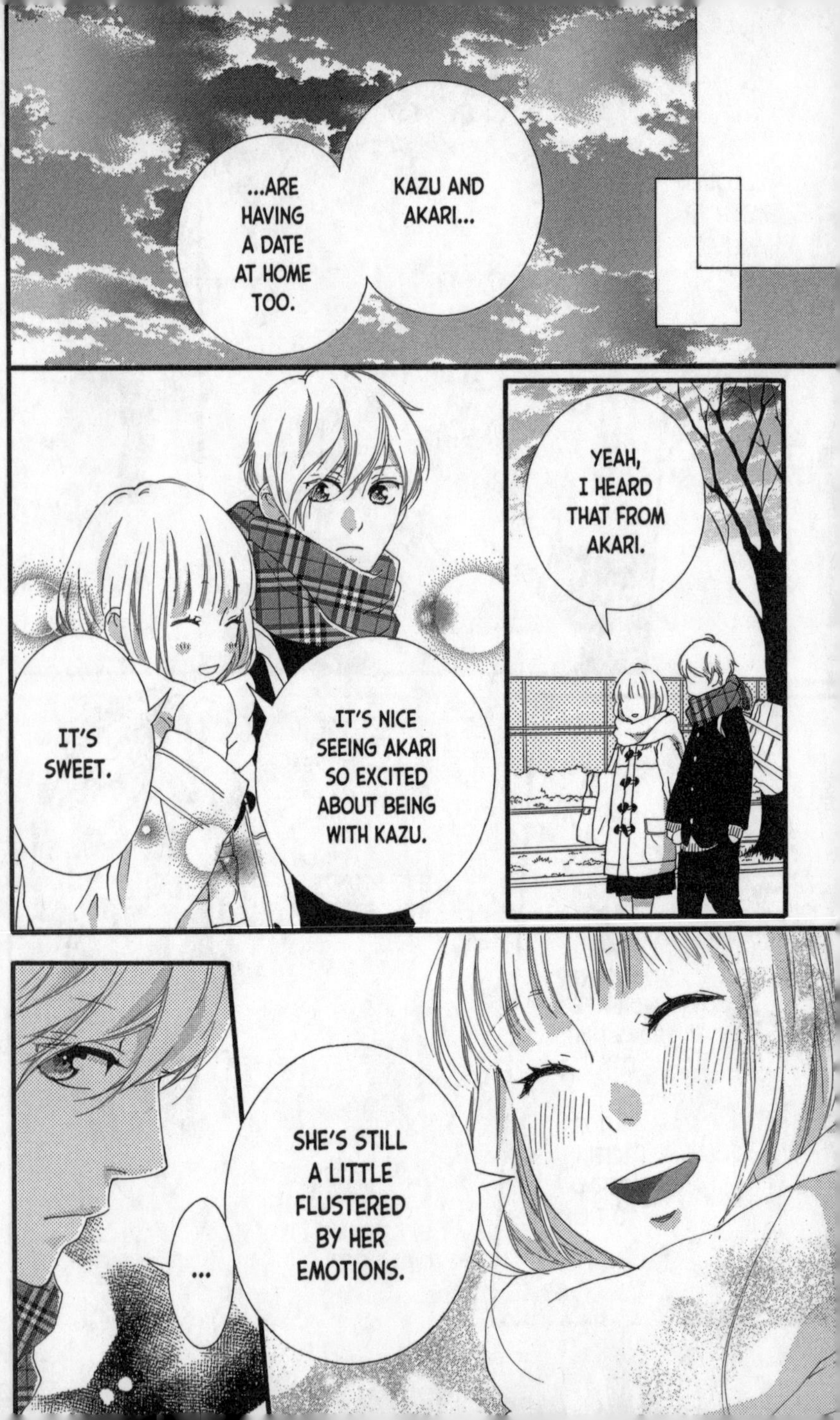
KAZU AND AKARI...
...ARE HAVING A DATE AT HOME TOO.
YEAH, I HEARD THAT FROM AKARI.
IT'S NICE SEEING AKARI SO EXCITED ABOUT BEING WITH KAZU.
IT'S SWEET.
SHE'S STILL A LITTLE FLUSTERED BY HER EMOTIONS.
...

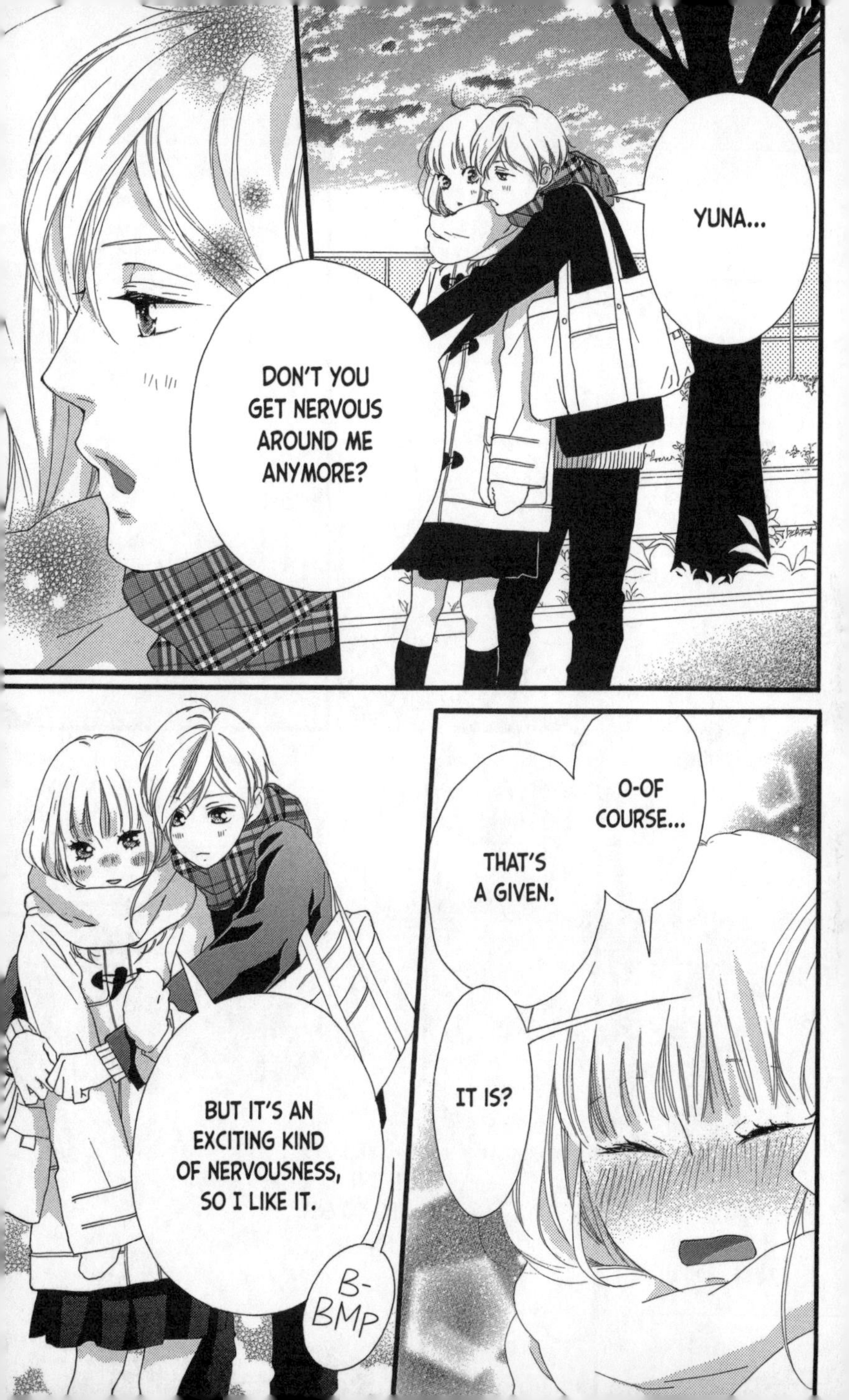
YUNA...
DON'T YOU GET NERVOUS AROUND ME ANYMORE?
O-OF COURSE...
THAT'S A GIVEN.
IT IS?
BUT IT'S AN EXCITING KIND OF NERVOUSNESS, SO I LIKE IT.
B-BMP

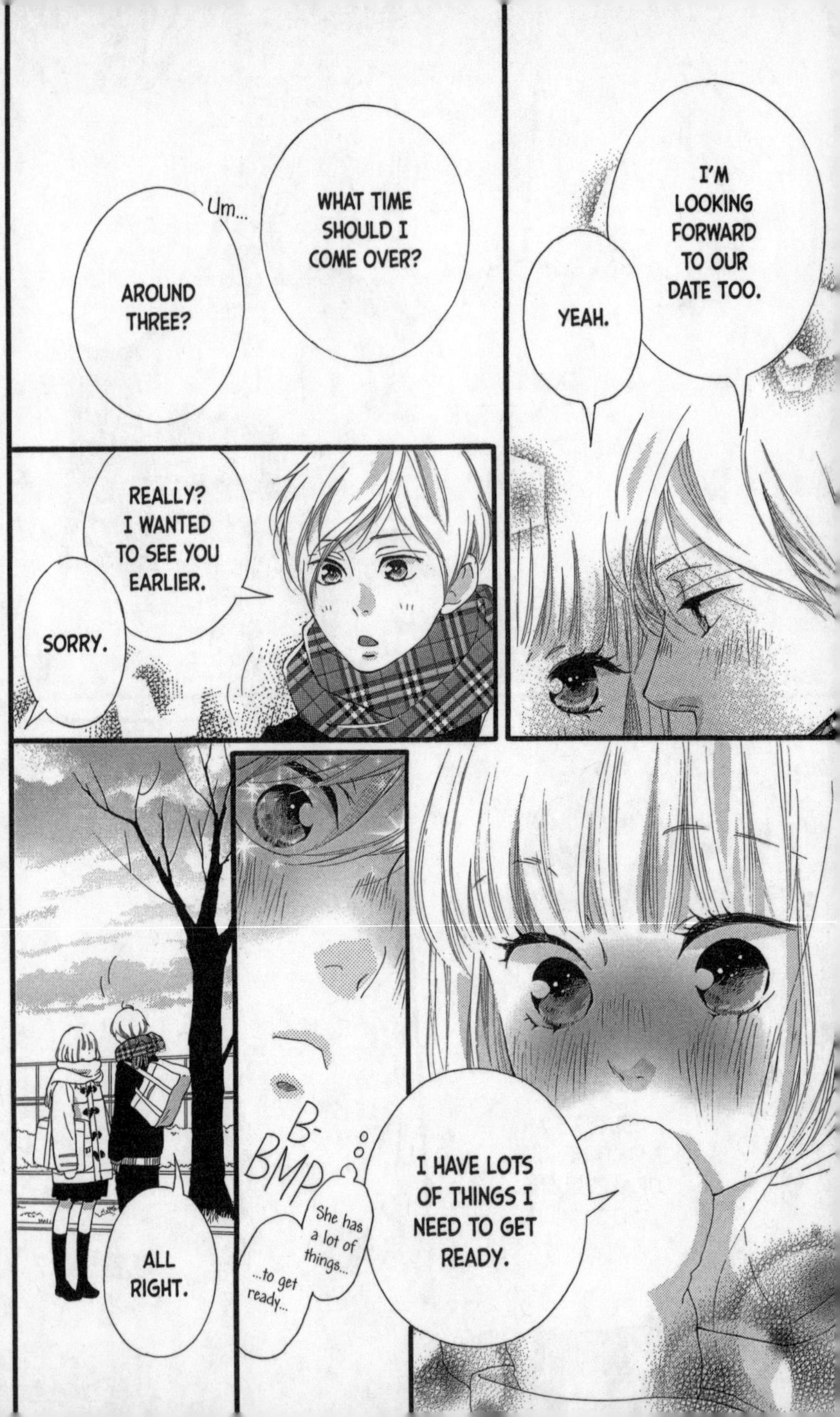
I'M LOOKING FORWARD TO OUR DATE TOO.
YEAH.
WHAT TIME SHOULD I COME OVER?
Um...
AROUND THREE?
REALLY? I WANTED TO SEE YOU EARLIER.
SORRY.
I HAVE LOTS OF THINGS I NEED TO GET READY.
B-BMP
She has a lot of things...
...to get ready...
ALL RIGHT.

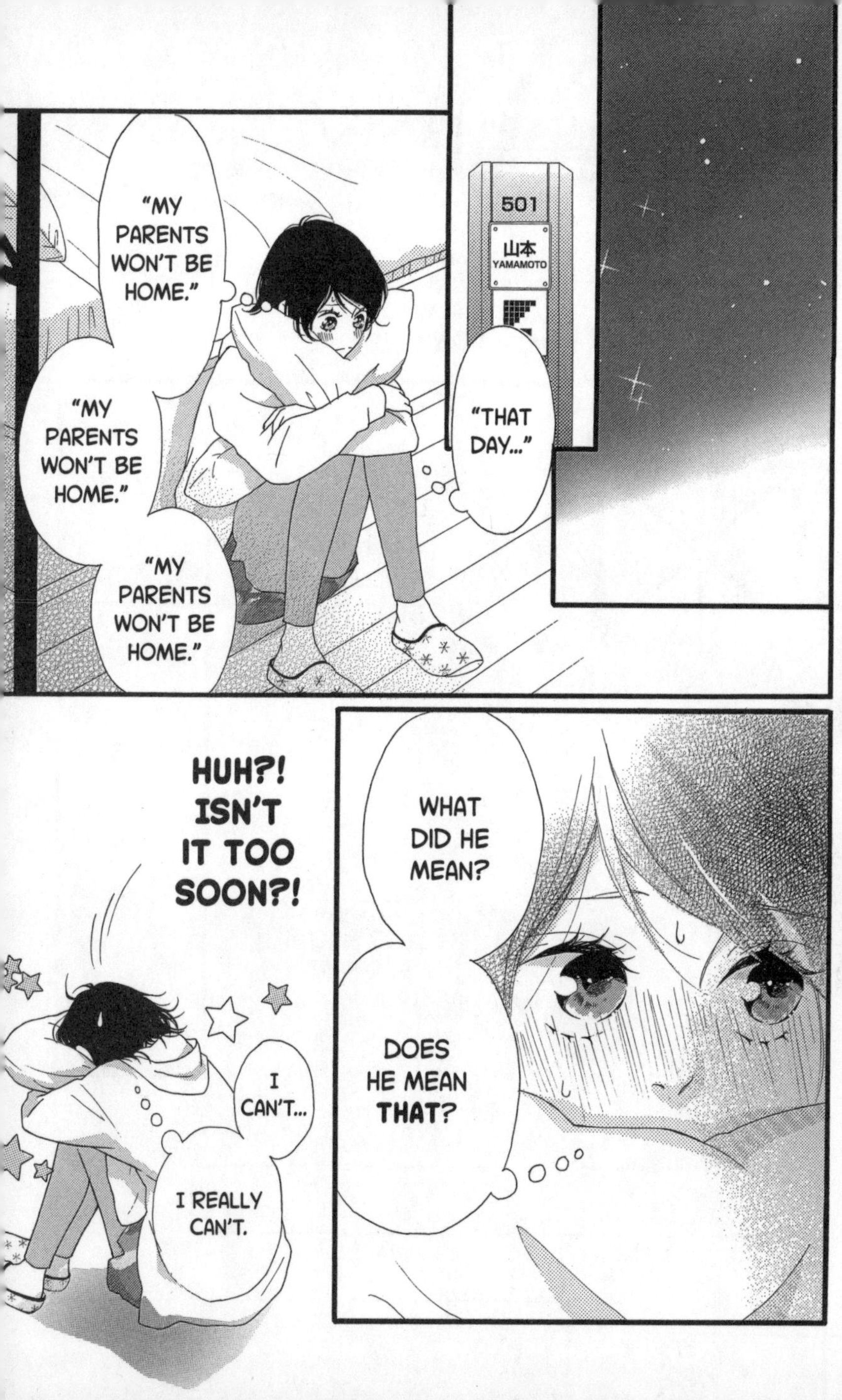
501
山本
YAMAMOTO
"THAT DAY..."
"MY PARENTS WON'T BE HOME."
"MY PARENTS WON'T BE HOME."
"MY PARENTS WON'T BE HOME."
WHAT DID HE MEAN?
DOES HE MEAN **THAT**?
HUH?! ISN'T IT TOO SOON?!
I CAN'T...
I REALLY CAN'T.

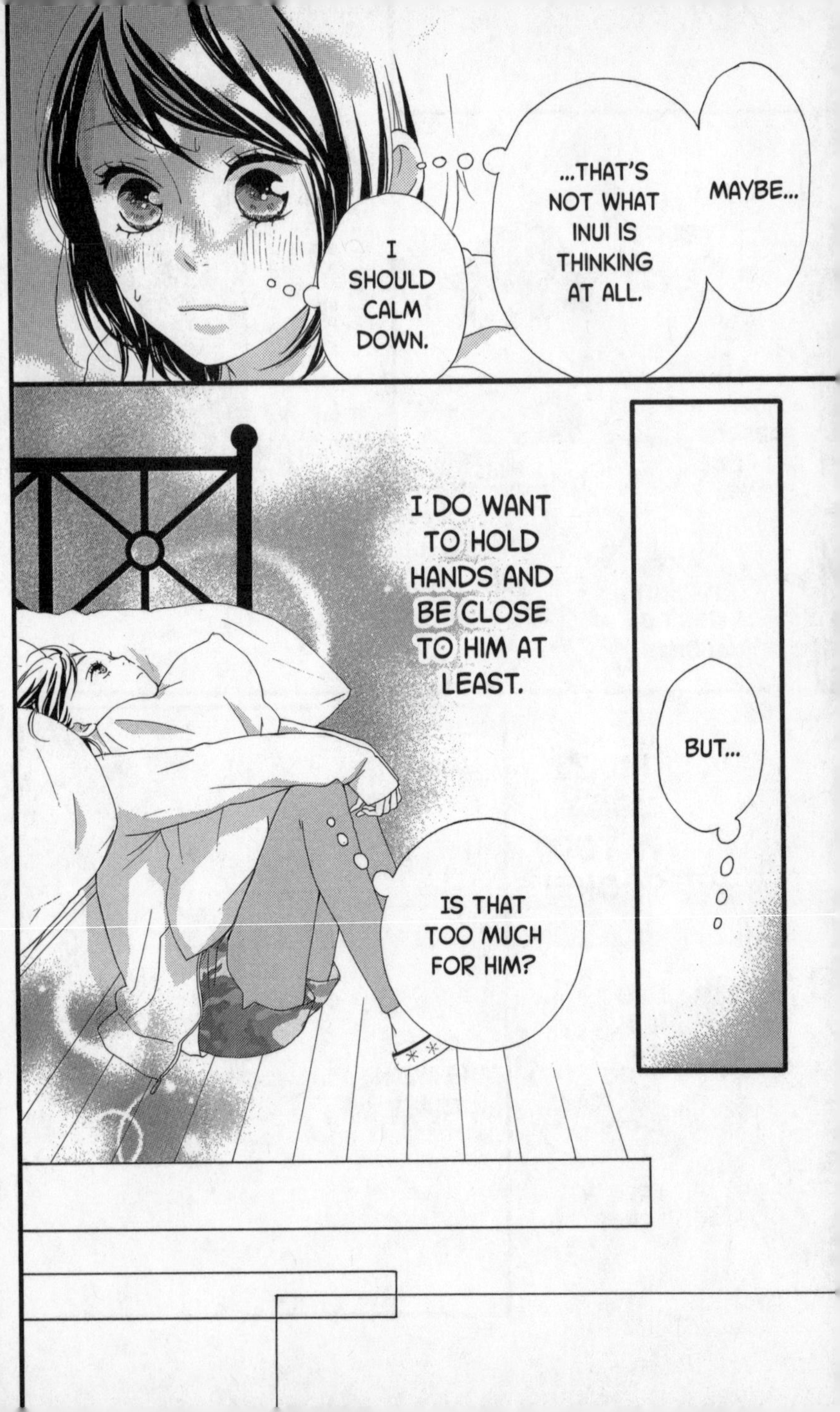
MAYBE...
...THAT'S NOT WHAT INUI IS THINKING AT ALL.
I SHOULD CALM DOWN.
BUT...
I DO WANT TO HOLD HANDS AND BE CLOSE TO HIM AT LEAST.
IS THAT TOO MUCH FOR HIM?

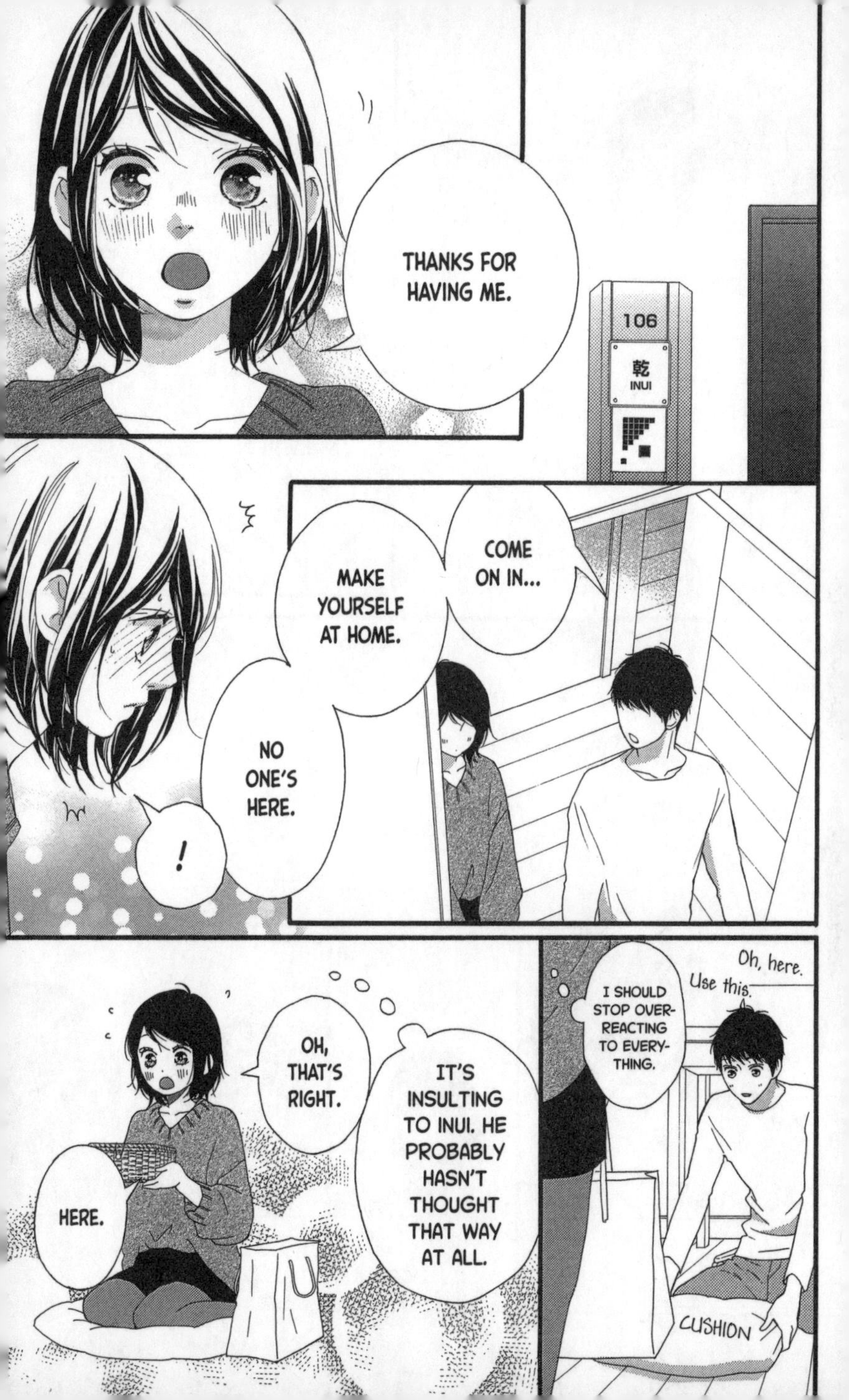
106
乾
INUI
THANKS FOR HAVING ME.
COME ON IN...
MAKE YOURSELF AT HOME.
NO ONE'S HERE.
!
Oh, here. Use this.
I SHOULD STOP OVER-REACTING TO EVERY-THING.
CUSHION
IT'S INSULTING TO INUI. HE PROBABLY HASN'T THOUGHT THAT WAY AT ALL.
OH, THAT'S RIGHT.
HERE.

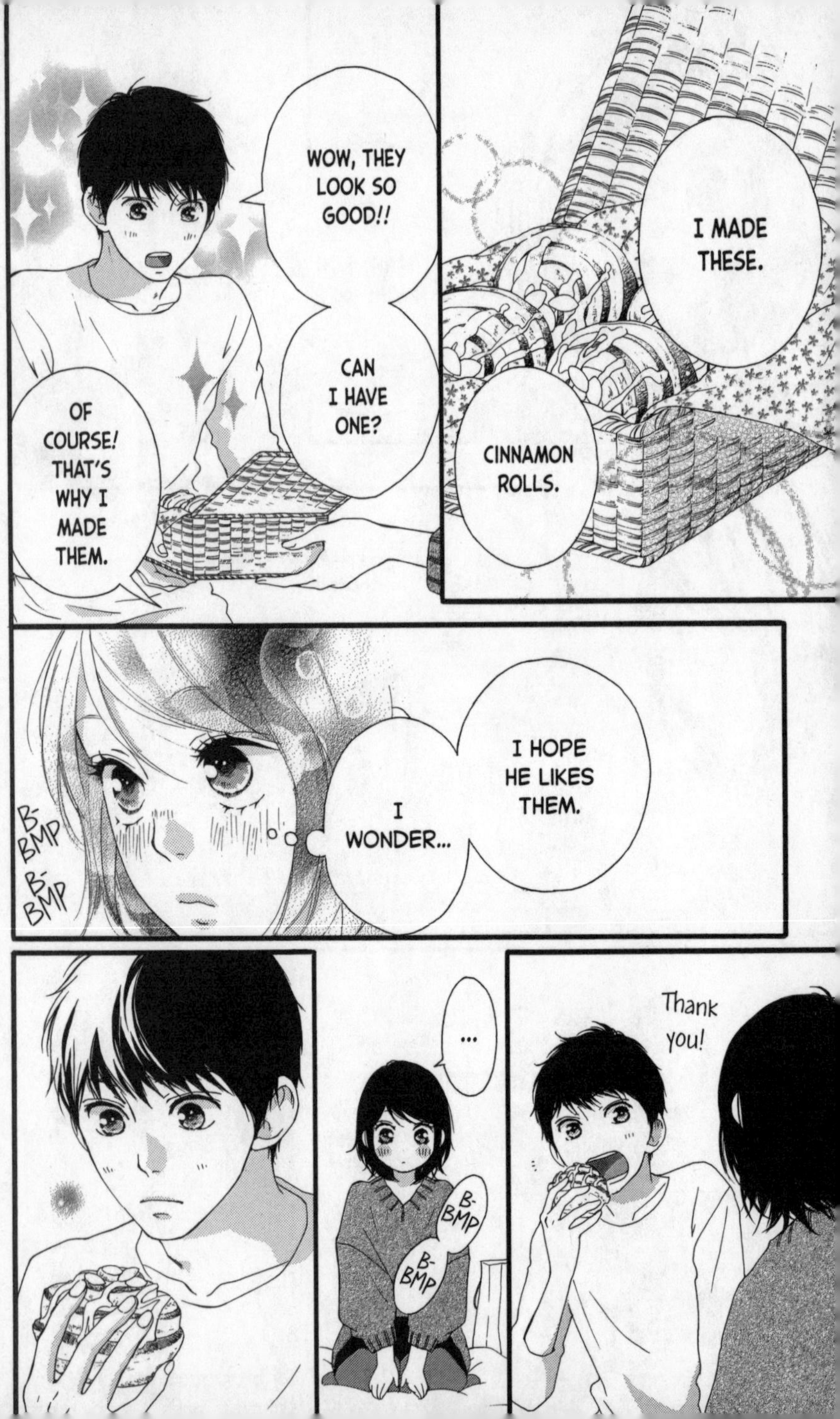
I MADE THESE.
CINNAMON ROLLS.
WOW, THEY LOOK SO GOOD!!
CAN I HAVE ONE?
OF COURSE! THAT'S WHY I MADE THEM.
I HOPE HE LIKES THEM.
I WONDER...
B-BMP B-BMP
Thank you!
...
B-BMP
B-BMP

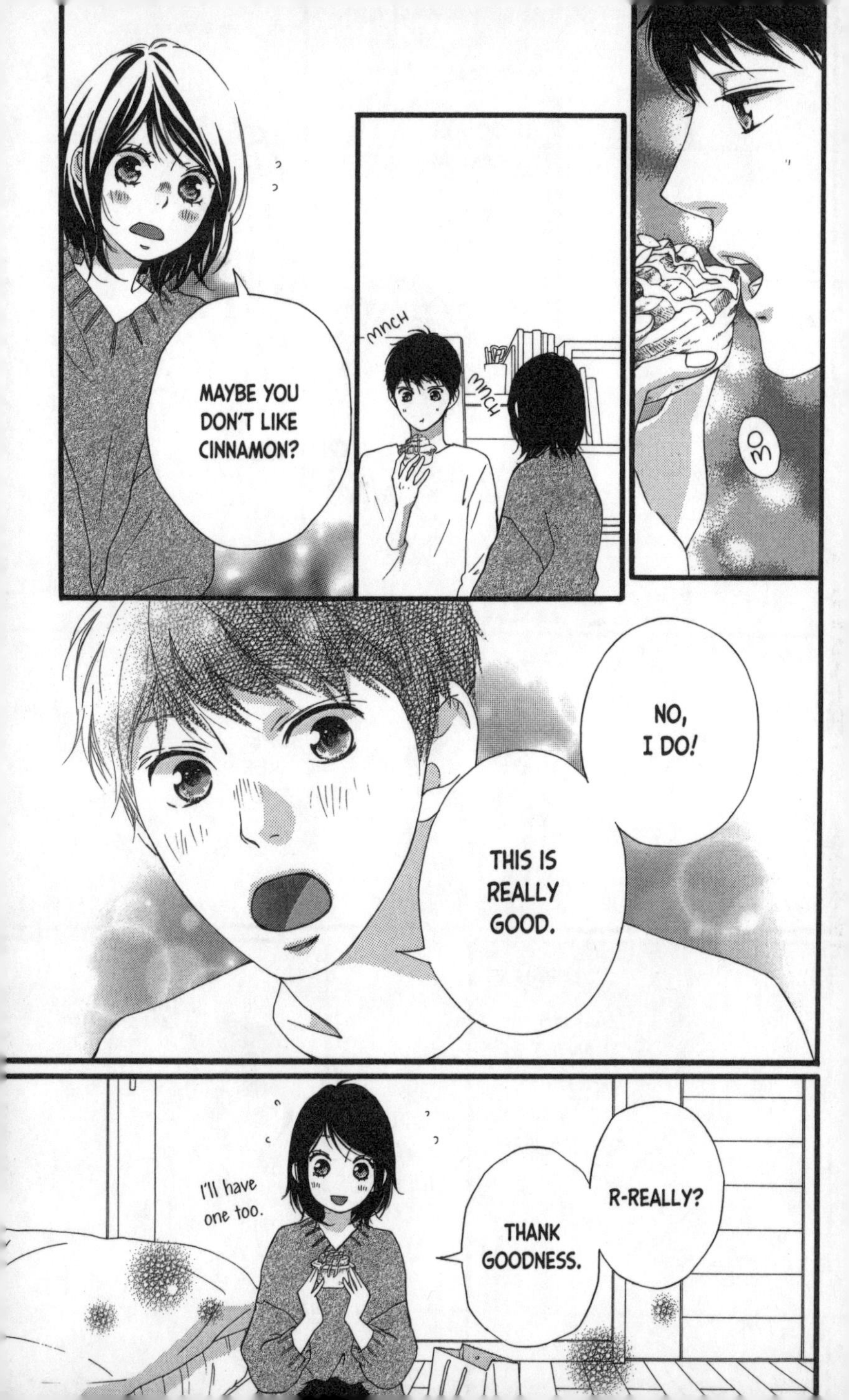
MOMO
MNCH
MNCH
MAYBE YOU DON'T LIKE CINNAMON?
NO, I DO!
THIS IS REALLY GOOD.
R-REALLY?
THANK GOODNESS.
I'll have one too.

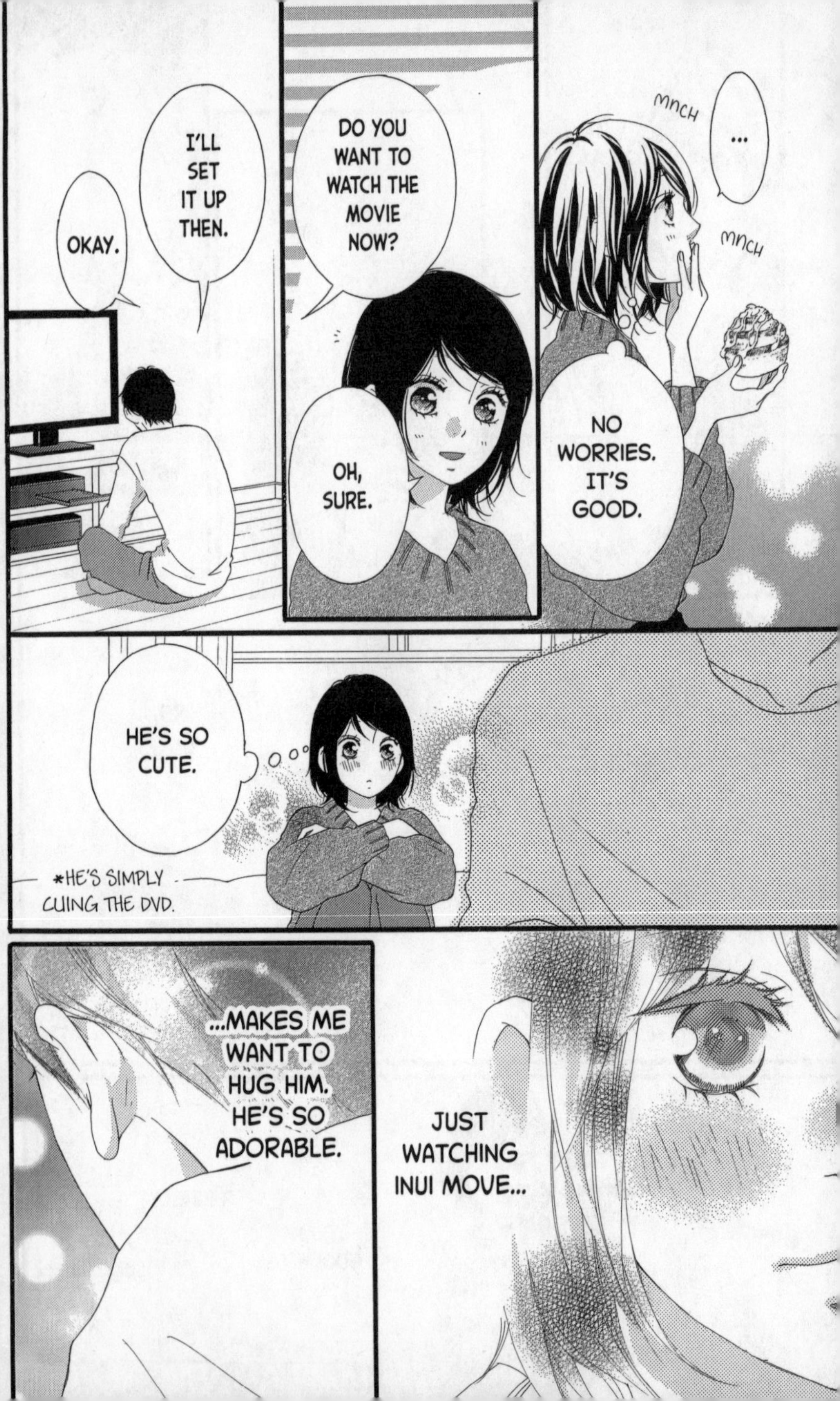
MNCH
...
MNCH
NO WORRIES. IT'S GOOD.
DO YOU WANT TO WATCH THE MOVIE NOW?
OH, SURE.
I'LL SET IT UP THEN.
OKAY.
HE'S SO CUTE.
*HE'S SIMPLY CUING THE DVD.
JUST WATCHING INUI MOVE...
...MAKES ME WANT TO HUG HIM. HE'S SO ADORABLE.

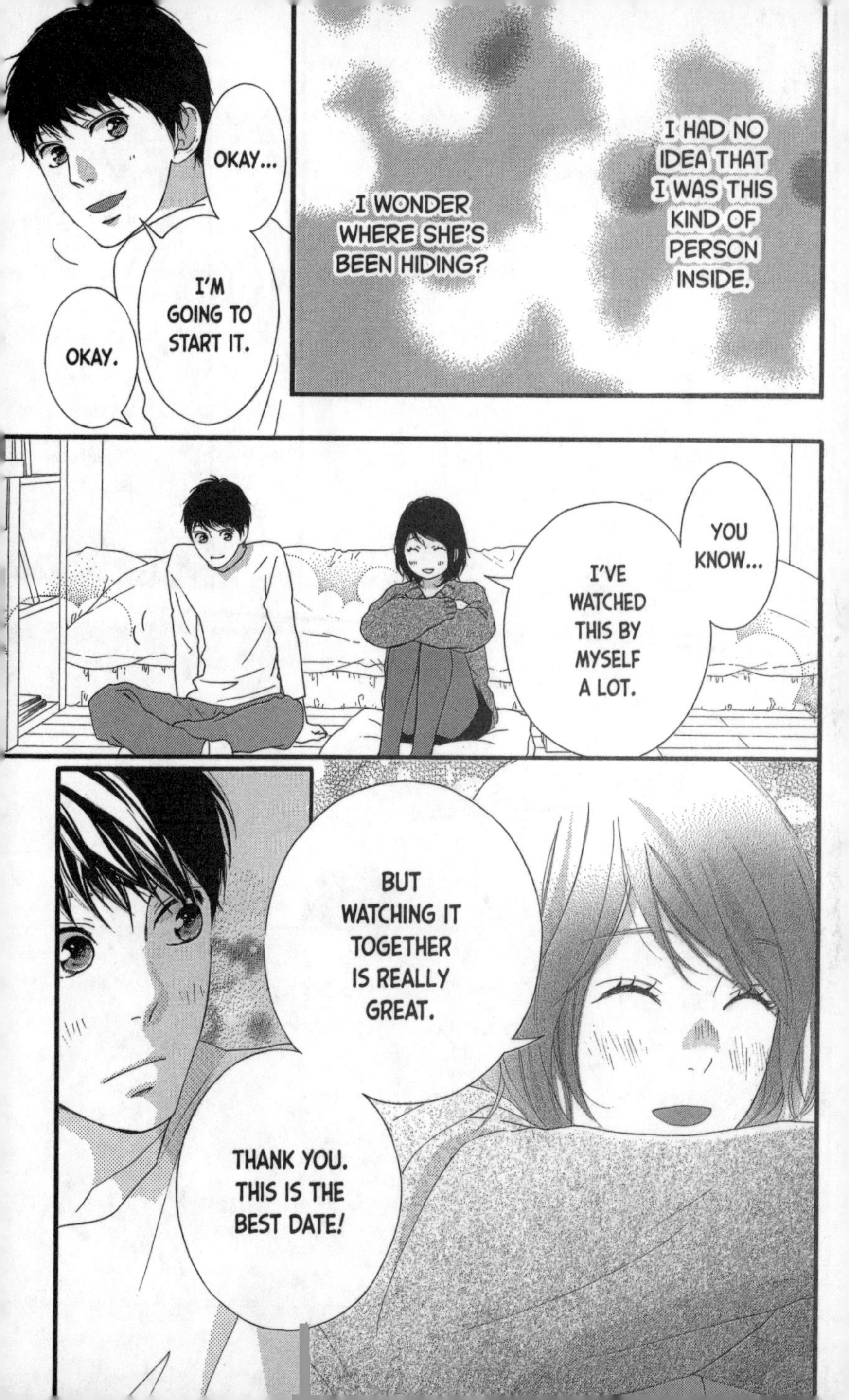
I HAD NO IDEA THAT I WAS THIS KIND OF PERSON INSIDE.
I WONDER WHERE SHE'S BEEN HIDING?
OKAY...
I'M GOING TO START IT.
OKAY.
YOU KNOW...
I'VE WATCHED THIS BY MYSELF A LOT.
BUT WATCHING IT TOGETHER IS REALLY GREAT.
THANK YOU. THIS IS THE BEST DATE!

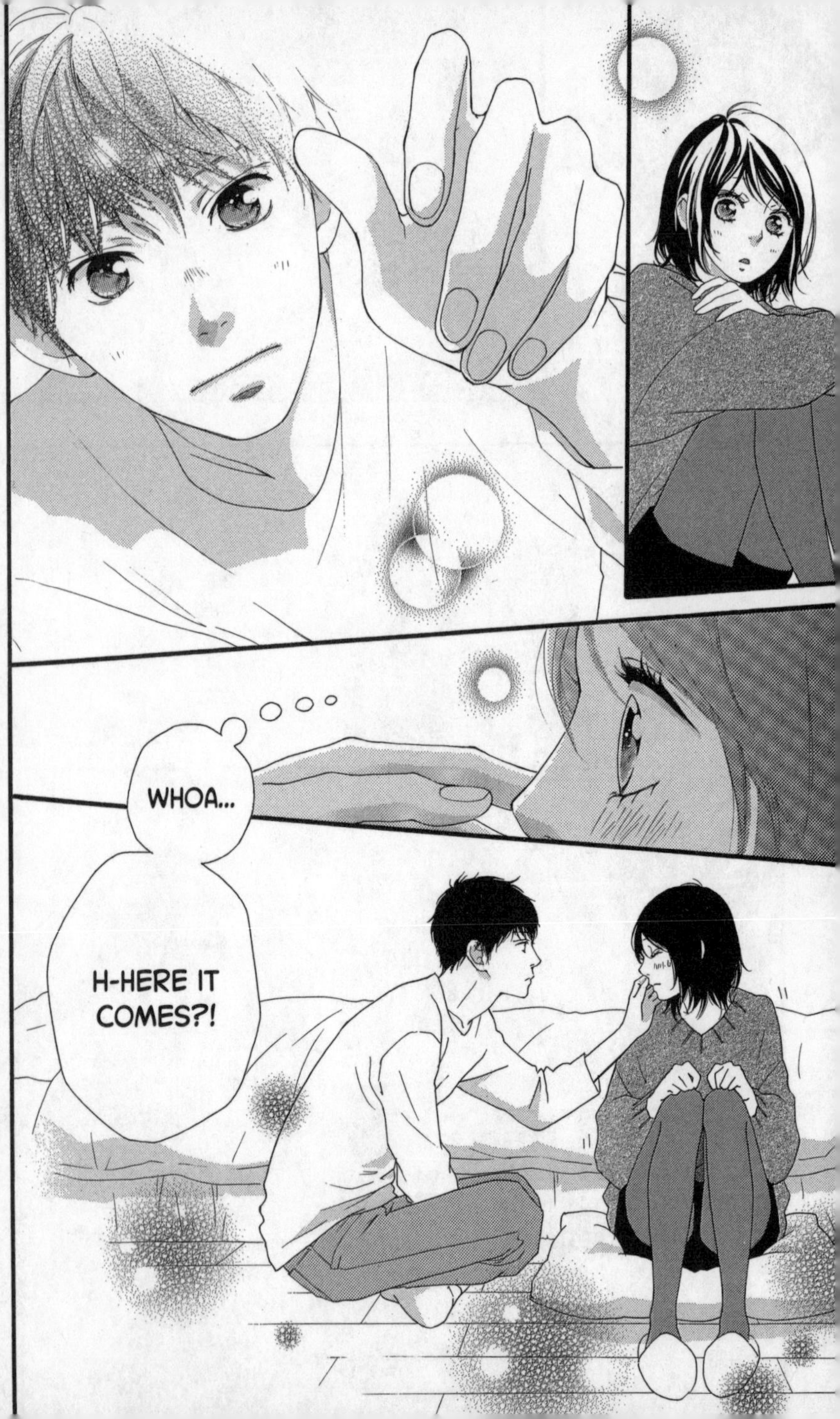
WHOA...
H-HERE IT COMES?!

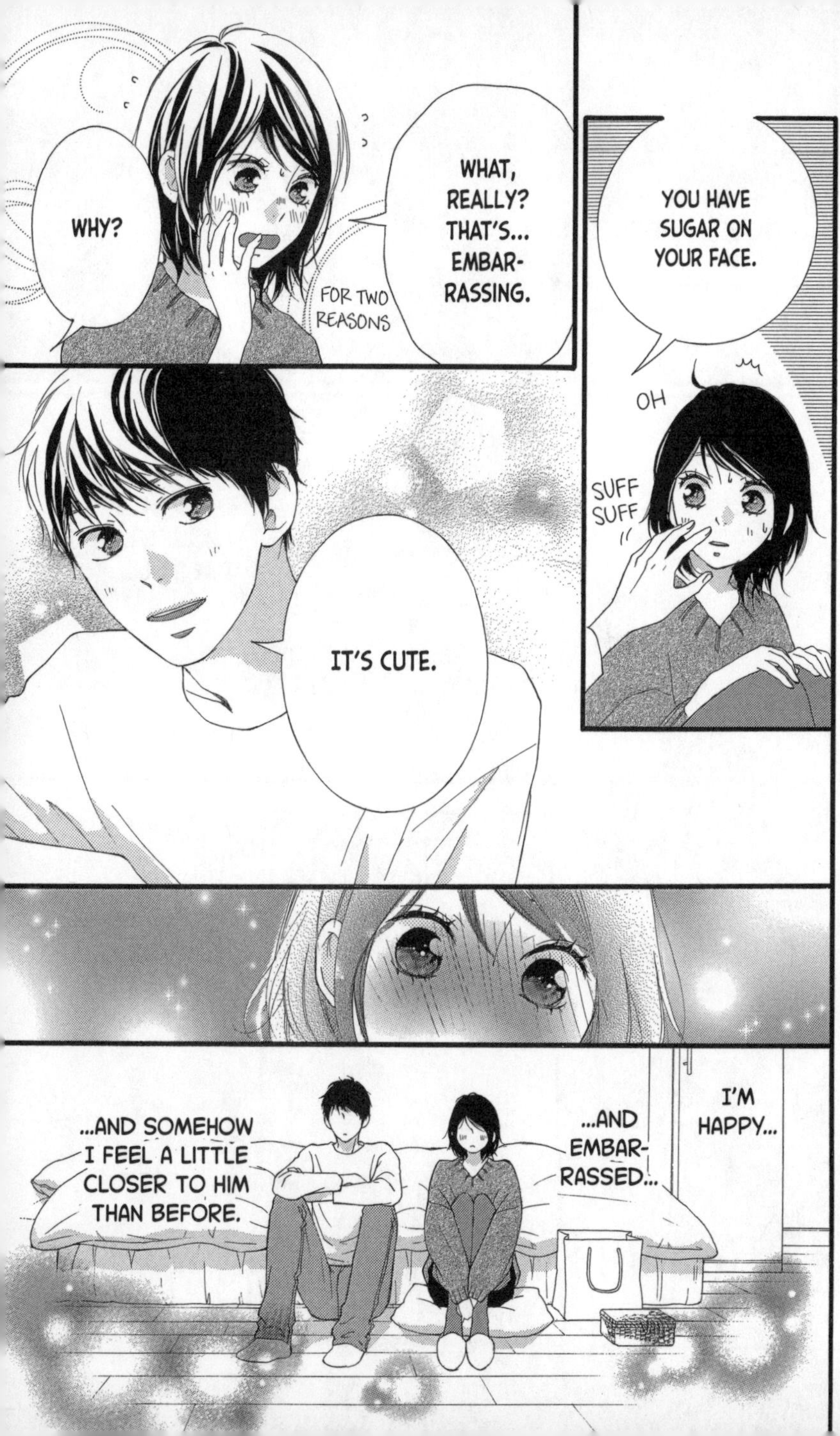
YOU HAVE SUGAR ON YOUR FACE.
OH
SUFF SUFF
WHAT, REALLY? THAT'S... EMBAR-RASSING.
FOR TWO REASONS
WHY?
IT'S CUTE.
I'M HAPPY...
...AND EMBAR-RASSED...
...AND SOMEHOW I FEEL A LITTLE CLOSER TO HIM THAN BEFORE.

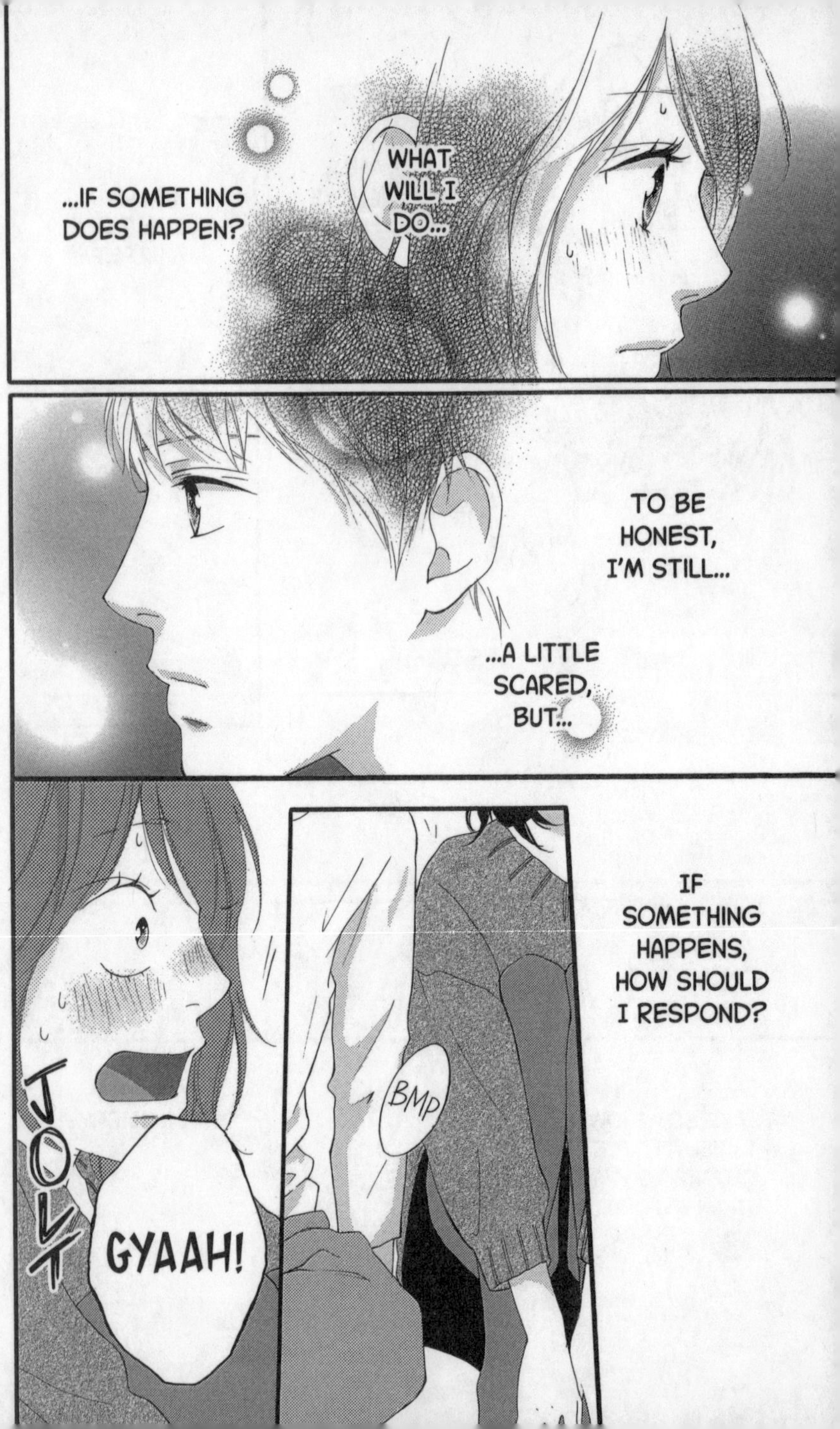
WHAT WILL I DO...
...IF SOMETHING DOES HAPPEN?
TO BE HONEST, I'M STILL...
...A LITTLE SCARED, BUT...
IF SOMETHING HAPPENS, HOW SHOULD I RESPOND?
BMP
GYAAH!
JOLT

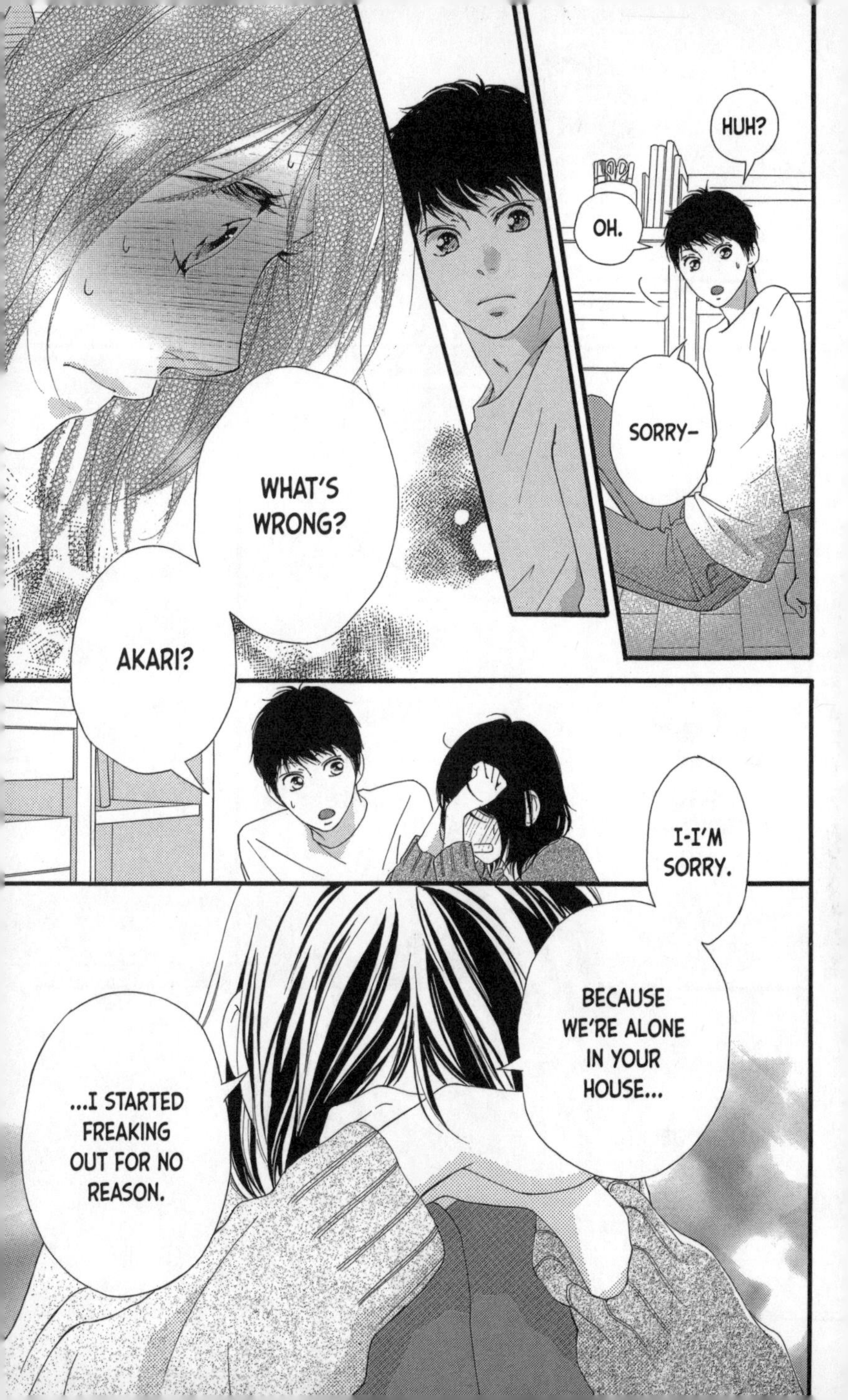
HUH?
OH.
SORRY–
WHAT'S WRONG?
AKARI?
I-I'M SORRY.
BECAUSE WE'RE ALONE IN YOUR HOUSE...
...I STARTED FREAKING OUT FOR NO REASON.

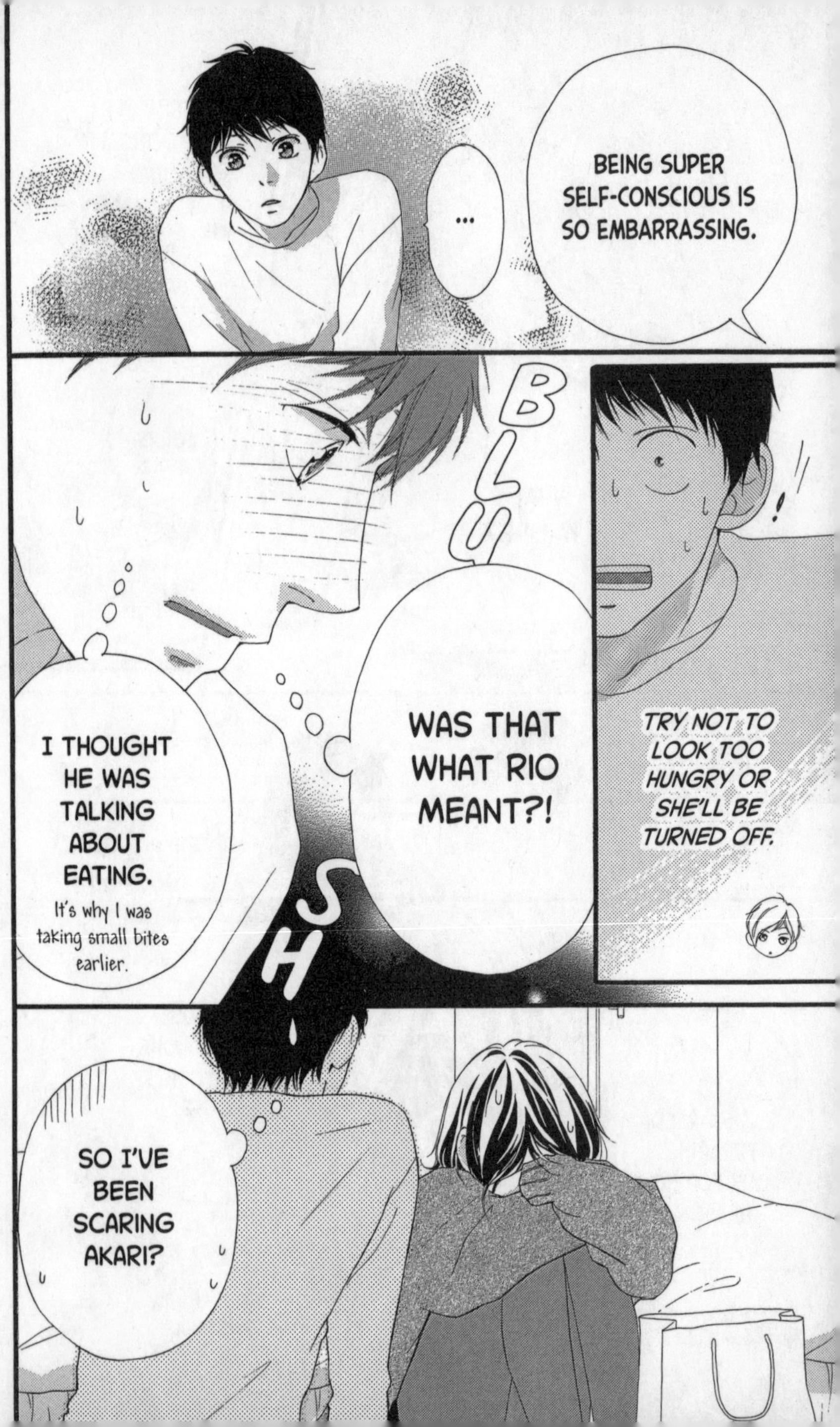
BEING SUPER SELF-CONSCIOUS IS SO EMBARRASSING.
...
TRY NOT TO LOOK TOO HUNGRY OR SHE'LL BE TURNED OFF.
!
BLUSH
WAS THAT WHAT RIO MEANT?!
I THOUGHT HE WAS TALKING ABOUT EATING.
It's why I was taking small bites earlier.
SO I'VE BEEN SCARING AKARI?

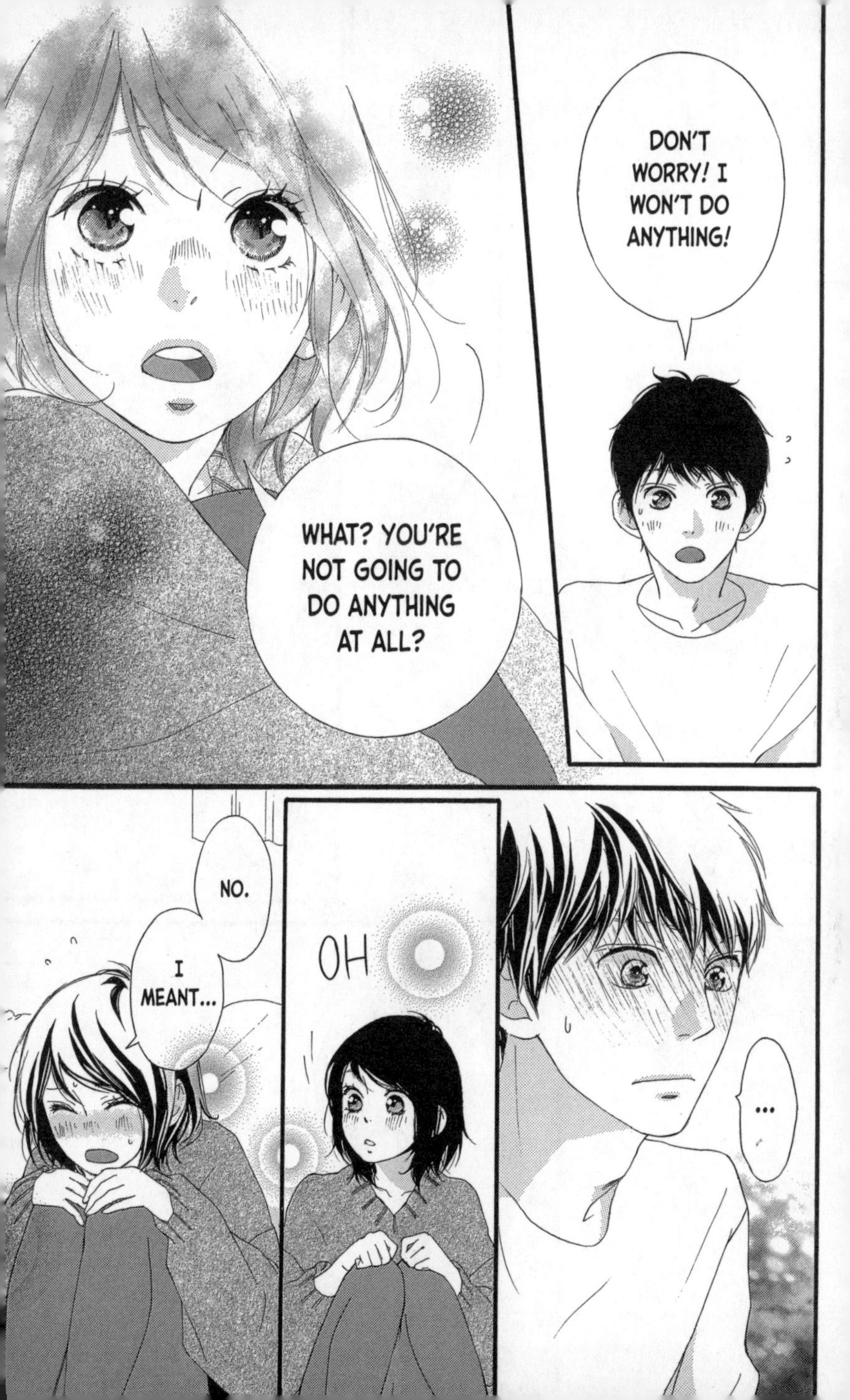
DON'T WORRY! I WON'T DO ANYTHING!
WHAT? YOU'RE NOT GOING TO DO ANYTHING AT ALL?
...
OH
NO.
I MEANT...

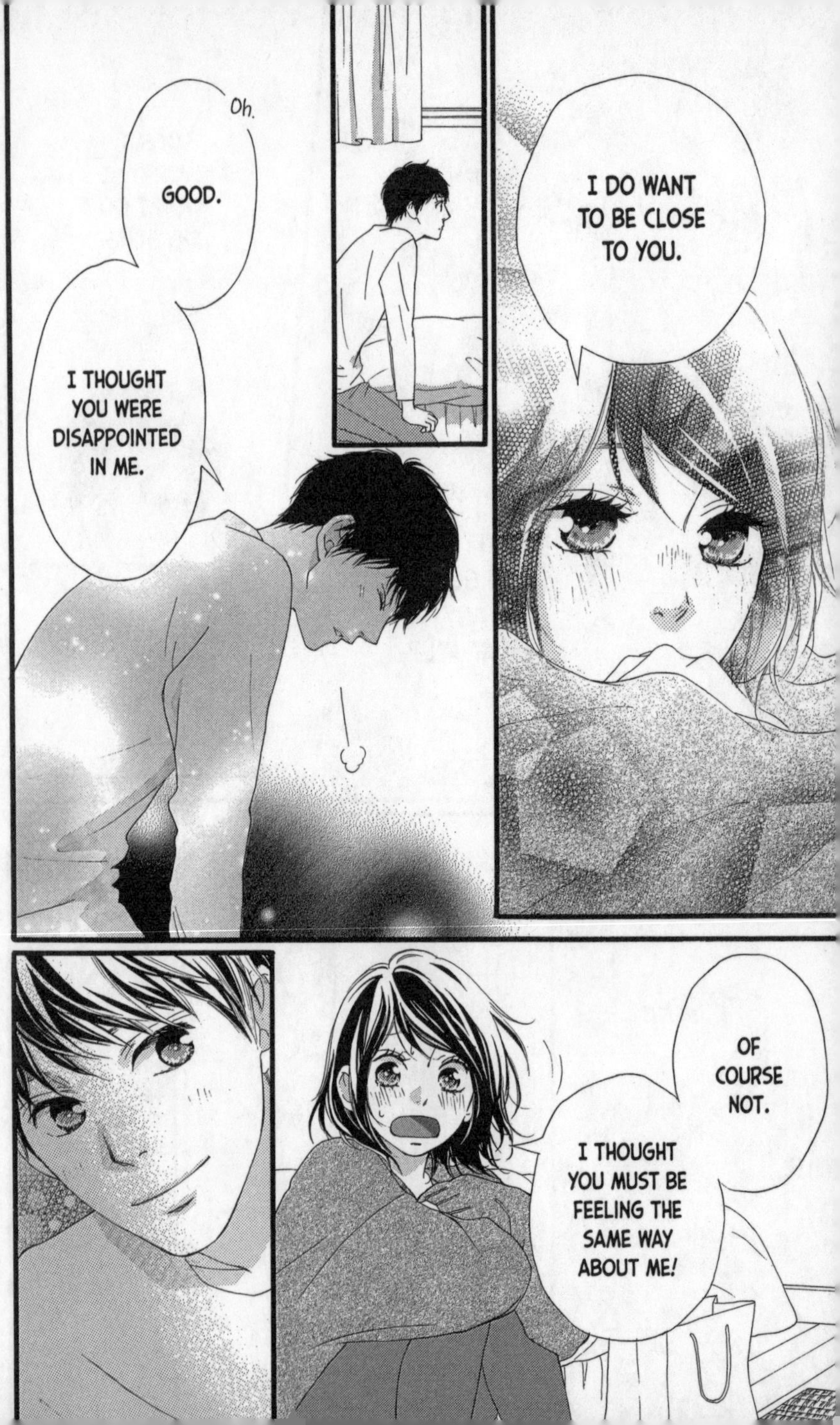
I DO WANT TO BE CLOSE TO YOU.
Oh.
GOOD.
I THOUGHT YOU WERE DISAPPOINTED IN ME.
OF COURSE NOT.
I THOUGHT YOU MUST BE FEELING THE SAME WAY ABOUT ME!

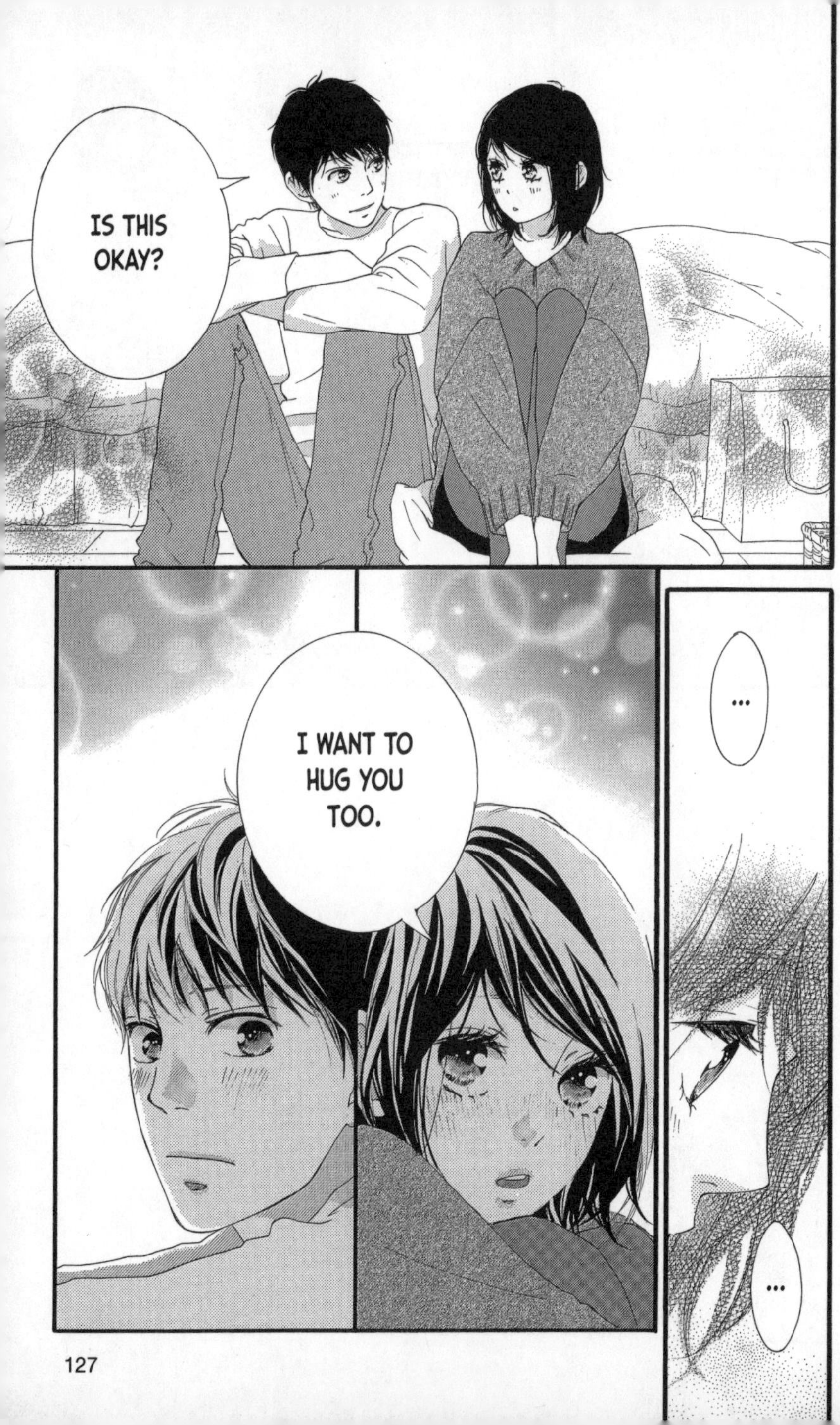
IS THIS OKAY?
...
...
I WANT TO HUG YOU TOO.

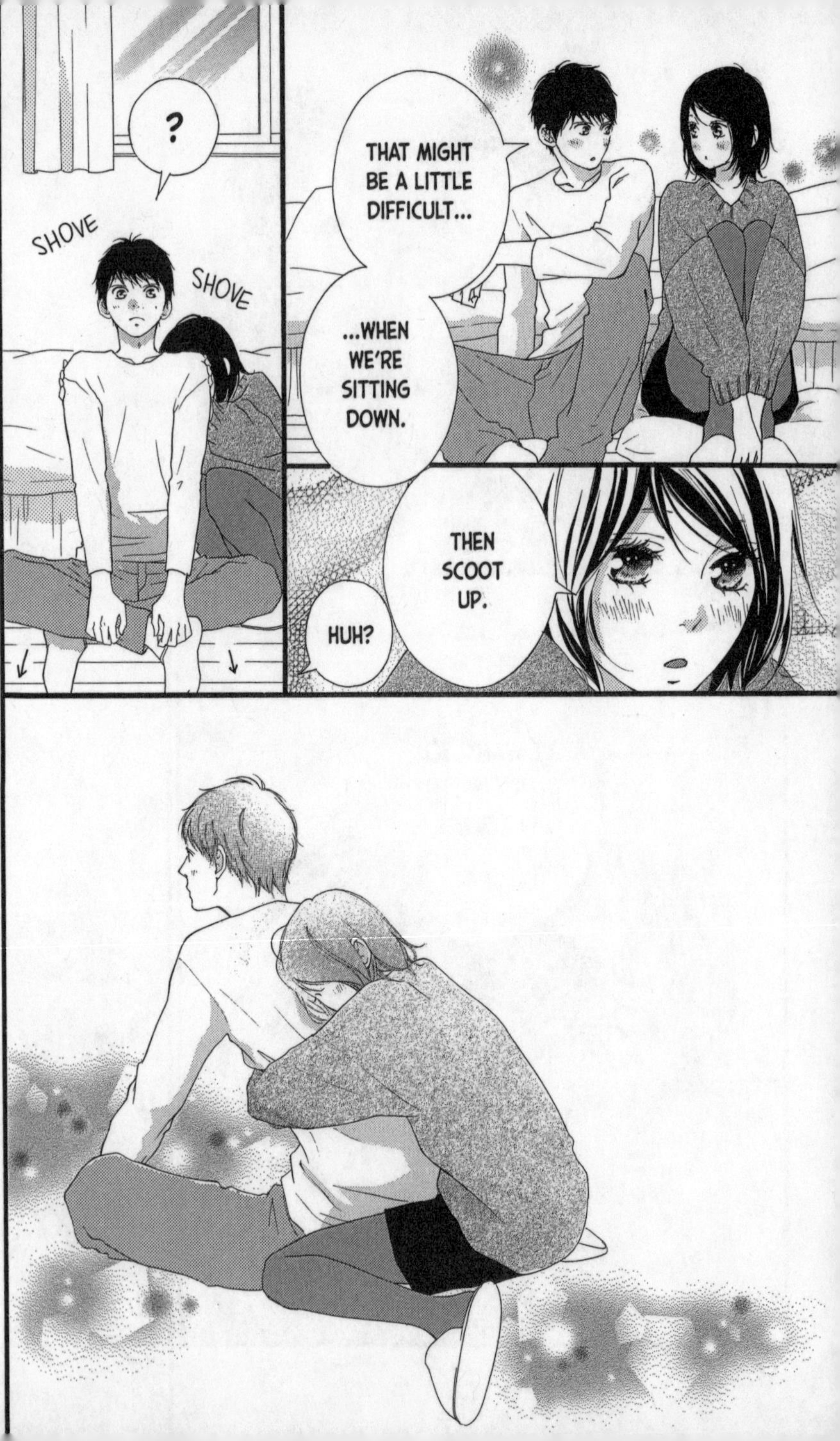
THAT MIGHT BE A LITTLE DIFFICULT...
...WHEN WE'RE SITTING DOWN.
THEN SCOOT UP.
HUH?
?
SHOVE
SHOVE

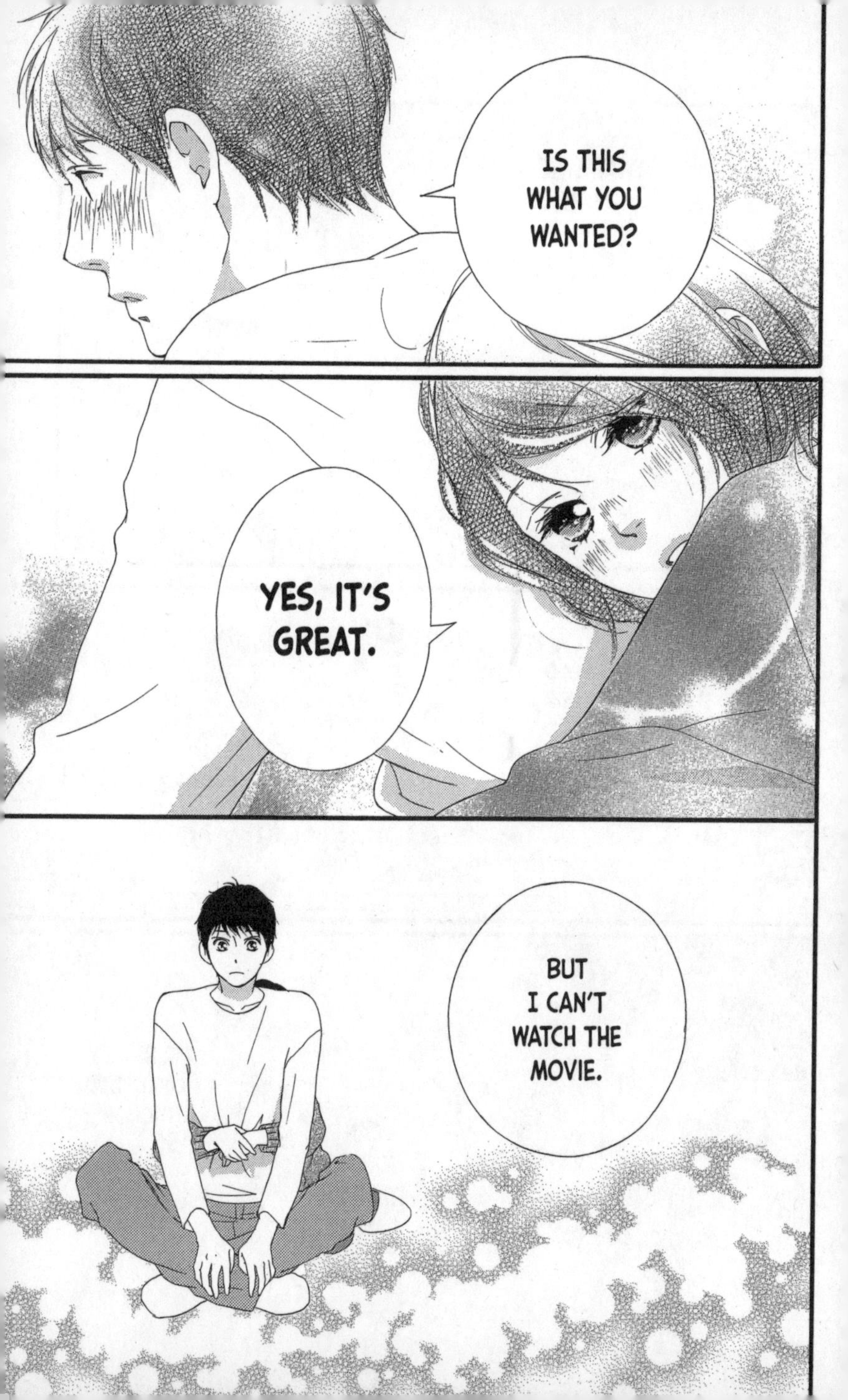
IS THIS WHAT YOU WANTED?
YES, IT'S GREAT.
BUT I CAN'T WATCH THE MOVIE.

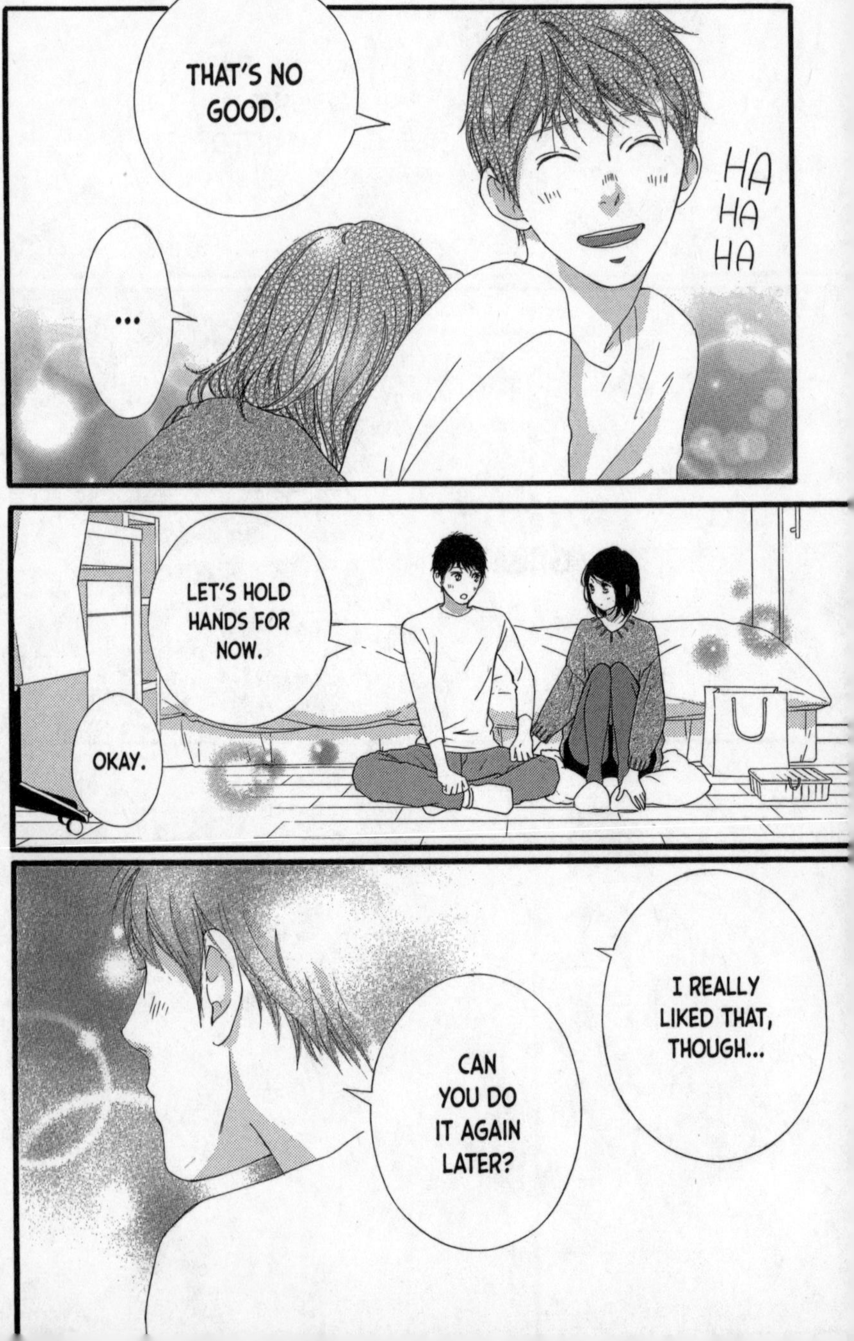
THAT'S NO GOOD.
HA HA HA
...
LET'S HOLD HANDS FOR NOW.
OKAY.
I REALLY LIKED THAT, THOUGH...
CAN YOU DO IT AGAIN LATER?

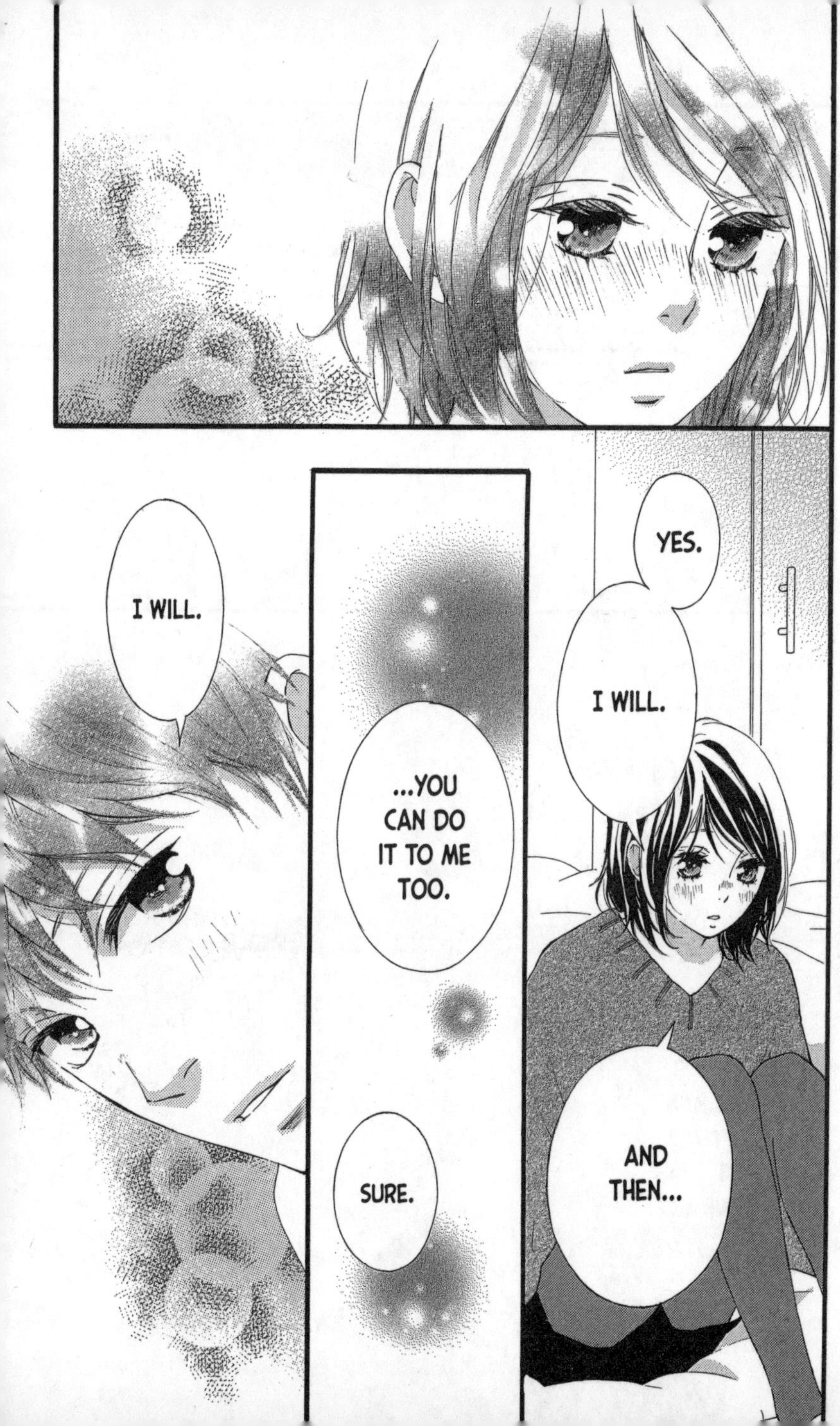
YES.
I WILL.
AND THEN...
...YOU CAN DO IT TO ME TOO.
SURE.
I WILL.

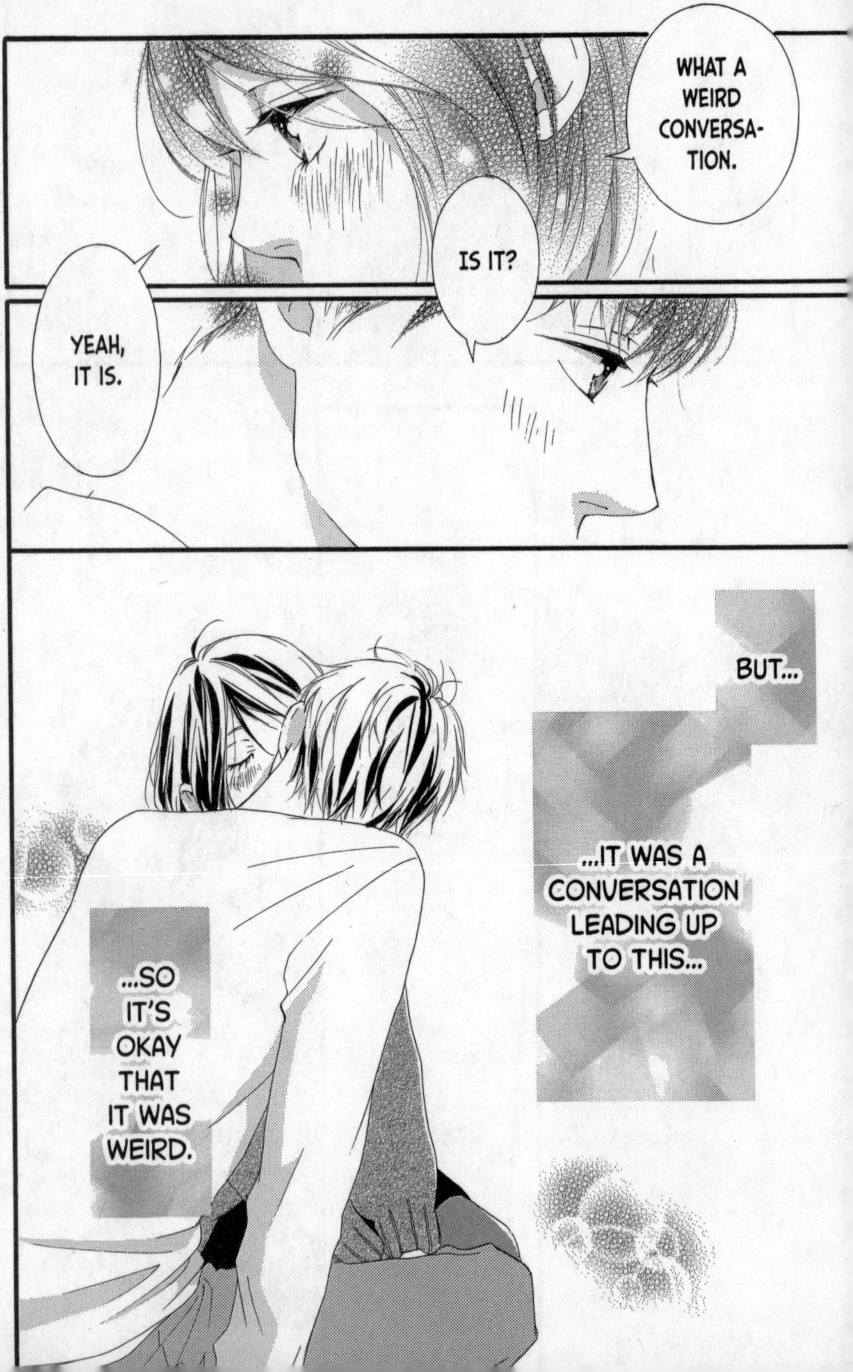
WHAT A WEIRD CONVERSATION.
IS IT?
YEAH, IT IS.
BUT...
...IT WAS A CONVERSATION LEADING UP TO THIS...
...SO IT'S OKAY THAT IT WAS WEIRD.

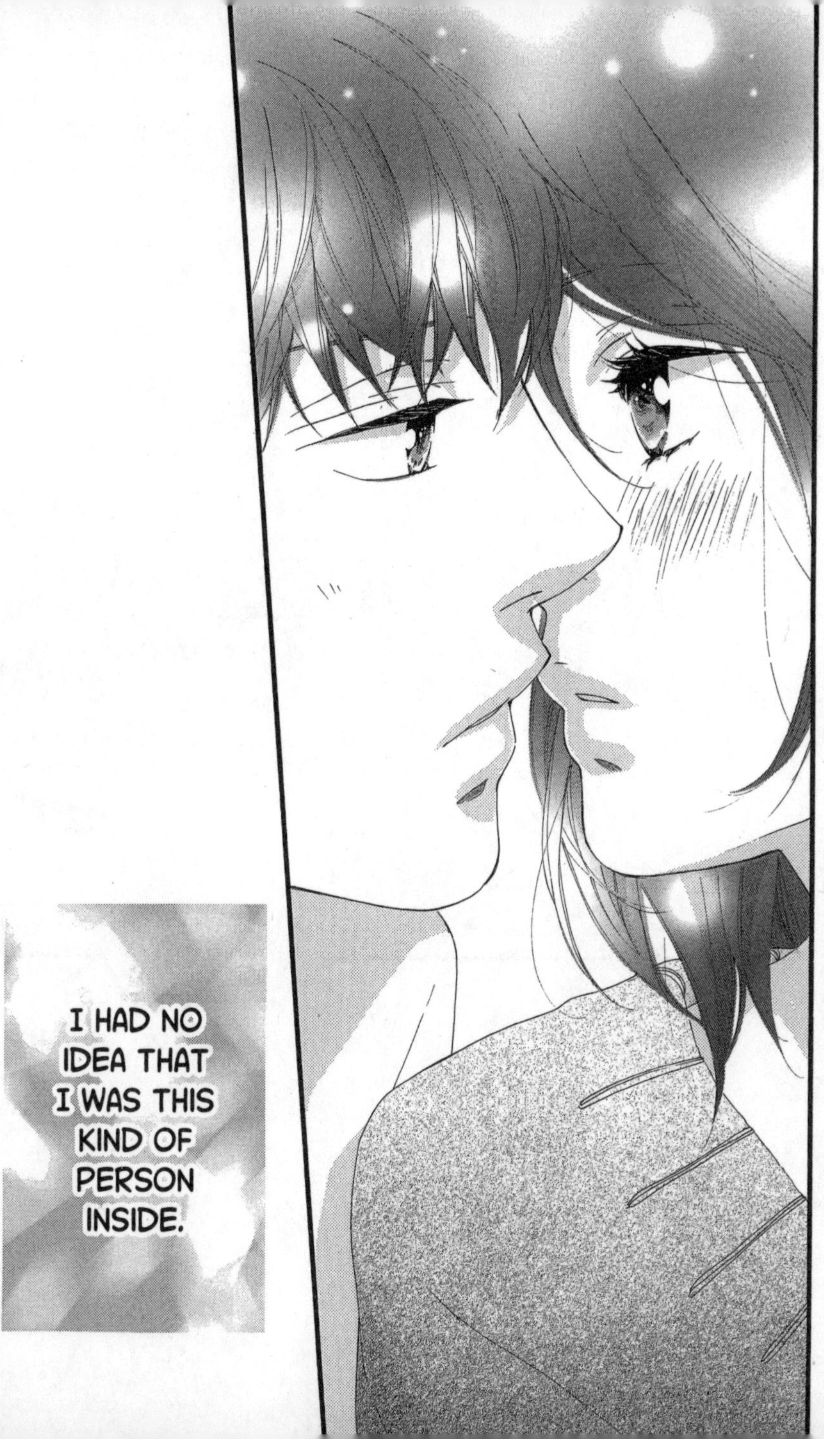
I HAD NO IDEA THAT I WAS THIS KIND OF PERSON INSIDE.

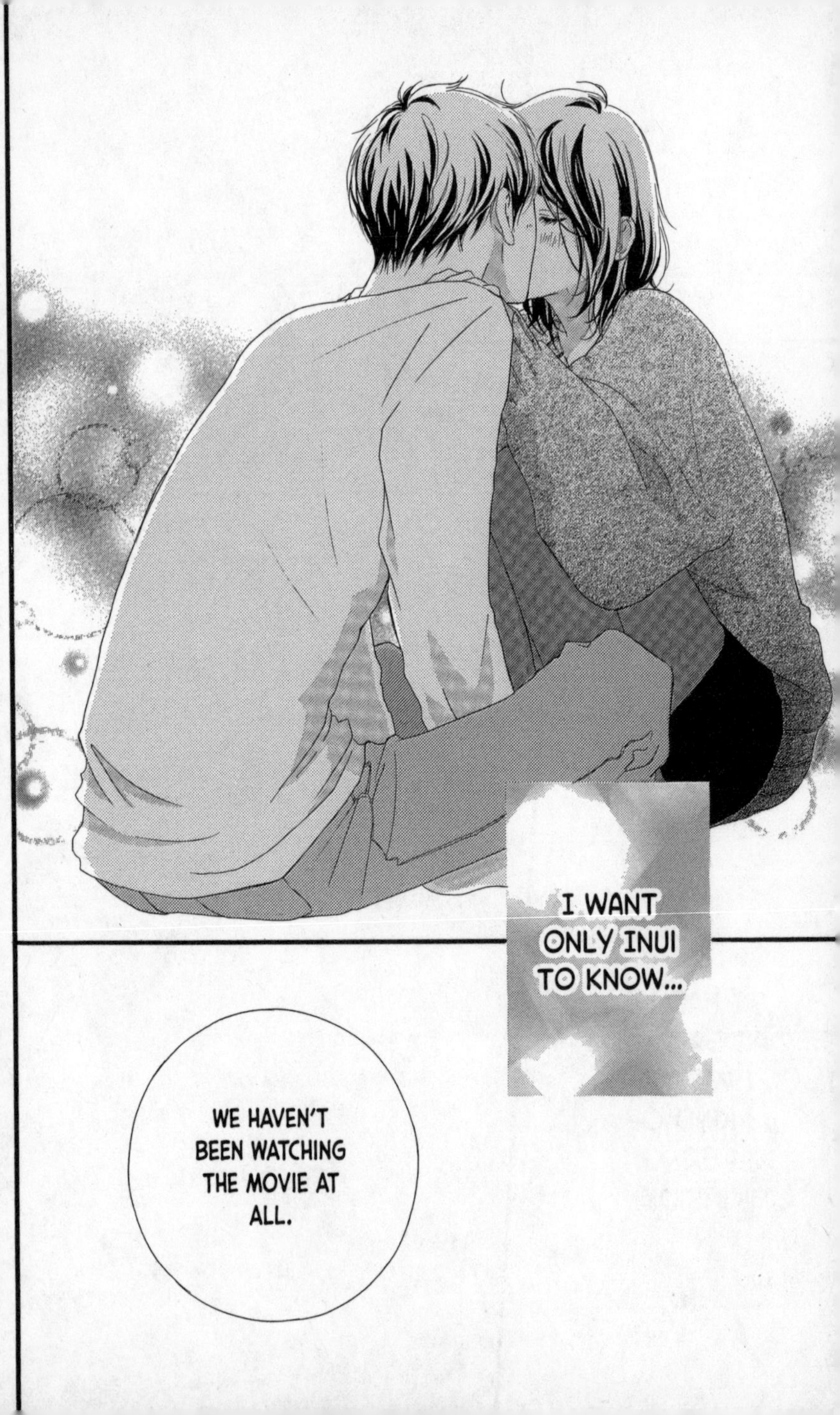
I WANT ONLY INUI TO KNOW...
WE HAVEN'T BEEN WATCHING THE MOVIE AT ALL.

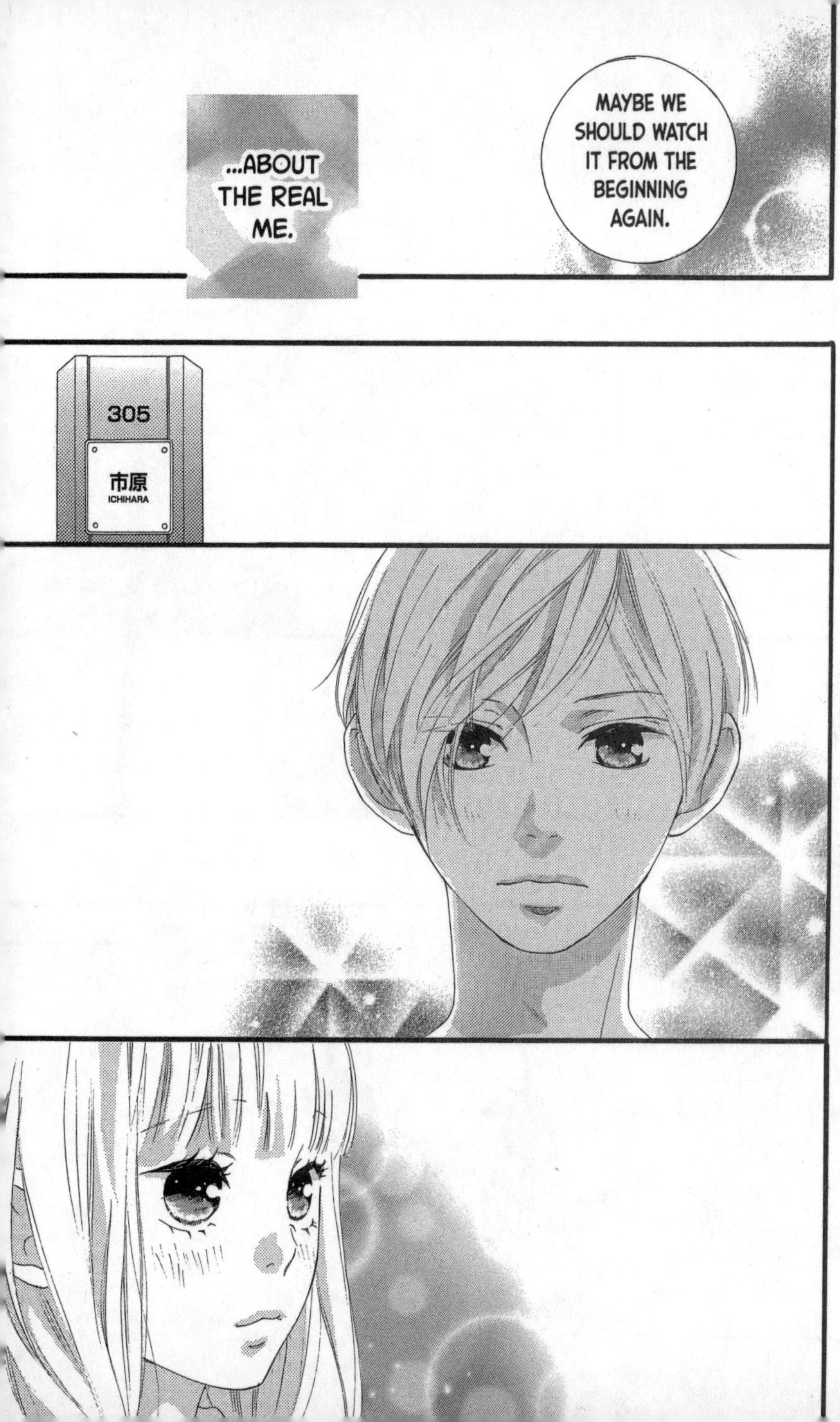
MAYBE WE SHOULD WATCH IT FROM THE BEGINNING AGAIN.
...ABOUT THE REAL ME.
305
市原
ICHIHARA

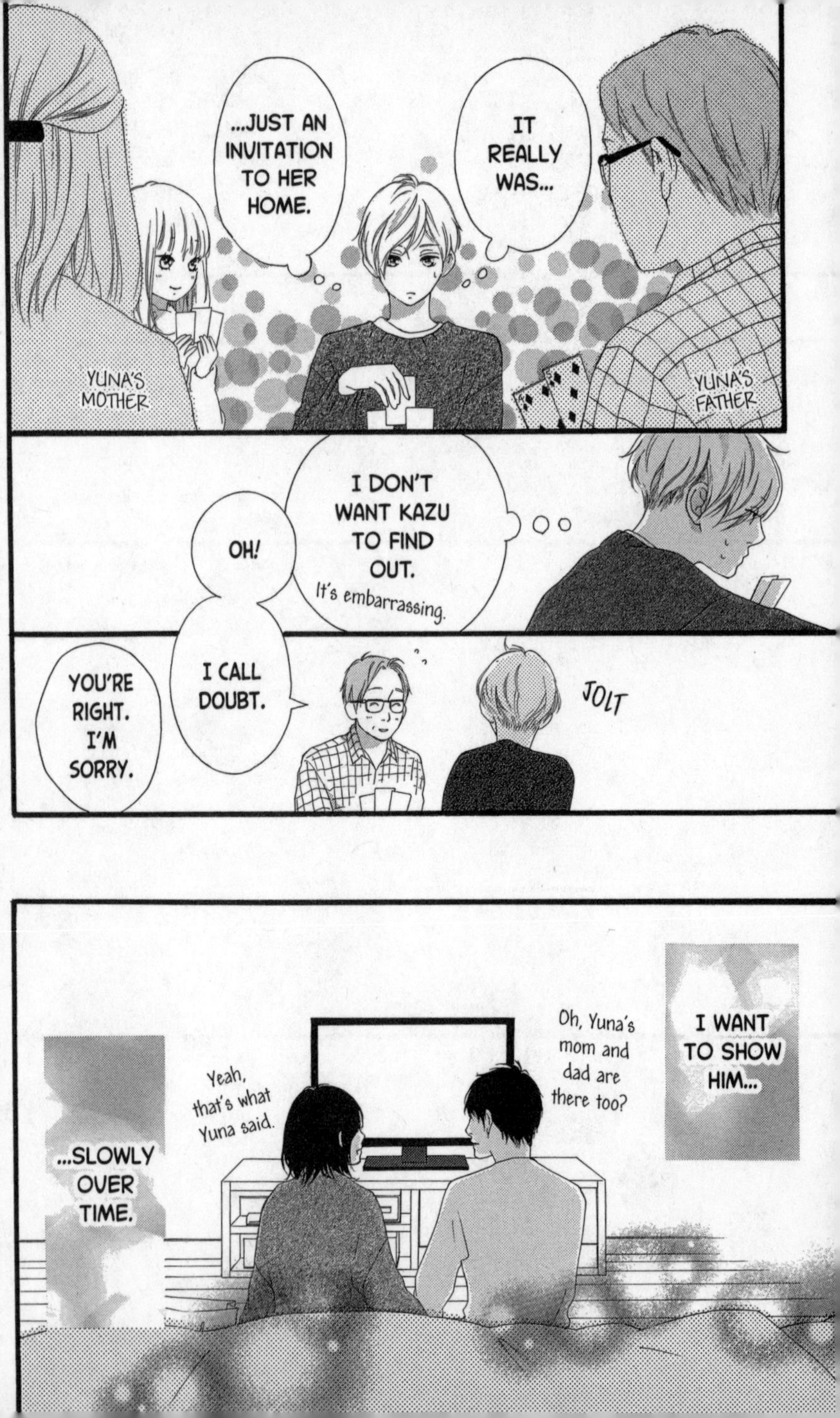
YUNA'S FATHER
IT REALLY WAS...
...JUST AN INVITATION TO HER HOME.
YUNA'S MOTHER
I DON'T WANT KAZU TO FIND OUT.
It's embarrassing.
OH!
JOLT
I CALL DOUBT.
YOU'RE RIGHT. I'M SORRY.
I WANT TO SHOW HIM...
Oh, Yuna's mom and dad are there too?
Yeah, that's what Yuna said.
...SLOWLY OVER TIME.

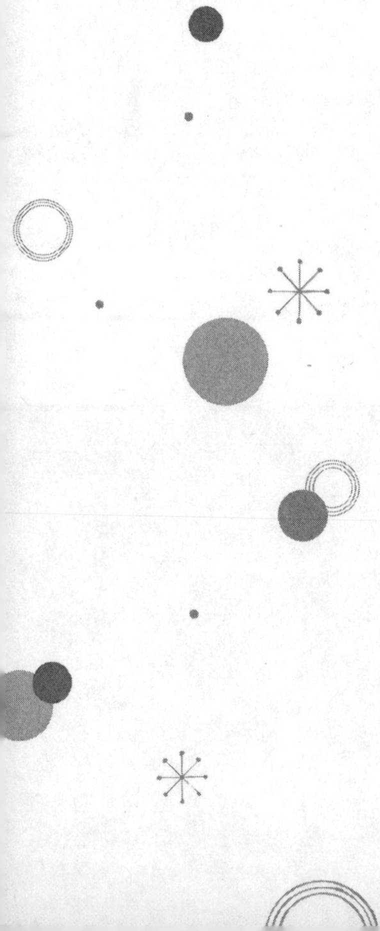

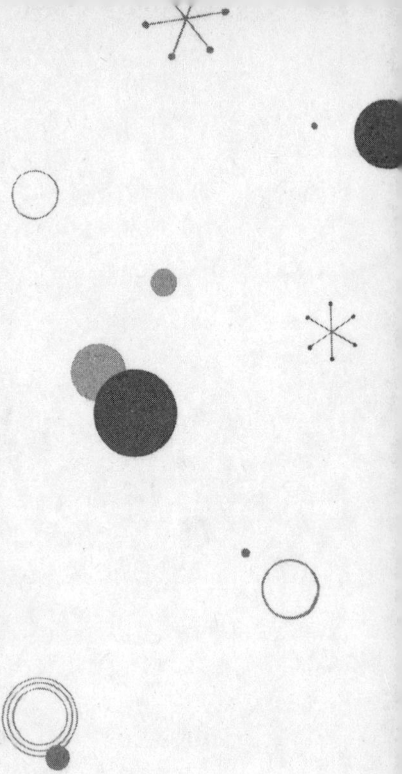

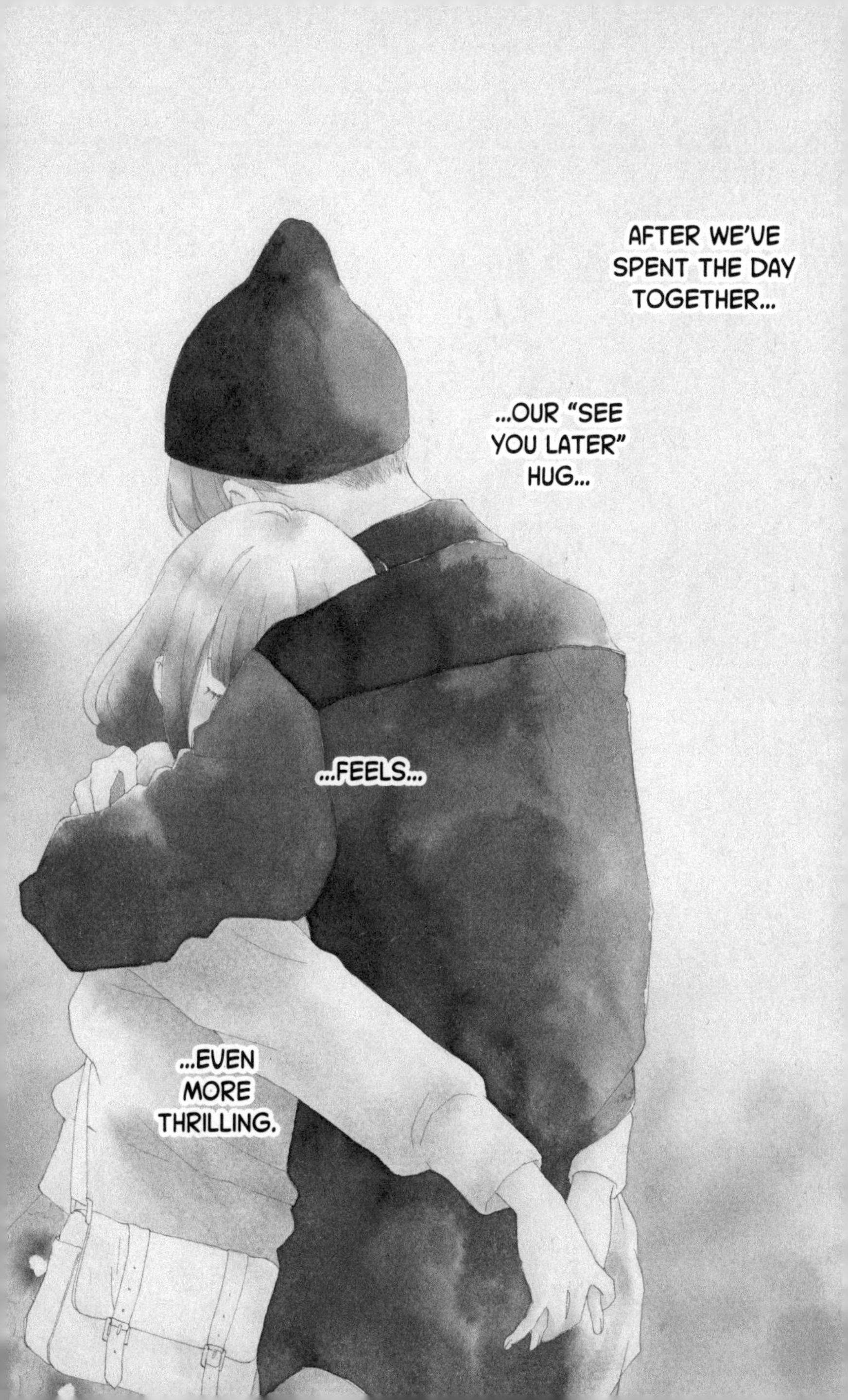
AFTER WE'VE SPENT THE DAY TOGETHER...
...OUR "SEE YOU LATER" HUG...
...FEELS...
...EVEN MORE THRILLING.

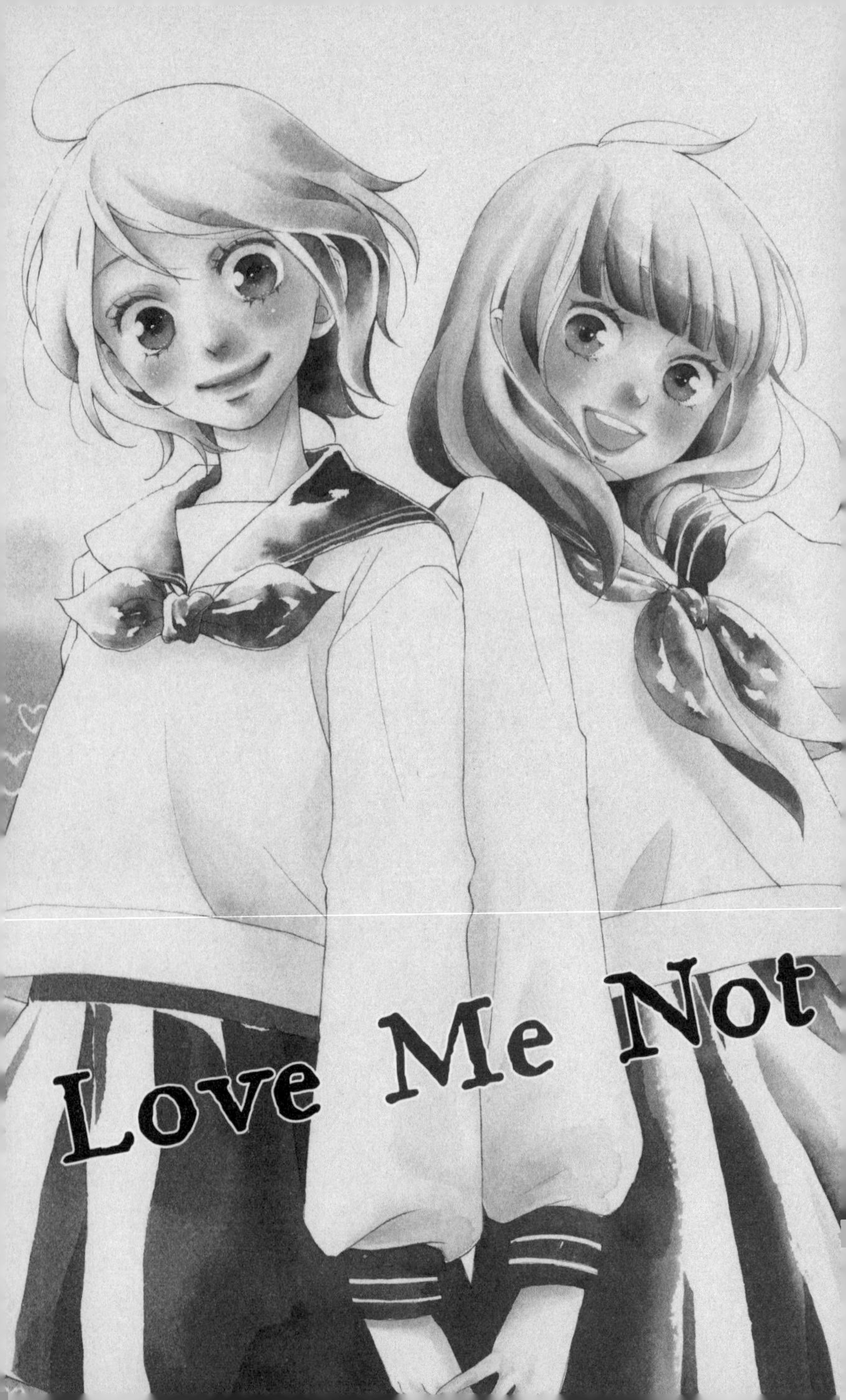
Love Me Not

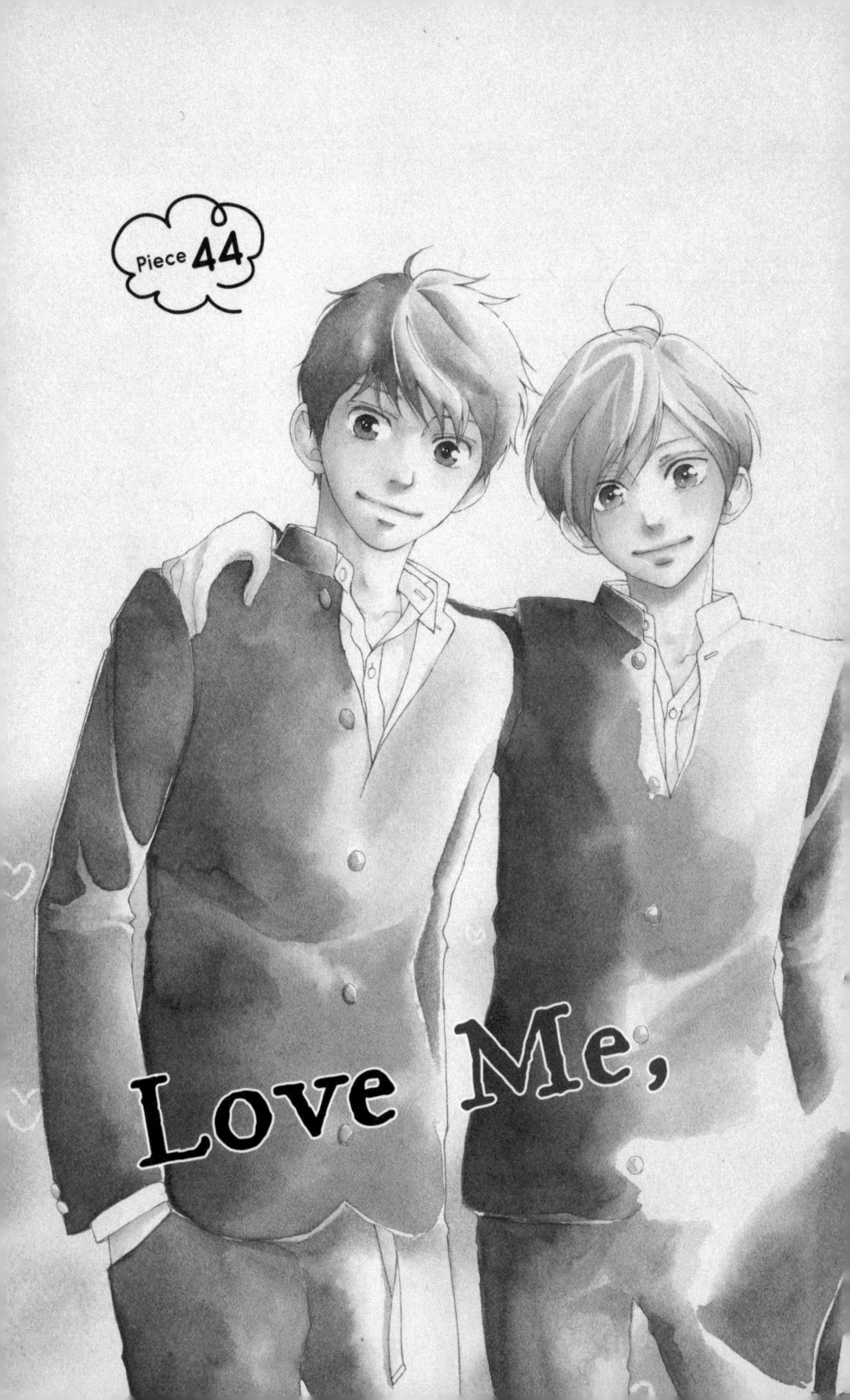
Piece 44
Love Me,

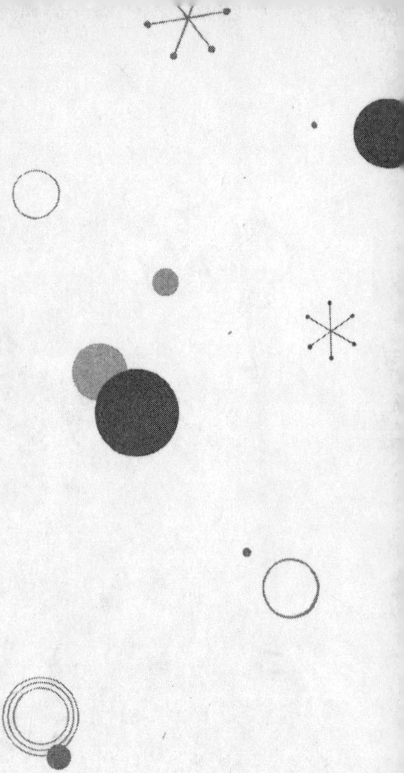

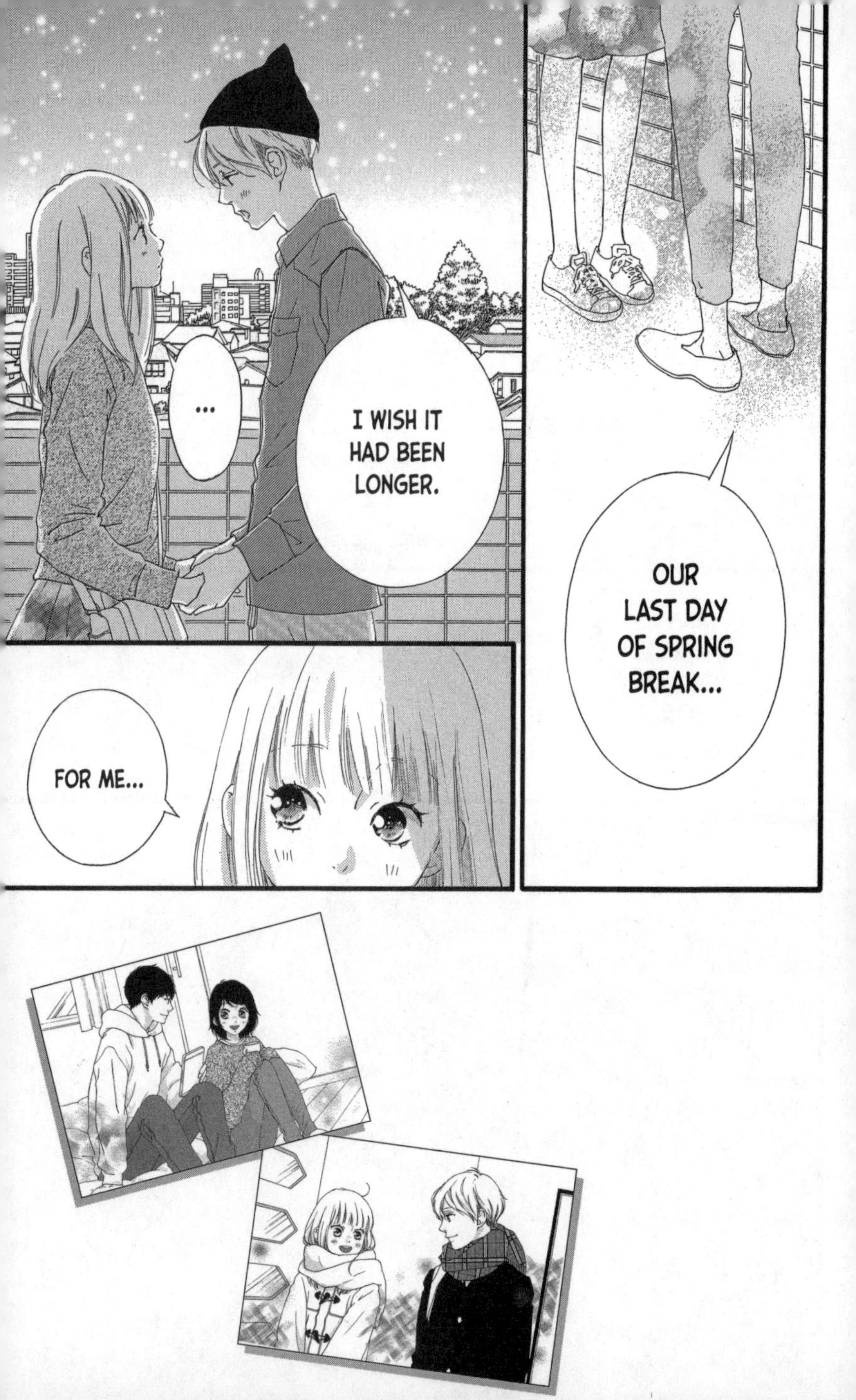
OUR LAST DAY OF SPRING BREAK...
I WISH IT HAD BEEN LONGER.
...
FOR ME...

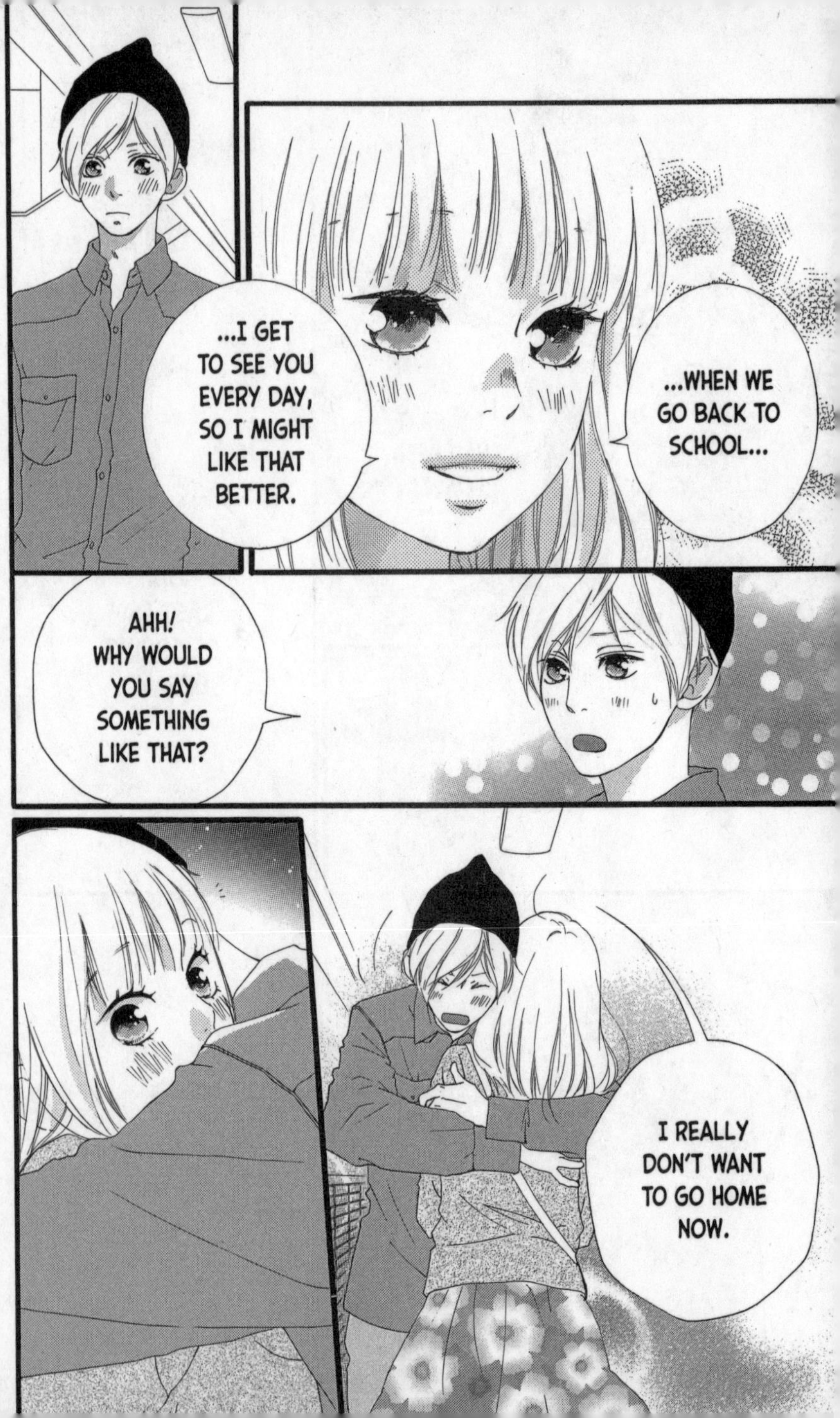
...WHEN WE GO BACK TO SCHOOL...
...I GET TO SEE YOU EVERY DAY, SO I MIGHT LIKE THAT BETTER.
AHH! WHY WOULD YOU SAY SOMETHING LIKE THAT?
I REALLY DON'T WANT TO GO HOME NOW.

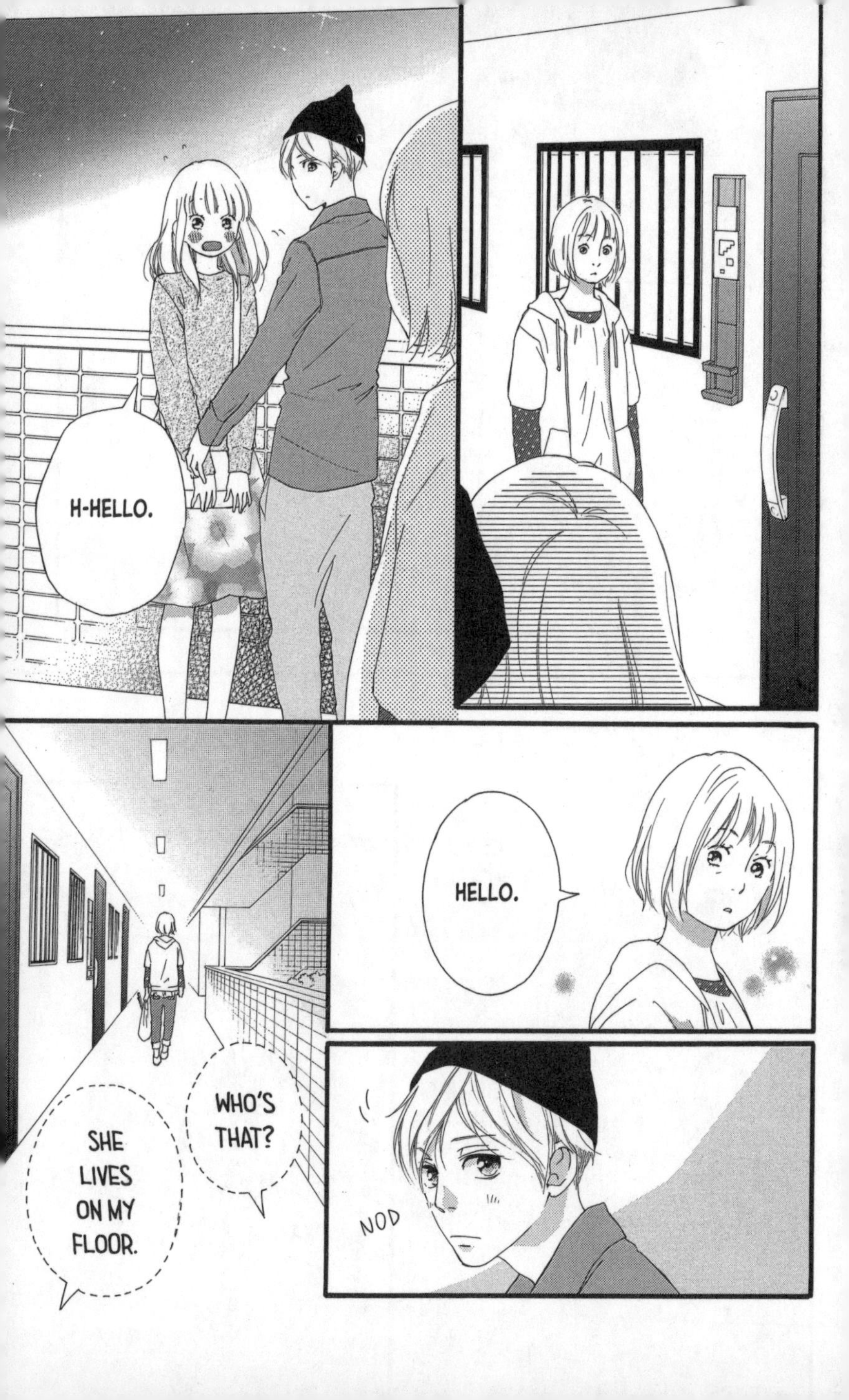
H-HELLO.
HELLO.
NOD
WHO'S THAT?
SHE LIVES ON MY FLOOR.

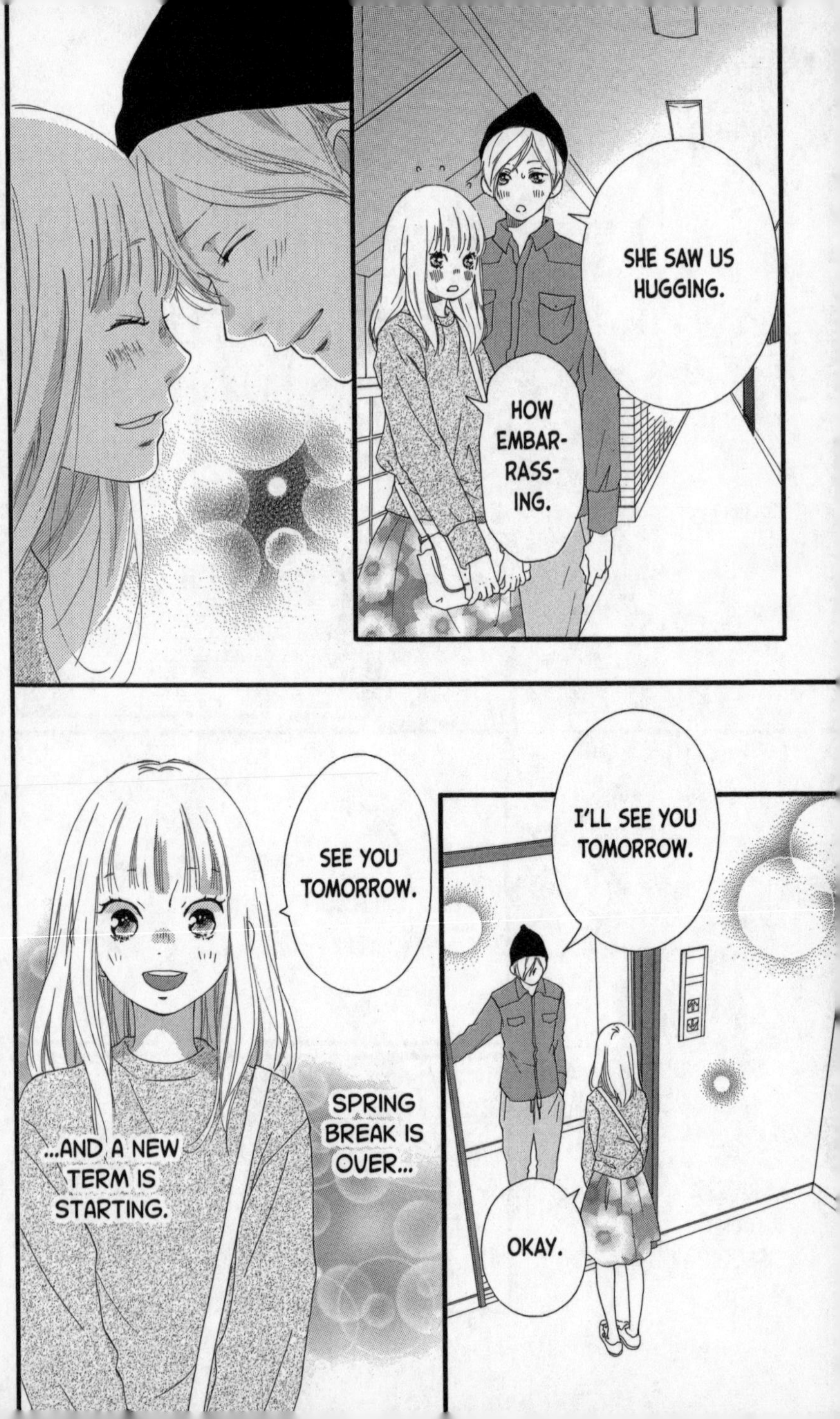
SHE SAW US HUGGING.
HOW EMBARRASSING.
I'LL SEE YOU TOMORROW.
OKAY.
SEE YOU TOMORROW.
SPRING BREAK IS OVER...
...AND A NEW TERM IS STARTING.

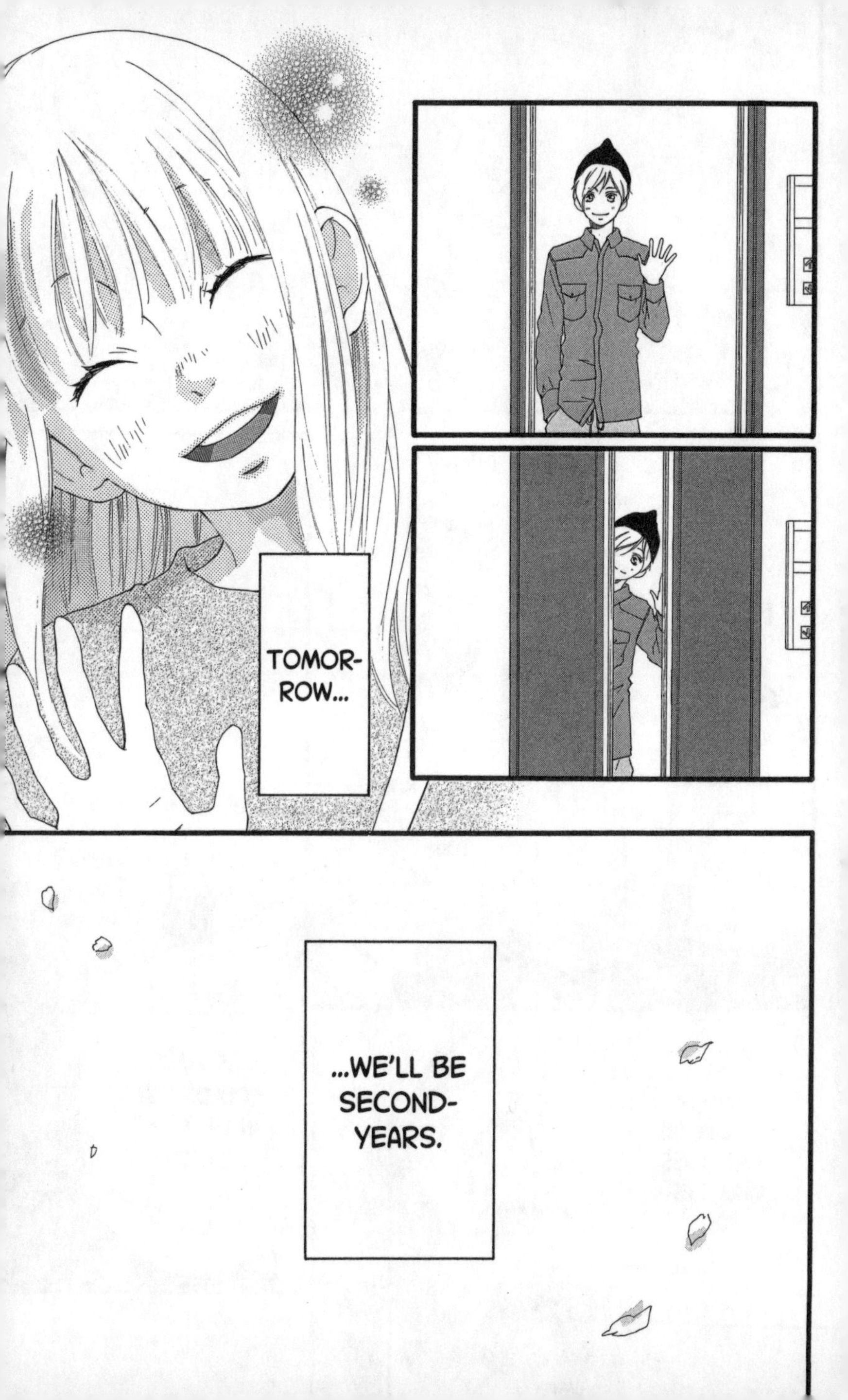
TOMOR-ROW...
...WE'LL BE SECOND-YEARS.

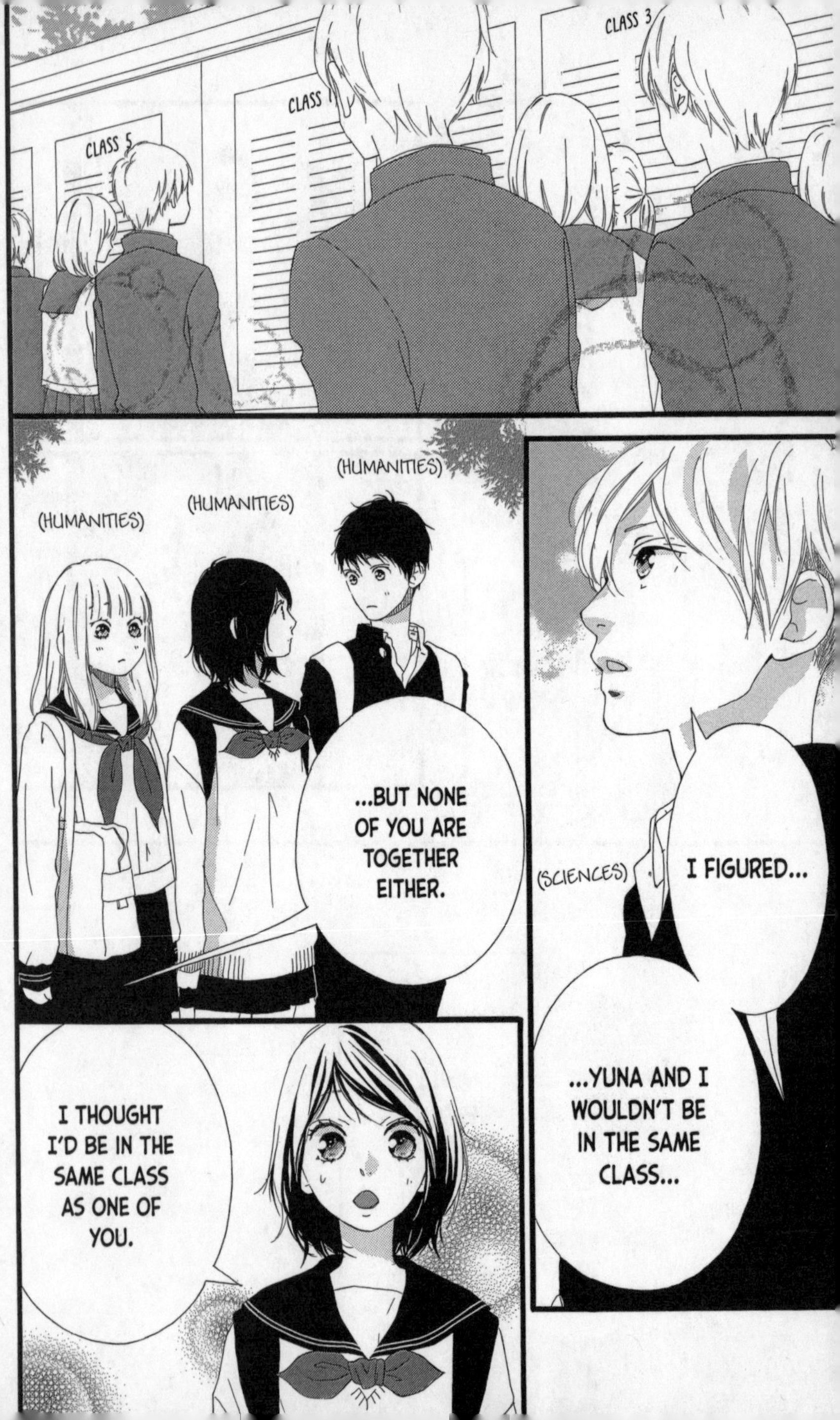
CLASS 3
CLASS 1
CLASS 5
I FIGURED...
(SCIENCES)
...YUNA AND I WOULDN'T BE IN THE SAME CLASS...
(HUMANITIES)
(HUMANITIES)
(HUMANITIES)
...BUT NONE OF YOU ARE TOGETHER EITHER.
I THOUGHT I'D BE IN THE SAME CLASS AS ONE OF YOU.

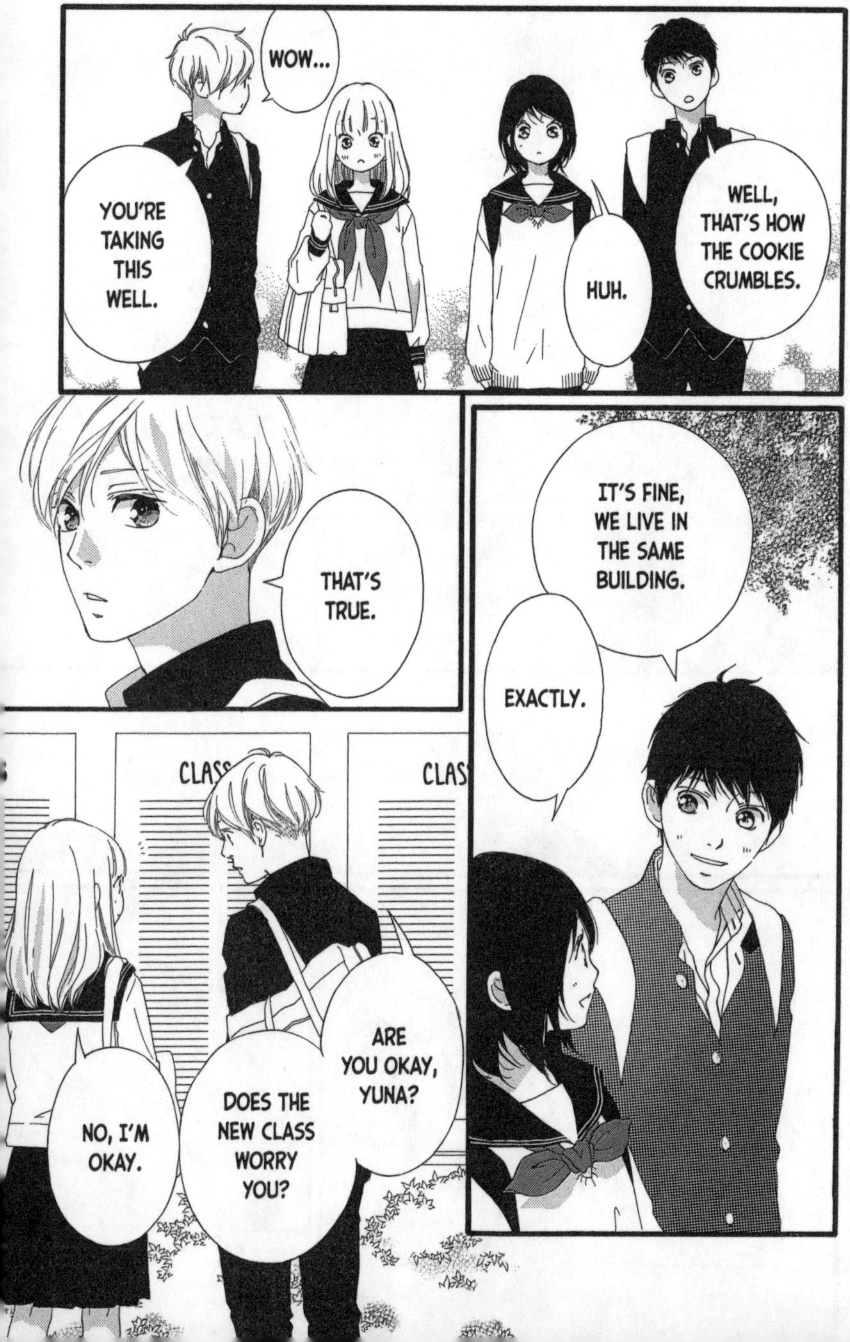
WELL, THAT'S HOW THE COOKIE CRUMBLES.
HUH.
WOW...
YOU'RE TAKING THIS WELL.
IT'S FINE, WE LIVE IN THE SAME BUILDING.
EXACTLY.
THAT'S TRUE.
CLAS
CLASS
ARE YOU OKAY, YUNA?
DOES THE NEW CLASS WORRY YOU?
NO, I'M OKAY.

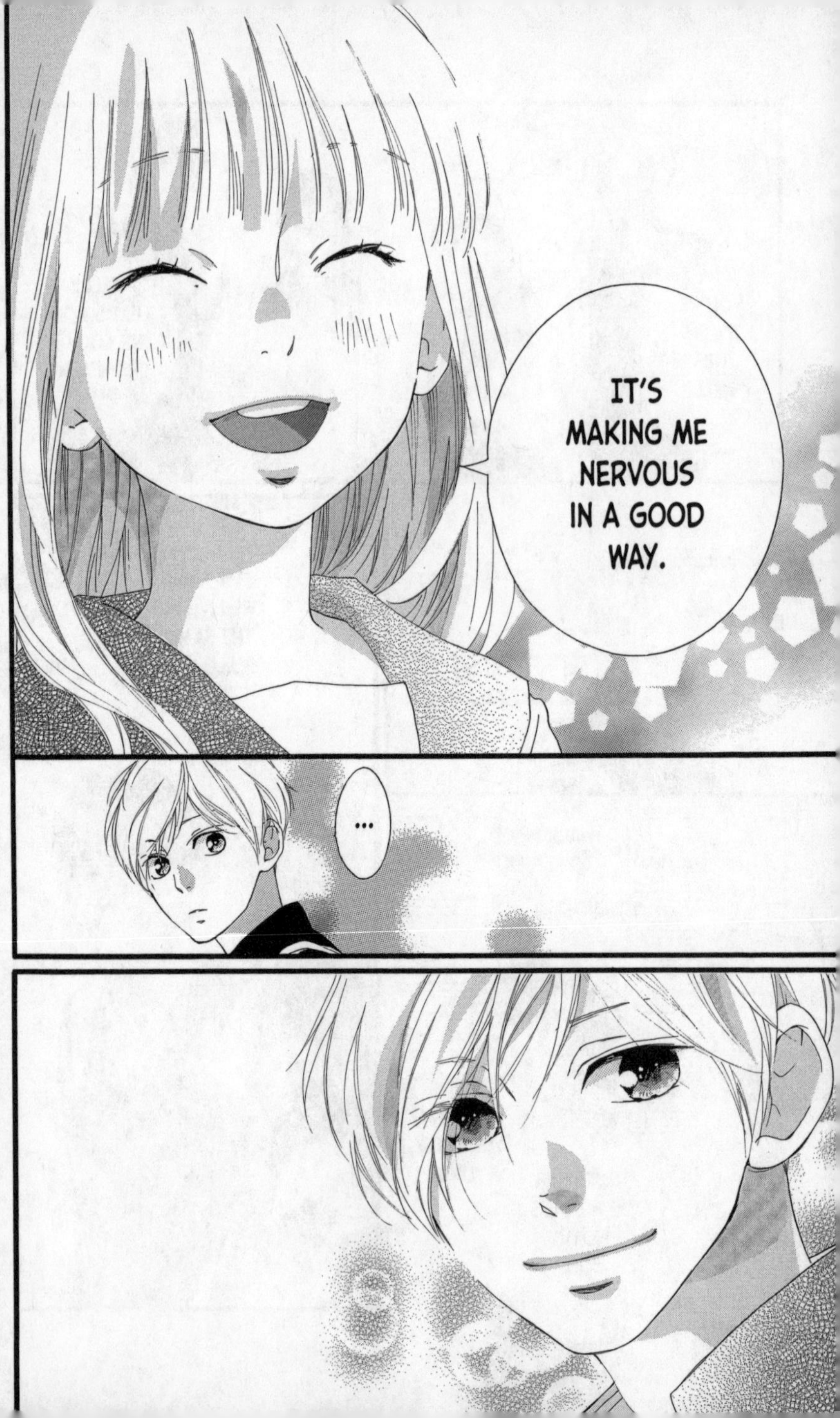
IT'S MAKING ME NERVOUS IN A GOOD WAY.
...

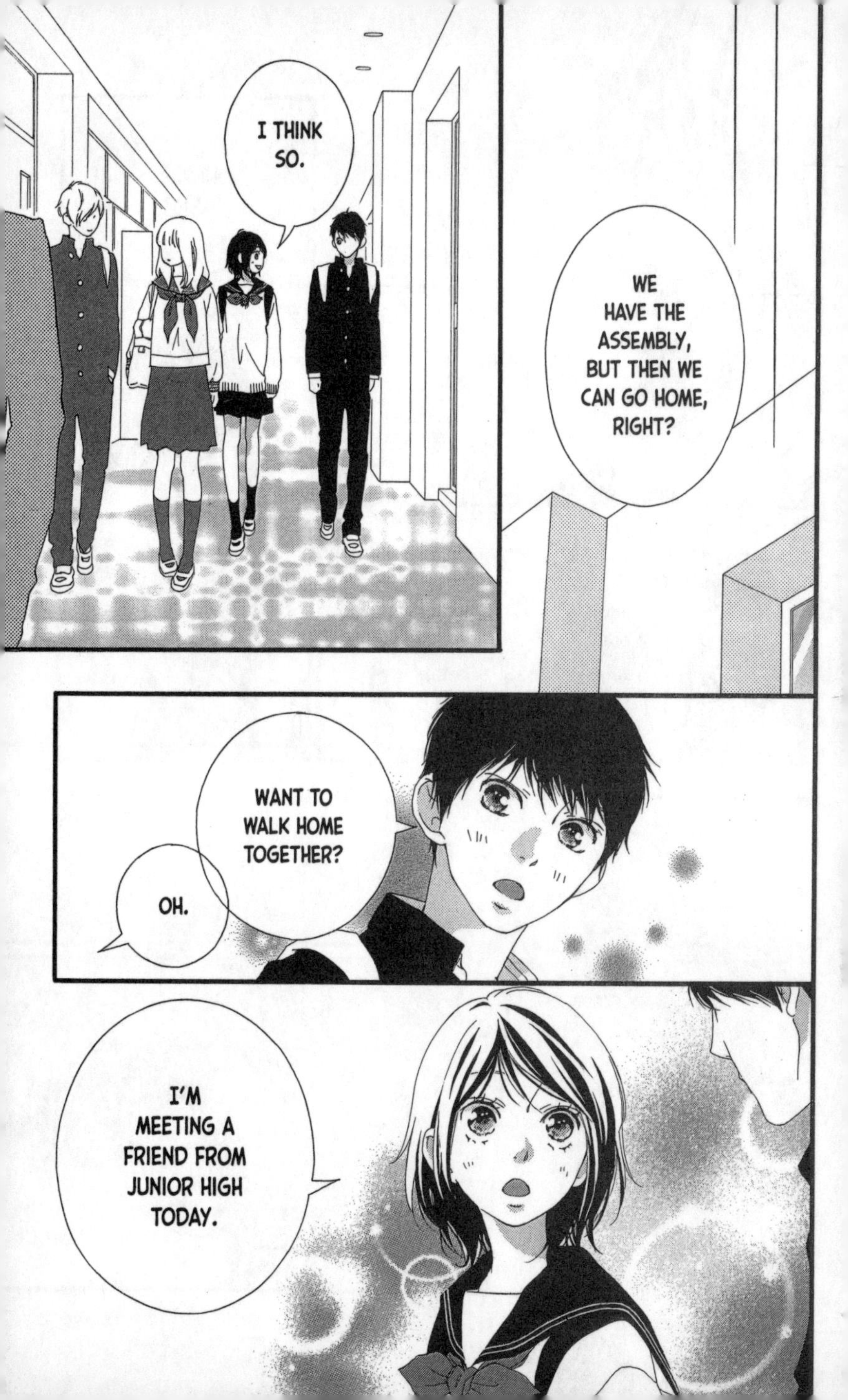
WE HAVE THE ASSEMBLY, BUT THEN WE CAN GO HOME, RIGHT?
I THINK SO.
WANT TO WALK HOME TOGETHER?
OH.
I'M MEETING A FRIEND FROM JUNIOR HIGH TODAY.

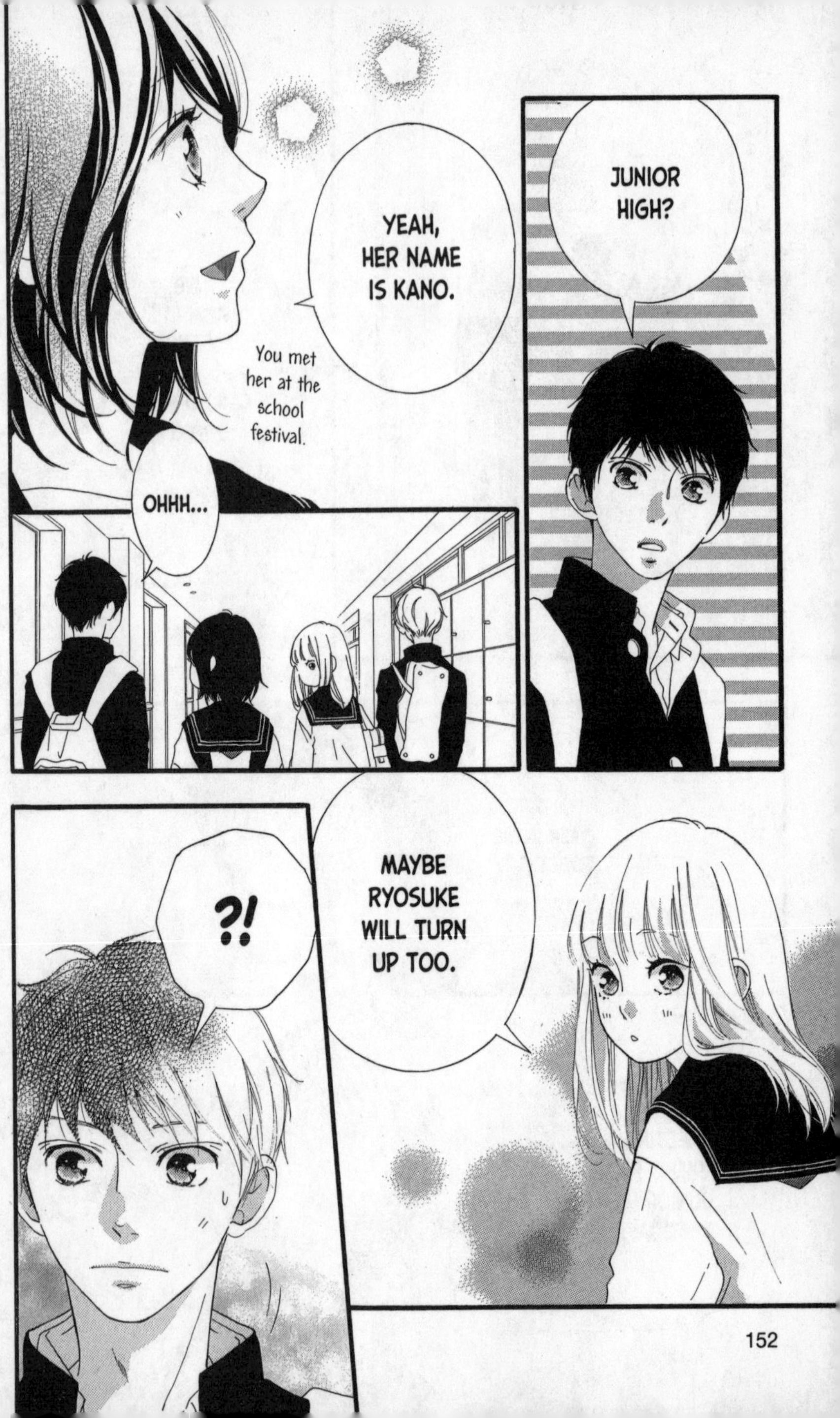
JUNIOR HIGH?
YEAH, HER NAME IS KANO.
You met her at the school festival.
OHHH...
MAYBE RYOSUKE WILL TURN UP TOO.
?!

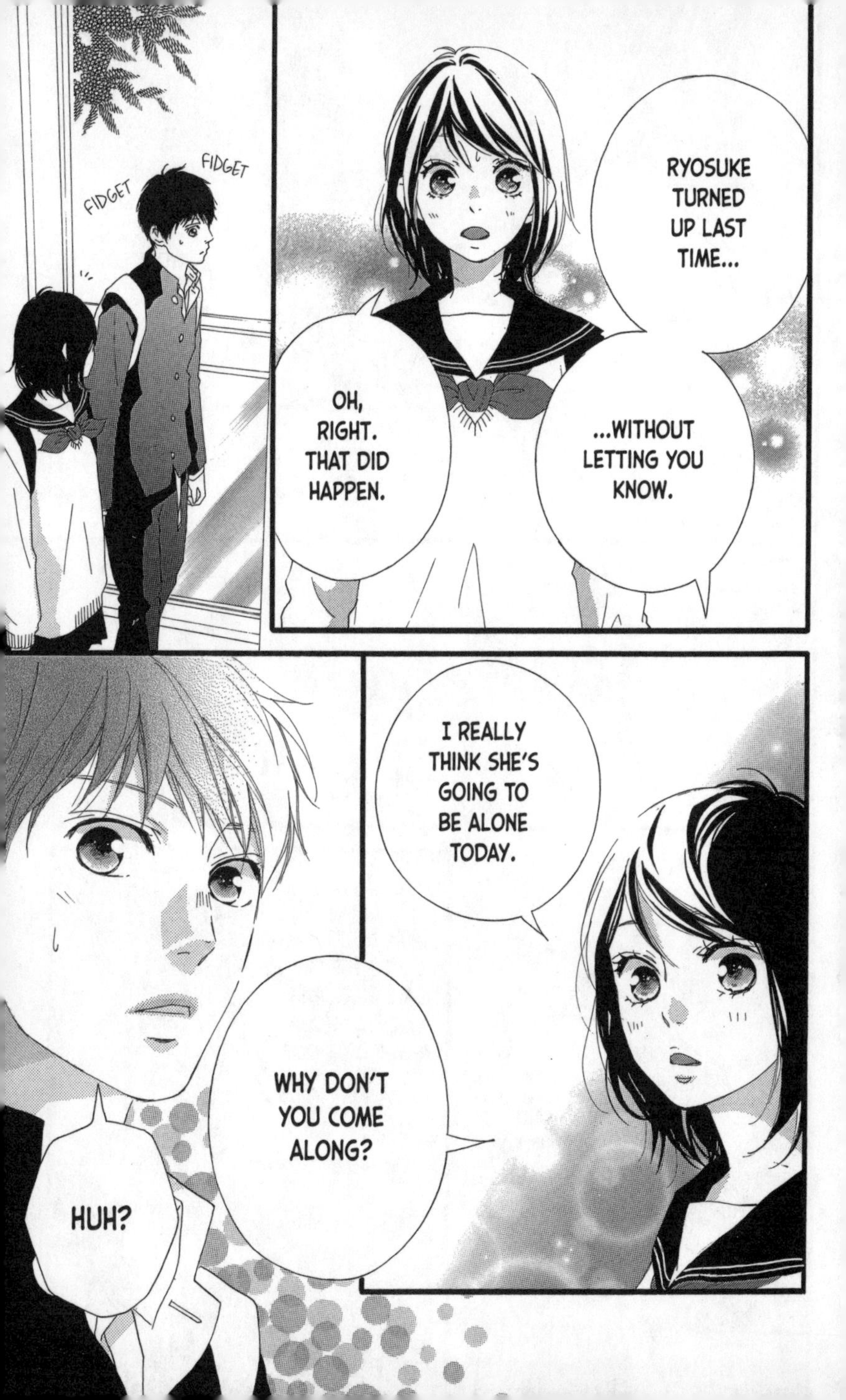
RYOSUKE TURNED UP LAST TIME...
...WITHOUT LETTING YOU KNOW.
OH, RIGHT. THAT DID HAPPEN.
FIDGET
FIDGET
I REALLY THINK SHE'S GOING TO BE ALONE TODAY.
WHY DON'T YOU COME ALONG?
HUH?

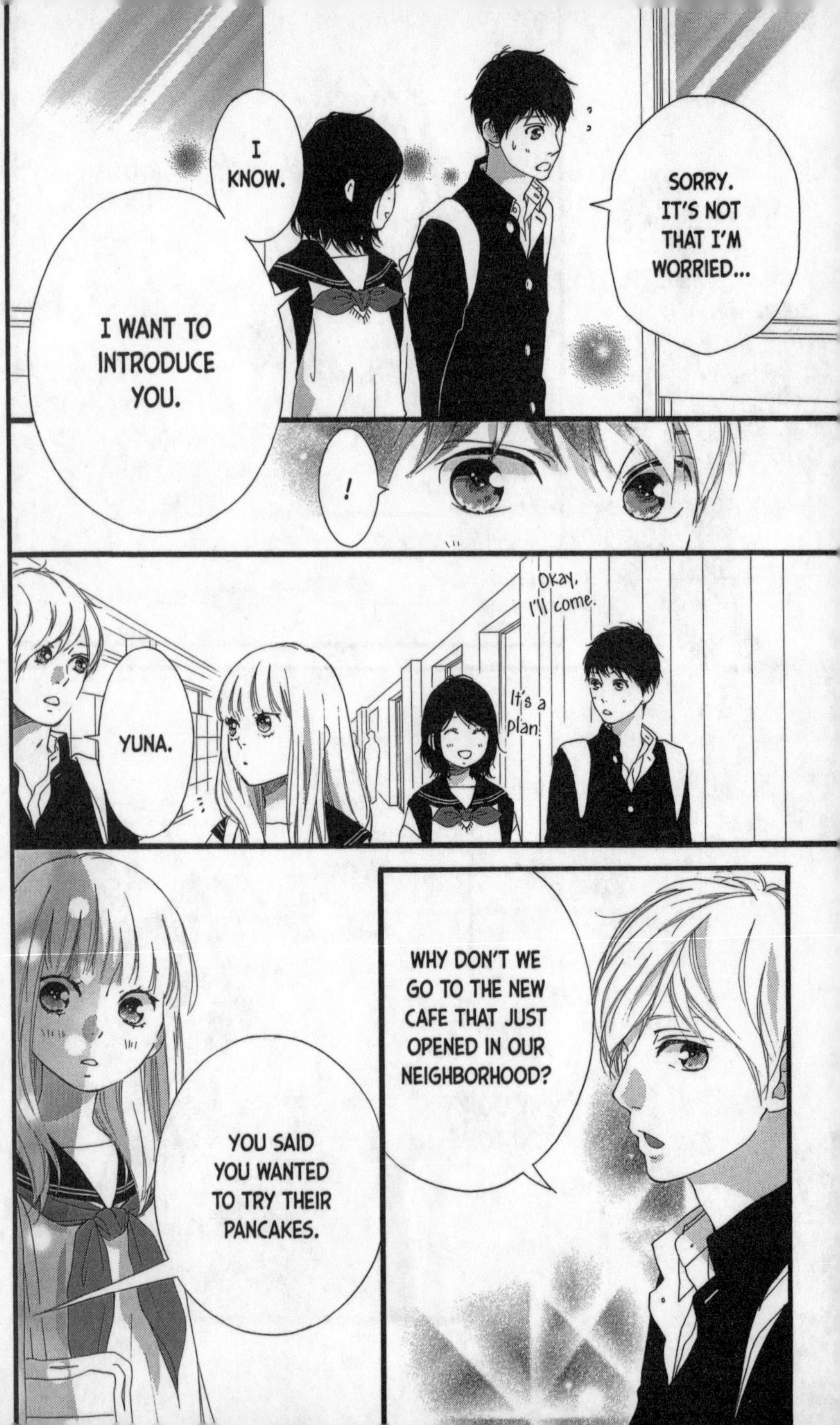
SORRY. IT'S NOT THAT I'M WORRIED...
I KNOW.
I WANT TO INTRODUCE YOU.
!
Okay, I'll come.
It's a plan!
YUNA.
WHY DON'T WE GO TO THE NEW CAFE THAT JUST OPENED IN OUR NEIGHBORHOOD?
YOU SAID YOU WANTED TO TRY THEIR PANCAKES.

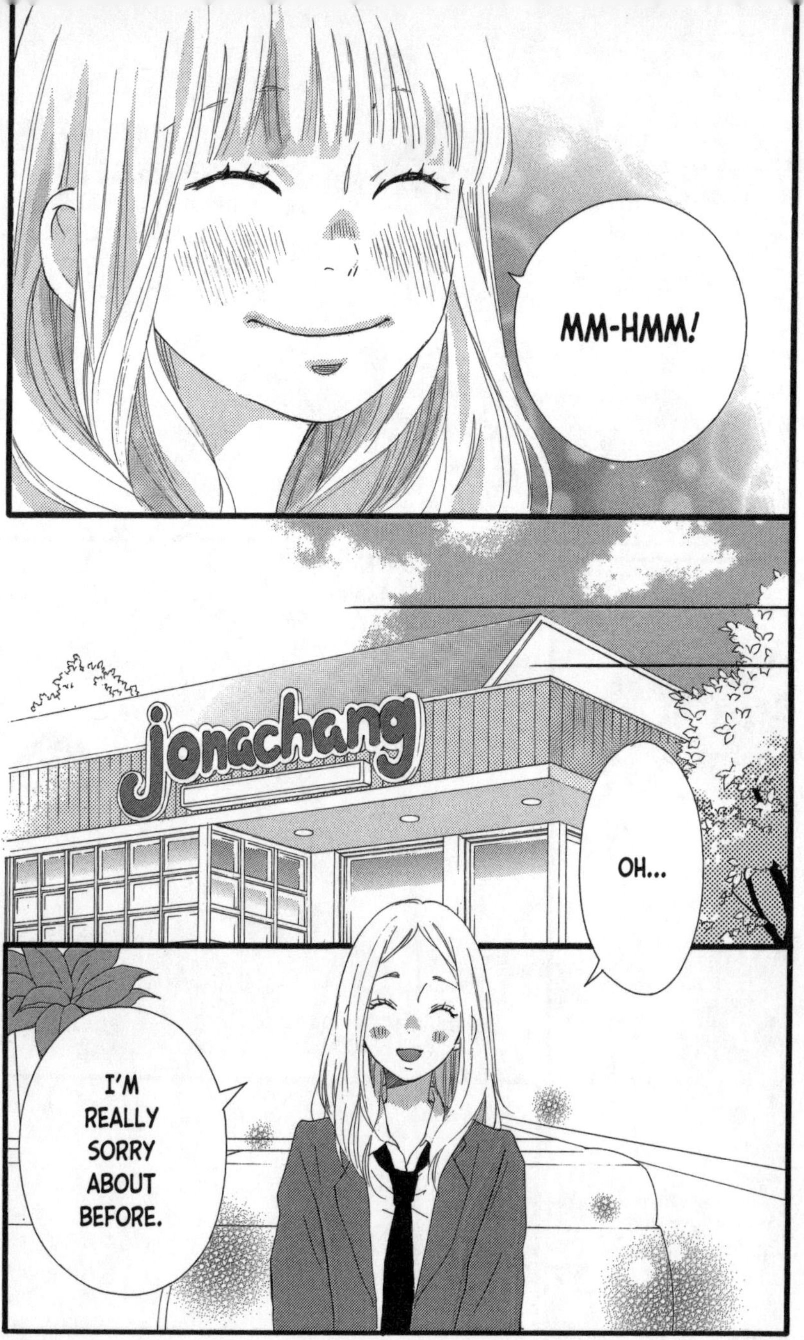
MM-HMM!
OH...
jonachang
I'M REALLY SORRY ABOUT BEFORE.

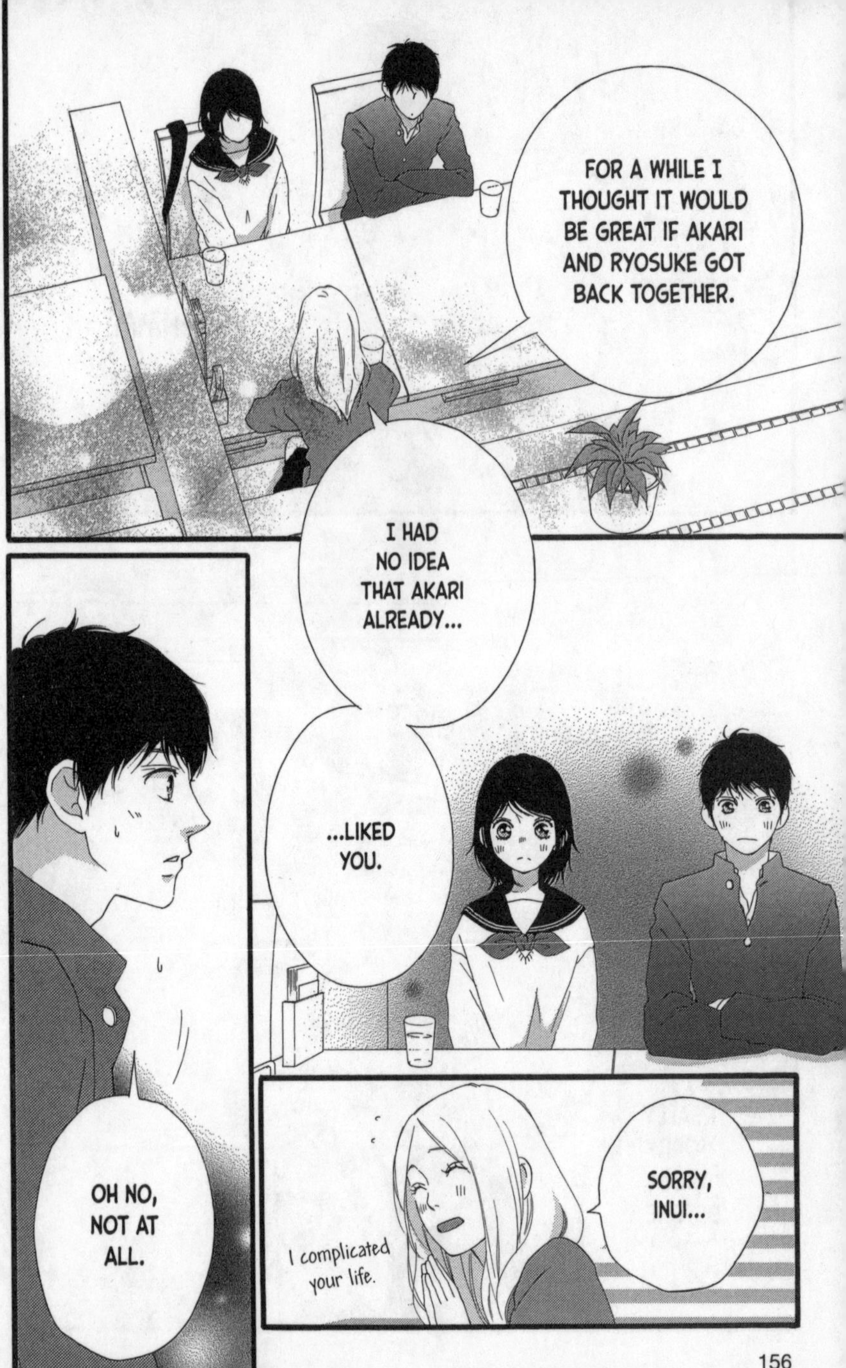
FOR A WHILE I THOUGHT IT WOULD BE GREAT IF AKARI AND RYOSUKE GOT BACK TOGETHER.
I HAD NO IDEA THAT AKARI ALREADY...
...LIKED YOU.
SORRY, INUI...
I complicated your life.
OH NO, NOT AT ALL.

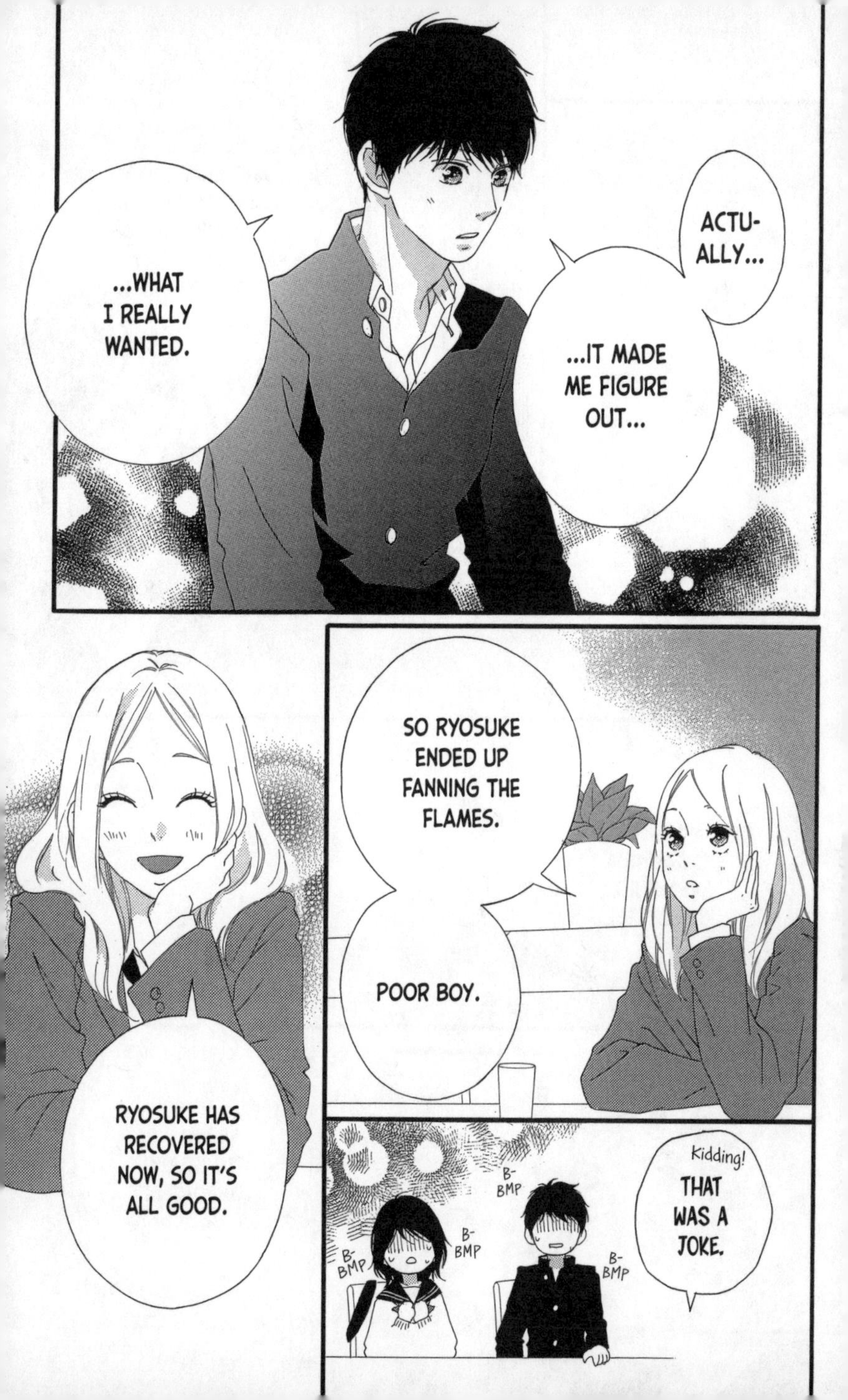
ACTU-ALLY...
...IT MADE ME FIGURE OUT...
...WHAT I REALLY WANTED.
SO RYOSUKE ENDED UP FANNING THE FLAMES.
POOR BOY.
Kidding!
THAT WAS A JOKE.
B-BMP
B-BMP
B-BMP
B-BMP
RYOSUKE HAS RECOVERED NOW, SO IT'S ALL GOOD.

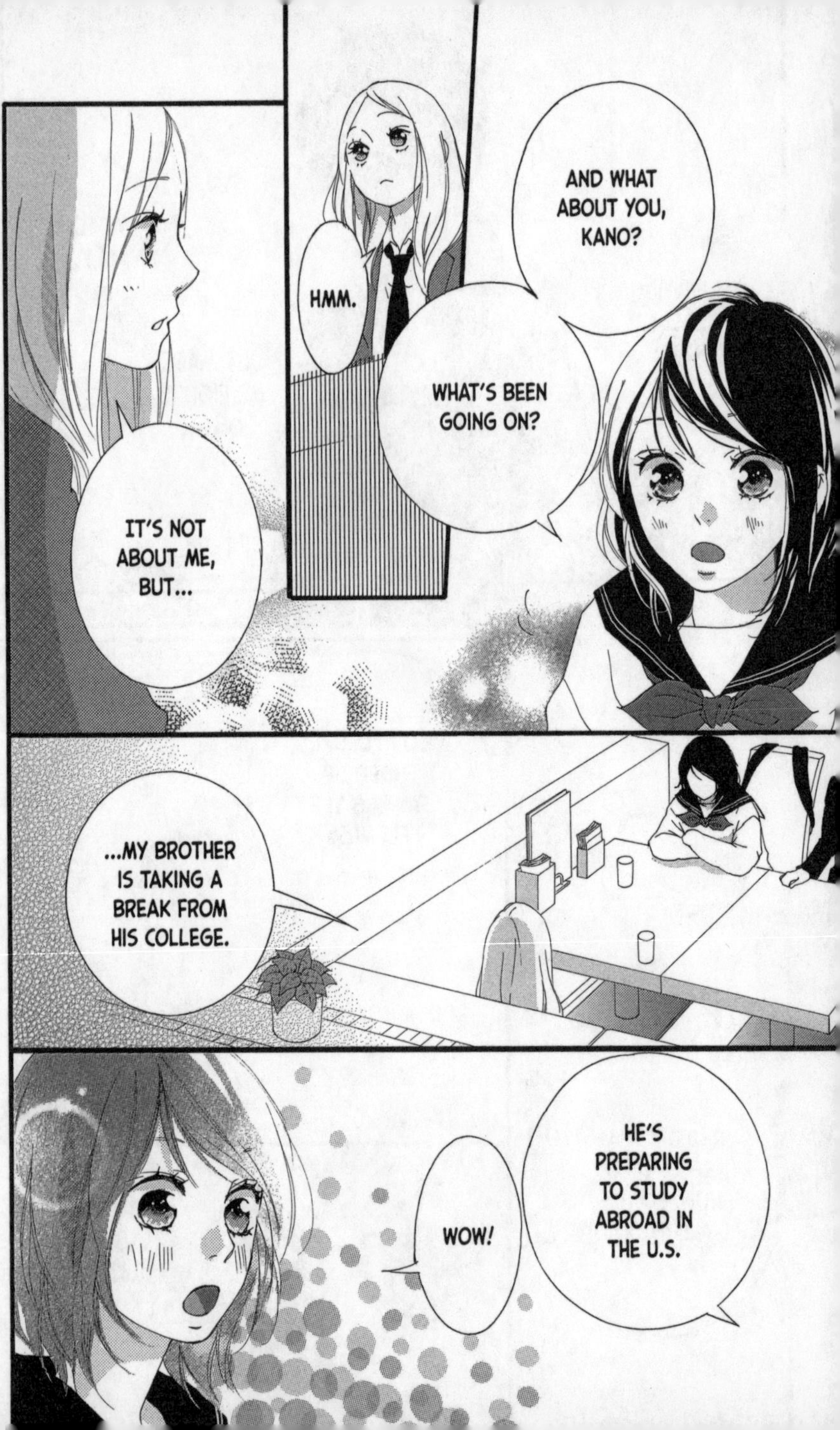
AND WHAT ABOUT YOU, KANO?
WHAT'S BEEN GOING ON?
HMM.
IT'S NOT ABOUT ME, BUT...
...MY BROTHER IS TAKING A BREAK FROM HIS COLLEGE.
HE'S PREPARING TO STUDY ABROAD IN THE U.S.
WOW!

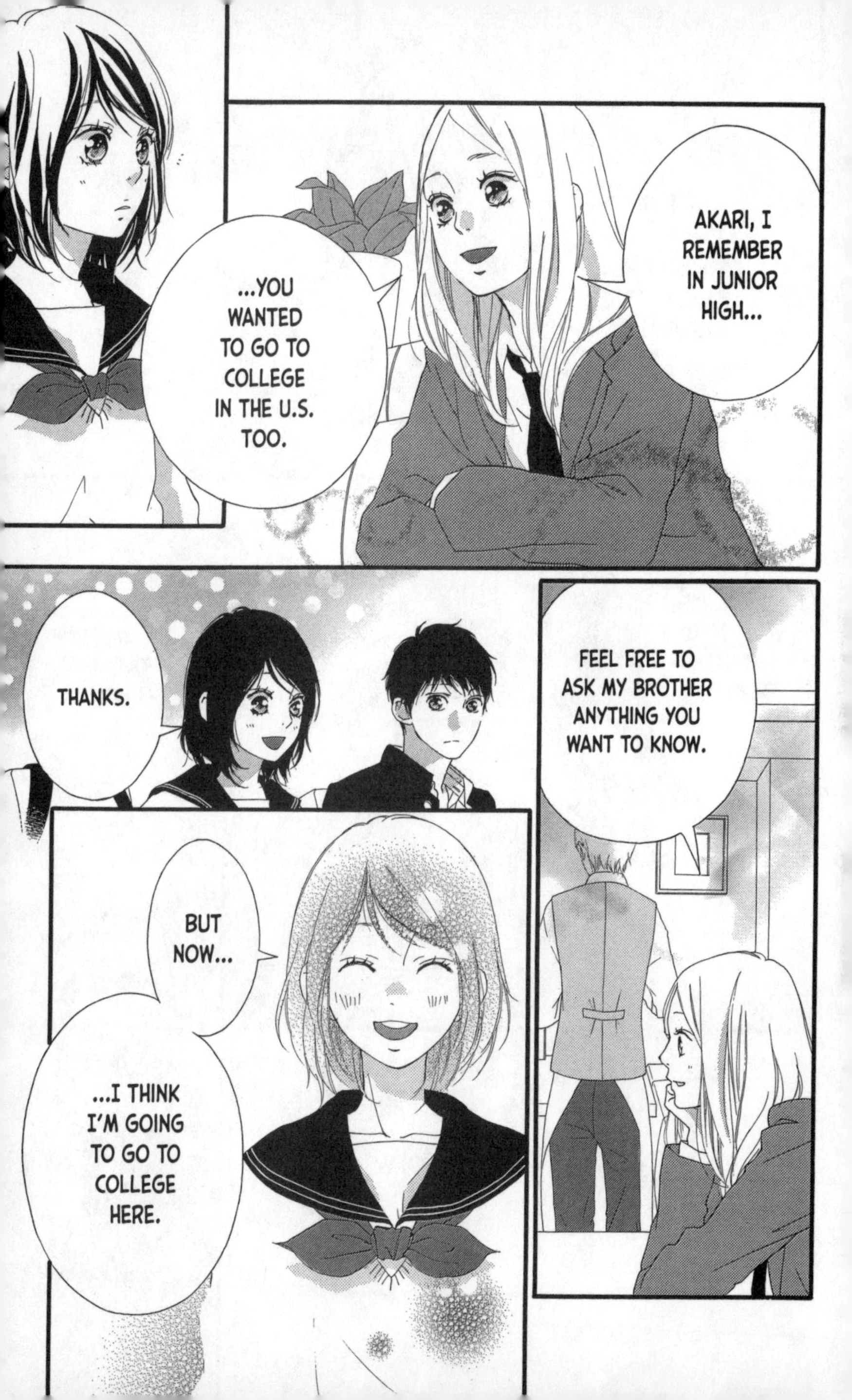
AKARI, I REMEMBER IN JUNIOR HIGH...
...YOU WANTED TO GO TO COLLEGE IN THE U.S. TOO.
FEEL FREE TO ASK MY BROTHER ANYTHING YOU WANT TO KNOW.
THANKS.
BUT NOW...
...I THINK I'M GOING TO GO TO COLLEGE HERE.

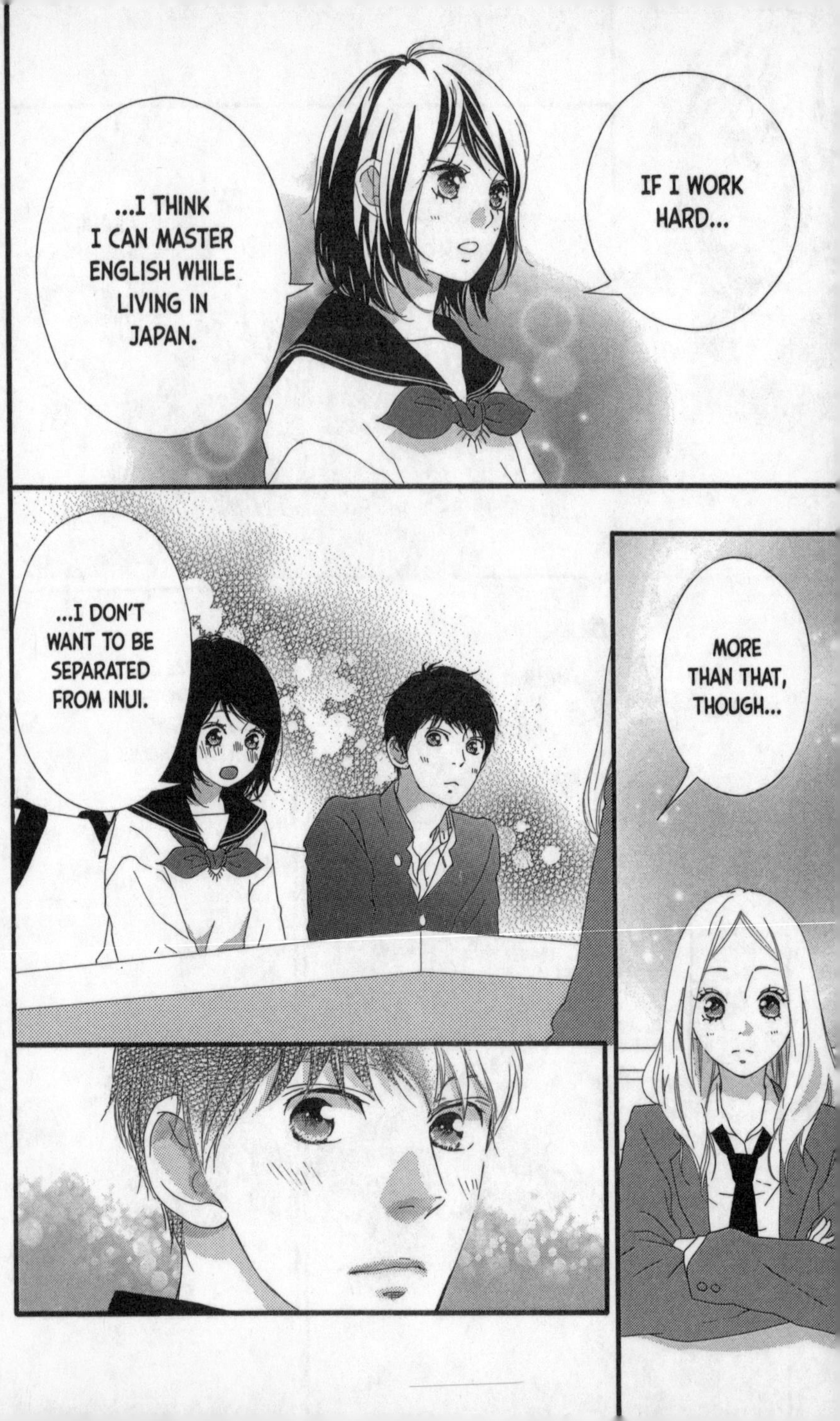
IF I WORK HARD...
...I THINK I CAN MASTER ENGLISH WHILE LIVING IN JAPAN.
MORE THAN THAT, THOUGH...
...I DON'T WANT TO BE SEPARATED FROM INUI.

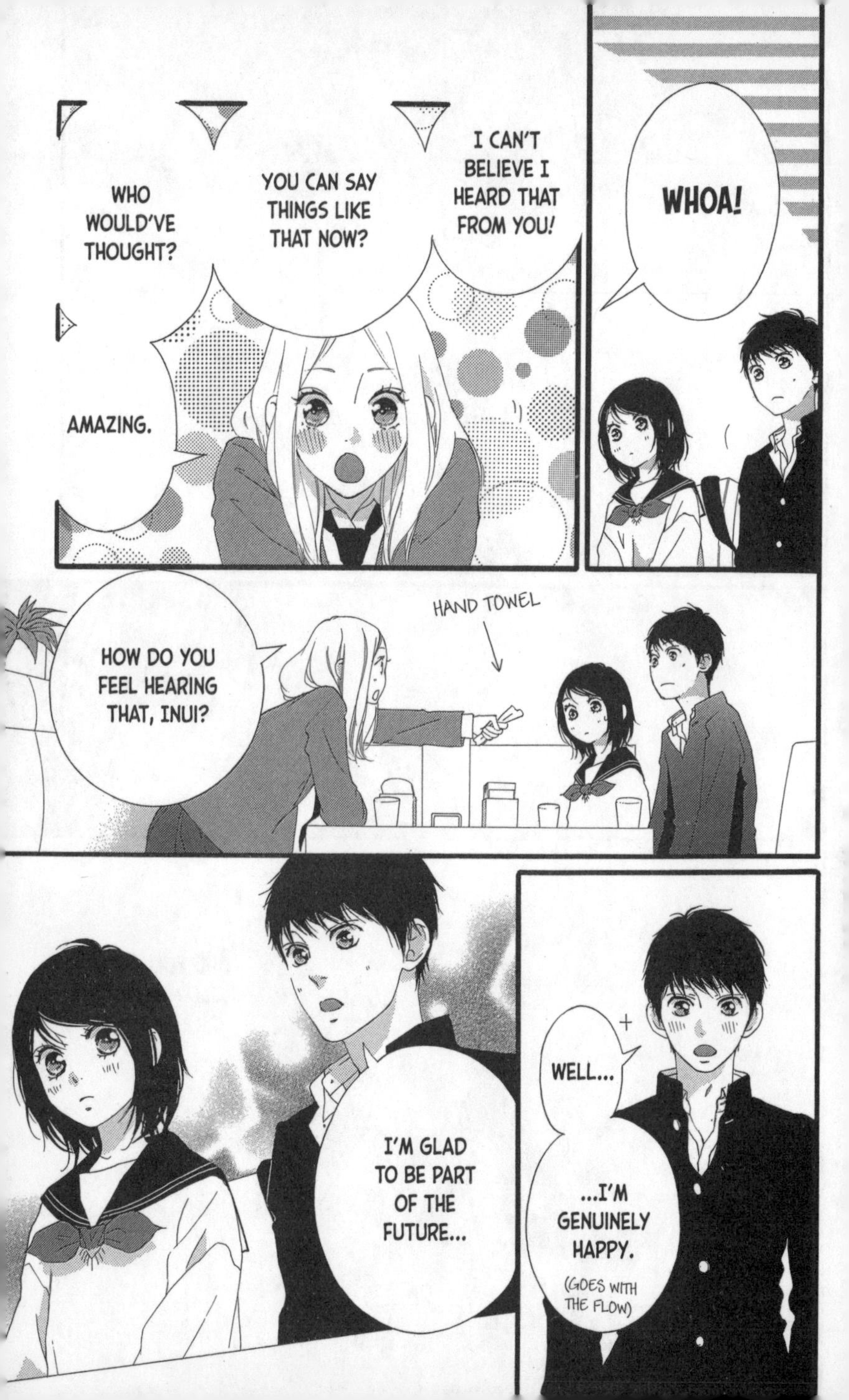
WHOA!
I CAN'T BELIEVE I HEARD THAT FROM YOU!
YOU CAN SAY THINGS LIKE THAT NOW?
WHO WOULD'VE THOUGHT?
AMAZING.
HAND TOWEL
HOW DO YOU FEEL HEARING THAT, INUI?
WELL...
...I'M GENUINELY HAPPY.
(GOES WITH THE FLOW)
I'M GLAD TO BE PART OF THE FUTURE...

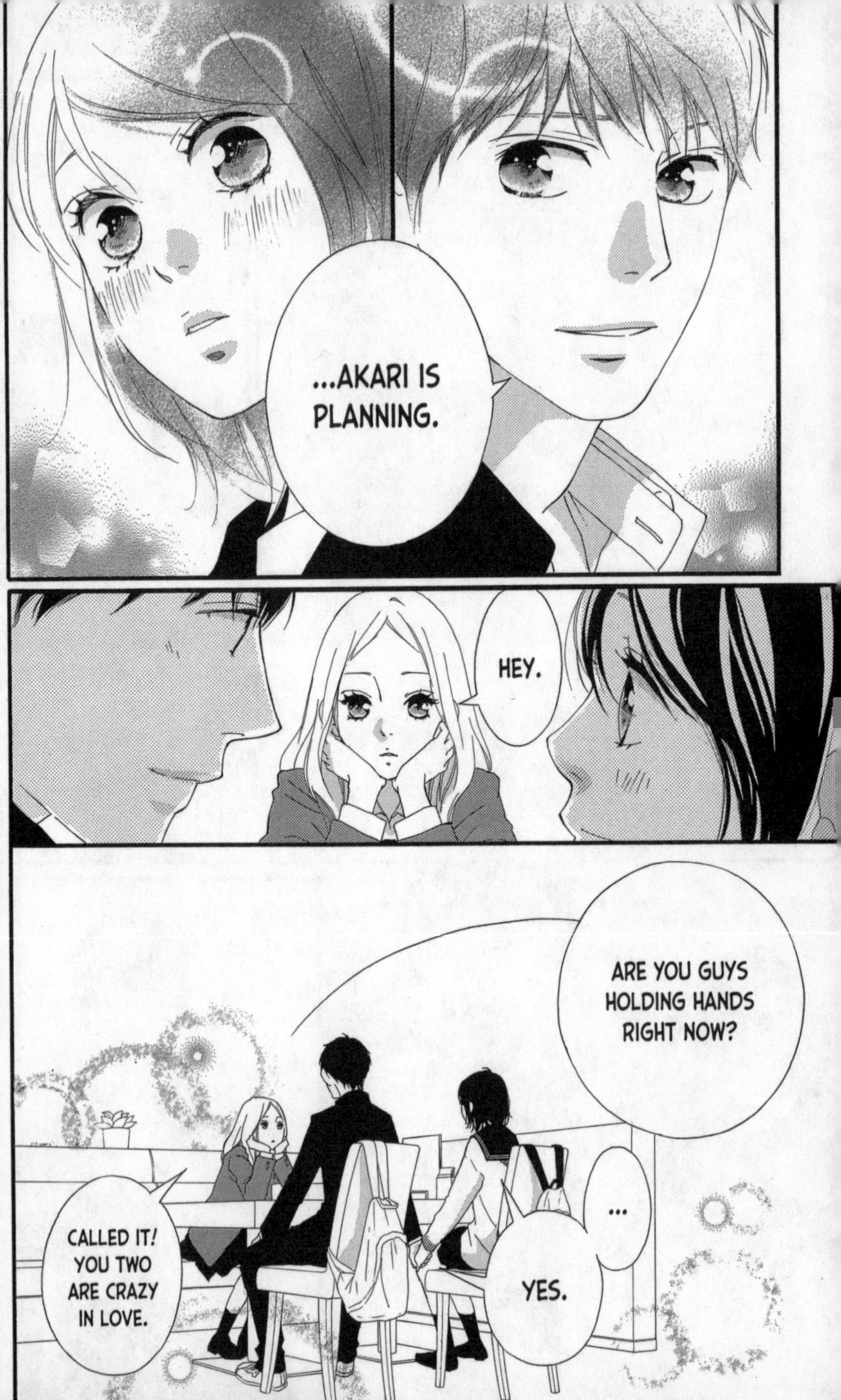
...AKARI IS PLANNING.
HEY.
ARE YOU GUYS HOLDING HANDS RIGHT NOW?
...
YES.
CALLED IT! YOU TWO ARE CRAZY IN LOVE.

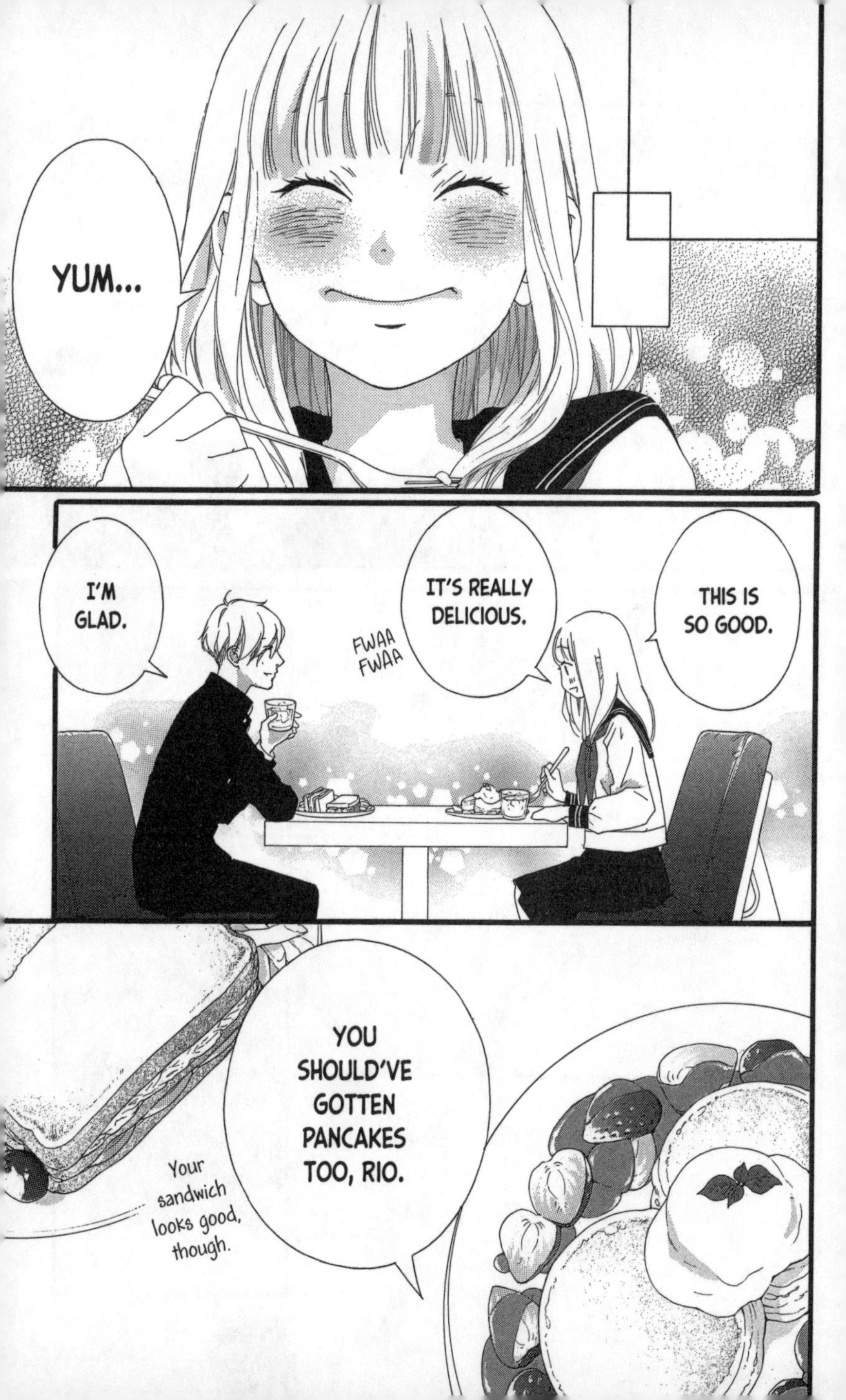
YUM...
THIS IS SO GOOD.
IT'S REALLY DELICIOUS.
FWAA FWAA
I'M GLAD.
YOU SHOULD'VE GOTTEN PANCAKES TOO, RIO.
Your sandwich looks good, though.

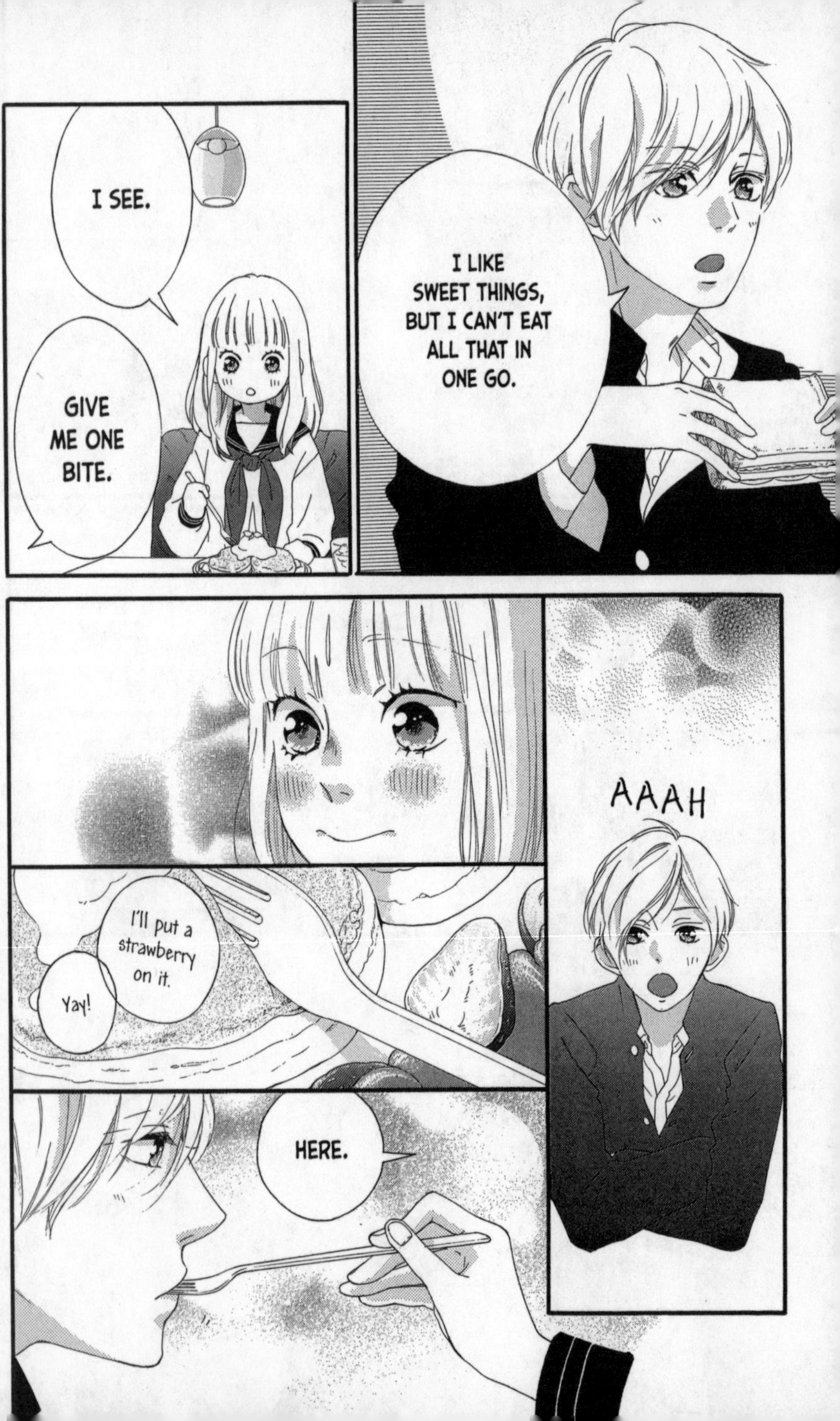
I LIKE SWEET THINGS, BUT I CAN'T EAT ALL THAT IN ONE GO.
I SEE.
GIVE ME ONE BITE.
AAAH
I'll put a strawberry on it.
Yay!
HERE.

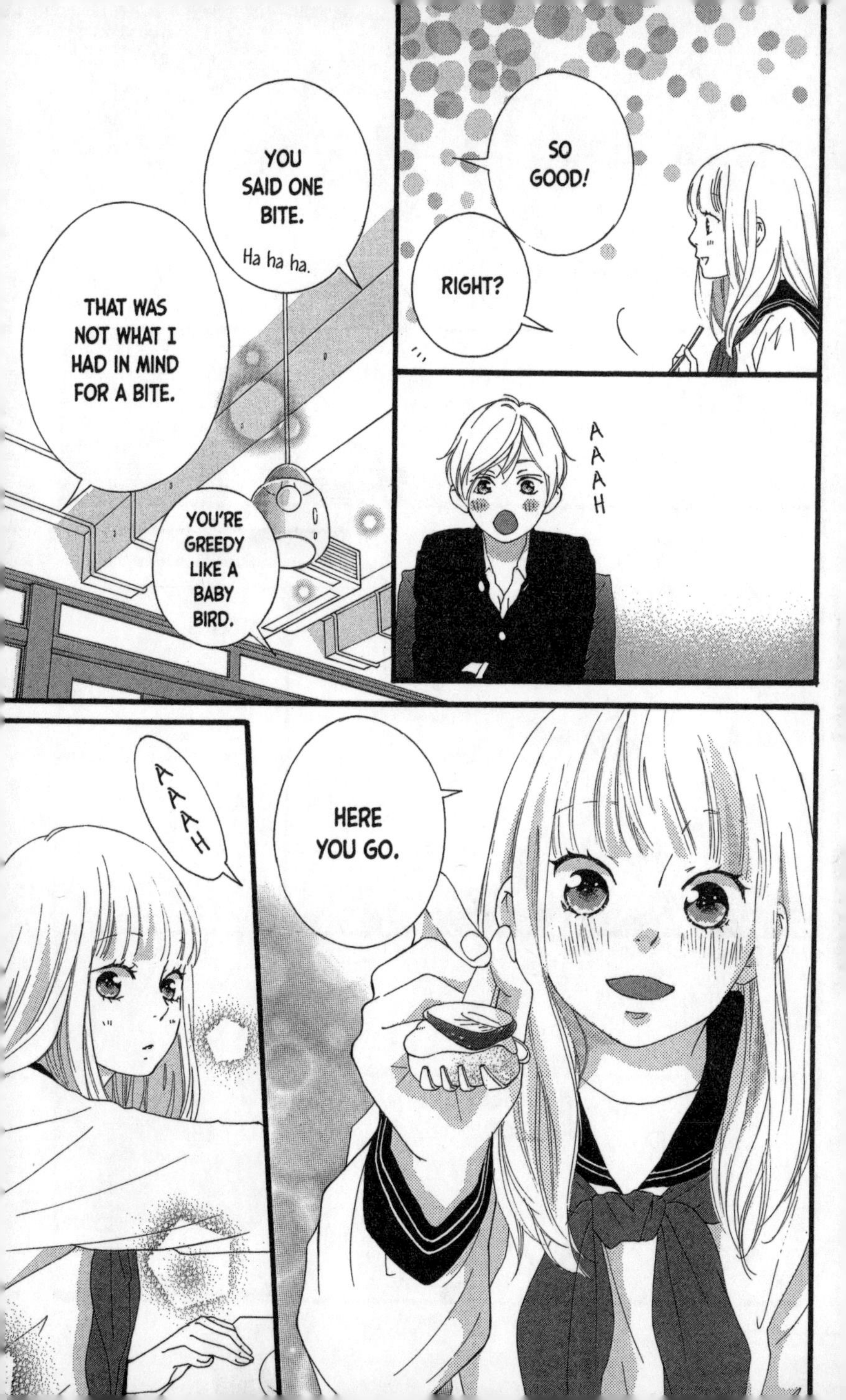
SO GOOD!
RIGHT?
AAAH
YOU SAID ONE BITE.
Ha ha ha.
THAT WAS NOT WHAT I HAD IN MIND FOR A BITE.
YOU'RE GREEDY LIKE A BABY BIRD.
HERE YOU GO.
AAAH

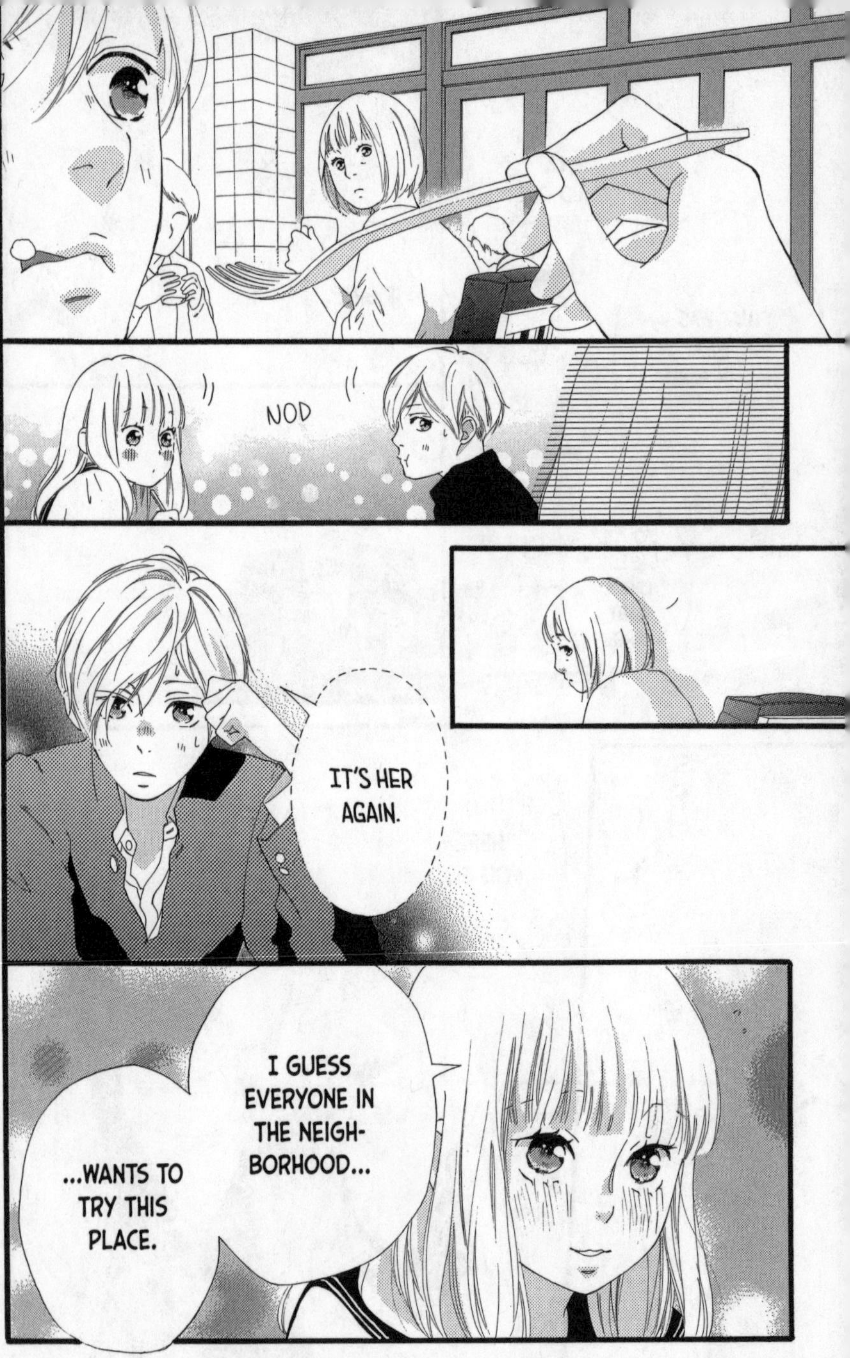
NOD
IT'S HER AGAIN.
I GUESS EVERYONE IN THE NEIGH-BORHOOD...
...WANTS TO TRY THIS PLACE.

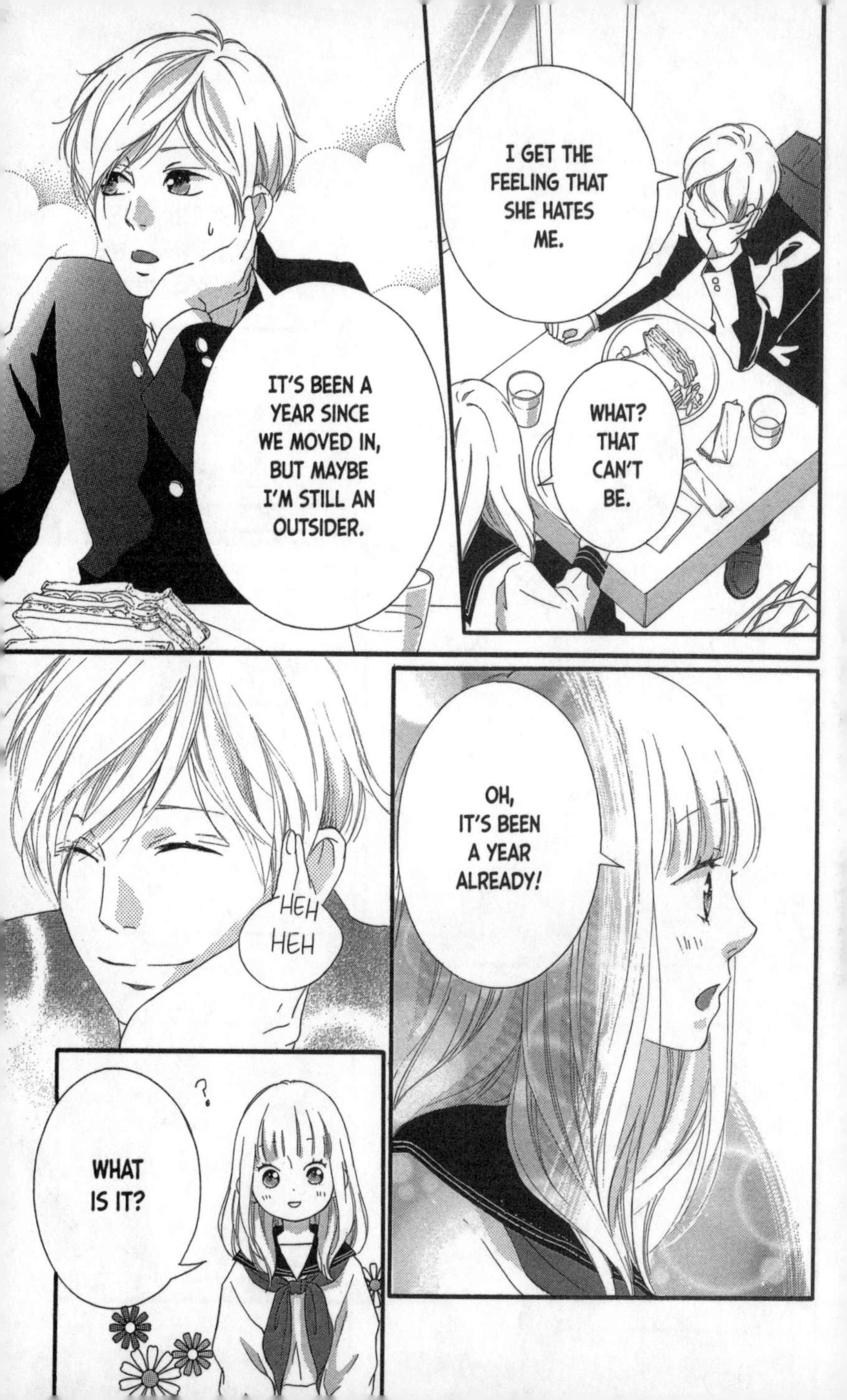
I GET THE FEELING THAT SHE HATES ME.
WHAT? THAT CAN'T BE.
IT'S BEEN A YEAR SINCE WE MOVED IN, BUT MAYBE I'M STILL AN OUTSIDER.
OH, IT'S BEEN A YEAR ALREADY!
HEH HEH
?
WHAT IS IT?

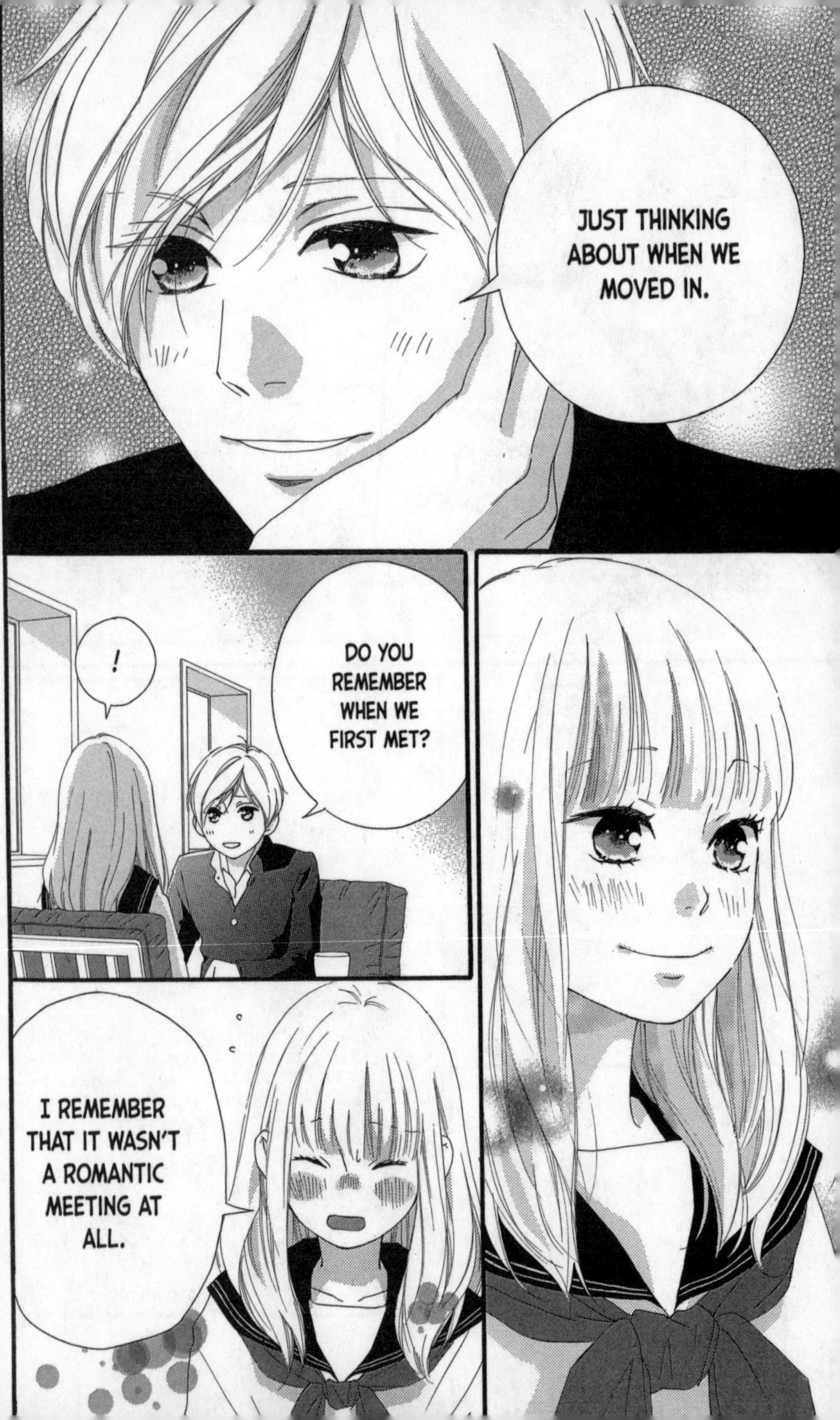
JUST THINKING ABOUT WHEN WE MOVED IN.
DO YOU REMEMBER WHEN WE FIRST MET?
!
I REMEMBER THAT IT WASN'T A ROMANTIC MEETING AT ALL.

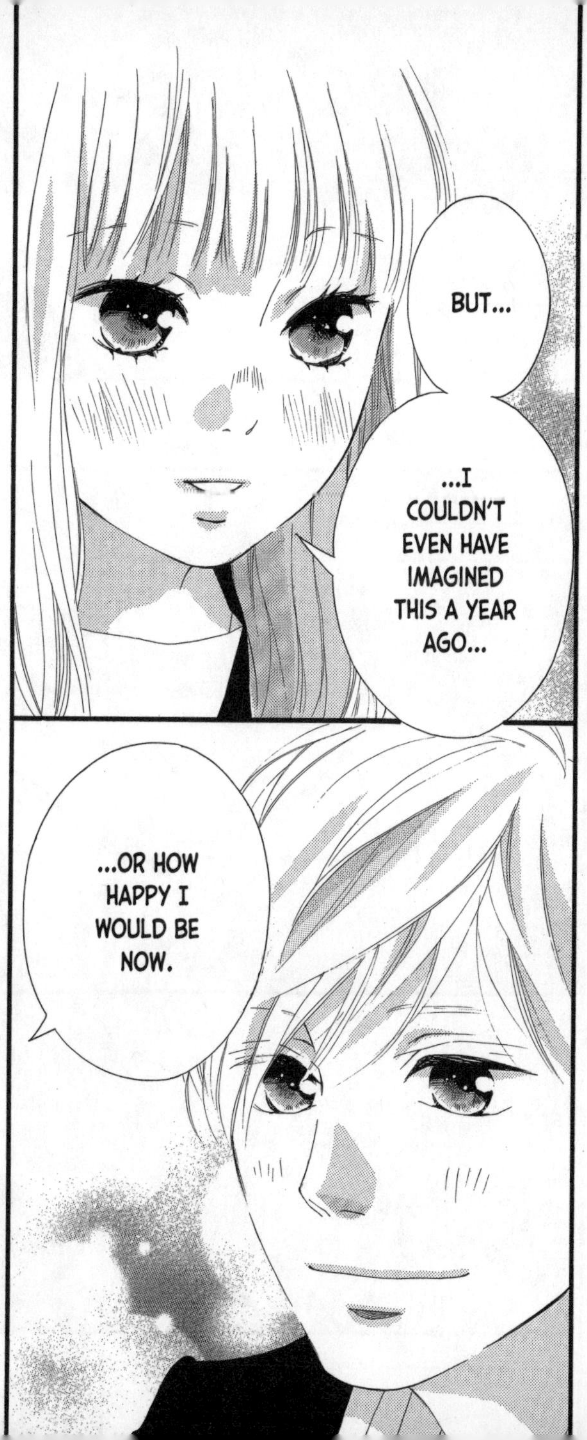
BUT...
...I COULDN'T EVEN HAVE IMAGINED THIS A YEAR AGO...
...OR HOW HAPPY I WOULD BE NOW.

I like planning trips. Whether or not I can actually go is beside the point; I just really like planning them. I'll buy a couple of guidebooks to plan out my route for sightseeing and what I'm going to eat where. I don't want to cram too much in, so I'll plan the number of days needed as well. I get so into it that I'll start going through travel blogs for information that's not in the guide-books. I really like the feeling of drawing a line from point to point and linking everything together. I have to be careful because if I go too far, I'll feel like I've already taken the trip and lose interest. Last year my schedule was too busy, so I couldn't go anywhere, but I hope I can go on a trip of my own this year.

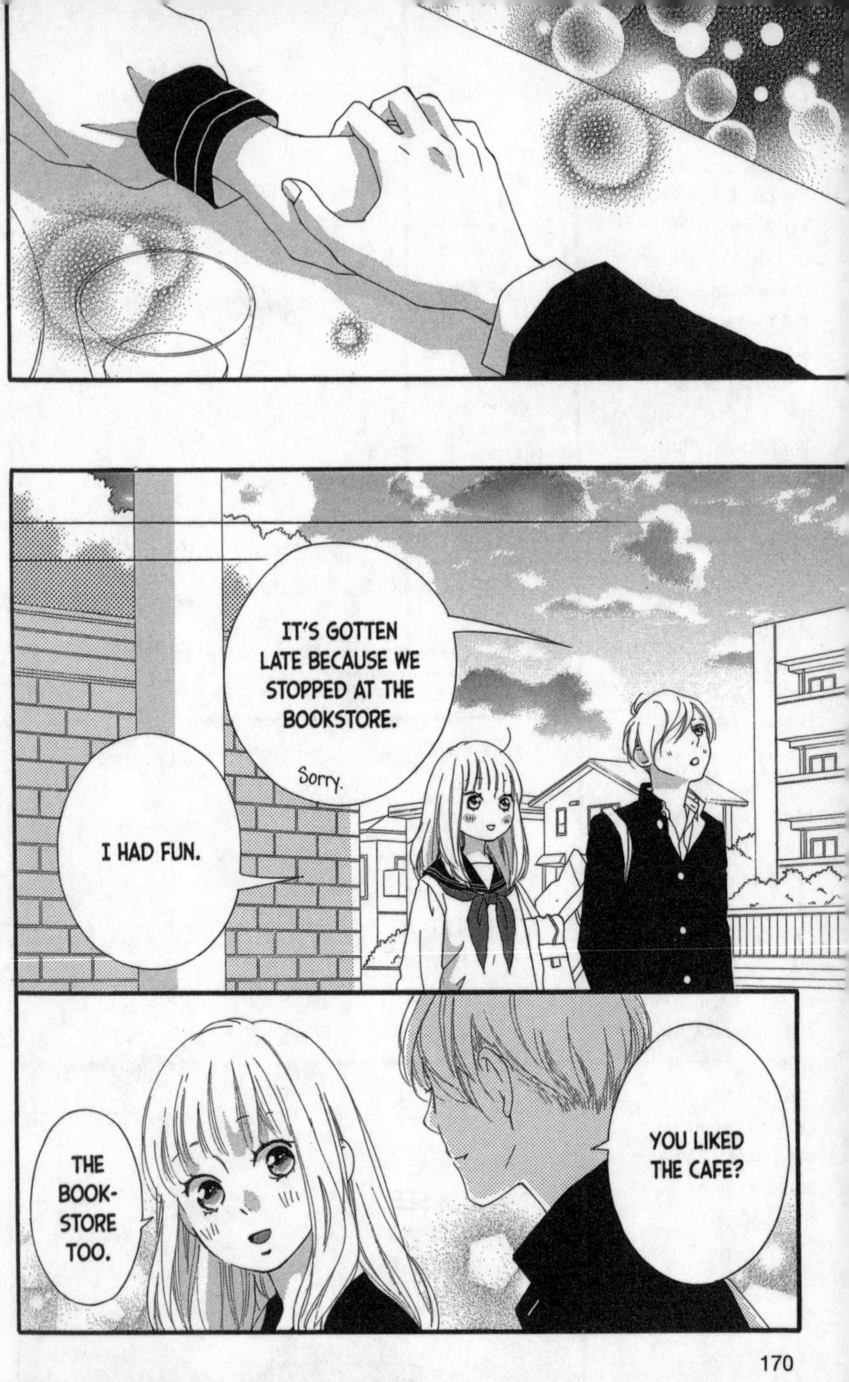
IT'S GOTTEN LATE BECAUSE WE STOPPED AT THE BOOKSTORE.
Sorry.
I HAD FUN.
YOU LIKED THE CAFE?
THE BOOK-STORE TOO.

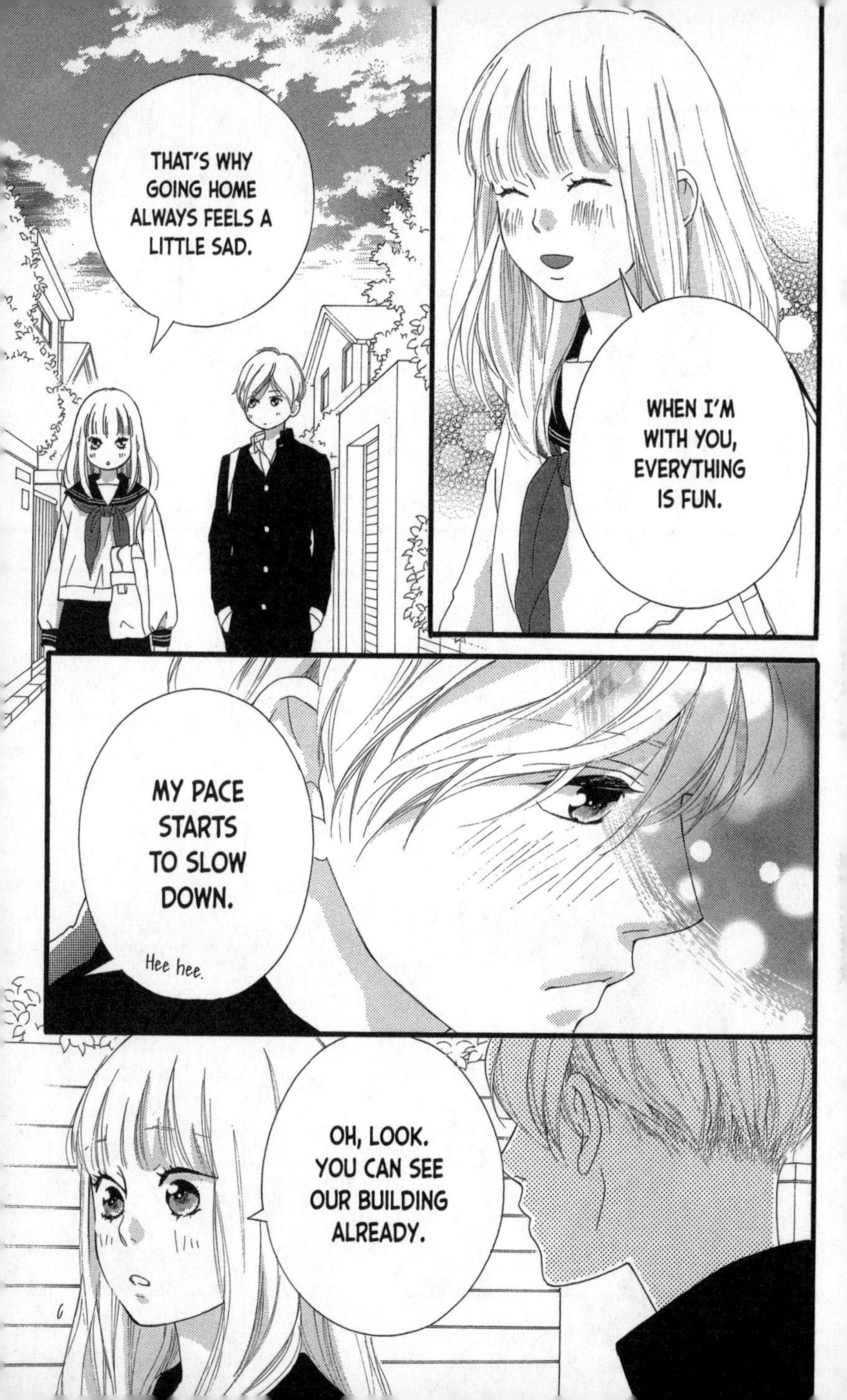
WHEN I'M WITH YOU, EVERYTHING IS FUN.
THAT'S WHY GOING HOME ALWAYS FEELS A LITTLE SAD.
MY PACE STARTS TO SLOW DOWN.
Hee hee.
OH, LOOK. YOU CAN SEE OUR BUILDING ALREADY.

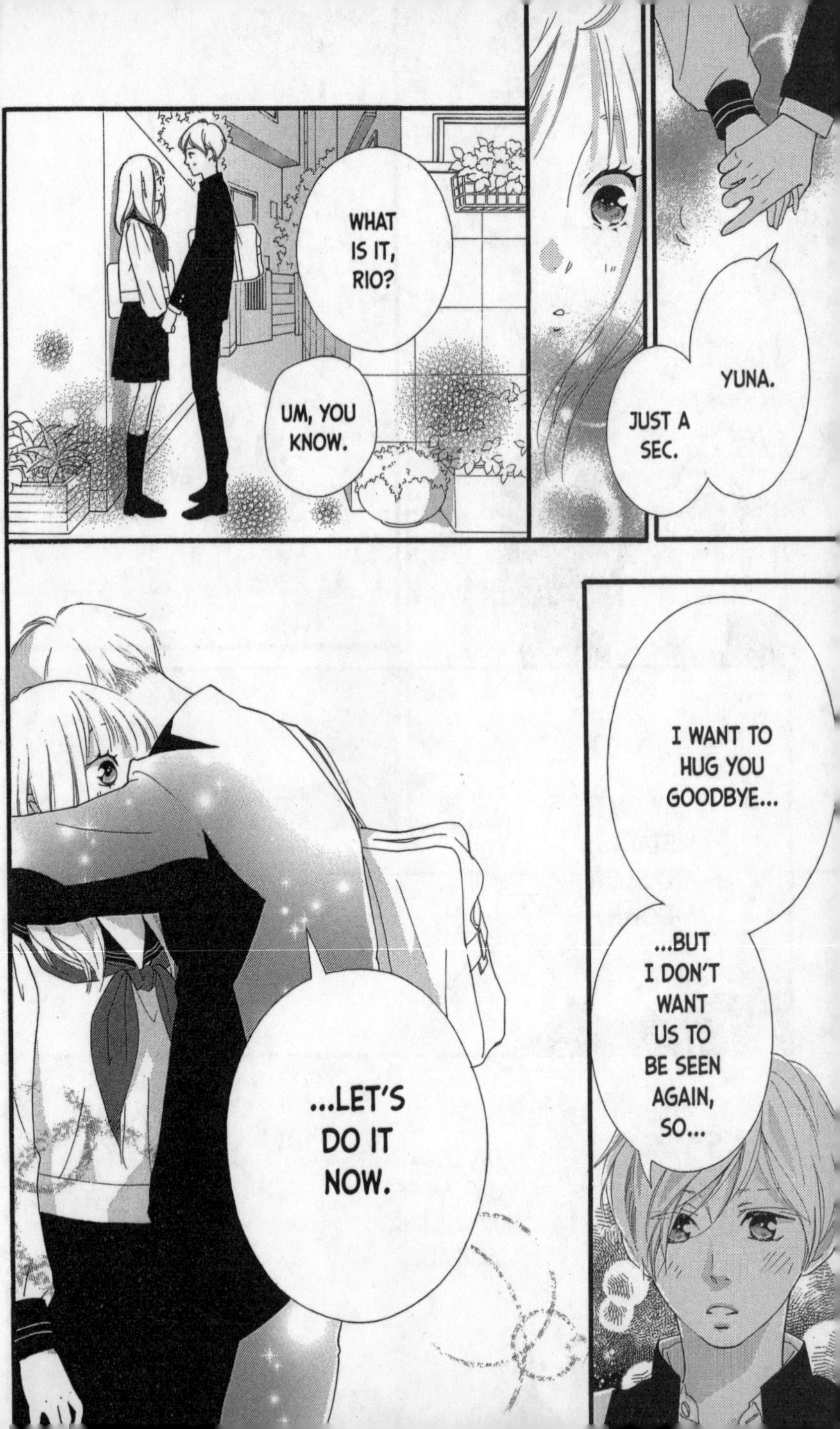
YUNA. JUST A SEC.
WHAT IS IT, RIO?
UM, YOU KNOW.
I WANT TO HUG YOU GOODBYE...
...BUT I DON'T WANT US TO BE SEEN AGAIN, SO...
...LET'S DO IT NOW.

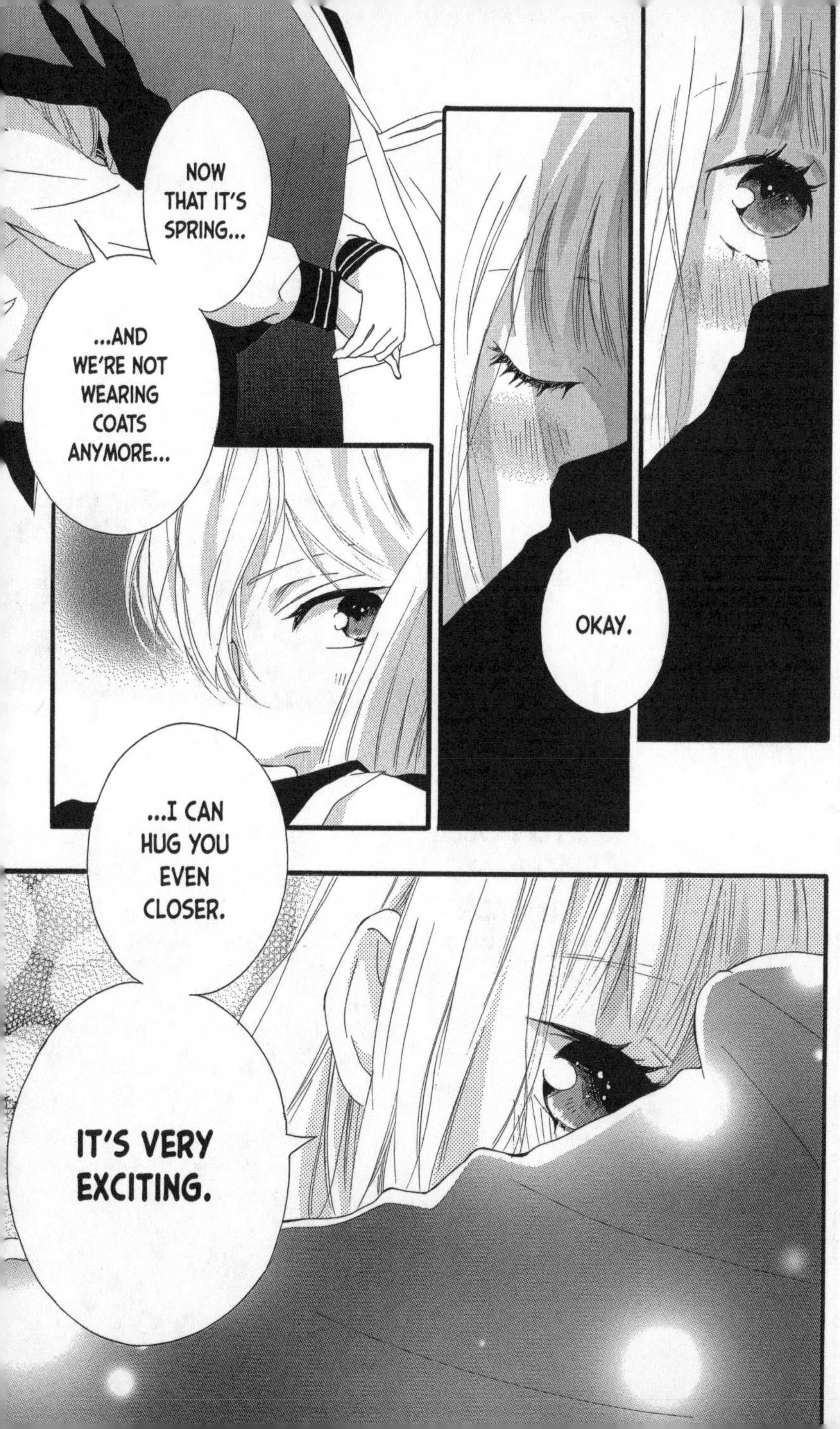
OKAY.
NOW THAT IT'S SPRING...
...AND WE'RE NOT WEARING COATS ANYMORE...
...I CAN HUG YOU EVEN CLOSER.
IT'S VERY EXCITING.

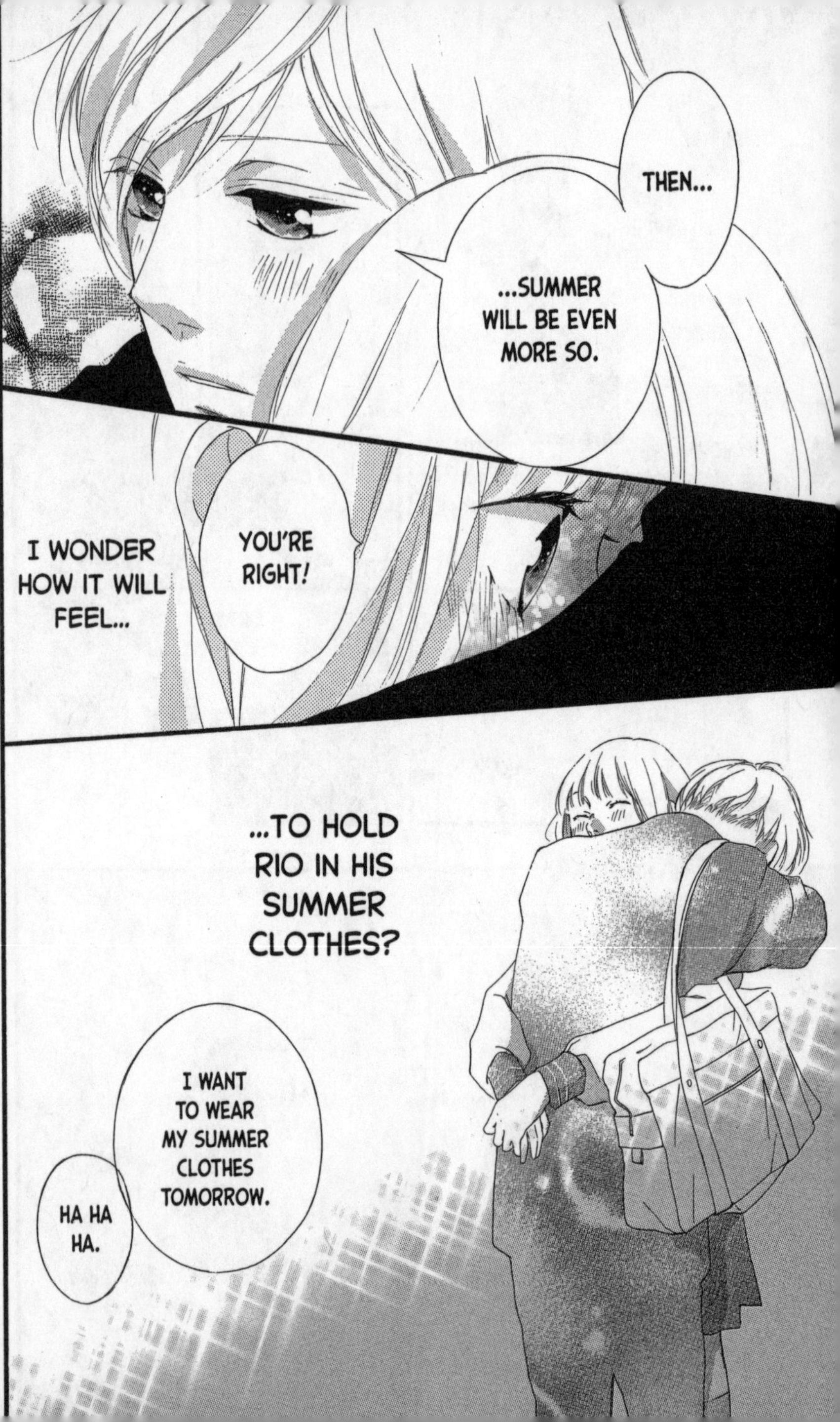
THEN...
...SUMMER WILL BE EVEN MORE SO.
YOU'RE RIGHT!
I WONDER HOW IT WILL FEEL...
...TO HOLD RIO IN HIS SUMMER CLOTHES?
I WANT TO WEAR MY SUMMER CLOTHES TOMORROW.
HA HA HA.

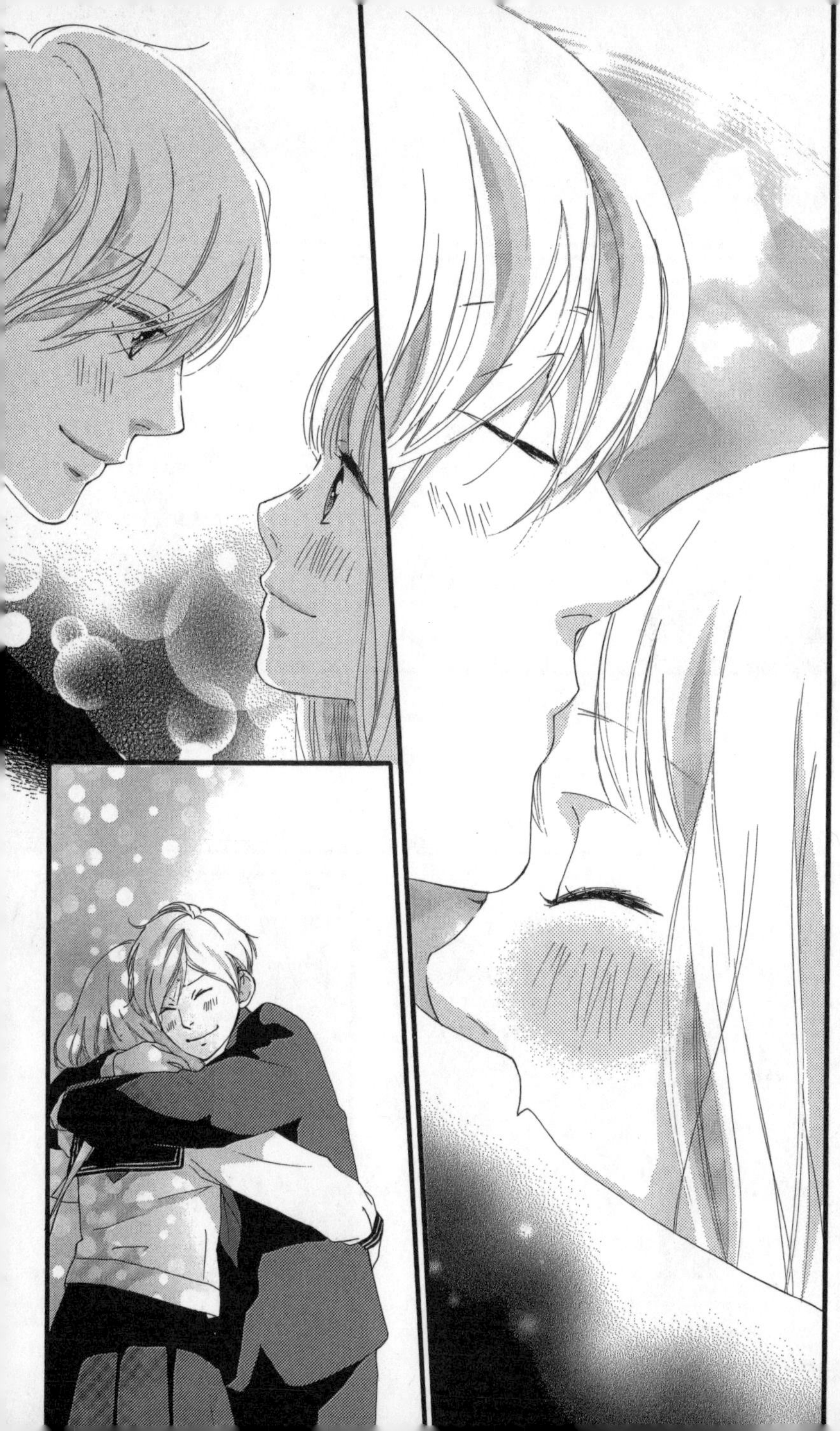

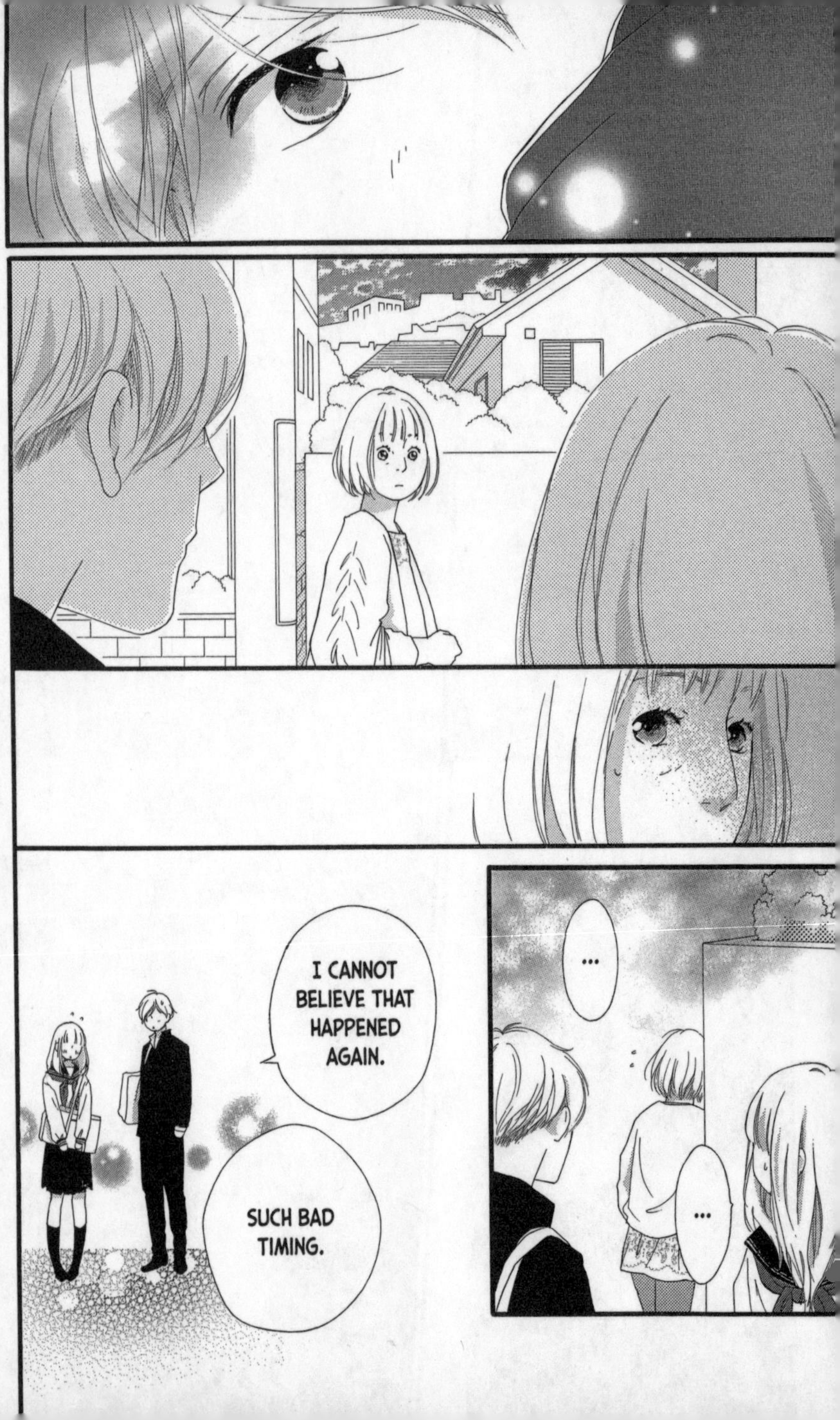
...
...
I CANNOT BELIEVE THAT HAPPENED AGAIN.
SUCH BAD TIMING.

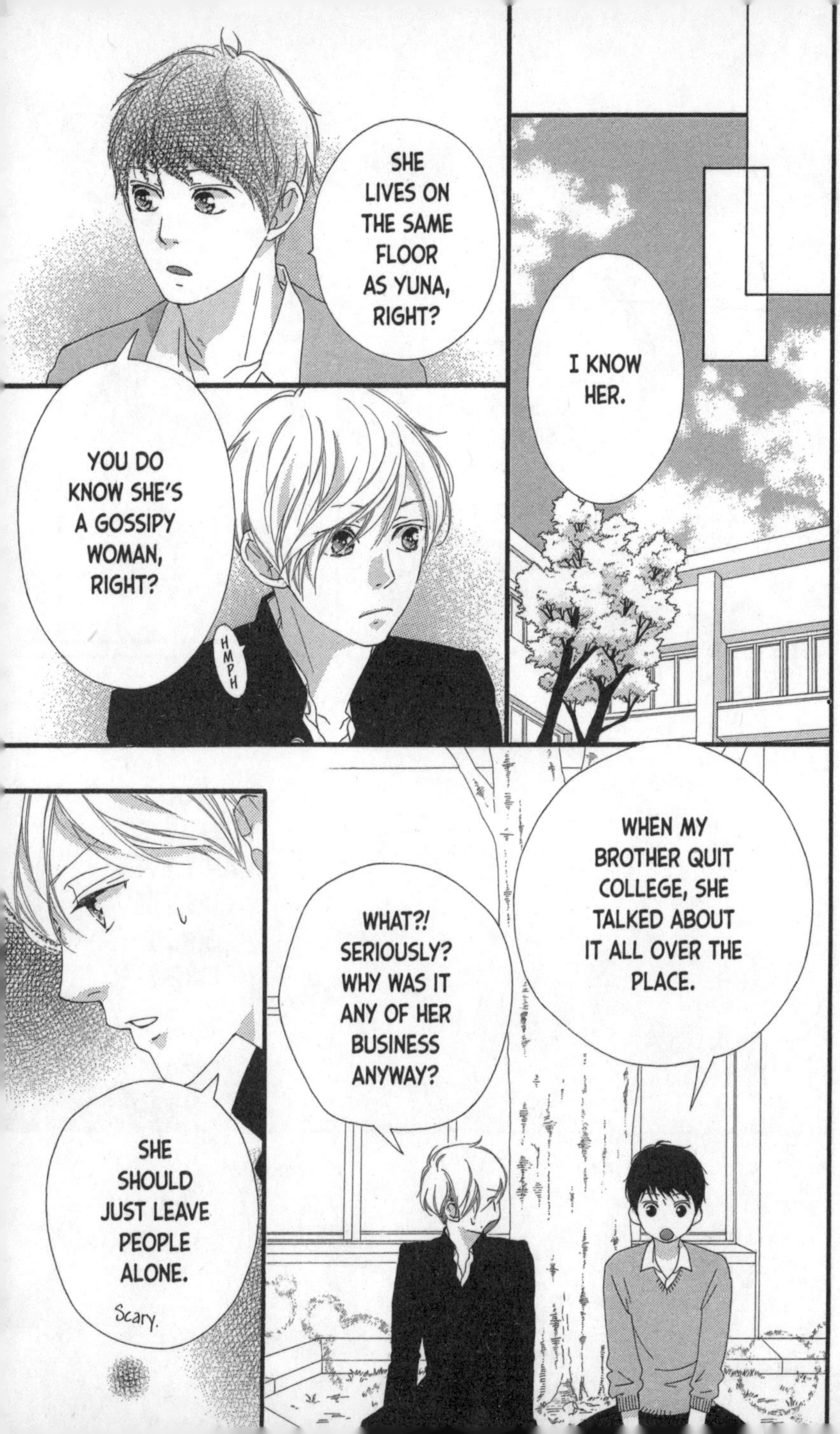
I KNOW HER.
SHE LIVES ON THE SAME FLOOR AS YUNA, RIGHT?
YOU DO KNOW SHE'S A GOSSIPY WOMAN, RIGHT?
HMPH
WHEN MY BROTHER QUIT COLLEGE, SHE TALKED ABOUT IT ALL OVER THE PLACE.
WHAT?! SERIOUSLY? WHY WAS IT ANY OF HER BUSINESS ANYWAY?
SHE SHOULD JUST LEAVE PEOPLE ALONE.
Scary.

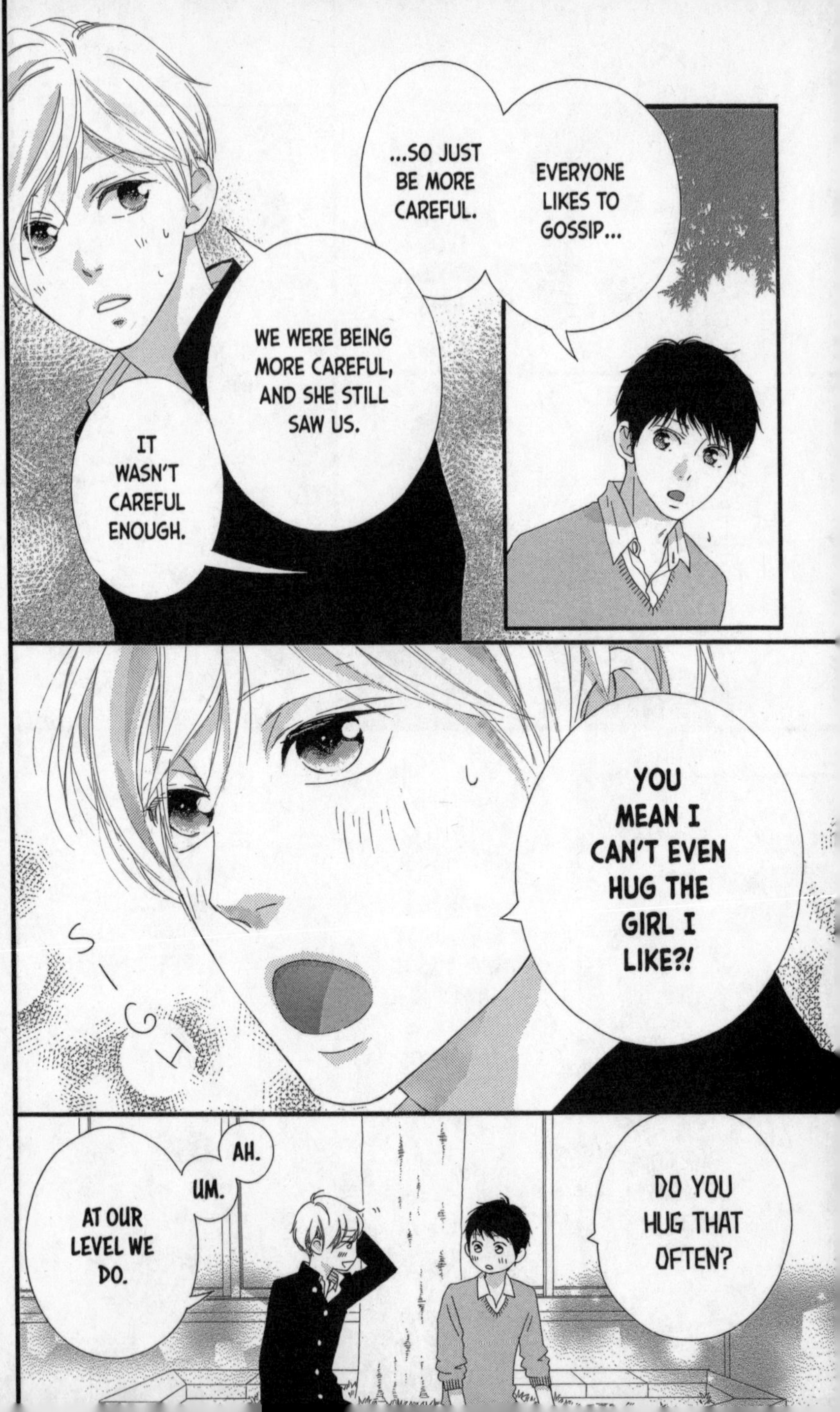
EVERYONE LIKES TO GOSSIP...
...SO JUST BE MORE CAREFUL.
WE WERE BEING MORE CAREFUL, AND SHE STILL SAW US.
IT WASN'T CAREFUL ENOUGH.
YOU MEAN I CAN'T EVEN HUG THE GIRL I LIKE?!
SIGH
DO YOU HUG THAT OFTEN?
AH.
UM.
AT OUR LEVEL WE DO.

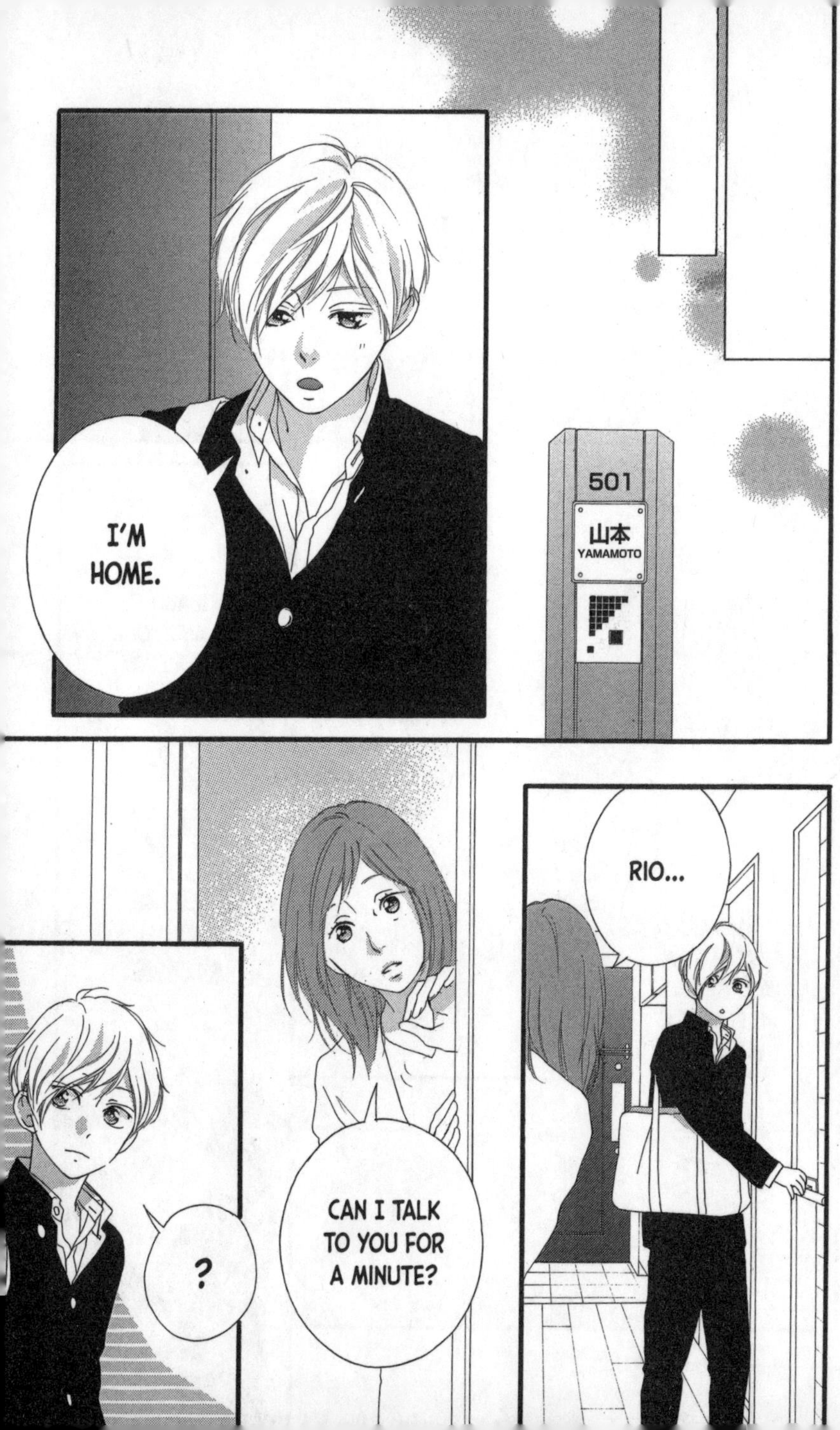
501
山本
YAMAMOTO
I'M HOME.
RIO...
CAN I TALK TO YOU FOR A MINUTE?
?

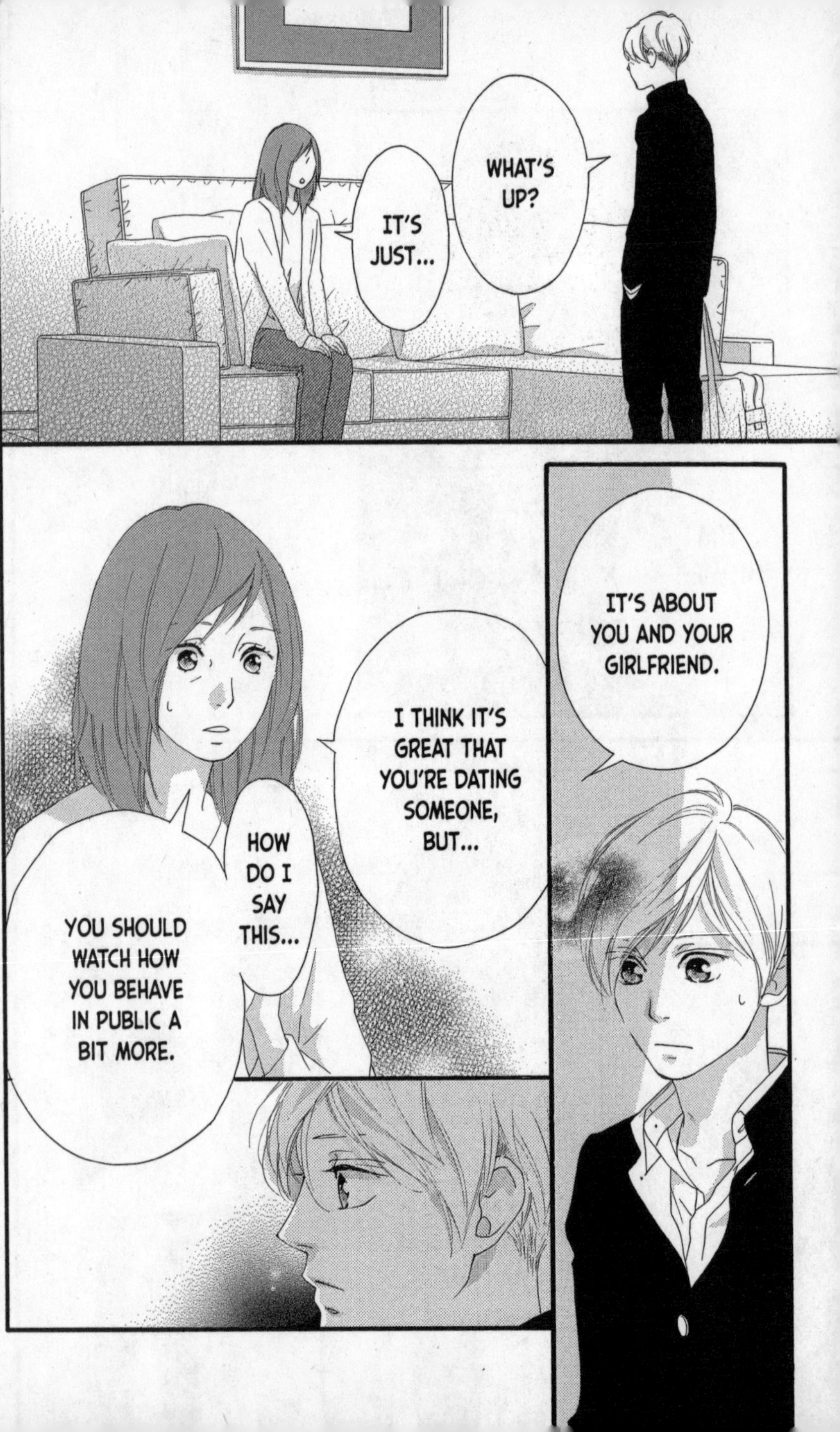
WHAT'S UP?
IT'S JUST...
IT'S ABOUT YOU AND YOUR GIRLFRIEND.
I THINK IT'S GREAT THAT YOU'RE DATING SOMEONE, BUT...
HOW DO I SAY THIS...
YOU SHOULD WATCH HOW YOU BEHAVE IN PUBLIC A BIT MORE.

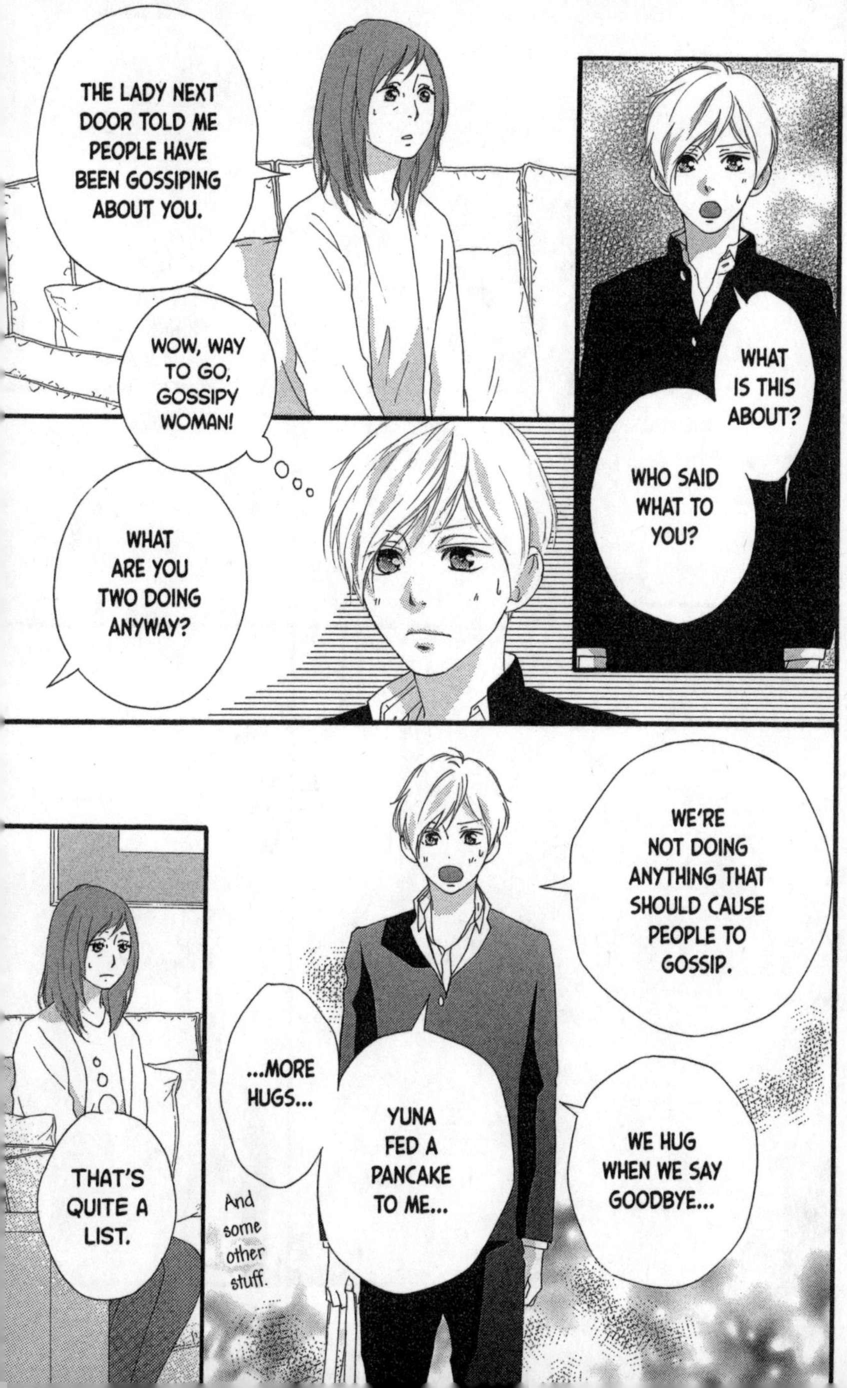
WHAT IS THIS ABOUT?
WHO SAID WHAT TO YOU?
THE LADY NEXT DOOR TOLD ME PEOPLE HAVE BEEN GOSSIPING ABOUT YOU.
WOW, WAY TO GO, GOSSIPY WOMAN!
WHAT ARE YOU TWO DOING ANYWAY?
WE'RE NOT DOING ANYTHING THAT SHOULD CAUSE PEOPLE TO GOSSIP.
WE HUG WHEN WE SAY GOODBYE...
YUNA FED A PANCAKE TO ME...
...MORE HUGS...
And some other stuff.
THAT'S QUITE A LIST.

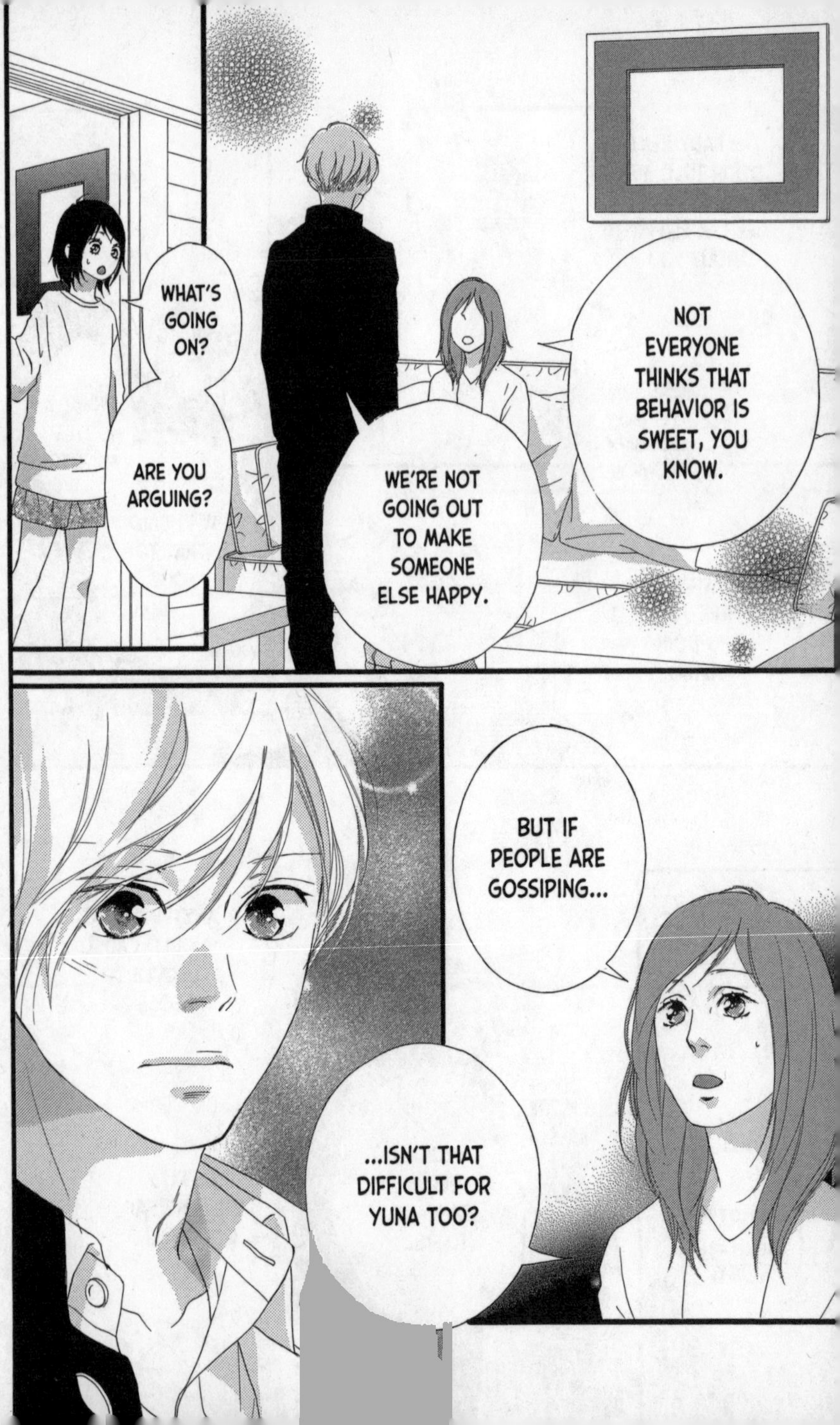
NOT EVERYONE THINKS THAT BEHAVIOR IS SWEET, YOU KNOW.
WE'RE NOT GOING OUT TO MAKE SOMEONE ELSE HAPPY.
WHAT'S GOING ON?
ARE YOU ARGUING?
BUT IF PEOPLE ARE GOSSIPING...
...ISN'T THAT DIFFICULT FOR YUNA TOO?

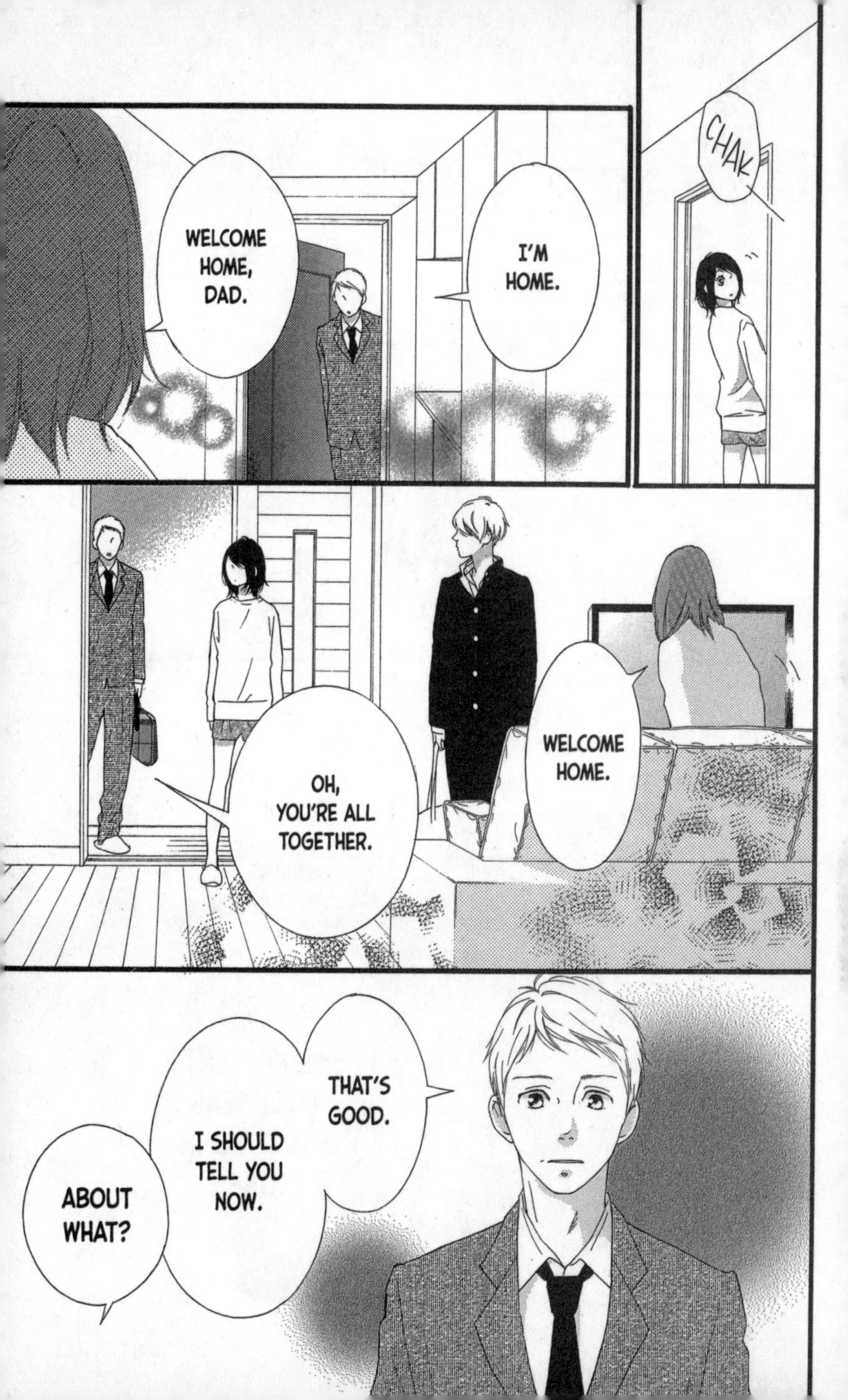
CHAK
I'M HOME.
WELCOME HOME, DAD.
WELCOME HOME.
OH, YOU'RE ALL TOGETHER.
THAT'S GOOD.
I SHOULD TELL YOU NOW.
ABOUT WHAT?

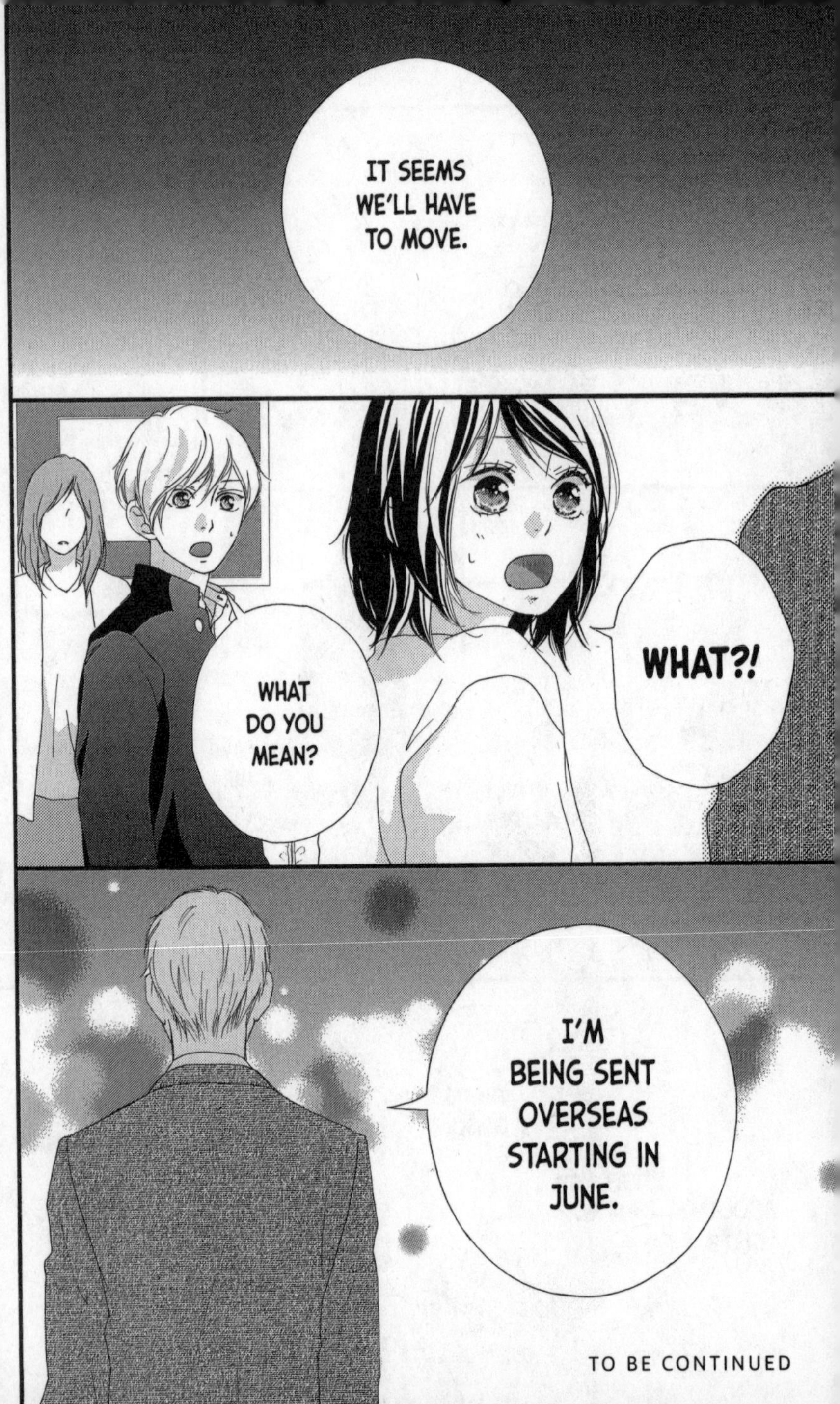
IT SEEMS WE'LL HAVE TO MOVE.
WHAT?!
WHAT DO YOU MEAN?
I'M BEING SENT OVERSEAS STARTING IN JUNE.

TO BE CONTINUED

AFTERWORD

Thank you for reading this to the end.

Every volume, I grapple with how I want the cover illustration to look. This time I've drawn Rio and Kazuomi. I had wanted to try out this pairing earlier, but because of how the story was unfolding, I couldn't do them. This time I thought it was okay to have them on the cover. It was probably the only place I could do it in terms of timing. I'm very satisfied with how the cover turned out. And in a spurt of impatience, I've already vaguely decided what the cover will be for the next volume. It will make me happy if you guess what it will be on your own and look forward to seeing if you are right. I'll see you in the next volume.

Io Sakisaka

When it's cold, I like putting a little bit of dark rum in my café au lait. I like the aroma and taste of rum. I drink so many café au laits that I now keep a bottle of rum on my desk. As soon as you put a bottle of alcohol anywhere near a work space, you really look like a degenerate, so I don't recommend this at all.

Io Sakisaka

Born on June 8, Io Sakisaka made her debut as a manga creator with *Sakura, Chiru*. Her series *Strobe Edge* and *Ao Haru Ride* are published by VIZ Media's Shojo Beat imprint. *Ao Haru Ride* was adapted into an anime series, and *Love Me, Love Me Not* was made into an animated feature film. In her spare time, Sakisaka likes to paint things and sleep.

Love Me, Love Me Not

Vol. 11

Shojo Beat Edition

STORY AND ART BY
Io Sakisaka

Adaptation/Nancy Thistlethwaite
Translation/JN Productions
Touch-Up Art & Lettering/Sara Linsley
Design/Yukiko Whitley
Editor/Nancy Thistlethwaite

First published in Japan in 2015 by SHUEISHA Inc., Tokyo.
English translation rights arranged by SHUEISHA Inc.

Printed in the U.S.A.

Published by VIZ Media, LLC
P.O. Box 77010
San Francisco, CA 94107

10 9 8 7 6 5 4 3 2 1
First printing, November 2021

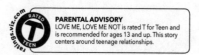

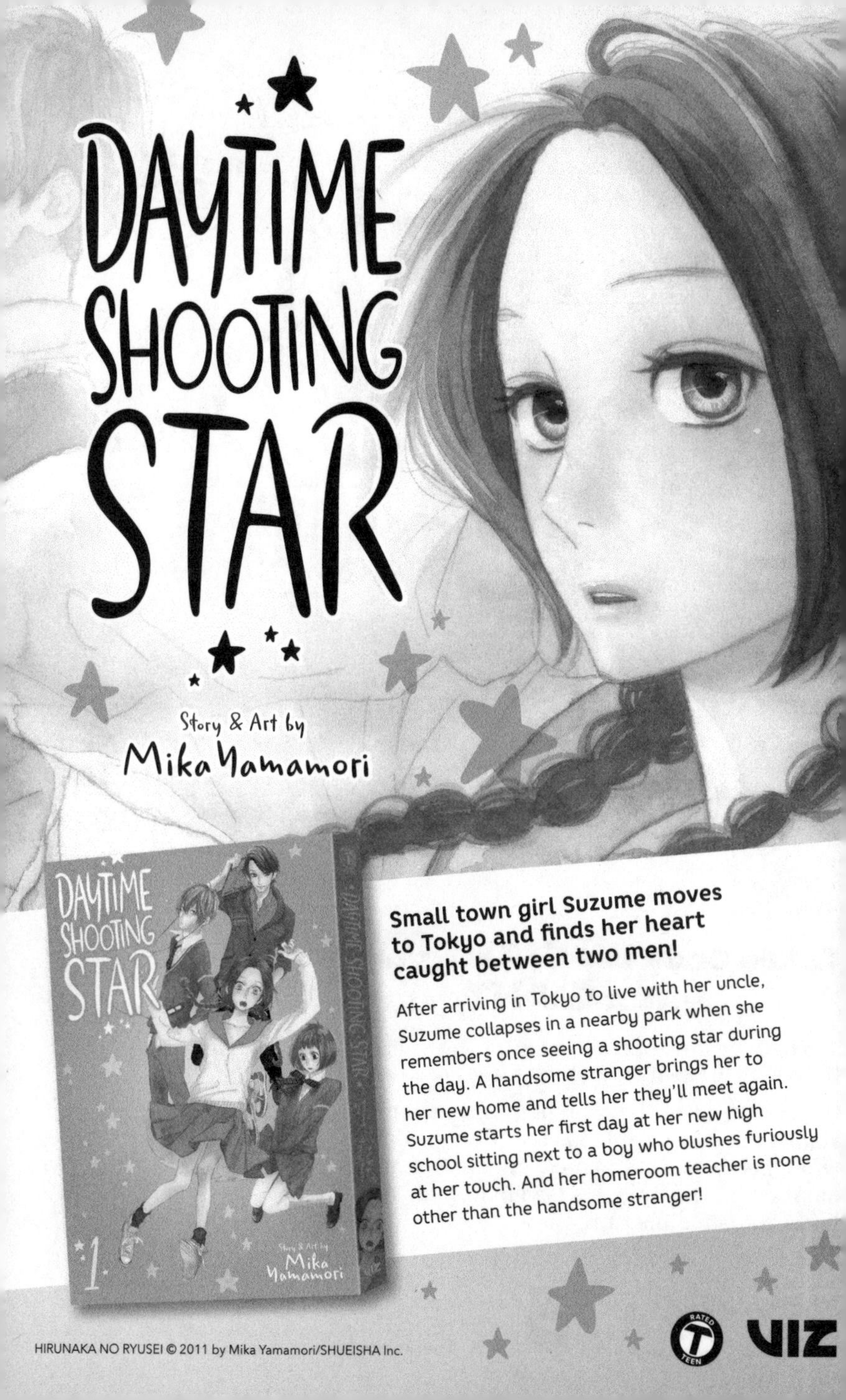
DAYTIME SHOOTING STAR
Story & Art by
Mika Yamamori
DAYTIME SHOOTING STAR
1
Story & Art by
Mika Yamamori
Small town girl Suzume moves to Tokyo and finds her heart caught between two men!
After arriving in Tokyo to live with her uncle, Suzume collapses in a nearby park when she remembers once seeing a shooting star during the day. A handsome stranger brings her to her new home and tells her they'll meet again. Suzume starts her first day at her new high school sitting next to a boy who blushes furiously at her touch. And her homeroom teacher is none other than the handsome stranger!
RATED T TEEN
VIZ
HIRUNAKA NO RYUSEI © 2011 by Mika Yamamori/SHUEISHA Inc.

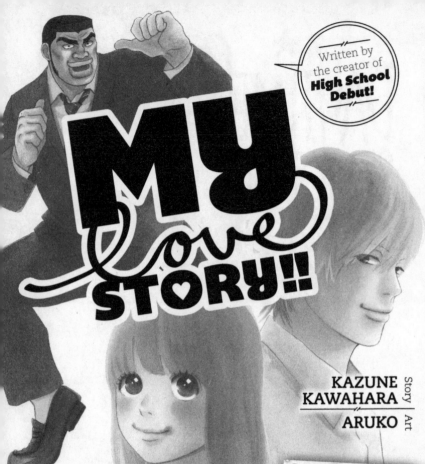

Written by the creator of **High School Debut!**

KAZUNE KAWAHARA — Story

ARUKO — Art

Takeo Goda is a GIANT guy with a GIANT *heart*

Too bad the girls don't want him!
(They want his good-looking best friend, Sunakawa.)

Used to being on the sidelines, Takeo simply stands tall and accepts his fate. But one day when he saves a girl named Yamato from a harasser on the train, his (love!) life suddenly takes an incredible turn!

Honey
So Sweet

Story and Art by Amu Meguro

Little did Nao Kogure realize back in middle school that when she left an umbrella and a box of bandages in the rain for injured delinquent Taiga Onise that she would meet him again in high school. Nao wants nothing to do with the gruff and frightening Taiga, but he suddenly presents her with a huge bouquet of flowers and asks her to date him—with marriage in mind! Is Taiga really so scary, or is he a sweetheart in disguise?

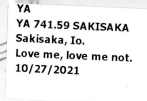

Stop!

You may be reading the wrong way.

In keeping with the original Japanese comic format, this book reads from right to left—so action, sound effects, and word balloons are completely reversed to preserve the orientation of the original artwork. Check out the diagram shown here to get the hang of things, and then turn to the other side of the book to get started!

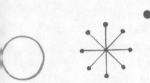

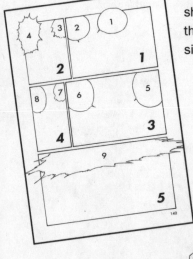